NON-PROLIFERATION LAW AS A SPECIAL REGIME

The fragmentation of international law is an undeniable phenomenon, and one that has met with increasing academic interest. This fragmentation is the result of the progressive expansion of both international legal activity and the subject-matter of international law. This expansion brings with it the risk of conflicting rules, principles and institutions.

Non-Proliferation Law as a Special Regime focuses on weapons of mass destruction, and aims to identify whether there are specific rules applying to this field that depart from the general rules of international law and the rules of other special regimes, in particular with regard to the law of treaties and the law of state responsibility. In providing a systematic analysis of a substantive area of international law, and applying the theory of fragmentation and special regimes, the book contributes to the on-going debate concerning one of the most topical issues in international law.

DANIEL H. JOYNER is Professor of Law at the University of Alabama School of Law.

MARCO ROSCINI is Reader in International Law at the University of Westminster School of Law.

NON-PROLIFERATION LAW AS A SPECIAL REGIME

A Contribution to Fragmentation Theory in International Law

Edited by
DANIEL H. JOYNER
and
MARCO ROSCINI

CAMBRIDGE
UNIVERSITY PRESS

CAMBRIDGE UNIVERSITY PRESS
Cambridge, New York, Melbourne, Madrid, Cape Town,
Singapore, São Paulo, Delhi, Mexico City

Cambridge University Press
The Edinburgh Building, Cambridge CB2 8RU, UK

Published in the United States of America by Cambridge University Press, New York

www.cambridge.org
Information on this title: www.cambridge.org/9781107009714

First published 2012

Printed and bound in the United Kingdom by the MPG Books Group

A catalogue record for this publication is available from the British Library

Library of Congress Cataloguing in Publication data
Non-proliferation law as a special regime: a contribution to fragmentation theory in international law / edited by Daniel H. Joyner and Marco Roscini.
p. cm.
Includes index.
ISBN 978-1-107-00971-4
1. Nuclear nonproliferation. 2. International obligations. 3. Treaties. I. Joyner, Daniel. II. Roscini, Marco.
KZ5675.N68 2012
341.7′34–dc23
2012011812

ISBN 978-1-107-00971-4 Hardback

CONTENTS

CONTRIBUTORS

MALGOSIA FITZMAURICE Professor of International Law, Queen Mary, University of London

DIETER FLECK Former Director, International Agreements and Policy, Federal Ministry of Defence, Germany

MATTHEW HAPPOLD Professeur en droit international public, Université du Luxembourg

JONATHAN HERBACH Lecturer in Public International Law and Researcher at the Centre for Conflict and Security Law, Utrecht University

DANIEL H. JOYNER Professor of Law, University of Alabama School of Law

PANOS MERKOURIS Teaching Associate, Queen Mary, University of London

ANDREW MICHIE Legal Officer, United Nations Industrial Development Organization (UNIDO)

ERIC MYJER Professor of International Law, Utrecht University

MARCO ROSCINI Reader in International Law, University of Westminster School of Law

SAHIB SINGH Visiting Lecturer in International Law, University of Vienna; Visiting Fellow, British Institute of International and Comparative Law

NIGEL D. WHITE Professor of International Law, University of Nottingham

ABBREVIATIONS

ABM	anti-ballistic missile
ABMT	Anti-Ballistic Missile Treaty
ARSIWA	Articles on the Responsibility of States for Internationally Wrongful Acts
BTWC	Biological and Toxin Weapons Convention [i.e., Convention on the Prohibition of the Development, Production and Stockpiling of Bacteriological (Biological) and Toxin Weapons and on their Destruction] *also known as* BWC
BWC	Biological Weapons Convention *see* BTWC
CBM	confidence-building measure
CBRN	chemical, biological, radiological and nuclear
CFE	Conventional [Armed] Forces in Europe
CFSP	Common Foreign and Security Policy
COP/MOP	conference of the parties serving as the meeting of the parties
CPPNM	Convention on the Physical Protection of Nuclear Material
CSA	Comprehensive Safeguards Agreement
CTBT	Comprehensive Nuclear-Test-Ban Treaty
CTBTO	Comprehensive Nuclear-Test-Ban Treaty Organization
CTFEU	Consolidated [version of the] Treaty on the Functioning of the European Union
CWC	Chemical Weapons Convention [i.e., Convention on the Prohibition of the Development, Production, Stockpiling and Use of Chemical Weapons and on their Destruction]
CWPF	chemical weapon production facility
DPRK	Democratic People's Republic of Korea (North Korea)
DSU	Directorate Service Unit
ECR	European Court Reports
ECJ	European Court of Justice
EHRR	European Human Rights Reports
ENMOD	environmental modification

ENMOD Convention	Environmental Modification Convention [i.e., Convention on the Prohibition of Military or any other Hostile Use of Environmental Modification Techniques]
GAOR	General Assembly Official Records
GATT	General Agreement on Tariffs and Trade
IAEA	International Atomic Energy Agency
ICAO	International Civil Aviation Organization
ICJ	International Court of Justice
ICTY	International Criminal Tribunal for the former Yugoslavia
IDC	International Data Centre
ILC	International Law Commission
ILM	*International Legal Materials*
IMCO	Inter-Governmental Maritime Consultative Organisation
IMO	International Maritime Organization (formerly IMCO)
IMS	International Monitoring System
IMSC	International Maritime Safety Committee
INF	Intermediate-range Nuclear Forces
ITU	International Telecommunications Union
LNTS	League of Nations Treaty Series
MARPOL	marine pollution [*and* International Convention for the Prevention of Pollution from Ships]
MEA	multilateral environmental agreement
MFN	most favoured nation
MSC	Maritime Safety Committee
NFZT	Nuclear-Free-Zone Treaty
NNWS	non-nuclear-weapon state
NPT	Nuclear Non-Proliferation Treaty [Treaty on the Non-Proliferation of Nuclear Weapons]
NTI	Nuclear Threat Initiative
NTM	national technical means
NWFZ	Nuclear-Weapon-Free Zone
NWS	nuclear-weapon state
OAS	Organization of American States
OPANAL	Organismo para la Proscripción de las Armas Nucleares en la América Latina y el Caribe [Agency for the Prohibition of Nuclear Weapons in Latin America and the Caribbean]
OPBW	Organization for the Prohibition of Biological Weapons
OPCW	Organization for the Prohibition of Chemical Weapons
OSI	on-site inspection
OST	Outer Space Treaty
PCA	Permanent Court of Arbitration

PCIJ	Permanent Court of International Justice
PFOS	perfluoroctane sulfonate
PNE	Peaceful Nuclear Explosions
PNET	Peaceful Nuclear Explosions Treaty
PTBT	Partial Test-Ban Treaty
PTS	provisional Technical Secretariat
RGDIP	*Revue Générale de Droit International Public*
RIAA	Reports of International Arbitral Awards
SALT	Strategic Arms Limitation Talks
SC Res	Security Council Resolution
SOLAS	Safety of Life at Sea
SORT	Strategic Offensive Reductions Treaty
START	Strategic Arms Reduction Treaty
SUA	Suppression of Unlawful Acts [Against the Safety of Maritime Navigation]
TEC	Treaty Establishing the European Communities
TFEU	Treaty on the Functioning of the European Union
TTBT	Threshold Test-Ban Treaty
UNCITRAL	United Nations Commission on International Trade Law
UNCLOS	United Nations Convention on the Law of the Sea
UNFCCC	United Nations Framework Convention on Climate Change
UNGA	United Nations General Assembly
UNIDIR	United Nations Institute for Disarmament Research
UNSC	United Nations Security Council
UNSC Res.	United Nations Security Council Resolutions
UNTS	United Nations Treaty Series
VCLT	Vienna Convention on the Law of Treaties
VEREX	verification experts
VERTIC	Verification Research, Training and Information Centre
WHO	World Health Organization
WMD	weapon of mass destruction
WMO	World Meteorological Organization
WTO	World Trade Organization
WTO DSU	World Trade Organization Dispute Settlement Understanding

Introduction

DANIEL H. JOYNER AND MARCO ROSCINI

It has been observed that 'much of the action in international law [has] shifted to specialized regimes'.[1] Indeed, 'international law has evolved into an elaborate, but fragmented, structure':[2] what was once regulated by 'public international law' is now governed by specialist systems such as, for instance, 'international humanitarian law', 'international environmental law', 'diplomatic law', 'human rights law', 'European Union law', 'the law of the World Trade Organization (WTO)'. Such regimes 'emerge from the informal activity of lawyers, diplomats, pressure groups, more through shifts in legal culture and in response to practical needs of specialization than as conscious acts of regime-creation'.[3] This fragmentation of international law has met with increasing academic interest and, often, concern. As observed in the Report of the International Law Commission (ILC)'s Study Group on the Fragmentation of International Law, fragmentation entails the risk of conflicting and incompatible rules, principles and institutions as between the general and specialized systems and between the specialized systems.[4]

The specialization of legal sources and processes and their adaptation to the needs of regulation of different areas of societal interaction is not a

[1] D. Bodansky and J. R. Cook, 'Introduction and Overview to Symposium: The ILC's State Responsibility Articles', *American Journal of International Law*, 96 (2002), 774.

[2] B. Simma and D. Pulkowski, 'Of Planets and the Universe: Self-contained Regimes in International Law', *European Journal of International Law*, 17 (2006), 485.

[3] 'Fragmentation of International Law: Difficulties Arising from the Diversification and Expansion of International Law', Report of the Study Group of the International Law Commission, A/CN.4/L.682, 13 April 2006, p. 84 (hereinafter ILC Report). As it has been observed, 'the history of fragmentation is also a story of professional specialization': A.-C. Martineau, 'The Rhetoric of Fragmentation: Fear and Faith in International Law', *Leiden Journal of International Law*, 22 (2009), 2.

[4] ILC Report, para. 14. The report was completed by the Chairman, Martti Koskenniemi, in April 2006 and is accompanied by forty-two conclusions. http://untreaty.un.org/ilc/texts/instruments/english/draft%20articles/1_9_2006.pdf.

phenomenon exclusively witnessed in international law. Indeed, it is a phenomenon which has long been observed and considered in domestic legal systems.[5] As Gunther Teubner and Andreas Fischer-Lescano persuasively argue, fragmentation and the appearance of subject-specific specialized regimes in any legal system are not primarily legal phenomena. Rather, they are essentially social phenomena which are only reflected epiphenomenally in the law.[6] Special regimes tend to evolve organically, through the efforts of communities of experts both inside and outside of state governments. These expert communities identify areas of social and political interaction they perceive to be in need of articulated and particularized regulation through legal sources. Different subject areas of such interaction will also frequently be perceived as implicating differing sets of political or other values and principles which should underpin and order the legal sources applicable to them. Vaughan Lowe has very usefully identified these extra-legal principles which 'direct the manner in which competing or conflicting norms … should interact in practice' as 'interstitial norms'.[7] By reference to these interstitial norms reflecting the values specific to the issue area, special rules emerge through both formal (hard law) and informal (soft law) legal sources. In many cases, special dispute settlement forums are also created for the substantive rules.

Special regimes, then, are designed better to take into account the peculiarities of the specific subject area involved and are generally perceived to regulate the area of social/political interaction more effectively than general international law.[8] However, in so doing, the formal and informal rules of special regimes, underpinned by their interstitial norms, will often come into conflict both with general international legal rules, procedures and principles, as well as with the rules, procedures and principles of other special regimes.

Again, the phenomena of legal fragmentation and the emergence of special legal regimes are ones common to domestic legal systems as well.

[5] R. Dworkin, 'Hard Cases', *Harvard Law Review*, 88 (1975), 1057, repr. in R. Dworkin, *Taking Rights Seriously* (Cambridge, Mass.: Harvard University Press, 1978); F.W. Maitland, 'A Prologue to a History of English Law', *Law Quarterly Review*, 14 (1898), 13.

[6] G. Teubner and A. Fischer-Lescano, 'Regime Collisions: The Vain Search for Legal Unity in the Fragmentation of Global Law', *Michigan Journal of International Law*, 25 (2004), 1999.

[7] V. Lowe, 'The Politics of Law-Making: Are the Method and Character of Norm Creation Changing?', in M. Byers (ed.), *The Role of Law in International Politics* (Oxford University Press, 2000), pp. 207, 216.

[8] M. Koskenniemi and P. Leino, 'Fragmentation of International Law?: Postmodern Anxieties', *Leiden Journal of International Law*, 15 (2002), 553–579.

One need only look to the first-year curriculum of a law school to see the special substantive rules, procedures and principles present in the law of contract, the law of tort, the law of property, constitutional law, administrative law and criminal law. The material difference between domestic legal systems and the international legal system in terms of the manner in which they deal with this phenomenon is to be found in the lack of both substantive and procedural hierarchies in international law, which do typically exist in domestic law, to bring both procedural and substantive unity to the legal system.[9]

In international law, however, there are a number of legal tools, discussed at length in the ILC Study Group Report and elsewhere, for dealing with the phenomenon of fragmentation and preserving a sense of unity and wholeness in the international legal system. As the Report concludes:

> [o]ne principal conclusion of this report has been that the emergence of special treaty-regimes ... has not seriously undermined legal security, predictability or the equality of legal subjects. The techniques of *lex specialis* and *lex posterior*, of *inter se* agreements and of the superior position given to peremptory norms and the (so far under-elaborated) notion of 'obligations owed to the international community as a whole' provide a basic professional tool-box that is able to respond in a flexible way to most substantive fragmentation problems.[10]

The ILC Report thus argues that international law currently possesses instruments which can serve in most cases to resolve conflicts, both as between special regimes and general international law and as between different special regimes. Similarly, a 1995 Study concludes that 'on balance, the relative autonomy of special fields has been used by different actors involved, as far as the secondary rules are concerned, in a way which, at the same time, promoted and guaranteed the growing effectiveness of their own particular set of primary rules, *without putting in jeopardy the unity or coherence of the international legal order*'.[11] One

[9] ILC Report, para. 26: 'Conflicts between rules are a phenomenon in every legal order. Every legal order is also familiar with ways to deal with them. Maxims such as *lex specialis* or *lex posterior* are known to most legal systems, and ... to international law. Domestic legal orders also have robust hierarchical relations between rules and rule-systems (in addition to hierarchical institutions to decide rule-conflicts). In international law, however, ... there are much fewer and much less robust hierarchies.'

[10] ILC Report, para. 492 (emphasis in original).

[11] K. C. Wellens, 'Diversity in Secondary Rules and the Unity of International Law: Some Reflections on Current Trends', in L. A. N. M. Barnhoorn and K. C. Wellens (eds.), *Diversity in Secondary Rules and the Unity of International Law* (The Hague: Martinus Nijhoff Publishers, 1995), p. 28 (emphasis added).

might share this conclusion or not. To a large extent, the answer to the question whether fragmentation is a 'beneficial antioxidant'[12] or a threat to the systemic unity of international law rests on the perspective that is adopted: to borrow a famous metaphor, '[d]epending on whether we choose a universalistic or a particularistic perspective, whether we first see the universe or the planets, the analysis tends to yield different results'.[13]

The doctrine of fragmentation is based on the existence of 'special' (or 'specialized') regimes.[14] A 'regime' is a system of interrelated norms addressing some problem. In a broader sense, such a system might comprise an entire substantive area of international law (e.g., international human rights law, international humanitarian law), while in a narrower sense it could be limited to a particular treaty or to certain provisions contained within a particular treaty. The latter might, however, better be seen as a special regime within a special regime, or, to borrow Riphagen's language, as a 'sub-system'.[15]

'Special' means 'not general': it does not necessarily entail uniqueness but implies a diversity from, yet also a common systemic nature with, general rules. We see special regimes essentially as a form of *lex specialis*. Different types of *leges speciales* can be identified according to (a) their special subject-matter, i.e., their primary rules (e.g., international humanitarian law with respect to international human rights law in situations of armed conflict);[16] (b) their special secondary rules, i.e., rules administering primary rules (e.g., the 'special rules' referred to in Article 55 of the 2001 International Law Commission's Articles on the Responsibility of States for Internationally Wrongful Acts (ILC Articles)); or (c) the limited number of subjects addressed by the rules (e.g., regional treaties).

[12] M. Craven, 'Unity, Diversity and the Fragmentation of International Law', *Finnish Yearbook of International Law*, 14 (2003), 4–5.

[13] Simma and Pulkowski, 'Of Planets and the Universe', 506.

[14] The expression 'special regime' was first used by the Special Rapporteur Roberto Ago in his Fifth Report on State Responsibility (UN Doc. A/CN.4/291 and Adds. 1 and 2). It was then used by the Special Rapporteur Willem Riphagen (Fourth Report, UN Doc. A/CN.4/366 and Add. 1 and Add. 1/Corr. 1, para. 127), who, however, also used other expressions, such as 'objective regimes' and 'peremptory subsystems'.

[15] Third Report on the Content, Forms and Degrees of International Responsibility (Pt. II of the Draft Articles), UN Doc. A/CN.4/354 and Corr. 1 and Adds. 1 and 2, para. 35.

[16] Legality of the Threat or Use of Nuclear Weapons, Advisory Opinion of 8 July 1996, ICJ Reports 1996, para. 25.

'Special regimes', in a technical sense, then, are only those forms of *lex specialis* where special primary rules on a certain subject-matter are supplemented by secondary rules specific to the regime in question.[17] Special secondary rules aim at enhancing the efficacy of primary rules and are often accompanied by functionally specialized institutions that contribute to the administration of the special rules, such as, in non-proliferation law: the Comprehensive Nuclear-Test-Ban Treaty Organization (CTBTO), the International Atomic Energy Agency (IAEA), the Agency for the Prohibition of Nuclear Weapons in Latin America and the Caribbean (Organismo para la Proscripción de las Armas Nucleares en la América Latina y el Caribe (OPANAL)) and the Organization for the Prohibition of Chemical Weapons (OPCW).

Our definition of 'special regime' includes both the first and second notions identified in the ILC Study Group Report, i.e., 'a special set of secondary rules that determine the consequences of a breach of certain primary rules (including the procedures of such determination)' and 'any interrelated cluster (set, regime, subsystem) of rules on a limited problem together with the rules for the creation, interpretation, application, modification, or termination – in a word, administration – of those rules'.[18] There is, however, a difference. The ILC Report seems to suggest that only the rules on state responsibility are secondary rules, while those on the creation, interpretation, application, modification or termination of rules are primary ones.[19] In his famous article on self-contained regimes, Simma also adopts a definition of 'self-contained regime' based on a narrow notion of secondary rules, i.e., 'a subsystem which is intended to exclude more or less totally the application of the general legal consequences of wrongful acts, in particular the application of countermeasures normally at the disposal of an injured party'.[20]

[17] Approaching the matter from the opposite perspective, that of unity, Dupuy distinguishes between the formal unity of the international legal order, based on the identity of secondary rules whatever the content of primary rules, and substantial unity, based on a set of unifying primary rules of customary nature, some of which even attain a peremptory status: P.-M. Dupuy, 'The Danger of Fragmentation or Unification of the International Legal System and the International Court of Justice', *New York University Journal of International Law and Politics*, 31 (1998–1999), 793–795.

[18] ILC Report, p. 81. [19] *Ibid.* See also the ILC Study Group conclusions, para. 12.

[20] B. Simma, 'Self-Contained Regimes', *Netherlands Yearbook of International Law*, 16 (1985), 117.

The identification of secondary rules with the law of state responsibility in the debate on special/self-contained regimes, accepted almost as a dogma by several commentators,[21] probably originates from the fact that the perspective from which the issue was approached was that of determining whether special regimes affected the right of the parties to take countermeasures under general international law.[22] This narrow approach, however, does not fully take into account what secondary rules are about.

In his *The Concept of Law*, Hart famously distinguished between primary and secondary rules. Although they have features in common, secondary rules differ from primary rules in that

> they are all about such rules; in the sense that while primary rules are concerned with the actions that individuals must or must not do, these secondary rules are all concerned with the primary rules themselves. They specify the ways in which the primary rules may be conclusively ascertained, introduced, eliminated, varied, and the fact of their violation conclusively determined.[23]

Such secondary rules can be classified into 'rules of recognition' (those that lead to the identification of the primary rules containing obligations and regulate possible conflicts), 'rules of change' (specifying how new primary rules are introduced) and 'rules of adjudication' (regulating the consequences of the violation of primary rules).[24] Whereas a primitive social structure is characterized by primary rules only, more

[21] For a different view, see A. Marschik, 'Too Much Order? The Impact of Special Secondary Norms on the Unity and Efficacy of the International Legal System', *European Journal of International Law*, 9 (1998), 212: 'Regimes of international law which combine certain primary norms with a distinct set of secondary norms designed to ensure the operation of those primary norms have since been termed "subsystems" of international law', where 'secondary norms' are those that 'regulate the primary rules: creation, modification, extinction, interpretation and operation'. See also J. Pauwelyn, *Conflict of Norms in Public International Law: How WTO Law Relates to other Rules of International Law* (Cambridge University Press, 2003), p. 159.

[22] It has, however, been doubted that certain rules contained in the Articles on State Responsibility, in particular those on circumstances precluding wrongfulness, are secondary rules. See E. David, 'Primary and Secondary Rules', in J. Crawford, A. Pellet and S. Olleson, *The Law of International Responsibility* (Oxford University Press, 2010), pp. 29–33. This author argues that '[t]he so-called secondary rules may become primary rules and vice-versa: the implementation of responsibility through mechanisms for dispute settlement refers to rules of conduct, and therefore primary rules, which are no less secondary rules, given that they are triggered by the violation of primary rules' (*ibid.* 32).

[23] H. L. A. Hart, *The Concept of Law*, 2nd edn. (Oxford University Press, 1994), p. 94.

[24] *Ibid.* 94–97.

sophisticated legal systems supplement the primary rules with secondary rules.[25] While acknowledging that '[p]erhaps international law is at present in a stage of transition ... which would bring it nearer in structure to a municipal system',[26] Hart eventually concludes that, in the absence of a legislature, courts with compulsory jurisdiction and organized sanctions, international law is similar to primitive societies, as it lacks rules of recognition, change and adjudication.[27]

Pierre-Marie Dupuy has, however, persuasively argued that international law is indeed provided with secondary rules.[28] In particular, Hart's secondary rules correspond, in the international legal order, to the rules on sources, responsibility and dispute settlement.[29] Not only the law of state responsibility, then, is of secondary nature, but also the law of treaties, which contains rules of recognition and rules of change[30] and also rules that determine certain consequences of wrongful acts.[31] This is implicitly confirmed by Article 56 of the Articles on State Responsibility, where it states that '[t]he applicable rules of international law continue to govern questions concerning the responsibility of a State for an internationally wrongful act to the extent that they are not regulated by these articles'. According to its Commentary, Article 56 has to be interpreted in the sense that the Articles on State Responsibility 'are not concerned

[25] *Ibid.* 91–94. [26] *Ibid.* 236.

[27] For Hart, then, international law is 'not "binding", and so not worth the title of "law"' (*ibid.* 214).

[28] P.-M. Dupuy, 'The Danger of Fragmentation', 793.

[29] Wellens, 'Diversity in Secondary Rules and the Unity of International Law', p. 8. Dupuy qualifies 'rules of international responsibility for wrongful acts' and rules that 'establish the conditions under which an injured State may have recourse to countermeasures' as 'norms of adjudication'. P.-M. Dupuy, 'The Danger of Fragmentation', 793.

[30] In the *Gabčíkovo-Nagymaros* case, the ICJ noted that the law of treaties determines 'whether a convention is or is not in force, and whether it has or has not been properly suspended or denounced'. *Gabčíkovo-Nagymaros Project (Hungary* v. *Slovakia)*, ICJ Reports 1997, para. 47.

[31] J. Verhoeven, 'The Law of State Responsibility and the Law of Treaties', in Crawford, Pellet and Olleson, *Law of International Responsibility*, p. 108. The author refers in particular to Arts. 49–52, 60 and, to the extent that they prevent the state responsible for the impossibility or the change of circumstances from invoking them as a ground for terminating its participation in the treaty, 61–62 of the 1969 Vienna Convention on the Law of Treaties. Verhoeven also notes that the ICJ's conclusion in para. 47 of the *Gabčíkovo-Nagymaros* judgment that the law of treaties and the law of state responsibility have distinct scopes 'does not preclude certain consequences of wrongful acts being drawn from the law of treaties, principally the invalidation or termination of certain engagements' (*ibid.*).

with any legal effects of a breach of an international obligation which . . . stem from the law of treaties or other areas of law.'[32]

The degree of 'specialness' of a special regime can of course vary. It could go from departure from general secondary rules (as intended above) on only one aspect to total replacement of such rules. Simma and Pulkowski note that, for the universalists, there is a presumption against the total exclusion of general rules, while for the particularists, rules outside the special regime can be resorted to only exceptionally.[33] Qualifying regimes replacing a single or few provisions of the general secondary rules as 'weak' and those excluding the application of secondary rules *in toto* as 'strong', as the two authors do, is, however, misleading:[34] the two types of regimes do not have different legal force but are, quite simply, more or less special. In any case, '[i]t is in the nature of "general law to apply generally" – namely inasmuch as it has not been specifically excluded'.[35] Contracting out of general rules might be explicit (by expressly stating that the special rules derogate from general international law) or result implicitly from an interpretation of the treaty in the light of its object and purpose.[36] There is of course some circularity: the special secondary rules have to be interpreted according to the general secondary rules on interpretation in order to ascertain whether they are intended as special, that is, as replacing the general ones, and whether general international law allows derogation.[37] This is so unless specific rules on interpretation are provided in the special regime.[38]

Special regimes are often confused with so-called 'self-contained regimes'. The expression was first used by the Permanent Court of

[32] J. Crawford, *The International Law Commission's Articles on State Responsibility: Introduction, Text and Commentaries* (Cambridge University Press, 2002), p. 309. The examples given in the Commentary are Arts. 52, 62 (2) (b) and 60 (1) of the 1969 Vienna Convention on the Law of Treaties.

[33] Simma and Pulkowski, 'Of Planets and the Universe', 501.

[34] *Ibid.* 490–491. The distinction between 'strong' and 'weak' forms of *lex specialis* is also contained in the Commentary to Art. 55 of the ILC Articles on State Responsibility. Crawford, *International Law Commission's Articles on State Responsibility*, p. 308.

[35] ILC Report, p. 96.

[36] Pauwelyn, *Conflict of Norms in Public International Law*, pp. 215–218.

[37] Several provisions of the 1969 Vienna Convention on the Law of Treaties are dispositive (see *ibid.* 392) and Art. 55 of the ILC Articles on State Responsibility provides that the Articles 'do not apply when and to the extent that the conditions for the existence of an internationally wrongful act or the content or implementation of the international responsibility of a State are governed by special rules of international law'.

[38] The possible existence of special rules on the interpretation of non-proliferation law is discussed by Nigel White in Chapter 3.

International Justice (PCIJ) in the *S.S Wimbledon* case with regard to the relationship between two sets of primary rules.[39] The International Court of Justice (ICJ) employed it in the context of the remedies available for violations of the law of diplomatic relations.[40] The International Criminal Tribunal for the former Yugoslavia (ICTY) also noted that '[i]n international law, every tribunal is a self-contained system (unless otherwise provided)', without specifying what 'self-contained' means.[41] An accurate definition of 'self-contained regime' sees it as an extreme case of special regimes where *all* secondary rules are special *and* totally exclude any fall-back on general rules. It has been correctly argued that no special system in existence today is 'self-contained' and thus fully isolated from general international law.[42] Indeed, there is a difference between a far-reaching special regime, that is, a regime with a high number of special secondary rules, and a 'self-contained' regime which excludes any fall-back on general international law.[43] If the former are rare,[44] the latter do not exist: they are 'a phantom with no legal basis in international law, a notion which, despite its persistent appearance in jurisprudential debate, is best confined to the lively world of myth and fable'.[45] The ICJ itself did not intend the expression 'self-contained

[39] *S. S. Wimbledon*, 1923 PCIJ, Ser. A, No. 1, 23–24. The Court had to establish whether the general provisions on German waterways contained in the 1919 Versailles Peace Treaty also applied to the Kiel Canal in spite of the existence of specific provisions in the same treaty on that canal.

[40] *US Diplomatic and Consular Staff in Teheran* (*US* v. *Iran*), Judgment of 24 May 1980, ICJ Reports 1980, para. 86. According to the Court, '[t]he rules of diplomatic law . . . constitute a self-contained regime which, on the one hand, lays down the receiving State's obligation regarding the facilities, privileges and immunities to be accorded to diplomatic missions and, on the other, foresees their possible abuse by members of the mission and specifies the means at the disposal of the receiving State to counter any such abuse. These means are by their nature, entirely efficacious.' See also *Military and Paramilitary Activities in and against Nicaragua* (*Nicaragua* v. *US*), Merits, Judgment of 27 June 1986, ICJ Reports 1986, paras. 267–268 (with regard to human rights law, but without using the expression 'self-contained regime').

[41] *Prosecutor* v. *Tadić*, Case No. IT-94-1, Decision on the Defence Motion for Interlocutory Appeal on Jurisdiction, 2 Oct. 1995, para. 11.

[42] See, e.g., ILC Report, para. 91; Simma and Pulkowski, 'Of Planets and the Universe', 492; G. Abi-Saab, 'Fragmentation or Unification: Some Concluding Remarks', *New York University Journal of International Law and Politics*, 31 (1998–1999), 926.

[43] Indeed, 'contracting out of *some* rules of international law does not mean contracting out of *all* of them, let alone contracting out of the system of international law'. Pauwelyn, *Conflict of Norms in Public International Law*, p. 40.

[44] An example is EU Law.

[45] A. Lindroos and M. Mehling, 'Dispelling the Chimera of "Self-Contained Regimes": International Law and the WTO', *European Journal of International Law*, 16 (2005), 877.

regime' to exclude any resort to general international law, but rather to emphasize that the remedies for violations of diplomatic law are those available under diplomatic law itself when they are 'entirely efficacious', without, however, ruling out the general remedies in case they are not.[46]

General international law then continues to apply, without a need for an explicit *renvoi*, from at least three points of view.[47] First, special regimes imply general notions such as 'statehood', 'jurisdiction', 'state succession', 'immunities', etc., the meaning of which is determined by general rules. Second, general international law would also apply to all substantial and procedural aspects not regulated by the special regime.[48] Finally, fall-back on general law would occur whenever the special regime fails, e.g., when it is violated by the parties and the remedies provided therein are not efficacious or when the regime institutions do not function as they were supposed to.[49]

The question that this book will address, then, is not whether non-proliferation law is a self-contained regime in 'splendid isolation'[50] from general international law, but rather whether it is a special regime containing specific secondary rules and principles that differ from rules and principles of general international law and with those of other special regimes. The point is one of degree, that is, how much of the non-proliferation regime is special: this could go from one to, at least in theory, all its secondary rules. But, as noted above, in neither case would fall-back on general international law be entirely ruled out.

As already noted, whenever a special regime, however limited, comes to existence, a potential normative conflict arises. The ILC Conclusions define a normative conflict as 'the case where two norms that are both valid and applicable point to incompatible decisions so that a choice must be made between them'.[51] The maxim *lex specialis derogat legi*

46 *US Diplomatic and Consular Staff in Teheran*, para. 86.

47 See ILC Report, pp. 92 ff.

48 See, for instance, the Iran–US Claims Tribunal: 'As a *lex specialis* in the relations between the two countries, the Treaty supersedes the *lex generalis*, namely customary international law. This does not mean, however, that the latter is irrelevant in the instant case. On the contrary, the rules of customary law may be useful in order to fill in possible lacunae of the law of the Treaty, to ascertain the meaning of undefined terms in its text or, more generally, to aid interpretation and implementation of its provisions.' *Amoco Int. Finance Corp.* v. *Iran* (1987), 15 Iran–US CTR 189, para. 112.

49 ILC Report, p. 98. The failure might be substantive (if the regime fails to achieve its purpose) or procedural (if, for instance, reparation was envisaged but has not been secured through the regime mechanisms).

50 Simma and Pulkowski, 'Of Planets and the Universe', 492.

51 ILC Conclusions, para. 2.

generali ensures that the secondary rules of the special regime will usually take priority over the application of the general secondary rules (without, however, invalidating them). As observed in the Commentary to Article 55 of the ILC Articles on State Responsibility, '[f]or the *lex specialis* principle to apply it is not enough that the same subject matter is dealt with by two provisions; there must be some actual inconsistency between them, or else a discernible intention that one provision is to exclude the other'.[52] The conflict, in other words, must exist and cannot be solved by way of harmonization. Normative conflicts can arise between a special regime and the general law, between a special regime and other special regimes and within the special regime itself. The ILC Report notes that 'increasing attention will have to be given to the collision of norms and regimes and the rules, methods and techniques for dealing with such collisions'.[53]

The present book takes up this recommendation and tries first to identify whether there are specific secondary rules, as well as underlying interstitial principles, present in non-proliferation law that depart from or conflict with general international legal rules or with specific secondary rules and interstitial principles present in other special regimes. To the extent that such specialized rules are found to exist in non-proliferation law, the second task will be to consider whether and to what extent these specialized rules can be considered as evidence sufficiently supporting the conclusion that non-proliferation law is a special regime explainable by fragmentation theory.

A word on definitions: 'non-proliferation law' is defined herein to include all weapon of mass destruction (WMD) related treaties (i.e., chemical, biological, radiological and nuclear (CBRN) weapons-related treaties and missile-related treaties, due to their CBRN delivery relevance). Essentially, this term is intended to include WMD-related arms control treaties (treaties by which states agree to limit or reduce the amount and kinds of weapons they are entitled to possess); WMD-related disarmament treaties (treaties by which states agree to renounce entirely the possession of certain weapons and relinquish entirely existing stockpiles); WMD-related non-proliferation treaties (treaties that aim to prevent the spread of weapons); as well as WMD-related treaties limiting certain specific conduct, such as those banning weapon testing. The term non-proliferation law is not herein intended to include treaties

52 Crawford, *International Law Commission's Articles on State Responsibility*, p. 307.
53 ILC Report, p. 249.

on conventional (i.e., non-CBRN) weapons.[54] Some norms of WMD non-proliferation law have customary law status (for instance, the prohibition of atmospheric nuclear tests)[55] but to a great extent non-proliferation law is still treaty based.[56]

As noted previously, there has been debate in fragmentation and special regime theory literature on whether there is any normative or explanatory usefulness in identifying an entire substantive area of law, like international human rights law or international criminal law, and enquiring whether the entire substantive area, comprised of many different treaties and rules of customary international law, is or is not a special regime *in toto*. Some commentators have argued that the only meaningful level of analysis of specialness is at the discrete source level (i.e., a particular treaty like, for example, the Treaty on the Non-Proliferation of Nuclear Weapons (Nuclear Non-Proliferation Treaty – NPT)).[57]

This view is understandable and is very probably correct when applied to some issue areas of law that are grouped together, sometimes rather arbitrarily and over-inclusively, under the heading of a particular substantive area of international law. Indeed, as Ian Brownlie has argued, one example of this over-inclusivity and false assertion of substantive homogeneity may be presented in the area of international human rights

[54] See, generally, D. H. Joyner, *International Law and the Proliferation of Weapons of Mass Destruction* (Oxford University Press, 2009), p. xiv. The UN Commission for Conventional Armaments defined WMDs as 'atomic explosive weapons, radioactive material weapons, lethal chemical and biological weapons, and any weapons developed in the future which have characteristics comparable in destructive effect to those of the atomic bomb or other weapons mentioned above'. UN Doc. RES/S/C. 3/30, 13 August 1948.

[55] M. Roscini, *Le zone denuclearizzate* (Turin: Giappichelli, 2003), pp. 276–82.

[56] We have chosen to use the term 'non-proliferation law' in this volume, as opposed to other terms of common use in this area including 'arms control law' and 'disarmament law', because of the relatively recent ascendance of use of 'non-proliferation law' as a term in both official and academic circles. 'Non-proliferation law' is useful as a term because it clearly covers only CBRN weapons and excludes conventional weapons. Thus, 'non-proliferation law' is essentially a lesser included term within the term 'arms control law', which does typically include conventional weapons sources.

[57] ILC Report, p. 17, para. 21: 'But this cannot be so inasmuch as the characterizations ("trade law", "environmental law") have no normative value per se. They are only informal labels that describe the instruments from the perspective of different interests or different policy objectives. Most international instruments may be described from various perspectives: a treaty dealing with trade may have significant human rights and environmental implications and vice versa. A treaty on, say, maritime transport of chemicals, relates at least to the law of the sea, environmental law, trade law, and the law of maritime transport. The characterizations have less to do with the "nature" of the instrument than the interest from which it is described.'

law.[58] There is no doubt that some of this critique applies to the present study as well. However, as will hopefully become clear in the contributions to this volume, non-proliferation law is an issue area of international law that, in terms of its unique interstitial principles, exclusively subject-committed sources of law, and its complexity and epistemic capture by a discrete community of technical, policy and legal experts, both inside and outside of government, arguably makes it a more defensible subject for the possible identification of patterns and standard clauses than would be possible with regard to other substantive areas of international law. This volume will proceed with this understanding as its working assumption. However, consideration will return to this point in the conclusions to the volume.

On methodology, the volume is divided into two parts. The first focuses on the law of treaties as it bears on non-proliferation law sources. The second focuses on the law of state responsibility relative to non-proliferation law sources. Each section is subdivided into discrete subjects dealing with an aspect of either treaty law or the law of state responsibility and a separate contributor has been invited to write a chapter on each discrete subject.

Thus, in Part I, on treaty law, Malgosia Fitzmaurice and Panos Merkouris have contributed a chapter on amendment and modification of non-proliferation treaties, Andrew Michie a chapter on the provisional application of non-proliferation treaties, Nigel White a chapter on the interpretation of non-proliferation treaties, Eric Myjer and Jonathan Herbach a chapter on the violation of non-proliferation treaties and related verification treaties, and your editors Daniel Joyner and Marco Roscini a chapter on withdrawal from non-proliferation treaties.

In Part II, on the law of state responsibility, Matthew Happold has contributed a chapter on the 'injured state' in the case of breach of a non-proliferation treaty and the legal consequences of such a breach, Sahib Singh a chapter on non-proliferation law and countermeasures, and Dieter Fleck a chapter on the consequences of termination of or withdrawal from non-proliferation treaties.

In each of the chapters, the author's primary research question has been to examine the topic of secondary rules assigned to them as it relates to non-proliferation treaties, and to determine whether, and to what extent, there exist within the law and legal practice related to non-

58 I. Brownlie, *Principles of Public International Law*, 6th edn (Oxford University Press, 2003), pp. 529–530.

proliferation treaties specific and specialized secondary rules on that topic that differ from the general rules of international law on that topic and/or from specialized rules on that topic found in other substantive areas of international law.

To the extent that such specialized rules are found to exist, the author's second task has been to consider whether these specialized rules present in non-proliferation treaties can be considered as evidence supporting the conclusion that non-proliferation law is a special regime, at least as to that particular topic, explainable by fragmentation and special regime theory. The analysis of the evidence produced through the various authors' subject-specific inquiries is finally consolidated and summarized, and its theoretical implications considered, in the Conclusions section of the volume.

Through this methodology, a fairly comprehensive examination and evaluation of non-proliferation law as a special regime in international law is possible. It is hoped that, through this systematic examination of one substantive area of international law and the analysis of the evidence obtained thereby and discussion of its theoretical implications, this volume will make a significant contribution to theoretical discussions concerning fragmentation and special regimes in international law.

I

The law of treaties

1

Amendment and modification of non-proliferation treaties

MALGOSIA FITZMAURICE AND PANOS MERKOURIS

I. Introduction

The aim of the present chapter will be to examine whether non-proliferation law constitutes a 'special regime' from the perspective of the rules on amendment and modification, or whether the relevant general rules as enshrined in Articles 39–41 of the Vienna Convention on the Law of Treaties (VCLT) are applicable.

In order to answer this question one must start from the relevant amendment/modification provisions included in the VCLT. To this effect, section II will present the main points and areas of consideration during the VCLT *travaux préparatoires*, that is, what purpose were they intended to serve, what degree of freedom was permitted to the states to regulate amendment and modification in a different manner and what were some main areas of contention. Before characterizing non-proliferation law as a 'special regime' with respect to amendment and modification, then, one has to examine the more general provisions. The VCLT provisions are an essential point of departure in establishing whether the amendment and modification provisions of non-proliferation treaties are indeed different and 'special'. In order to do so the analysis will begin with an examination of the text of the relevant VCLT provisions, read in the light of the ILC discussions which led up to the Vienna Conferences on the Law of Treaties.[1] This will facilitate the demonstration of the intention of the parties, the meaning and the

[1] Although most judicial bodies and authors when applying and interpreting the VCLT often resort to the ILC discussions, they do so automatically. A neglected aspect is whether these discussions can indeed be considered as *travaux préparatoires* of the VCLT. It should come as no surprise that this question was actually raised during the ILC discussions relating to various drafts of a Convention on the Law of Treaties. Most members of the ILC agreed that they should be considered as *travaux préparatoires* or at least as *travaux préparatoires of a second order*. In any event, however, even if

function that Articles 39–41 were intended to have as well as certain problematic areas.

Based on the previous analysis, this chapter will continue by focusing on the amendment and modification provisions of non-proliferation treaties themselves. In this section, the analysis will focus on specific examples of non-proliferation treaties and the solutions adopted therein. In order to ensure that the conclusions reached are truly representative of the amendment/modification approaches found in non-proliferation treaties, examples will be taken from:

(i) multilateral treaties (e.g., the 1968 Treaty on the Non-proliferation of Nuclear Weapons – NPT; the 1963 treaty banning nuclear weapon tests in the atmosphere, in outer space and under water (the Partial Test-Ban Treaty) – PTBT; the 1993 Convention on the prohibition of the development, production, stockpiling and use of chemical weapons and on their destruction (the Chemical Weapons Convention) – CWC);
(ii) regional treaties (e.g., the 1996 African Nuclear-Weapon-Free-Zone Treaty; the 1985 South Pacific Nuclear-Free Zone; the 1995 Treaty on the Southeast Asia Nuclear-Weapon-Free Zone); and
(iii) bilateral treaties (e.g., the Strategic Arms Limitation Talks – SALT I; SALT II; the Strategic Offensive Reductions Treaty – SORT; the Strategic Arms Reduction Treaty – START I; START II; the Peaceful Nuclear Explosions – PNE Treaty; the Intermediate-range Nuclear Forces – INF Treaty).

What will be determined is whether non-proliferation treaties diverge significantly from the VCLT provisions and, if so, whether their provisions on amendment and modification are similar.[2]

This analysis will then be followed by an examination of the contemporary issues and problems that both institutional and normative proliferation has brought to the forefront in the field of treaty amendment and modification. A regime should be considered as 'special' if the

such documents are not considered as preparatory work, they nevertheless can be considered as 'other supplementary means' of Art. 32. In more detail, see P. Merkouris, 'Article 31(3)(c) of the VCLT and the Principle of Systemic Integration', unpub. Ph.D. thesis, Queen Mary, University of London, 2010, p. 6.

[2] This need for an existence of such an 'attractor', that is, a set or point towards which a dynamical system evolves over time, is essential for the existence of a special regime. If there are no such 'attractors' or points of convergence then one cannot talk of a 'special regime' but rather of ad hoc and relatively unconnected, both causally and systemically, solutions to a particular problem.

adopted solutions are not only different from those provided for by general international law but also from the approaches adopted by other regimes,[3] or other 'branches' of international law. Consequently, building on the analysis of the two previous sections, the amendment and modification provisions of non-proliferation treaties will be examined to determine whether and in what manner they deviate from the solutions adopted in treaties relating to other 'branches' of international law, and if so what is the *raison d'être* of such deviation.

II. An analysis of the VCLT provisions on amendment and modification

The main question that this chapter aims to address is whether non-proliferation law is a special regime with respect to amendment and modification procedures. No accurate response can be provided to this, unless one examines what are the (for lack of a better term) 'general-application rules' on amendment and modification that would apply to treaties unless the parties have otherwise agreed.[4] The starting point of our analysis will be the VCLT provisions. The relevant provisions are: Article 39, which is an introductory provision reiterating the *jus dispositivum* character of the VCLT provisions regulating amendment and modification, Article 40, which focuses on amendment, and Article 41, which tackles *inter se* agreements. However, in order for the VCLT analysis to be complete, one has to examine not only the provisions that found their way into the official text but also some draft provisions relating to modification, which were eventually left out. For this reason, Draft Article 68 of the 1964 ILC Draft on the Law of Treaties, which referred to modification by subsequent treaty, subsequent practice and subsequent custom, and Draft Article 38 of the 1966 ILC Draft on the law of Treaties will also be looked into to gain a holistic view of all the arguments and approaches to amendment and modification, as they waxed and waned during the ILC meetings.

i. Article 39 of the VCLT

The variety of forms that amendment and modification clauses take in treaties, combined with the fact that the wording selected for Article 39

[3] 'Special' or not is immaterial.
[4] Based on the fact that such 'general-application rules' are *jus dispositivum*.

stipulates that the provisions on amendment and modification of the VCLT apply 'except insofar as the treaty may otherwise provide', would seem to indicate that it would be extremely difficult for the ILC to draft provisions that attempt to regulate in a coherent manner the amendment and modification of multilateral treaties.

Yet the Commission took upon itself exactly that task. The reason for this was threefold: first, the process of amendments was of concern to international organizations; secondly, the proliferation of multilateral treaties 'has led to an increased awareness of the importance of making provision in advance, in the treaty itself, for the possibility of its future amendment'; and thirdly, the growth of multilateral treaties has rendered the unanimity rule[5] impractical.[6]

One of the first problems that the ILC faced was the lack of homogeneity of the amendment and modification clauses, which made it difficult, as the Commission was the first to admit, to 'deduce from the treaty practice the development of detailed customary rules regarding the amendment of multilateral treaties'.[7] For that reason, the approach that was selected was not to try to 'frame a comprehensive code of rules regarding the amendment of treaties' but to 'include a formulation of the basic rules concerning the process of amendment'.[8] In essence, the Articles of the VCLT would be of a 'residual character'.[9]

Another problem that the ILC had to face was the relatively loose and sometimes interchangeable use of terms such as 'amendment', 'revision' and 'modification'; for instance, in the UN Charter, 'amendment' is used to denote a process that affects individual provisions, whereas 'revision' affects the treaty in its entirety.[10] However, such a practice was far from uniform. It is for this reason that the ILC

> considered it sufficient in the present articles to speak of 'amendment' as being a term which covers both the amendment of particular provisions and a general review of the whole treaty. As to the term 'revision', the Commission recognized that it is frequently found in State practice and that it is also used in some treaties. Nevertheless, having regard to the

[5] i.e., that an amendment could enter into force only if it was accepted by *all parties* to the treaty.

[6] *Yearbook of the International Law Commission, 1966*, vol. 2, pp. 231–232, para. 1.

[7] *Ibid.*, para. 2. [8] *Ibid.*

[9] i.e. that they would apply only if the parties to the treaty had not inserted in its text any specific provisions on amendment and modification. See also *Ibid.* 233, para. 7.

[10] See Arts. 108 and 109 of the UN charter. For additional examples, see United Nations, *Handbook of Final Clauses* (ST/LEG/6), pp. 130 and 150.

> nuances that became attached to the phrase 'revision of treaties' in the period preceding the Second World War, the Commission preferred the term 'amendment'. This term is here used to denote *a formal* amendment of a treaty intended to alter its provisions with respect to all the parties. The more general term 'modification' is used in Article 37 [now Article 41 of the VCLT] in connexion with an *inter se* agreement concluded between certain of the parties only, and intended to vary provisions of the treaty between themselves alone, and also in connexion with a variation of the provisions of a treaty resulting from the practice of the parties in applying it [which was included in Draft Article 38, but was eventually left out of the text of the VLCT].[11]

A final interesting point was that the Commission considered it self-evident that the amending agreement may take any form that the parties agree to. It could be agreed by an *oral agreement* or also a *tacit agreement*.[12] This was reinforced for the former by the fact that the legal force of an oral agreement would be preserved by the provisions of Article 3(a) and (b) of the VCLT, and by Draft Article 38 for the latter, which provided for modification of a treaty by subsequent practice of states.[13]

ii. Treaty Amendment – Article 40

Article 40 of the VCLT bears the title 'Amendment of multilateral treaties'. This was not an oversight of the ILC but a conscious choice. The Commission elected to draft Article 40 of the VCLT as applying only to multilateral treaties, as it had concluded that the formulation of any rule designated specifically for bilateral treaties would not serve any useful purpose.[14] 'Where only two parties are involved, the question is essentially one of negotiation and agreement between them.'[15]

In its Commentary to Article 39 VCLT (then Draft Article 35) the ILC had clarified the distinction between the various terms of 'amendment', 'modification' and 'revision'.[16] Although the Commission recognized the fact that in many cases the amendment would enter into force between only certain of the parties to the treaty, it nevertheless felt that this was not sufficient grounds to treat 'amendment' and 'modification' in a similar manner. According to the ILC,

[11] *Yearbook of the International Law Commission, 1966*, vol. 2, p. 232, para. 3.
[12] *Ibid.*, p. 233, para. 4.
[13] *Ibid.*; eventually Draft Art. 38 was deleted by the Committee as a whole. For a more detailed analysis of the importance of Draft Art. 38, see section II.iv, below.
[14] *Yearbook of the International Law Commission, 1966*, vol. 2, p. 233, para. 5.
[15] *Ibid.* [16] See section II.i, above.

> there is an essential difference between amending agreements designed to amend a treaty between the parties generally and agreements designed *ab initio* to modify the operation of the treaty as between certain of the parties only. Although an amending instrument may equally turn out to operate only between certain of the parties, the Commission considered that a clear-cut distinction must be made between the amendment process *stricto sensu* and *inter se* agreements modifying the operation of the treaty between a restricted circle of the parties.[17]

The fact that in the past certain treaties had been amended or revised without notification of or consultation with the other parties did not prevent the ILC from adopting a solution that according to it 'seemed to flow directly from the obligation assumed by the parties to perform the treaty in good faith'.[18] Article 40(3) of the VCLT also was a matter of debate. The question was whether parties should be given only a right to become parties to the amended treaty or whether they should also be granted a right to participate in the negotiations of the amendment. The ILC held that the latter solution struck a fair balance between the various competing rights.[19]

Finally, Article 40(5) was the result of, on the one hand, the residuary character of Article 40[20] and, on the other hand, the lack of a provision in the majority of treaties to regulate the relationship and the manner in which the consent to be bound would be expressed with respect to the original treaty and the amended version.[21] The ILC

> [c]onsidered that [Article 40(5)] should be based on two principles: (a) the right of the State, on becoming a party to the treaty, to decide whether to become a party to the treaty alone, to the treaty plus the amending agreement or to the amended treaty alone; (b) in the absence of any indication by the State, it is desirable to adopt a solution which will bring the maximum number of States into mutual relations under the treaty. Paragraph 5 therefore provides that, failing an expression of a different intention, a State which becomes a party after the amending agreement has come into force is to be considered as: (a) a party to the treaty as amended, and (b) a party also to the unamended treaty in its relations with any party to the treaty which is not bound by the amending agreement.[22]

[17] *Yearbook of the International Law Commission, 1966*, vol. 2, p. 233, para. 6.
[18] *Ibid.*, paras. 8–9. [19] *Ibid.*, pp. 233–234, para. 10. [20] *Ibid.*, p. 233, para. 7.
[21] Art. 40(5) reflects the 'principle of simultaneous acceptance'.
[22] *Yearbook of the International Law Commission, 1966*, vol. 2, p. 234, para. 13.

iii. Inter se *agreements – Article 41*

As mentioned above, the main difference between 'amendment' and 'modification' is that whereas the former relates to a change to the treaty that affects *all the parties*, the latter is a change that is applicable only between the parties that undertake to such an *inter se* agreement, without affecting the remainder of relationships and rights and obligations created by the original treaty. All three Special Rapporteurs on the Law of Treaties, Sir Hersch Lauterpacht, Sir Gerald Fitzmaurice and Sir Humphrey Waldock, were in agreement that *inter se* agreements were the most used and perhaps most desirable method of revising multilateral treaties.[23] International treaty practice has to offer a multitude of examples of *inter se* agreements.[24] Despite the fact that there are examples of treaties that include specific provisions permitting modification,[25] such as Article 311 of UNCLOS and Article 19 of the Paris Convention for the Protection of Industrial Property of 1979, nevertheless, in the majority of cases, a treaty will not contain clauses permitting or prohibiting *inter se* agreements.[26]

Although, as previously mentioned, Articles 39–41 of the VCLT were meant to be of a residuary nature,[27] it was with respect to Article 41 that the Commission felt it imperative to include explicitly two limitations on the freedom of states to enter into *inter se* agreements: such a modification should not '(i) affect the enjoyment by the other parties of their rights under the treaty or the performance of their obligations; [and]

[23] See H. Lauterpacht, *Second Report on the Law of Treaties* (A/CN.4/87), *Yearbook of the International Law Commission*, 1954, vol. 2, p. 136; G. Fitzmaurice, *Third Report on the Law of Treaties* (A/CN.4/115), *Yearbook of the International Law Commission, 1958*, vol. 2, p. 43, para. 89; H. Waldock, *Third Report on the Law of Treaties* (A/CN.4/167 and Add. 1–3), *Yearbook of the International Law Commission*, 1964, vol. 2, p. 49.

[24] See, for instance, the 1995 Treaty on the Southeast Asia Nuclear-Weapon-Free Zone, 35 *ILM* 635 (1995); the 1985 South Pacific Nuclear-Free-Zone Treaty, 24 *ILM* 1440 (1985); the 1996 African Nuclear-Weapon-Free Zone Treaty, 35 *ILM* 698 (1996). For more examples, see United Nations, *Final Clauses of Multilateral Treaties – Handbook* (New York: United Nations, 2003), available at http://treaties.un.org/doc/source/publications/FC/English.pdf (accessed 15 July 2011); S. A. Sadat-Akhavi, *Methods of Resolving Conflicts between Treaties* (Leiden: Martinus Nijhoff, 2003), pp. 114–119; Study Group of the International Law Commission, *Report on Fragmentation of International Law: Difficulties Arising from the Diversification and Expansion of International Law – Finalized by Martti Koskenniemi* (A/CN.4/L.682), 13 April 2006 (hereinafter ILC Study Group), paras. 297 *et seq.*

[25] Sometimes these provisions will be conflict clauses.

[26] ILC Study Group, para. 315.

[27] *Yearbook of the International Law Commission, 1966*, vol. 2, p. 233, para. 7.

(ii) [should not] relate to a provision, derogation from which is incompatible with the effective execution of the object and purpose of the treaty as a whole'.[28]

The possibility of a modification agreement affecting the rights of the other parties to the treaty had been raised by Mr. Bartos and Mr. Paredes in the 764th Meeting of the ILC[29] and was an integral part of the discussions on Article 41 of the VCLT.[30] The requirement of non-incompatibility of an *inter se* agreement with the object and purpose of the treaty is very similar to the same requirement in the context of reservations,[31] and is reflected in a number of VCLT provisions.[32]

Both of these limitations imposed on possible *inter se* agreements and the manner in which they may be applied touch upon another crucial aspect that arose several times in the ambit of the ILC discussion on the law of treaties with reference to several of the VCLT provisions: that of the typology of international obligations. Sir Gerald Fitzmaurice identified two categories of obligations: reciprocal and non-reciprocal. The reciprocal obligations, which can be subdivided into bilateral or bilateralizable obligations, are owed by each party to a bilateral or multilateral treaty *individually* to each of the other parties and are 'based on contractual reciprocity consisting of a reciprocal interchange between the parties, each giving certain treatment to, and receiving it from, each of the parties'. The non-reciprocal obligations, on the other hand, are further subdivided into two categories. (i) '[Interdependent] obligations,

[28] Art. 41 of the VCLT.

[29] Comments by Bartos, ILC 764th Meeting on 13 July 1964, *Yearbook of the International Law Commission, 1964*, vol. 1, p. 272, para. 79; Comments by Paredes, ILC 764th Meeting on 13 July 1964, *Yearbook of the International Law Commission, 1964*, vol. 1, p. 272, para. 84. This limitation that '*inter se* agreements' should not affect the rights or performance of the duties of other states parties to the original treaty is reflected in Art. 311(3) UNCLOS, which provides that *inter se* agreements should not affect the 'application of the [Convention's] basic principles or the other States parties' enjoyment of their rights or performance of their obligations under the Convention'.

[30] Comments by Verdross, ILC 860th Meeting on 13 July, 1964, *Yearbook of the International Law Commission, 1966*, vol. 1, part II, p. 126, para. 58; Comments by Castrén, ILC 860th Meeting on 13 July 1964, *Yearbook of the International Law Commission, 1966*, vol. 1, part II, p. 126, para. 59.

[31] See also 'Reservations to the Convention on the Prevention and Punishment of the Crime of Genocide', Advisory Opinion of 28 May 1951, ICJ Reports 1951 15.

[32] ILC Study Group, para. 309. An example of a provision giving voice to this limitation is Art. 311 (6) UNCLOS, which provides that 'States Parties agree that there *shall be no amendments to the basic principle relating to the common heritage of mankind set forth in article 136 and that they shall not be party to any agreement in derogation thereof* (emphasis added).

which, by reason of the character of the treaty, are necessarily dependent on a *corresponding performance by all other parties*'. A typical example of a treaty creating interdependent obligations and very relevant for the purposes of the chapter was offered by Sir Gerald Fitzmaurice himself: disarmament treaties.[33] (ii) Integral/absolute obligations, where 'the obligation of each party [is] altogether independent of performance by any other of the others, and would continue for each party even if defaults by others occurred'.[34] Although this typology was not adopted *expressis verbis* in the VCLT text, it had a profound effect in the course of the discussions and still permeates the reasoning of international judges and academics. Based on this typology one can come to the conclusions that with respect to treaties creating bilateral or bilateralizable obligations it would be much easier for an *inter se* agreement to be in conformity with both requirements of Article 41(1)(b) (i) and (ii). The case would be much more difficult to argue in case of treaties creating interdependent, and, even more so, integral, obligations.

Another point of consideration for the ILC, with respect to *inter se* agreements, was that of notification. Originally, the Commission was of the view that notification should be given of every proposal to conclude an *inter se* agreement, but later on, prompted by the Comments of the Governments and most notably those of the Government of the Netherlands, it opted for the solution that the intention to conclude an *inter se* agreement should be transmitted to the other parties *only* when the treaty itself made provision for the conclusion of such agreements.[35] Another aspect of the issue of notification was when such agreements

33 ILC Study Group, para. 309.

34 G. Fitzmaurice, *Third Report on the Law of Treaties* (A/CN.4/115), *Yearbook of the International Law Commission, 1958*, vol. 2, p. 44, para. 91; and, in more detail, pp. 41–45, paras. 77–94; p. 27, para. 2. See also G. Fitzmaurice, *Second Report on the Law of Treaties* (A/CN.4/107), *Yearbook of the International Law Commission, 1957*, vol. 2, p. 54; H. Waldock, *Third Report on the Law of Treaties* (A/CN.4/167 and Add. 1–3), *Yearbook of the International Law Commission*, 1964, vol. 2, p. 39, para. 17. Sir Gerald Fitzmaurice suggested as an example of a treaty creating 'interdependent' obligations, a disarmament treaty, whereas the Convention against Torture or the Genocide Convention would be examples of treaties creating 'integral' or 'absolute' obligations. See also J. Pauwelyn, 'A Typology of Multilateral Treaty Obligations: Are WTO Obligations Bilateral or Collective in Nature?'', *European Journal of International Law*, 14 (2003), 907–951; A.-L. Sicilianos, 'The Classification of Obligations and the Multilateral Dimensions of the Relations of International Responsibility', *European Journal of International Law*, 13 (2002), 1127–1145.

35 This was the solution that was finally adopted in the text of Art. 41(2). See also *Yearbook of the International Law Commission, 1966*, vol. 2, p. 87, para. 3.

should be notified to the other parties to the treaty. Should such a notification be made immediately, as soon as certain parties expressed an intention to conclude an *inter se* agreement, or should this occur after the publication of the agreement?[36]

Eventually the solution that was adopted by the Commission and found its way in the text of the VCLT (i.e., that states wishing to conclude an *inter se* agreement 'shall notify the other parties of their intention to conclude the agreement and of the modification to the treaty for which it provides') reflects the compromise that was achieved:

> [The] parties should be given time to react and that could only be done if concrete proposals were communicated to them, whence the wording in paragraph 2 . . . In other words, *notification must be given at a relatively advanced stage in the negotiation of the inter se agreement but nevertheless sufficiently prior to its conclusion so as to enable a meaningful reaction.*[37]

iv. *Draft Article 68 – the abandoned provision*

a. Modification by subsequent practice

Apart from Articles 39–41 of the VCLT, which ended up making it to the final text of the VCLT, during the ILC discussions another article relating to modification of treaties was taken into consideration. This was Article 68 of the 194 ILC Draft that read as follows:

> Article 68. Modification of a treaty by a subsequent treaty, by subsequent practice or by customary law

[36] *Yearbook of the International Law Commission, 1966*, vol. 1, part II, pp. 123 *et seq.* See also ILC 745th Meeting on 15 June 1964, *Yearbook of the International Law Commission, 1964*, vol. 1, pp. 141 *et seq.* and the comments by Mr. Reuter at ILC 754th Meeting on 29 June 1964, *Yearbook of the International Law Commission, 1964*, vol. 1, p. 201, para. 50.

[37] ILC Study Group, para. 318. The ILC Study Group also rightly pointed out that Art. 41 leaves two questions open: (i) the legal effect of the conclusion of an '*inter se* agreement' in contravention to the requirements set by Art. 41(1) of the VCLT; and (ii) the legal effect of an objection raised after the notification of Art. 41(2). See ILC Study Group, para. 319. See also Mr. Briggs at the ILC 860th Meeting on 27 May 1966, *Yearbook of the International Law Commission, 1966*, vol. 1, part II, pp. 126–127, paras. 71–72. Despite the theoretical importance of these issues, they fall outside the scope of the present article and the authors will restrict themselves to just indicating that the first question touches upon issues of material breach whereas the second is similar to the situation faced in the context of reservations.

The operation of a treaty may also be modified:

(a) By a subsequent treaty between the parties relating to the same subject matter to the extent that their provisions are incompatible;
(b) By subsequent practice of the parties in the application of the treaty establishing their agreement to an alteration or extension of the provisions; or
(c) By the subsequent emergence of a new rule of customary law relating to matters dealt with in the treaty and binding upon all the parties.[38]

Although this Article was eventually dropped, nevertheless, an examination of the issues relating to it can prove extremely useful for addressing contemporary challenges to the law of amendment and modification of treaties.[39] Even more so if one bears in mind that this very topic of the importance of subsequent agreements and subsequent practice has once again been taken up by the ILC for consideration. In 2008, the ILC at its sixtieth session decided to include in its programme of work the topic 'treaties over time in particular: subsequent agreement and practice', and to establish a study group.[40]

One of the observations that Special Rapporteur Waldock made with respect to this Article was that, especially with respect to bilateral treaties, 'the effect of subsequent practice as evidence of a new agreement modifying a treaty may be indistinguishable for practical purposes from subsequent practice as evidence of an agreement giving an authentic interpretation of the treaty'.[41] The *Temple of Preah Vihear* case, which dealt with this issue, showed, according to Waldock, that for practical purposes it may be irrelevant whether subsequent practice is considered as having effect either in the context of interpretation or in that of modification,[42] whereas in the *Air Services Agreement* case the tribunal had explicitly held that subsequent practice by the states had modified the treaty in question.[43]

This course of conduct may, in fact, be taken into account not merely as a means useful for interpreting the Agreement, but also as something more: that is, as a possible source of a subsequent modification, arising out of certain actions or certain attitudes, having a bearing on the

[38] *Yearbook of the International Law Commission, 1964*, vol. 2, p. 198.
[39] As will be shown below in the section on contemporary issues of amendment and modification of treaties.
[40] ILC 2997th Meeting on 8 August 2008 (A/63/10), para. 353 and Annex A.
[41] *Yearbook of the International Law Commission, 1966*, part II, pp. 89–90, para. 8
[42] *Ibid.* [43] *Ibid.*

> juridical situation of the parties and on the rights that each of them could properly claim.[44]

Furthermore, irrespective of the practical use of a distinction between subsequent practice as an interpretative or modification tool in the context of bilateral treaties, the issue remains of import with respect to multilateral treaties. The reason for this differentiation is that whereas in Article 31 of the VCLT the subsequent practice must establish the understanding of *all the parties* the proposed Draft Article 68 had no such mention. This would allow for some of the parties to 'apply the treaty in somewhat different ways; or that some parties apply the treaty in a way which the others do not accept as a correct interpretation of it'.[45] Such cases should be considered as modification. As Special Rapporteur, Waldock succinctly summarizes:

> Clearly, on the plane of interpretation, *the treaty has only one correct interpretation*. But in practice it may have applications between particular parties which diverge from the interpretation and application of it by the general body of the parties. It hardly seems possible to classify such cases under the head of 'interpretation by subsequent practice' without seeming to throw overboard the essential concept of the integrity of the text of a multilateral treaty.[46]

A further issue that troubled the Commission was whether it was necessary to distinguish between subsequent practice 'amending' the treaty and subsequent practice 'modifying' it, along similar lines as the provisions relating to 'amending' and '*inter se*' agreements. The Special Rapporteur observed:

> [i]f it may be inadvisable to try to carry the parallelism between express agreement and agreement evidenced by subsequent conduct too far, it seems desirable for the Commission to consider how far the conditions set out in [the present Article 41 of the VCLT] may be applicable also to '*inter se*' modification by subsequent practice.[47]

Whereas the ILC in its Report to the General Assembly held that the (at that point) Draft Article 38[48] dealt with the effect of subsequent practice

44 *Air Transport Services Agreement Arbitration* (US v. France), Award of 22 December 1963, 3 *ILM* 713 (1964).

45 *Yearbook of the International Law Commission, 1966*, part II, p. 90, para. 9

46 *Ibid.* (emphasis added). 47 *Ibid.*, para. 10.

48 '*Article 38. Modification of treaties by subsequent practice.* A treaty may be modified by subsequent practice in the application of the treaty establishing the agreement of the

in amending a treaty as a case of modification of treaties.[49] The ILC decided to dispense with the two paragraphs of Draft Article 68 relating to modification via a subsequent treaty relating to the same subject-matter and via emergence of a new customary rule. The former was left out because it was considered to be sufficiently covered by what would become Article 30 of the VCLT.[50] The latter was considered to

> depend to a large extent on the particular circumstances and on the intentions of the parties to the treaty . . . [and that] the question formed part of the general topic of the relation between customary norms and treaty norms which is too complex for it to be safe to deal only with one aspect of it in the present article.[51]

Despite the ILC's recommendation, the Committee of the Whole during the Vienna Conferences on the Law of Treaties deleted Article 38. There were some concerns expressed by some delegates based on a *stricto sensu* understanding of the *pacta sunt servanda* principle[52] and whether the *Temple of Preah Vihear* and *Air Services Agreement* cases reflected the law as it stood at the time.[53] However, the considerations that were the proverbial straw that broke the camel's back and led to the eventual rejection of Article 38 related to evidentiary issues of the notion of 'practice', e.g., what would be considered as constituting 'practice', how general and/or consistent such a practice should be, what would be the *gravitas* of any element taken into consideration and whether objections should also be factored in.[54] For all the above reasons, 'subsequent practice' was retained only within the ambit of interpretation as enshrined in Article 31 of the VCLT[55] but deleted Draft Article 38 in its entirety.

b. Modification by subsequent emergence of a new rule of customary law

During the VCLT *travaux préparatoires* the effects of the emergence of a new customary rule had been taken into consideration in various

parties to modify its provisions'. *Yearbook of the International Law Commission, 1966*, part II, p. 236.

49 *Ibid.*, para. 1 50 *Ibid.*, para. 2. 51 *Ibid.* This issue will be further analysed below.

52 UN Conference on the Law of Treaties, 37th Meeting of the Committee of the Whole (A/CONF.39/C.1/SR.37) (1968), para. 63.

53 *Ibid.*, paras. 58, 75. See also 38th Meeting of the Committee of the Whole (A/CONF.39/C.1/SR.38) (1968), paras. 1–5.

54 (A/CONF.39/C.1/SR.37), paras. 65–74 and (A/CONF.39/C.1/SR.38), paras. 1–60.

55 Specifically, Art. 31(3)(b) of the VCLT.

contexts. Originally an article to that effect was put to discussion, which provided that

> The interpretation at any time of the terms of a treaty ... shall take account of: (a) the emergence of any later rule of customary international law affecting the subject – matter of the treaty and binding upon all the parties.[56]

However, because it was felt that this principle essentially dealt with modification of treaties, it was later incorporated in the draft Article pertaining to modification:

> The operation of a treaty may also be modified ... (c) by the subsequent emergence of a new rule of customary law relating to matters dealt with in the treaty and biding upon all the parties.[57]

Although originally the comments by the Governments seemed to favour such a provision,[58] the objections raised by Greece that argued that it could not envisage how an *opinio juris* necessary for the creation of custom could be established when it so blatantly contradicted previous conventional commitments,[59] and more importantly the United Kingdom that argued that the aforementioned provision disregarded the principle that treaties should not be modified but with the consent of the parties,[60] seemed to sway the ILC in its direction.[61] In the end, the reference to supervening custom was deleted from the Articles of the VCLT, because it was felt that such an absolute rule did not admit of automatic application. In each case it should be examined whether the parties intended for their treaty to be a *lex specialis* not to be modified by any subsequently emerging customary norm.[62]

[56] H. Waldock, *Third Report on the Law of Treaties* (A/CN.4/167 and Adds. 1–3), *Yearbook of the International Law Commission, 1964*, vol. 2, p. 53.

[57] ILC, *Report of the International Law Commission Covering the Work of its Sixteenth Session, 11 May–24 July 1964 – Draft Articles on the Law of Treaties* (A/5809), *Yearbook of the International Law Commission, 1964*, vol. 2, p. 198.

[58] See N. Kontou, *The Termination of Treaties in Light of New Customary International Law* (Oxford: Clarendon Press, 1994), p. 137.

[59] Comments by Greece on 845th Meeting, *Yearbook of the International Law Commission, 1966*, vol. 2, p. 38, para. 41.

[60] Comments by United Kingdom, ANNEX: *Comments by Governments on Parts I, II and III of the Draft Articles on the Law of Treaties Drawn up by the Commission at its Fourteenth, Fifteenth and Sixteenth Sessions* (A/6309/Rev. l), *Yearbook of the International Law Commission, 1966*, vol. 2, p. 345.

[61] See Kontou, *The Termination of Treaties in Light of New Customary International Law*, p. 138 and references therein.

[62] *Ibid.*

More recently, the *Institut de Droit International* in its 1995 Resolution on 'Problems Arising from a Succession of Codification Conventions on a Particular Subject' avoided making any pronouncements on the issue of supervening custom.[63] In an earlier draft of Conclusion 11, however, there was a specific reference to that effect, that is, that a later customary law could modify an earlier treaty,[64] which was left out in the end because it was too complex an issue to be dealt with 'as an ancillary point at the end of a Conclusion'.[65]

Although this issue is an extremely intricate one and touches upon the relationship between the principles of *lex posterior* and *lex specialis*, it would be outside the scope of this chapter to delve deep into it. However, what can very cursorily be said, is that, since both these principles stand on par, whether a supervening custom indeed supersedes or modifies an earlier treaty will depend on an *ad hoc* examination of which set of rules is more reflective of the current state of consent of the parties. This approach seems also to be implied by the four conditions that Kontou sets for the supervening custom;[66] especially the fourth condition – although referring to the notion of *lex specialis* is actually more of a safeguard against the automatic application of supervening custom.[67]

63 Institut de Droit International, *Resolution of 1 September 1995 on Problems Arising from a Succession of Codification Conventions on a Particular Subject, Annuaire de l'Institut de Droit International*, 66 (1995/I), p. 248.

64 *Ibid.*

65 Comments by Higgins, in Institut de Droit International, *Resolution of 1 September 1995*, p. 207.

66 'New customary law may be invoked as a ground of termination or revision of a prior treaty if: (i) it is incompatible with the treaty provisions; (ii) it is different from the customary international law in force at the time of the conclusion of the treaty; and (iii) is binding upon all parties to the treaty, unless (iv) the parties intended that the treaty should continue applying as special law.' Kontou, *The Termination of Treaties in Light of New Customary International Law*, p. 146. Kontou also mentions the following cases as supporting her conclusions: C-812/79, *A-G* v. *Burgoa*, Judgment of 14 October 1980, ECR 2787; *Dispute Concerning Filleting within the Gulf of St Lawrence ('La Bretagne' Arbitration) (Canada* v. *France), RGDIP* 90 (1986), 716; *Fisheries Jurisdiction case (Merits)* (United Kingdom v. Iceland), Judgment of 25 July 1974, ICJ Reports 1974 3; *UK–France Continental Shelf Arbitration* (1989), 18 *ILM* 397 (1989).

67 See also Pauwelyn, who argues that there must be a presumption in favour of the later custom. The burden of proof is then on the states to reverse this presumption and show that *their intention* was for the earlier rule to continue to apply. J. Pauwelyn, *Conflict of Norms in Public International Law: How WTO Law Relates to other Rules of International Law* (Cambridge University Press, 2003), p. 141, *contra* M. Villiger, who argues in favour of such an automatic application. M. Villiger, *Customary International Law and Treaties: A Manual on the Theory and Practice of the Interrelation of Sources* (The Hague: Kluwer Law International, 1997), para. 324.

What this condition asks for is that the true intent of the parties is revealed: the reference to *lex specialis* is only incidental and should not be construed as a sort of hierarchy between *lex posterior* and *lex specialis*. The guiding principle for resolving this issue is *the intention of the parties*.

III. Approaches of non-proliferation law and other branches of international law to amendment and modification

In the previous section, the scope of Articles 39–41 of the VCLT was analysed. The key element was the great degree of freedom that was provided to states in adopting any procedures they felt would better serve the objects and purposes of the treaties they became parties to. Articles 39–41 were designated as having a 'residual' character.

This section will now focus on the approaches that have been adopted by non-proliferation treaties as to amendment and modification. These will be scrutinized to reveal whether they deviate not only from the 'general-application rules' of the VCLT but also from creative solutions that have been adopted in the context of other 'branches of international law'.

It has to be noted that the exponential increase in treaties being negotiated, signed and ratified in the last few years, as well as the expansion of the areas of international cooperation and regulation, has prompted some interesting approaches as to amendment and modification of treaties and also brought about situations that will test the limits and levels of adaptability of the relevant provisions. In the following pages the most notable examples will be addressed.

i. Following the paradigm of the VCLT?

a. Amendment of bilateral treaties

As mentioned in the previous section, Article 40 of the VCLT has the title 'Amendment of multilateral treaties', as any rules relating to amendment of bilateral treaties would be essentially pointless.[68] In bilateral agreements the issue of amendment or modification becomes almost tautological with that of negotiation and subsequent agreement.[69] It is no surprise then that in a number of bilateral non-proliferation treaties one cannot find any provision on amendment. For instance, the following bilateral non-proliferation

[68] *Yearbook of the International Law Commission, 1966*, vol. 2, p. 233, para. 5. [69] *Ibid.*

agreements do not establish an amendment/modification procedure: the Strategic Arms Limitation Talks (SALT I, SALT II); the Strategic Offensive Reductions Treaty (SORT); the 1994 USA–DPRK (Democratic People's Republic of Korea) Agreed Framework; the 1992 Joint Declaration of South and North Korea on the Denuclearization of the Korean Peninsula; the 1988 India–Pakistan Non-Attack Agreement; the 1999 Lahore Declaration between Indian and Pakistan; and the 1991 Mendoza Agreement.[70] However, this is not an approach that is always adhered to. There are some notable exceptions of bilateral non-proliferation agreements that actually do provide for an amendment procedure, such as the treaties between the United States of America and the Union of Soviet Socialist Republics on strategic offensive reductions (START I,[71] START II[72]); the treaty between the United States of America and the Union of Soviet Socialist Republics on underground nuclear explosions for peaceful purposes (PNE Treaty);[73] the treaty between the United States of America and the Union of Soviet Socialist Republics on the elimination of their intermediate-range and shorter-range missiles (INF Treaty);[74] the treaty on the limitation of anti-ballistic missile systems (ABM Treaty);[75] the Treaty between the United States of America and the Russian Federation on measures for the further reduction and limitation of strategic offensive arms (New START).[76]

All of these non-proliferation treaties include a provision to the effect: 'Each Party may propose amendments to this Treaty. Agreed amendments shall enter into force in accordance with the procedures governing entry into force of this Treaty.' This wording is identical in Article XVIII of SALT I, Article VII of SALT II, Article XIV of the ABM Treaty and Article XV of the New START.[77] The remaining two treaties, PNE

[70] This last one is actually a mini-lateral treaty (only three parties), but still no amendment procedure.

[71] Available at www.state.gov/www/global/arms/starthtm/start/treatytc.html#TREATYTOC (accessed 15 July 2011).

[72] Available at www.state.gov/www/global/arms/starthtm/start2/stiitoc.html#TREATYTOC (accessed 15 July 2011).

[73] Available at www.nti.org/media/pdfs/PNE.pdf?_=1316645666&_=1316645666 (accessed 15 July 2011).

[74] Available at www.nti.org/media/pdfs/aptinf.pdf?_=1316643952&_=1316643952 (accessed 15 July 2011).

[75] 944 UNTS 13 (1972).

[76] Available at www.state.gov/documents/organization/140035.pdf (accessed 15 July 2011).

[77] However, it has to be noted here that Art. XV of the New START has a second paragraph, which reads as follows: '2. If it becomes necessary to make changes in the Protocol to this

(Article VIII) and INF (Article XVI), have only minor linguistic differences that do not affect the content of that provision.

The question that arises is whether the inclusion of a specific provision relating to the amendment of a bilateral agreement serves any purpose. As the ILC commented, during the discussions on the law of treaties, the formulation of any rule on amendment designated specifically for bilateral treaties would have no purpose. In the case of bilateral agreements, the question of amendment was tantamount to 'a question . . . of negotiation and agreement between them'.[78] However, in the case of the treaties under consideration, the inclusion of an amendment provision may actually serve a purpose. First of all, an amendment proposal would leave intact the remainder of the text. Only the amendment would be discussed and consequently all the other provisions would be left out of the negotiating process. Of course, this reasoning seems somewhat artificial, as even if a new treaty had to be negotiated, the parties could agree to adopt the same text with the exception of a few agreed changes. Another argument could be the federal nature of the two parties of the bilateral agreement. The inclusion of an amendment provision could be as a safeguard against fears of a possible dissolution of one of the contracting states, or emergence of successor states. Of course, in such a scenario, issues of fundamental change of circumstances and state succession would arise. Nevertheless, a situation could arise where the bilateral agreement would be transformed into a multilateral one. If this were to occur, then a lack of an amendment provision would mean that the amendment of the relevant treaty would be regulated by the VCLT provisions or, if they were not temporally applicable, by customary international law.

It is, perhaps, for these reasons, and in order to be absolutely safe and clear as to the amendment procedure applicable, that the drafters of the above treaties decided to include amendment provisions in bilateral treaties.

b. Following the VCLT Article 40

Similarly, despite the fact that even during the ILC meetings it was explicitly acknowledged that the proliferation of international treaties had as a direct consequence the rendering of the unanimity rule as

Treaty that do not affect substantive rights or obligations under this Treaty, the Parties shall use the Bilateral Consultative Commission to reach agreement on such changes, without resorting to the procedure for making amendments that is set forth in paragraph 1 of this Article.' This approach will be discussed in more detail below.

[78] *Yearbook of the International Law Commission, 1966*, vol. 2, p. 233, para. 5.

impractical,[79] in modern practice one can still find examples of non-proliferation treaties that adhere to this all-or-nothing approach. Indicatively, we mention the 1985 South Pacific Nuclear-Free Zone (Treaty of Rarotonga) (Article 11);[80] the 1995 Treaty on the Southeast Asia Nuclear-Weapon-Free Zone (Bangkok Treaty) (Article 19);[81] and the 2006 Central Asian Nuclear-Weapon-Free Zone (Treaty of Semipalatinsk) (Article 17).[82]

The unanimity rule has its disadvantages, most notably the increased degree of difficulty in passing amendments. It is for this reason that the ILC considered it as impracticable.[83] It is, perhaps, indicative, that out of the conventions mentioned above, none has been amended so far, although this might be partly due to the object of regulation. In this context it is interesting to note that all of the abovementioned conventions that have adopted the 'unanimity rule' are regional Nuclear-Weapon-Free Zones (NWFZs). A NWFZ is

> deemed to be any zone, recognized as such by the General Assembly of the United Nations, which any group of States, in the free exercise of their sovereignty, has established by virtue of a treaty or convention whereby:
>
> (a) The statute of total absence of nuclear weapons to which the zone shall be subject, including the procedure for the delimitation of the zone, is defined;
> (b) An international system of verification and control is established to guarantee compliance with the obligations deriving from that statute.[84]

Although not all regional NWFZs have gone the way of the 'unanimity rule',[85] the fact that these treaties establish zones that are characterized by a complete absence of nuclear weapons and that they address specific regional concerns are elements that may have factored, and may continue to factor, heavily in the adoption of the unanimity rule over other less strict amendment procedures.

[79] *Ibid.* 231–232, para. 1. [80] 24 *ILM* 1442 (1985). [81] 35 *ILM* 635 (1995).
[82] Available at www.nuclearweaponsfreezones.org/docs/CANWFZ_treaty.pdf (accessed 15 July 2011).
[83] *Yearbook of the International Law Commission, 1966*, vol. 2, pp. 231–232, para. 1.
[84] United Nations General Assembly, 'Comprehensive Study of the Question of Nuclear-Weapon-Free Zones in All its Aspects', GA Res. 3472 (XXX) (A/RES/3472), adopted 11 December 1975.
[85] See, for instance, Art. 30 of the 1967 Treaty for the Prohibition of Nuclear Weapons in Latin America and the Caribbean (Treaty of Tlatelolco), 634 UNTS 281 (1967).

c. Following the VCLT rules – majority requirement

Other non-proliferation treaties tend to make use of the rather flexible nature of Article 40 and impose a variety of majorities for adoption and/or entry into force of amendments. These majorities range from (i) simple majority – e.g., the 1971 Treaty on the Prohibition of the Emplacement of Nuclear Weapons and other Weapons of Mass Destruction on the Seabed and the Ocean Floor and in the Subsoil thereof (Seabed Treaty)[86] and the 1972 Convention on the Prohibition of the Development, Production and Stockpiling of Bacteriological (Biological) and Toxin Weapons and on their Destruction (the Biological and Toxin Weapons Convention – BTWC *also known as* the Biological Weapons Convention – BWC)[87] to (ii) two-thirds majority – as in the 2005 International Convention for the Suppression of Acts of Nuclear Terrorism,[88] the 1980 Convention on the Physical Protection of Nuclear Material (CPPNM)[89] and the 1967 Treaty for the Prohibition of Nuclear Weapons in Latin America and the Caribbean (Treaty of Tlatelolco).[90] The Treaty of Tlatelolco is one of the NWFZs that have deviated from the 'unanimity rule'. However, whereas the NWFZs that require unanimity for the amendment process have not so far been amended, the Treaty of Tlatelolco has already been amended three times: in 1990, amending Article 7, relating to the legal denomination of the treaty;[91] in 1991, amending paragraph 2 of the former Article 25 (now Article 26), following the wording of Article 8 of the Organization of American States (OAS) Charter. This made it possible for countries that previously were impeded to adhere to the System of Tlatelolco;[92] in 1992, amending Articles 14, 15, 16, 19 and 20, which aimed at reassuring the confidentiality of industrial secrets of member states in nuclear matters and clarifying how the IAEA would intervene during special

[86] Art. VI; 606 UNTS 267 (1971). [87] Art. XI; 1015 UNTS 163 (1972).

[88] Art. 26; 44 *ILM* 815 (2005). [89] Art. 20; 18 *ILM* 1419 (1980).

[90] Art. 30; 634 UNTS 281 (1967).

[91] Agency for the Prohibition of Nuclear Weapons in Latin America and the Caribbean, *Modification to the Treaty for the Prohibition of Nuclear Weapons in Latin America* (*Treaty of Tlatelolco*), Resolution 267 (E-V) (CG/E/Res.267 (E-V)), adopted 3 July 1990.

[92] Agency for the Prohibition of Nuclear Weapons in Latin America and the Caribbean, *Resolution Adopted by the Second Meeting of Signatories of the Treaty of Tlatelolco – Amendment of the Treaty for the Prohibition of Nuclear Weapons in Latin America and the Caribbean*, Resolution 268 (XII) (CG/Res.268), adopted 9 May 1991.

investigations.[93] This goes to show one of the main disadvantages of the 'unanimity rule', that is, the difficulty in securing an amendment in a multilateral treaty. The common element of all the above treaties is that they adhere strictly to Article 40(4) VCLT, which stipulates that '[t]he amending agreement does not bind any State already a party to the treaty which does not become a party to the amending agreement'. Only states that have accepted or ratified the amendment are bound. States that have refused to do so remain bound only by the original text of the treaty.

In this context two further treaties need to be mentioned: the 1963 treaty banning nuclear weapon tests in the atmosphere, in outer space and under water (Partial Test-Ban Treaty – PTBT)[94] and the 1968 Treaty on the Non-Proliferation of Nuclear Weapons (Nuclear Non-Proliferation Treaty – NPT).[95] Both these treaties, in Articles II and VIII, respectively, require for the adoption of the proposal for an amendment a simple majority of the parties, but with a caveat. In the case of the PTBT, that '[a]ny amendment to this Treaty must be approved by a majority of the votes of all the Parties to this Treaty, *including the votes of all of the Original Parties*',[96] whereas in the case of the NPT, 'any amendment to this Treaty must be approved by a majority of the votes of all the Parties to the Treaty, *including the votes of all nuclear-weapon States Party to the Treaty and all other Parties which, on the date the amendment is circulated, are members of the Board of Governors of the International Atomic Energy Agency*'.[97] In the case of the NPT the caveat extends even to the entry into force of the relevant amendment, since it is predicated upon the submission of instruments of ratification by a majority of the states, including those of '*all nuclear-weapon States Party to the Treaty and all other Parties which, on the date the amendment is circulated, are members of the Board of Governors of the International Atomic Energy Agency*'.[98]

d. Deviating from Article 40(4) VCLT

A similar extension occurs also in the case of the PTBT, but with one important twist. Instruments of ratification are required by all original parties, as in the adoption phase; however, the result of the submission of

[93] Agency for the Prohibition of Nuclear Weapons in Latin America and the Caribbean, *Amendments to the Treaty for the Prohibition of Nuclear Weapons in Latin America and the Caribbean*, Resolution 290 (E-VII) (CG/E/Res.290), adopted 26 August 1992.

[94] 480 UNTS 43 (1963). [95] 7 *ILM* 809 (1968). [96] Art. II(2) (emphasis added).

[97] Art. VIII(2) (emphasis added). [98] *Ibid.*

the instruments of ratification by a majority of parties is that '*all Parties are bound by such an amendment and not just the ratifying ones*'.[99] This breaks clear from Article 40(4) VCLT by binding states without them having become parties to the amending agreement. A similar approach to amendment procedures has been incorporated in the text of the 1996 African Nuclear-Weapon-Free Zone Treaty (Pelindaba Treaty),[100] where a submission of instruments of acceptance or ratification by a majority of the parties suffices to bind all the parties.[101]

This approach, which on its surface seems to break tradition with the primacy of intention in international affairs, should not come as a surprise. It is a response to the same concerns that gave rise to the 'tacit acceptance procedure' that will be analysed in more detail in section III, below. The fast pace of scientific development has made it essential for drafters to find ways to ensure that treaties will be able to adapt and address the new challenges, while at the same time fighting against their 'molecularization': a string of consecutive amendments that are binding on different sets of contracting parties has the disadvantage of creating a kaleidoscopic legal landscape, instead of a single unified approach. This impacts negatively on legal certainty and on the presumed efficacy of the treaty in question.

Furthermore, the fact that *all parties* are bound even if they have not ratified the amendment is not in conflict with the principle of *pacta sunt servanda*. On the contrary it actually stems from it. Although the parties have not given their intention for each and every particular amendment, that does not mean that intention is completely lacking. It is to be found in the drafting, signing and ratification of the original text of the treaty. Since both the VCLT and customary international law allow states to agree on any amendment procedure they wish, there is no obstacle in them expressing their intention not to have to express their intention for any future amendment. The original expression of intention is sufficient legally to explain the lack of any such expression for future amendments.

All the above examples illustrate in a crystal-clear manner that with respect to amendment and modification procedures there is no one single formula that is adopted consistently throughout all the non-proliferation instruments. On the contrary, a great variety of solutions has been put to use, ranging from strict adherence to the unanimity rule, adherence to Article 40 in a less stringent manner, e.g., by requiring

[99] Art. II(2) PTBT. [100] 35 *ILM* 698 (1996). [101] Art. 19(3).

majority,[102] to a clean break from 40(4) VCLT leading to states being bound without having explicitly agreed to the amending agreement. It is this last possibility that introduces the next part of the analysis.

ii. Technical or administrative character of treaty provisions as a decisive factor for divergence from the VCLT

a. The 'bifurcated procedure' of the CWC and the CTBT

The PTBT and NPT are not the only non-proliferation treaties that provide for the possibility of states being bound by amendments without their express agreement. A similar end result occurs in certain instances under the amendment procedures of the 1993 Convention on the Prohibition of the Development, Production, Stockpiling and Use of Chemical Weapons and on their Destruction (Chemical Weapons Convention – CWC)[103] and the 1996 Comprehensive Nuclear-Test-Ban Treaty (CTBT).[104] The reason that these two instruments are examined separately is twofold. First, they adopt a bifurcated procedure based on the nature of the provisions that are suggested should be amended and, secondly, they incorporate what is known as the 'tacit acceptance procedure'.[105]

In more detail, Article XV of the CWC outlines two procedures of amendment: a general one and a more specific one applying only to provisions of a particular nature. Article XV(3) stipulates that:

> Amendments shall enter into force for all States Parties 30 days after deposit of the instruments of ratification or acceptance by all the States Parties referred to under subparagraph (b) below:
>
> . . .
>
> (b) Ratified or accepted by all those States Parties casting a positive vote at the Amendment Conference.

This does not seem to be any different from what was analysed in the previous section. However, in the immediately following paragraph the parties to the convention establish another procedure applicable only to certain provisions. The first question that has to be answered is why such a solution was adopted. It is rather interesting to note that the parties to the CWC felt it was necessary to explain themselves by the first sentence

[102] Simple of two-thirds, unqualified or qualified. [103] 32 *ILM* 800 (1993).
[104] 35 *ILM* 1439 (1996).
[105] This will be analysed in more detail below during the presentation of the SOLAS Convention 1974 amendment procedure.

of Article XV(4) by stating that this second procedure was included in the system of the CWC '[i]n order to ensure the viability and the effectiveness of this Convention'.[106] The provisions that fall under this alternative procedure are mainly provisions of the Annexes and relate to matters of an administrative or technical nature.[107]

The procedure reserved for such provisions is the following: the text of the proposed amendment is submitted to the Director General, who in turn submits it to the parties, the Executive Council and the Depository[108] and evaluates it.[109] The Executive Council submits its proposal whether to adopt or reject the amendment.[110] If no state objects within a reasonable time-frame[111] it is assumed that they have tacitly accepted the Executive Council's recommendation.[112] If the recommendation was one for acceptance, then, lacking an objection by a state, the amendment is approved and finally enters into force.[113] This is done without the need for any instrument of ratification or any specific act by a state, just a mere lack of explicitly objecting to the Executive Council's recommendation. For that reason this procedure is known as 'tacit acceptance procedure'.

The CTBT in Article VII has a similar amendment procedure that is characterized by a bifurcated approach as to amendment and also by the inclusion of elements of a 'tacit acceptance procedure'. The critical question is whether this solution is unique to these two non-proliferation instruments. An answer to this question requires examination of treaties from other branches of international law. The relevant examples from the law of the sea area will be given.

b. The 'tacit acceptance procedure' of International Maritime Organization conventions

The 1974 International Convention for the Safety of Life at Sea (SOLAS)[114] is regarded as one of the most successful and important

106 Art. XV(4) CWC.

107 In detail, Art. XV(4) provides that 'Provisions in the Annexes shall be subject to changes in accordance with paragraph 5, if proposed changes are related only to matters of an administrative or technical nature. All changes to the Annex on Chemicals shall be made in accordance with paragraph 5. Sections A and C of the Confidentiality Annex, Part X of the Verification Annex, and those definitions in Part I of the Verification Annex which relate exclusively to challenge inspections, shall not be subject to changes in accordance with paragraph 5.'

108 Art. XV(5)(a) CWC. 109 Art. XV(5)(b) CWC. 110 Art. XV(5)(d) CWC.

111 In this case, ninety days. 112 Art. XV(5)(d) CWC. 113 Art. XV(5)(g) CWC.

114 The 1974 International Convention for the Safety of Life at Sea (SOLAS), adopted 1 November 1974 and entered into force 25 May 1980, 14 *ILM* 959 (1974).

treaties relating to maritime safety. The first version of SOLAS was adopted in 1914, as a response to the tragedy of the Titanic. It was followed by several other versions.[115] One of the main innovations of the 1974 SOLAS was the shift from more classical forms of amendment procedure to the inclusion of what is known as the 'tacit acceptance procedure'. Earlier versions of the SOLAS Convention provided that amendments came into force only by unanimous acceptance by the contracting parties[116] or after a percentage of the parties, usually two-thirds, had accepted them.[117]

However, such procedures were extremely time-consuming and, in fact, became an obstacle to the emergence and adoption of amendments to the various versions of SOLAS. The fact that none of the proposed amendments to the 1960 SOLAS received sufficient acceptance to enter into force speaks volumes.[118] It was, thus, recognized that a simplified and quick amendment procedure was necessary to ensure that the SOLAS Convention and the other IMO-related conventions could keep pace with the technological advances and the rapid evolution of all aspects relating to shipping. If this did not happen, then the aforementioned conventions would soon become outdated and the 'IMO's role as the international forum for technical issues involving shipping would have been placed in jeopardy'.[119]

In 1968, the IMO,[120] responding to concerns by several of its member states regarding the ability of the IMO to respond to contemporary challenges,[121] decided to establish a working group to identify areas for

[115] The second in 1929, the third in 1948 and the fourth in 1960; see IMO, 'International Convention for the Safety of Life at Sea (SOLAS), 1974', www.imo.org/About/Conventions/ListOfConventions/Pages/International-Convention-for-the-Safety-of-Life-at-Sea-(SOLAS),-1974.aspx (accessed 15 July 2011).

[116] SOLAS 1914, Art. 74 (referring to 'common consent') available at www.imo.org/knowledgecentre/referencesandarchives/documents/solas%201914.pdf (accessed 23 March 2012); SOLAS 1929, Art. 61, available at www.austlii.edu.au/au/other/dfat/treaties/1936/9.html (accessed 15 July 2011). It is interesting to note that the term used in SOLAS 1924 is 'modification'; however, the description of the process and effect of such 'modifications' clearly demonstrate that what we are dealing with are 'amendments'.

[117] SOLAS 1948, Art. 9, available at www.austlii.edu.au/au/other/dfat/treaties/1960/1.html (accessed 15 July 2011); SOLAS 1960, Art. 9, available at www.austlii.edu.au/au/other/dfat/treaties/1968/7.html (accessed 15 July 2011).

[118] IMO, Conventions, Introduction: 'Adopting a Convention, Entry into Force, Accession, Amendment, Enforcement, Tacit Acceptance Procedure', available at www.imo.org/About/Conventions/Pages/Home.aspx (accessed 15 July 2011).

[119] *Ibid.*

[120] Then named the Inter-Governmental Maritime Consultative Organisation (IMCO).

[121] It is helpful to bear in mind that the *Torrey Canyon* incident had taken place in March 1967.

improvement of the functioning of the IMO, and in 1969 it came back with a series of proposal, the most important of which concerned the amendment procedures of the IMO.[122]

The Working Group in its proposal drew inspiration from the procedures of four other UN agencies: the International Civil Aviation Organization (ICAO), the International Telecommunications Union (ITU), the World Meteorological Organization (WMO) and the World Health Organization (WHO).[123]

This process would lead to the eventual adoption of the 'tacit acceptance procedure' of Article VIII of the 1974 SOLAS Convention.[124] Similar tacit acceptance procedures can now be found in most of the IMO's technical conventions.[125]

Although the tacit acceptance procedure is the most notable element of Article VIII of the 1974 SOLAS Convention, it is not the only one. Article VIII is an amalgam of different amendment procedures. First, it distinguishes between two methods of an amendment being proposed: (i) amendments after consideration within the organization (Article VIII (b)) and (ii) amendments by a conference (Article VIII(c)). This dual approach echoes the distinction between 'amendment' and 'revision', which, as was mentioned in the previous sections, was not adopted in the end by the ILC. It is for this reason that the drafters of the 1974 SOLAS Convention correctly make no use of the term 'revision' and include both of these processes within the same article on amendments.

The main difference between these two methods is the manner in which the proposed amendments are to be adopted. In the first case, the whole process takes place by use of the IMO organs, and specifically the International Maritime Safety Committee (IMSC). In the second case, a conference is convened for the explicit purpose of adopting amendments to the SOLAS Convention. However, as to the substantive effects of these two processes, that is, when the amendments are deemed to have been adopted and enter into force, Article VIII provides that:

[122] IMO, 'Adopting a Convention'. [123] *Ibid.*

[124] A detailed history of the evolution of the 'tacit acceptance procedure' in the IMO can be found at IMO, 'Adopting a Convention'.

[125] e.g., the 1972 Convention on the International Regulations for Preventing Collisions at Sea, 1050 UNTS 16 (1972); the 1973 International Convention for the Prevention of Pollution from Ships, as amended by the Protocol of 1978 (MARPOL 73/78), 17 *ILM* 546 (1973); the 1972 International Convention for Safe Containers, 29 UST 3707 (1972). See also Z. O. Özçayır, 'IMO Conventions: The Tacit Consent Procedure and Some Recent Examples', *Journal of International Maritime Law*, 10/2 (2004), 204–211.

> (iii) Unless the Conference decides otherwise, the amendment shall be deemed to have been accepted and shall enter into force in accordance with the procedures specified in subparagraphs (b)(vi) and (b)(vii) respectively of this article, provided that references in these paragraphs to the expanded Maritime Safety Committee shall be taken to mean references to the Conference.[126]

These provisions create a bifurcated system. A different process is set out for acceptance and entry into force of amendments relating to Articles of the Convention or Chapter I of the Annex, on the one hand, and a completely different process[127] for any amendments to any part of the Annex other than Chapter I, on the other. The reason for that is the different nature of the provisions in question. The Articles of the Convention and Chapter I of the Annex contain general provisions that affect the functioning and workings of the entire Convention, whereas the Chapters of the Annex, with the exception of Chapter I, are of a technical nature and therefore need to be constantly updated in order to keep up with technological advances. The amendment system that thus is created is the following. For amendments to Articles of the Convention and Chapter I of the Annex, the more 'classical' approach to amendments has been followed:

> (vi) (1) An amendment to an article of the Convention or to chapter I of the annex shall be deemed to have been accepted on the date on which it is accepted by two thirds of the Contracting Governments . . .
> (vii) (1) An amendment to an article of the Convention or to chapter I of the annex shall enter into force with respect to those Contracting Governments which have accepted it, six months after the date on which it is deemed to have been accepted, and with respect to each Contracting Government which accepts it after that date, six months after the date of that Contracting Government's acceptance.[128]

On the other hand, for amendments to all parts of the Annex, apart from Chapter I, the tacit acceptance procedure has been followed. This means that an amendment that has been adopted by the IMSC, in accordance with the procedure set out in Article VIII(b)(i)–(v), will be considered as adopted and enter into force after the expiration of the required amount of time.[129] Member states do not need to proceed to any action. The amendment enters into force automatically. The only caveat is if

[126] 1974 SOLAS Convention, Art. VIII(c)(iii). [127] The 'tacit acceptance procedure'.
[128] 1974 SOLAS Convention, Art. VIII(b)(vi)(1) and (vii)(1).
[129] *Ibid.*, Art. VIII(b)(vi)(2) and (vii)(2).

> within the specified period either more than one third of Contracting Governments, or Contracting Governments the combined merchant fleets of which constitute not less than fifty per cent of the gross tonnage of the World's merchant fleet, notify the Secretary-General of the Organization that they object to the amendment, it shall be deemed not to have been accepted.[130]

Deemed as not having been accepted, the amendment does not enter into force. It is evident from the above that the tacit acceptance procedure is designed to ensure speed, effectiveness and adaptability of the SOLAS Convention. The numerous amendments of the SOLAS Convention attest to this fact.[131]

The presentation of the 1974 SOLAS amendment procedure demonstrates that 'bifurcated systems' of amendment procedure and 'tacit acceptance procedures' are not a creation of non-proliferation treaties. The 1993 CWC and the 1996 CTBT were adopted much later than the 1974 SOLAS Convention and the other relevant IMO Conventions. If anything, it is probably these IMO Conventions that functioned as a template for designing the amendment procedures of CWC and CTBT. Furthermore, the system adopted in all the abovementioned treaties are not a direct result of the treaties themselves falling within the limits of a specific 'branch of law', e.g., law of the sea or non-proliferation law. They are the direct response to the nature of certain provisions within the treaties being of an extremely technical or administrative character that needed constant updating to avoid becoming obsolete, a 'dead letter'. As the parties themselves have explicitly stated in CWC and CTBT, such a procedure allowing for a much speedier amendment procedure is essential '[i]n order to ensure the viability and the effectiveness of this Convention'.[132]

iii. Limitations to right of proposing amendments

The proliferation of international treaties and organizations, which was one of the main considerations for the ILC in including in the text of the VCLT a set of 'residual rules' relating to amendment and modification, can also have a restrictive effect on the rights of states to propose

130 1974 SOLAS Convention, Art. VIII(b)(vi)(2).

131 The Amendments adopted by the IMSC are listed in IMSC Resolutions, which can be found at http://www5.imo.org/SharePoint/mainframe.asp?doc_id=3710&topic_id=435 (accessed 15 July 2011).

132 Art. XV(4) CWC; similarly, Art. VII(7) CTBT.

amendments or enter into '*inter se* agreements', especially when these states are parties to regional organizations.

Two recent cases taken from the jurisprudence of the ECJ[133] seem to indicate the trend that although a convention may provide for the possibility of a state to propose amendments this may no longer suffice for that state to exercise that right. It will have to be examined and balanced alongside its other international obligations stemming from international treaties and/or participation in international organizations. Both of these cases revolved around Article 351 of the CTFEU (ex Article 307 TEC).[134] According to the jurisprudence of the ECJ, Article 351 of the CTFEU refers to rights of third states and obligations of member states, *but not to rights of member states.*[135]

In case C-45/07, *Commission* v. *Greece*, Greece had submitted a proposal to the MSC of the IMO regarding the adoption of certain safety measures under SOLAS.[136] The Court held that since the EU enjoyed exclusive competence in that area[137] and since Greece *had a right but not*

[133] C-45/07, *Commission* v. *Greece*, Judgment of 12 February 2009, available at http://curia.europa.eu/jurisp/cgi-bin/form.pl?lang=EN&Submit=Rechercher$docrequire=alldocs&numaff=C-45/07 (accessed 15 July 2011) and Case C-246/07, *Commission* v. *Sweden*, Judgment of 20 April 2010, available at http://curia.europa.eu/jurisp/cgi-bin/form.pl?lang=EN&Submit=Rechercher$docrequire=alldocs&numaff=C-246/07 (accessed 15 July 2011).

[134] Art. 351 TFEU provides that 'The rights and obligations arising from agreements concluded before 1 January 1958 or, for acceding States, before the date of their accession, between one or more Member States on the one hand, and one or more third countries on the other, shall not be affected by the provisions of the Treaties.

To the extent that such agreements are not compatible with the Treaties, the Member State or States concerned shall take all appropriate steps to eliminate the incompatibilities established. Member States shall, where necessary, assist each other to this end and shall, where appropriate, adopt a common attitude.

In applying the agreements referred to in the first paragraph, Member States shall take into account the fact that the advantages accorded under the Treaties by each Member State form an integral part of the establishment of the Union and are thereby inseparably linked with the creation of common institutions, the conferring of powers upon them and the granting of the same advantages by all the other Member States.'

[135] C-10/61, *Commission of the European Economic Community* v. *Italy*, Judgment of 27 February 1962, ECR 1, para. II B 3. On the problematic aspects of this distinction between 'rights' and 'obligations', see J. Klabbers, 'Re-Inventing the Law of Treaties: The Contribution of the EC Courts', *Netherlands Yearbook of International Law*, 30 (1999), pp. 63–65.

[136] IMO, 'Measures to Enhance Maritime Security' (MSC 80/5/11), 18 March 2005, available at www.sjofartsverket.se/upload/4017/80-5-11.pdf (accessed 15 July 2011).

[137] Case C-45/07, paras. 14–19, by virtue of the fact that setting of a common policy in the area of transport is one of the objectives of the Community (as affirmed in C-22/70, *Commission* v. *Council* [1971] ECR 263, para. 20) and Arts. 90, 91 and 100 of the CTFEU in combination

an obligation to submit such an amendment proposal,[138] it should have abstained from such an action, which was in violation of its obligations under EU law. By its amendment proposal Greece 'set in motion . . . a procedure with the contested proposal, [and] took an initiative likely to affect the provisions of the Regulation, which is an infringement of the obligations under [EU law]'.[139] The fact that the proposal of Greece did not mean *ipso facto* that these amendments would be adopted, let alone enter into force, was considered by the Court as irrelevant.[140] The mere exercise of that right was in violation of EU law.

Similarly, in case C-246/07, *Commission* v. *Sweden*, Sweden had submitted on its own behalf a proposal for an amendment to Annex A of the Stockholm Convention on Persistent Organic Pollutants (Stockholm Convention).[141] The problem was that prior to the Swedish submission the Commission had presented a proposal for a Decision[142] asking for authorization to submit on behalf of the EU similar amendment proposals for the inclusion of certain chemical substances in the Annexes to the Aarhus Convention and the Stockholm Convention. In reasoning similar to that of Case C-45/07, *Commission* v. *Greece*, the ECJ held that Sweden's actions and amendment proposal was in violation of EU law.[143]

Of course, one could wonder about the relevance of these two cases with respect to non-proliferation law. The argument could be made that non-proliferation law does not fall within the competences of the EU and therefore the above cases are not relevant. However, this is not as clear-cut as may initially seem. First of all, the above cases demonstrate a rather dynamic and expansive interpretation and application of Article 351 CTFEU, with the main objective to ensure the unity and

with Regulation (EC) No. 725/2004 of the European Parliament and of the Council of 31 March 2004 on enhancing ship and port facility security.

138 Case C-45/07, paras. 34–38. 139 *Ibid.*, para. 23.

140 This can be seen from the adoption of the expression 'likely to affect [the Community rules]' in order to describe the possible repercussions of the proposal of Greece. *Ibid.*, paras. 23 and 29. Greece also submitted that 'an obligation to abstain from active participation in the IMO will not ensure that the Community interest is protected, since the Community is not a member of that international organisation'. *Ibid.*, para. 30. However, the Court did not accept this line of argument because '[t]he mere fact that the Community is not a member of an international organisation in no way authorises a Member State, acting individually in the context of its participation in an international organisation, to assume obligations likely to affect Community rules promulgated for the attainment of the objectives of the Treaty'. *Ibid.*

141 This amendment proposal consisted of the inclusion of a substance, perfluorooctane sulfonate (PFOS), in Annex A.

142 COM (2004) 537 final. 143 Case C-246/07, *Commission* v. *Sweden*, paras. 69–105.

unencumbered application of the policies of the EU. Secondly, the Treaties of the EU are constantly updated and amended and the competences of the EU have significantly changed through time. So, despite the fact that security policy, which some non-proliferation instruments may relate to, falls outside EU competence, one may speculate that this will not always be the case.[144]

Thirdly, and perhaps most importantly, many treaties in modern practice cover a wide area of issues, some of which will fall outside EU competence – for example, UNCLOS, which the EU has ratified, but can exercise its competence with respect to only certain parts of the Convention.[145] Similarly, several non-proliferation treaties may deal with security, but can also have aspects relating to protection of the environment, maritime transport and safety or trade, which, depending on the exact circumstances, may or may not fall within the EU competence. Consequently, any amendment to those provisions, as long as the requirements of Article 351 CTFEU are met, would have to be coordinated with the Commission in order to avoid the situations of the aforementioned ECJ cases. In the same note, the issue of 'dual use' material, technology, equipment or chemicals[146] can only increase the

[144] See, for instance, the evolution of the provisions relating to environmental protection within the EU from the late 1970s until today. Also notable is the fact that EU activity with respect to WMDs has increased in the last few years. See, for instance, 'Commission Communication on Addressing the International Challenge of Nuclear Safety and Security', COM(2008) 312 final, 22 May 2008; 'Commission Communication on Nuclear Non-Proliferation', COM(2009) 143 final, 26 March 2009; Council decision 2010/212/CFSP of 29 March 2010; Council of the European Union, 'Basic Principles for an EU Strategy against Proliferation of Weapons of Mass Destruction', 10352/03, 10 June 2003; Council of the European Union, Action Plan for the Implementation of the Basic Principles for an EU Strategy against Proliferation of Weapons of Mass Destruction, 10354/1/03, 13 June 2003; Council of the European Union, 'Fight against the Proliferation of Weapons of Mass Destruction: Mainstreaming Non-proliferation Policies into the EU's Wider Relations with Third Countries', Council Note, 14997/03, 19 November 2003, available at www.consilium.europa.eu/showPage.aspx?id=718 (accessed 15 July 2011).

[145] Only with respect to those areas that fall within its competence.

[146] On this issue, see A. Schaper, 'Controlling the Spread of Dual-Use Nuclear Technologies', in D. Carlton (ed.), *Controlling the International Transfer of Weaponry and Related Technology* (Aldershot: Dartmouth, 1994); Nuclear Suppliers Group, 'Memorandum of Understanding Implementing Guidelines for Transfers of Nuclear-Related Dual-Use Equipment, Material and Related Technology (3 April 1992)', 31 *ILM* 1094–1134 (1992); S. J. Lundin, *Verification of Dual-Use Chemicals under the Chemical Weapons Convention: The Case of Thiodiglycol* (Oxford University Press, 1991).

possibility that amendments to certain provisions of non-proliferation agreements may be in violation of Article 351 CTFEU.

All the above demonstrates that no branch of law exists in a vacuum and that the proliferation of regional organizations may indirectly affect the amendment and modification procedures of non-proliferation instruments and restrict the right of states to propose any amendments they may wish.

iv. 'Institutional' elements in amendment and modification procedures

A final issue that needs to be considered is whether the non-proliferation treaties share among them a unique feature in the form of inclusion of 'institutional' elements in their amendment and modification provisions. What is meant by 'institutional' elements is whether the treaty text provides either (i) for a committee, commission or other permanent body to take part in the amendment/modification procedure or (ii) for the establishment of or cooperation with an international organization that will ensure the compliance with the obligations stemming from the treaty and that among its functions it will have certain duties relating to amendment/modification.

Not all non-proliferation treaties have opted for the inclusion of 'institutional' elements, but out of those that have, examples can be found of both methods of incorporation. For instance, the ABM Treaty provided that a Standing Consultative Commission had to be established that among its many functions would 'consider, as appropriate, possible proposals for further increasing the viability of this Treaty; including proposals for amendments in accordance with the provisions of this Treaty'.[147] The New START, as well, while in the first paragraph of Article XV follows to the letter the understanding that in bilateral agreements everything is a matter of agreement and negotiation between the two contracting parties, in paragraph 2 introduces the Bilateral Consultative Commission for changes to Protocol to the treaty that do not affect *substantive rights or obligations* under the treaty.[148] The Treaty

[147] ABM Treaty, Art. XIII(1)(f).

[148] '2. If it becomes necessary to make changes in the Protocol to this Treaty that do not affect substantive rights or obligations under this Treaty, the Parties shall use the Bilateral Consultative Commission to reach agreement on such changes, without resorting to the procedure for making amendments that is set forth in paragraph 1 of this Article'; New START, Art. XV(2).

of Rarotonga in Annex III establishes a Consultative Committee that 'shall consider proposals for amendment' and only when 'a proposal is agreed upon by consensus by the Consultative Committee shall it be communicated to the Director who shall circulate it for acceptance to all Parties'.[149] Finally, the Treaty of Semipalatinsk provides that '[t]he Parties agree to hold annual meetings of their representatives, on a rotating basis, as well as extraordinary meetings, at the request of any Party, in order to review compliance with this Treaty or other matters related to its implementation'.[150] Any amendment must be submitted to these annual meetings called Consultative Meetings at least ninety days before the meeting.[151]

Other non-proliferation treaties have gone even further. Instead of establishing permanent committees or other bodies of similar type, they provide that the treaty itself establishes an international organization. This organization will ensure the review, compliance with and general well-functioning of the treaty. Tied to these functions is, of course, the amendment procedure, in which the organization may have a substantive or a procedural role, depending on the treaty. The Treaty of Tlatelolco by Article 7 established the 'Agency for the Prohibition of Nuclear Weapons in Latin America', or in short, 'the Agency'. The amendment procedure is initiated and executed through the organs of 'the Agency'.[152] Similarly, the CTBT established the 'Comprehensive Nuclear Test-Ban Treaty Organization' ('the Organization'), whose aim is to 'to achieve the object and purpose of this Treaty, to ensure the implementation of its provisions, including those for international verification of compliance with it, and to provide a forum for consultation and cooperation among States Parties'.[153] The CWC established for similar reasons the 'Organization for the Prohibition of Chemical Weapons'.[154] In both conventions, as in the case of the Treaty of Tlatelolco, the international organizations established are key elements throughout the whole process of amendment.[155]

Treaties other than non-proliferation treaties have developed and elaborated a sophisticated system of 'institutional elements'. Multilateral environmental agreements (MEAs), for instance, have a long history of holding annual meetings of the parties, the so-called COP/MOP

149 Treaty of Rorotonga, Art. 11. 150 Treaty of Semipalatinsk, Art. 10.
151 *Ibid.*, Art. 17. 152 Treaty of Tlatelolco, Art. 30.
153 Art. II CTBT: The Organization A. General Provisions, para. 1.
154 Art. VIII CWC: The Organization A. General Provisions.
155 Art. VII CTBT; Art. XV CWC.

(conference of the parties serving as the meeting of the parties) meetings[156] that are instrumental in the attainment of the object and purpose of the MEA and compliance with its provisions, and of course have a role to play in the amendment procedure.[157] Furthermore, during COP/MOP meetings, further bodies are established to aid them in securing that the treaty functions properly, and these bodies may also be implicated in the amendment process, either directly or indirectly by examining the possible solutions to problems that the treaty is facing and proposing solutions.[158] So the holding of annual meetings and the establishment of permanent committees and other bodies cannot be said to be a characteristic unique only to non-proliferation treaties.

As for treaties that associate their amendment procedures with organs of international organizations, the classical example would be, as in the case of the 'tacit acceptance procedure', the so-called IMO Conventions, i.e., the conventions adopted under the auspices of IMO or for which it is responsible. Conventions, such as the SOLAS Convention, the 1972 Convention on the Prevention of Marine Pollution by Dumping of Wastes and Other Matter (London Dumping Convention),[159] the 1973 International Convention for the Prevention of Pollution from Ships (MARPOL 73/78),[160] the 1988 Convention for the Suppression of Unlawful Acts Against the Safety of Maritime Navigation (SUA),[161] all are closely connected to the workings of the IMO. One of the many ways this is reflected is by the fact that the IMO and its bodies are directly

[156] 'Conference of the Parties' and 'Meeting of the Parties', respectively. The Kyoto Protocol has CMP ('Conference of the Parties Serving as the Meeting of the Parties to the Kyoto Protocol') meetings.

[157] See, e.g., 1971 Ramsar Convention on Wetlands of International Importance Especially as Waterfowl Habitat (Ramsar Convention), 996 UNTS 245, Art. 10*bis* (1971); 1987 Montreal Protocol on Substances that Deplete the Ozone Layer (Montreal Protocol), 1522 UNTS 29 (1987), Art. 11(4)(h); 1992 United Nations Framework Convention on Climate Change (UNFCCC), 1771 UNTS 107, Art. 15 (1992); 1997 Kyoto Protocol to the United Nations Framework Convention on Climate Change (Kyoto Protocol), 37 *ILM* 22, Art. 20 (1997).

[158] See, for a list of the relevant bodies of (i) the Ramsar Convention, www.ramsar.org/cda/en/ramsar-about-bodies/main/ramsar/1-36-71_4000_0__ (accessed 15 July 2011); (ii) the Montreal Protocol, UNEP, *Handbook for the Montreal Protocol on Substances that Deplete the Ozone Layer*, 8th edn (Nairobi: UNEP, 2009), available at www.ozone.unep.org/Publications/MP_Handbook/MP-Handbook-2009.pdf (accessed 15 July 2011); the UNFCCC, http://unfccc.int/essential_background/convention/convention_bodies/items/2629.php (accessed 15 July 2011); the Kyoto Protocol, www.unfccc.int/kyoto_protocol/kyoto_protocol_bodies/items/2772.php (accessed 15 July 2011).

[159] 1046 UNTS 120 (1972). [160] 1340 UNTS 61 (1979). [161] 1678 UNTS 221 (1988).

implicated in the amendment procedures of each and every one of these conventions.[162] Consequently, even in the case of the incorporation of 'institutional' elements in their amendment procedures, the non-proliferation treaties cannot claim that they are a 'special regime'.

IV. Amendment and modification procedures of non-proliferation law as a special regime

The amendment and modification procedure of treaties has always been one of the main tools allowing for a treaty to change and adapt to new challenges and to new legal and technological advancements and to ensure its vitality and effectiveness. The question that was addressed in this chapter was whether any amendment and modification procedures had arisen that would substantiate the characterization of non-proliferation law as a special regime.[163]

In its final report the ILC Study Group, which had been established to examine the issue of fragmentation/diversification of international law,[164] came to the conclusion that the term 'self-contained regime' was a misnomer,[165] the reason being that there is no basis, either theoretical or jurisprudential,[166] to support the 'idea of special systems or regimes

[162] SOLAS Convention, Art. VIII; London Dumping Convention, Art. XV; MARPOL 73/78, Art. 16; SUA Convention, Art. 20.

[163] i.e., non proliferation law specific.

[164] GAOR, 57th Session, Supplement No. 10 (A/57/10), chap. 9.A, paras. 492–494 and 511.

[165] ILC Study Group, para. 152§5. See also para. 193.

[166] There have been several cases where the various courts and tribunals have referred to a variety of international norms in order to interpret a specific treaty. See, e.g., *United States – Standards for Reformulated and Conventional Gasoline*, Appellate Body Report of 29 April 1996, WT/DS2/AB/R, p. 17; *Korea – Measures Affecting Government Procurement*, Panel Report of 1 May 2000, WT/DS163/R, para. 7.96; *Velásquez Rodríguez* case, Judgment of 29 July 1988, OC-4/88, *Inter-American Yearbook on Human Rights* (1988) p. 990, para. 184; *Al-Adsani* v. *United Kingdom*, Judgment of 21 November 2001, 34 EHRR 11, paras. 55–56 (2001); *Fogarty* v. *United Kingdom*, Judgment of 21 November 2001, 34 EHRR 12, paras. 36–37 (2001); *McElhinney* v. *Ireland*, Judgment of 21 November 2001, 34 EHRR 13, paras. 36–37 (2001); *Arbitration Regarding the Iron Rhine ('Ijzeren Rijn') Railway* (Belgium *v.* The Netherlands), Award of 24 May 2005, PCA, para. 58 (hereinafter *Iron Rhine Arbitration*), accessible at www.pca-cpa.org/upload/files/BE-NL%20Award%20corrected%20200905.pdf (accessed 1 March 2010); *Mamatkulov and Askarov* v. *Turkey*, Judgment of 4 February 2005, 41 EHRR 494, para. 111 (2005); *Georges Pinson* case (France v. United Mexican States), Award of 13 April 1928, 5 RIAA 422, para. 50(4) (1952); *Esphahanian* v. *Bank Tejarat*, Award of 29 March 1983, *Iran-USCTR* 2 (1983/I), p. 161; *Case No. A/18*, Award of 6 April 1984, *Iran-USCTR* 5 (1984/I), p. 260. In most of these cases it has to be noted that various norms of public international law came into consideration for the purposes of

that would be fully isolated from general international law'.[167] Consequently, the term 'special regime' was considered more appropriate. Furthermore, the ILC Study Group identified three possible types of special regimes: in a narrow sense, 'a special set of secondary rules under the law of State responsibility that claims primacy to the general rules concerning consequences of a violation'; in a broader sense, as 'interrelated wholes of primary and secondary rules, sometimes also referred to as "systems" or "subsystems" of rules that cover some particular problem differently from the way it would be covered under general law'; and finally in a third sense, 'special regimes' could be understood as branches of international law.[168]

Irrespective of which approach is adopted with respect to non-proliferation law, for the purposes of the analysis of the present chapter, what has to be identified is whether the amendment and modification procedures outlined in non-proliferation law treaties have the required amount of specificity and difference from the procedures described in the VCLT. If no such differentiation can be established then it cannot be maintained that the amendment and modification procedures of non-proliferation treaties are an element with special characteristics deviating from the rules established under the VCLT. Consequently, they will also not be able to substantiate in and of themselves that non-proliferation law is a special regime.

The analysis of the VCLT provisions and the discussions that led to their eventual adoption revealed that Articles 39–41 of the VCLT were envisaged as having a 'residuary character', thus allowing states a great degree of flexibility on how to regulate the amendment and modification procedures within the treaties they became parties to.

This freedom has been used extensively in the context of non-proliferation instruments, in the sense that a variety of procedures have been adopted that cover a wide range of possibilities. Some treaties followed the rather stringent 'unanimity rule', others leaned towards adoption of amendments through various formulas of majorities. But even in these treaties the procedures were not identical. Some required simply an adoption by a two-thirds majority, while others qualified this by requiring additional elements, e.g. that the vote of all original parties must be included (PTBT) or 'the votes of all nuclear-weapon States Party to the Treaty and all other Parties which, on the date the amendment is

interpretation of the relevant treaty provision or term through the medium of Art. 31(3)(c) of the Vienna Convention on the Law of Treaties (VCLT).

167 ILC Study Group, para. 152§5. 168 *Ibid.*, paras. 128–129.

circulated, are members of the Board of Governors of the International Atomic Energy Agency' (PNE Treaty). Furthermore, some treaties followed the rules set out in the VCLT, while others deviated from it, and particularly Article 40(4) VCLT, by binding states to an amendment agreement even without their explicit consent.[169]

An interesting subset of this last category is the CWC and CTBT, which provided for a 'bifurcated amendment system' based on the nature of the provisions to be amended, and for the more technical and administrative of those they applied the 'tacit acceptance procedure'. Although this procedure deviated from the provisions of the VCLT, this does not make it a unique solution, characteristic of only non-proliferation treaties. On the contrary, similar procedures have been adopted in treaties in other branches of international law,[170] such as the SOLAS and the MARPOL Conventions. It would thus seem that even the 'bifurcated system' and the 'tacit acceptance procedure' are logical and practical solutions to address the issues that arise from highly technical treaties that are in dire need of regular updating.

It was also shown that when and if 'institutional' aspects are introduced in the amendment and modification procedures of non-proliferation treaties, these also are far from being unique to that particular area of law. IMO Conventions and MEAs are the most notable examples of treaties that share this characteristic approach. Finally, it was demonstrated that the issue of amendment and modification is far from settled, both with respect to non-proliferation law and more generally all branches of international law. The cases of the Court of Justice C-45/07, *Commission* v. *Greece* and C-246/07, *Commission* v. *Sweden* have brought to the forefront of academic discourse the possibility of restrictions to the rights of states freely to propose amendments to treaties they are parties to. This scenario may have not materialized in the context of non-proliferation treaties yet, but this does not mean that it is entirely impossible. On the contrary, the ever-increasing competences of the EU, combined with the expansive interpretation of Article 351 CTFEU and the composite nature of many modern treaties, make this scenario a possible and plausible one.

Let us return then to our original question of whether the amendment and modification procedures of the non-proliferation instruments reflect the special regime character of that branch of law. The multiplicity of

[169] See, for instance, the PTBT and the Pelindaba Treaty.

[170] e.g., the international law of the sea.

approaches adopted in a variety of instruments, ranging from strict adherence to the 'residual rules' of the VCLT to the more innovative approaches of 'bifurcated systems' and 'tacit acceptance procedures', all seem to indicate that, at least for the moment, the amendment and modification procedures of the non-proliferation treaties do not have the necessary degree of coherence and systematicity that would allow us to conclude that they by themselves demonstrate beyond a shadow of a doubt that non-proliferation law is a special regime as to what pertains to those procedures.

2

Provisional application of non-proliferation treaties

ANDREW MICHIE[1]

I. Introduction

The focus of efforts to prevent the proliferation of weapons of mass destruction has traditionally been to conclude binding international agreements between states.[2] Even though alternative instruments are sometimes used, treaties remain the principal means of regulating horizontal and vertical non-proliferation at bilateral, regional and global levels. Yet the formalities associated with the conclusion of treaties, which may partly explain their enduring supremacy in this area of international law, also entail certain risks and drawbacks. Where a treaty requires ratification or a similar act of confirmation in order to bind the state, there may be a temporal gap following signature during which the necessary domestic approvals are obtained. If this period is protracted, it may in turn lead to a detrimental delay in the entry into force of the treaty and the implementation of the measures for which it provides. A particularly useful rule in the treaty-maker's repertoire, therefore, is that of provisional application, which allows the signatories to give immediate but conditional effect to a treaty or part of a treaty pending its ratification and definitive entry into force.[3]

The practice now known as provisional application emerged in the second half of the nineteenth century following the increasing

[1] The views expressed herein are the author's only, and do not necessarily represent the views of UNIDO.

[2] G. den Dekker, *The Law of Arms Control: International Supervision and Enforcement* (The Hague: Martinus Nijhoff, 2001), p. 50.

[3] On provisional application, generally, see R. Lefeber, 'The Provisional Application of Treaties', in J. Klabbers and R. Lefeber (eds.), *Essays on the Law of Treaties* (The Hague: Martinus Nijhoff, 1998), p. 81; M. A. Rogoff and B. E. Gauditz, 'The Provisional Application of International Agreements', *Maine Law Review*, 39 (1987), 29.

democratization of the treaty-making process and the introduction of constitutional constraints on the sovereign's ratifying power, including the requirement of prior parliamentary approval.[4] Largely, though not completely, codified in Article 25 of the Vienna Convention on the Law of Treaties of 1969, the procedure is most often employed where there is some urgency or necessity to give effect to a treaty or part of a treaty immediately upon signature.[5] Provisional application is also relied upon in situations which are not strictly urgent, such as to circumvent political or administrative hindrances to entry into force;[6] to achieve legal continuity between successive treaties;[7] to attain consistency of obligations among the parties when amending or modifying a treaty;[8] or to prepare for the establishment of a new international organization or treaty regime.[9] In certain categories of agreements, such as air transport agreements[10] or commodity agreements,[11] clauses on provisional application

[4] H.-G. Krenzler, '*Die vorläufige Anwendung völkerrechtlicher Verträge*', doctoral thesis, Heidelberg, 1963, p. 16.

[5] For example, General Agreement on Tariffs and Trade of 1947 (55 UNTS 187); Geneva Convention on Long-range Transboundary Air Pollution of 1979 (1302 UNTS 217); Energy Charter Treaty of 1994 (2080 UNTS 99); and Agreement Relating to the Implementation of Part XI of the 1982 UN Convention on the Law of the Sea of 1994 (1836 UNTS 3).

[6] For example, Maritime Boundary Agreement of 1977 between the US and Cuba, which has been provisionally applied since 1978. See Rogoff and Guaditz, 'The Provisional Application of International Agreements', 35.

[7] For example, various international commodity agreements and agreements of the European Community renewing the fixed-term fishery rights of EU vessels in foreign waters.

[8] For example, the plenipotentiary conference of the International Telecommunication Union has called for the provisional application of the amended constitution and convention of the ITU in order to ensure a uniform normative framework among the member states of the Union. See ITU Resolution 69, Kyoto, 1994.

[9] See 'Examples of Precedents of Provisional Application, Pending their Entry into Force, of Multilateral Treaties, Especially Treaties which have Established International Organizations and/or Regimes', UN doc. A/AC.138/88, dated 12 June 1973; and US Congressional Research Service, 'Law of the Sea Treaty: Alternative Approaches to Provisional Application', 13 *ILM* 454 (1974).

[10] For example, Civil Air Transport Agreement between the US and Japan of 1952 (212 UNTS 27); Agreement Relating to Air Services between Switzerland and the Union of South Africa of 1959 (559 UNTS 19); Air Transport Agreement on Scheduled Services between Argentina and Sweden of 1988 (2437 UNTS 231); Air Transport Agreement between the US and Colombia of 10 May 2011 (available at www.state.gov).

[11] For example, International Sugar Agreement of 1992 (1703 UNTS 203); International Cocoa Agreement of 2001 (2229 UNTS 2); International Coffee Agreement of 2001 (2161 UNTS 308); and International Tropical Timber Agreement of 2006 (doc. TD/TIMBER.3/12, available at www.unctad.org).

may be the norm rather than the exception.[12] In such treaties, a recurrent pattern of similar provisions may lead to the formation of a distinctive system or 'regime' of provisional application with its own distinctive function and normative characteristics.

Although widely utilized in treaty relations, no non-proliferation instrument included a clause on provisional application before the end of the Cold War.[13] Since the conclusion in 1991 of the first Strategic Arms Reduction Treaty (START) between the United States and the Soviet Union,[14] almost all major bilateral and multilateral non-proliferation treaties have, to a greater or lesser degree, been provisionally applied, the most recent being the New START of 2010.[15] On the face of it, this innovative and at times unusual body of non-proliferation practice bears little resemblance to the traditional practice of provisional application in other areas of international law. While complex clauses on provisional application are not unknown, hardly any achieve the level of technical elaboration found in certain non-proliferation treaties. The twofold aims of this chapter, then, are to conduct a brief survey of the non-proliferation practice of provisional application and to consider the degree to which it may be considered special or unique when compared to state practice in other areas of international law. In keeping with the theme of this book, the underlying question will be whether and to what extent the non-proliferation practice serves any distinctive normative functions or displays any distinctive normative characteristics which may thus be evidence of the existence of a special regime of provisional application for non-proliferation treaties and, more generally, of a special regime of non-proliferation law.

However, before examining the various instances of provisional application of important non-proliferation treaties, it is necessary to provide a brief overview of the procedure under Article 25 of the Vienna Convention. This will be done in section II below. Section III then

[12] Historically, the first major system or regime of provisional application was probably that associated with the network of bilateral trade treaties concluded mainly by European states in the decades before and after the First World War. See Krenzler, 'Die vorläufige Anwendung völkerrechtlicher Verträge', 18.

[13] The first arms control treaty to be provisionally applied was the Treaty on Conventional Armed Forces in Europe of 1990. Unusually, the CFE Treaty was subject to two phases of provisional application: the first pursuant to the final protocol to the Treaty (provisional application in part) and the second pursuant to the final act of an extraordinary conference of the parties held in Helsinki in July 1992 (provisional application of the entire Treaty).

[14] See section V.i, below. [15] See section V.iii, below.

considers the manner in which non-proliferation treaties are brought into force, while section IV makes a few general observations on the role of provisional application in a non-proliferation context. Sections V and VI survey non-proliferation treaties which have been provisionally applied using the two methods envisaged in Article 25, that is, where the treaty itself provides for provisional application (section V) and where the negotiating states have reached agreement on the provisional application in some manner other than in the treaty (section VI). Section VII goes on to assesses whether the non-proliferation practice of provisional application can be considered to be a special system or 'regime' of provisional application in its own right, while section VIII concludes with a few final remarks on the subject.

II. Article 25 of the Vienna Convention

The Vienna Convention of 1969 accords states wide discretion when exercising their treaty-making powers. Article 25 on provisional application is no exception in this respect. In terms of paragraph 1 of Article 25, some or all of the negotiating states may agree, either in terms of the treaty or in some other manner, to apply a treaty or part of a treaty provisionally pending its entry into force.[16] The undertaking to apply a treaty provisionally may accordingly be reflected in the final clauses of the treaty, in a protocol or annex forming part of the treaty, or in a collateral agreement or arrangement, which may or may not itself be a treaty under international law. In principle, an agreement on provisional application may even be inferred from the practice of the states concerned in giving effect to a treaty pending its entry into force since that practice may constitute their tacit agreement or tacit acquiescence in the matter.[17]

In general, treaties are provisionally applied from the date of their signature. Signature is not, however, a prerequisite for provisional application.[18] It is therefore open to the negotiating states to choose another

[16] Art. 25, para. 1 reads as follows: '1. A treaty or a part of a treaty is applied provisionally pending its entry into force if: (a) the treaty itself so provides; or (b) the negotiating States have in some other manner so agreed.'

[17] In 1977, the legal bureau of the Canadian foreign ministry issued an opinion to the effect that the conduct of the USA and Canada in implementing a bilateral agreement before it had entered into force constituted tacit acquiescence that it should be applied provisionally. See LXI *Canadian Yearbook of International Law* (1978), 366.

[18] Lefeber, 'The Provisional Application of Treaties', pp. 84–85.

event or date upon which the provisional application will take effect. Since some states may not favour provisional application in a particular situation, multilateral treaties often provide signatories with the possibility to opt into or out of the procedure by means of a notification or declaration to that effect, which is deposited at the time of signature or thereafter.[19] The result of an 'opt-in' clause, though, may be that the treaty is provisionally applied by only a few states,[20] or perhaps by none.[21]

Pursuant to paragraph 2 of Article 25, unless the treaty otherwise provides, or the negotiating states have otherwise agreed, a state may terminate the provisional application of a treaty with respect to itself at any time if it decides not to become a party to the treaty and so notifies the other states between which the treaty is being provisionally applied.[22] The default rule on termination in paragraph 2 thus gives expression to the underlying principle that signatories enjoy a discretionary right of ratification. The opening proviso to the paragraph, 'Unless the treaty otherwise provides or the negotiating States have otherwise agreed', nevertheless allows states to regulate the question of termination as they see fit, which they may do, for instance, by fixing a time limit for the provisional period; by providing that termination of the provisional application by one party will result in termination for all; or by reaching a subsequent agreement on the matter. The proviso also suggests that the consequence of an express regulation of termination may be to *exclude* the right of unilateral termination which a signatory would otherwise enjoy.[23]

[19] See, for example, Art. 7(1) of the Agreement Relating to the Implementation of Part XI of the 1982 United Nations Convention on the Law of the Sea of 1994 and Art. 45(2) of the Energy Charter Treaty of 1994.

[20] Thus far the Convention on Cluster Munitions of 2008 has been provisionally applied by just one state (Norway). See G. Nystuen and S. Casey-Maslen, *The Convention on Cluster Munitions: A Commentary* (Oxford University Press, 2010), p. 532.

[21] For example, no state notified the depositary of its wish to apply provisionally the Fish Stocks Agreement of 1995. See 'Oceans and the Law of the Sea: Law of the Sea, Report by the Secretary-General', UN doc. A/52/487, dated 20 October 1997.

[22] Art. 25, para. 2 reads as follows: '2. Unless the treaty otherwise provides or the negotiating States have otherwise agreed, the provisional application of a treaty or a part of a treaty with respect to a State shall be terminated if that State notifies the other States between which the treaty is being applied provisionally of its intention not to become a party to the treaty.'

[23] See Lefeber, 'The Provisional Application of Treaties', p. 87, who argues that an explicit provision on termination of the provisional application at entry into force would mean that the rule on unilateral termination would no longer apply.

In the case of bilateral treaties, termination by one negotiating state will end the provisional application of the treaty as a whole unless the negotiating states have expressly provided for, or agreed to the contrary. In the case of multilateral instruments, on the other hand, termination by one negotiating state will normally not affect the rights and obligations of the others, among which the treaty will continue to be applied provisionally unless they agree otherwise. While the provisional application of a treaty usually ends with its definitive entry into force, it may extend beyond that date with respect to those signatories of a multilateral treaty for which the treaty has yet to enter into force.[24]

Although the Vienna Convention does not explicitly say so, customary international law holds that an undertaking to apply a treaty or part of a treaty provisionally gives rise to a legal obligation to observe the terms in question as if they were in force.[25] *Pacta sunt servanda*, the most important principle in all the law of treaties, thus applies equally during the period of provisional application.[26] Unless the provisional application is made subject to national laws or regulations or a similar limitation,[27] a provisionally applied treaty must be performed in good faith until the treaty enters into force or the provisional application is lawfully terminated.[28]

24 A. Aust, *Modern Treaty Law and Practice* (Cambridge University Press, 2000), p. 139.

25 See Lefeber, 'The Provisional Application of Treaties', p. 90.

26 Though holding, rather oddly, that the basis for a rule of customary international law *allowing for* provisional application may be lacking, the arbitral tribunal in *Kardassopoulos (Greece)* v. *Georgia* nonetheless found that '[w]here what is in issue is . . . the provisional application of the whole treaty, then such provisional application imports the application of all its provisions as if they were already in force, even though the treaty's proper or definitive entry into force has not yet occurred.' See Decision on Jurisdiction, ICSID Case No. ARB/05/18 (6 July 2007), paras. 218–219. See also M. Belz, 'Provisional Application of the Energy Charter Treaty: *Kardassopoulos v. Georgia* and Improving Provisional Application in Multilateral Treaties', *Emory International Law Review*, 22 (2008), 727.

27 See, for example, Art. 45(1) of the Energy Charter Treaty of 1994, which provides for provisional application by each signatory 'to the extent that such provisional application is not inconsistent with its constitution, laws or regulations'. However, in the *Yukos* case, the Permanent Court of Arbitration recently interpreted this article to mean that the Russian Federation had 'agreed that the Treaty *as a whole* would be applied provisionally pending its entry into force unless *the principle* of provisional application itself was inconsistent "with its constitution, laws or regulations"'. See Interim Award on Jurisdiction and Admissibility, PCA Case Nos. AA 226–229 (30 November 2009), paras. 301 ff.

28 At the Vienna conference on the law of treaties, Yugoslavia had proposed a new article expressly clarifying that every treaty applied provisionally in whole or in part is binding on the contracting states and must be performed in good faith. However, the drafting

III. Entry into force of non-proliferation treaties

Treaties relating to weapons of mass destruction self-evidently deal with subjects of the greatest significance to states. Besides having potential implications for their sovereignty and national security, non-proliferation treaties may affect the interests of powerful domestic constituencies such as the armed forces, armaments producers and commercial corporations. They may also require legislative and other national enforcement measures, as well as the allocation of substantial additional resources to cover the costs of verification and other implementing activities. In view of these and other possible ramifications, it is understandable that governments are reluctant to assume new non-proliferation treaty commitments without an opportunity to consult internally and, where necessary, obtain parliamentary approval or bring national law into line with the treaty. Non-proliferation treaties therefore seldom bind a state on signature alone but normally stipulate that there should be a further confirmatory act, such as ratification, acceptance, approval or accession, by which the state is said to express its consent to be bound by the treaty.[29] Given the nature of non-proliferation treaties, this additional step provides states with an indispensable procedural safeguard.

Besides providing for ratification, acceptance, approval or accession by each state, non-proliferation treaties usually contain discrete clauses governing their entry into force. In bilateral non-proliferation treaties, such clauses typically provide for entry into force upon exchange of instruments of ratification, as in the case of various bilateral treaties between the United States and the Russian Federation, of which the Threshold Test-Ban Treaty of 1974[30] and the series of START treaties[31] are notable examples. Another, less formal, route is notification by each signatory of completion of the requisite domestic procedures for entry into force. This procedure is reflected in certain

committee considered that the proposal was 'self-evident and that provisional application also fell within the scope of . . . the *pacta sunt servanda* rule'. Believing that it would be better not to state such an obvious fact, the committee did not recommend the adoption of the proposed new article. See UN doc. A/CONF.39/11/Add.1, at 157.

[29] In accordance with Art. 2(1)(b) of the Vienna Convention of 1969, 'ratification', 'acceptance', 'approval' and 'accession' mean in each case the international act so named whereby a state establishes on the international plane its consent to be bound by a treaty.

[30] 13 *ILM* 906; opened for signature 3 July 1974; entered into force 11 December 1990.

[31] See sections V.i–V.iii, below.

US–Russian agreements as well, such as the Plutonium Management and Disposition Agreement of 2000.[32]

Multilateral non-proliferation treaties may, like other multilateral conventions, call for the deposit of a particular number of instruments of ratification, acceptance or approval in order for the treaty to enter into force. The number of instruments required in a particular case will generally reflect a balance of considerations, such as the desire to bring the treaty into force as rapidly as possible (the lower the number of ratifications, the shorter the likely waiting period) and the need for a sense of legitimacy and effectiveness (the higher the number of ratifications, the greater the likely legitimacy and effectiveness). The figure selected may, at first sight and without an intimate knowledge of the negotiations, seem somewhat arbitrary. The Chemical Weapons Convention of 1992,[33] for example, provided that it would enter into force 180 days after the deposit of the 65th instrument of ratification but in no case earlier than two years after its opening for signature. On this occasion, it seems that the negotiating states selected a comparatively high number so as to allow sufficient time to prepare for the extensive obligations assumed under the Convention.[34]

Although the entry-into-force provisions of the Chemical Weapons Convention are similar to those found in many other multilateral treaties on other subjects, the same cannot be said of the entry-into-force provisions of multilateral non-proliferation treaties generally. What distinguishes most multilateral non-proliferation treaties from other multilateral instruments is that in addition to, or instead of, ratification by a certain number of states, their entry into force is made conditional upon the adherence of those states which are militarily or technologically the most relevant to the subject matter of the treaty.[35] This objective may be achieved by providing for the ratification of certain named states or a category or group of states, or by using some other formula that includes the most relevant players. The reason for such a requirement is obvious. A non-proliferation treaty which failed to attract the adherence of the states actually possessing the weapons, technology or material it

[32] See section V.iv, below. [33] See section VI.i, below.

[34] J. Klabbers, 'Strange Bedfellows: The "Interim Obligation" and the 1993 Chemical Weapons Convention', in E. P. J. Myjer (ed.), *Issues of Arms Control Law and the Chemical Weapons Convention* (The Hague: Martinus Nijhoff, 2001), pp. 11, 15.

[35] This observation is true of arms control treaties, generally. See A. Michie, 'The Provisional Application of Arms Control Treaties', *Journal of Conflict and Security Law*, 10 (2005), 345, 349.

circumscribed would be of little practical value. In fact, it might even compromise the interests of those states becoming parties to it while others were able to pursue a strategic advantage by remaining outside.

The Partial Test-Ban Treaty (PTBT) of 1963[36] thus provided for its entry into force after deposit of the instruments of ratification of the original parties, which were the principal nuclear-weapon states at the time, namely the United States, the USSR and the United Kingdom.[37] In the decade following the conclusion of the PTBT, a number of non-proliferation treaties seem to have been influenced by its conditions for entry into force. The Treaty on the Non-Proliferation of Nuclear Weapons (Nuclear Non-Proliferation Treaty – NPT) of 1968[38] stipulated that it would enter into force upon ratification by the states, the governments of which were designated as depositaries of the treaty – that is, the same three nuclear-weapon states – and by forty other states. A similar requirement appeared in the Seabed Treaty of 1971[39] and in the Biological Weapons Convention of 1972,[40] both of which called for ratification by twenty-two governments, including the governments designated as depositaries of the Convention, namely the governments of the United Kingdom, the United States and the USSR.

The most remarkable set of provisions governing the entry into force of a non-proliferation treaty are those found in the Comprehensive Nuclear Test-Ban Treaty (CTBT) of 1996.[41] In accordance with paragraph 1 of Article XIV of the CTBT, it will enter into force 180 days after it has been ratified by the forty-four states listed in annex 2 to the treaty, that is by

> States members of the Conference on Disarmament as at 18 June 1996 which formally participated in the work of the 1996 session of the Conference and which appear in Table 1 of the International Atomic Energy Agency's April 1996 edition of 'Nuclear Power Reactors in the World', and of States members of the Conference on Disarmament as at 18 June 1996 which formally participated in the work of the 1996 session of the Conference and which appear in Table 1 of the International

[36] 480 UNTS 43; opened for signature 5 and 8 August 1963; entered into force 10 October 1963.

[37] Only France, which had tested its first nuclear weapon in 1960, was excluded.

[38] 729 UNTS 161; opened for signature 1 July 1968; entered into force 5 March 1970.

[39] 955 UNTS 115; opened for signature 11 February 1971; entered into force 18 May 1972.

[40] 1015 UNTS 163; opened for signature 10 April 1972; entered into force 26 March 1975.

[41] See section VI.ii, below.

> Atomic Energy Agency's December 1995 edition of 'Nuclear Research Reactors in the World'.[42]

Devised to capture the handful of recognized and non-recognized nuclear-weapon states without singling them out, this unique formula will ensure that no state even remotely capable of possessing nuclear weapons will become definitively bound by the treaty until all the others are too.

IV. Provisional application in a non-proliferation context

The intervening period between signature and entry into force of a non-proliferation treaty is one of particular sensitivity. Having made significant concessions during long and arduous negotiations in order to achieve an acceptable compromise, the negotiating states will usually wish to ensure that nothing undermines the new treaty before it comes into force. They will therefore keenly observe each other's conduct with respect to the treaty, which may have a determining influence on the pace of their domestic approval and whether they ratify at all. Against this background, a signatory's obligation to refrain from acts which would defeat the object and purpose of a treaty, as reflected in Article 18 of the Vienna Convention of 1969,[43] has special relevance. The significance of this interim obligation of good faith is well illustrated by the strategic arms limitation agreements of 1972 (SALT I).[44] At the

[42] i.e., Algeria, Argentina, Australia, Austria, Bangladesh, Belgium, Brazil, Bulgaria, Canada, Chile, China, Colombia, the Democratic People's Republic of Korea, Egypt, Finland, France, Germany, Hungary, India, Indonesia, Iran, Israel, Italy, Japan, Mexico, the Netherlands, Norway, Pakistan, Peru, Poland, Romania, the Republic of Korea, the Russian Federation, Slovakia, South Africa, Spain, Sweden, Switzerland, Turkey, Ukraine, the United Kingdom, the United States, Viet Nam and Zaire (now the Democratic Republic of the Congo).

[43] Art. 18 provides: 'A State is obliged to refrain from acts which would defeat the object and purpose of a treaty when: (a) it has signed the treaty or has exchanged instruments constituting the treaty subject to ratification, acceptance or approval, until it shall have made its intention clear not to become a party to the treaty; or (b) it has expressed its consent to be bound by the treaty, pending the entry into force of the treaty and provided that such entry into force is not unduly delayed.'

[44] See J. S. Charme, 'The Interim Obligation of Article 18 of the Vienna Convention on the Law of Treaties: Making Sense of an Enigma', *George Washington Journal of International Law and Economics*, 25 (1991), 71, 79. The SALT I agreements are reproduced at www.state.gov.

time of concluding the agreements, the USA and the USSR signed certain common understandings, among which was Common Understanding E, entitled 'Standstill', which recorded their understanding that, 'pending ratification and acceptance, neither side would take any action prohibited by the agreements after they had entered into force'. While this formulation could be read as requiring actual observance of treaty provisions prior to ratification, the understanding is best viewed as an interpretative statement regarding the scope of the obligation to refrain from conduct that would defeat the object and purpose of the agreements prior to their entry into force.[45]

Important as the interim obligation under Article 18 may be, it cannot satisfy all normative requirements prior to the entry into force of a treaty. Given the sensitive character of non-proliferation treaties and the signatories' need to safeguard their respective positions in the intervening period, provisional application offers several additional advantages. In addition to facilitating the implementation of urgent measures, the provisional application of a treaty or part of a treaty may provide a more effective guarantee that limits or restrictions will not be evaded or undermined before the treaty takes effect. By maintaining the goodwill and momentum of the negotiations, provisional application may reduce the risk that one of the negotiating states will reconsider its position following signature and refuse to ratify the treaty. During the provisional phase, the signatories will also have the opportunity to test the practical merits of their accord: if the provisional application proves successful, they will have an added incentive for proceeding with ratification. If the treaty provides for a complex monitoring or verification system, that system may have to be operational by the time the treaty enters into force, necessitating some arrangement to apply to at least part of the treaty upon signature or shortly thereafter. The provisional application of institutional provisions, for instance, may facilitate agreement on technical implementing details of the system by creating an appropriate forum for the continuation of negotiations on the subject.

In the cautious world of non-proliferation, where so much emphasis is placed on the value of treaty commitments, it is especially important that an undertaking to apply a treaty or part of a treaty provisionally gives rise

[45] Declarations issued in 1976 by the USA and the USSR by which they undertook to observe, pending ratification, limitations contained in the Threshold Test Ban Treaty of 1974 and the Peaceful Nuclear Explosion Treaty of 1976 should probably be viewed in a similar light.

to a binding international obligation during the provisional period. Indeed, a signatory's breach, whether by omission or commission, of a provision that it is applying provisionally, could conceivably upset the entire pact. Provided that the provisional application had not been lawfully terminated beforehand, such a breach would in principle constitute a breach of an international obligation owed by the signatory to the other signatory or signatories between which the treaty is being provisionally applied.[46] As such, the breach would engage the signatory's responsibility for an internationally wrongful act, for which the other signatory or signatories could seek appropriate redress, such as strict compliance with the obligation breached. At the same time, the breach might involve a violation of the signatory's duty to refrain from acts which would defeat the object and purpose of the treaty before its entry into force. The potential dual nature of the breach again illustrates the nexus between Articles 18 and 25 of the Vienna Convention and the extent to which the technique of provisional application may supplement and reinforce the restraints imposed by Article 18 in a non-proliferation context.

In the area of non-proliferation, perhaps more so than in any other, the question whether to apply a treaty or part of a treaty provisionally is a delicate one. Proposals for provisional application are sometimes made but not accepted, as transpired in the case of the CTBT.[47] Whether provisional application is appropriate in a particular case, and to which extent, are questions which cannot be answered in the abstract but which will depend on a multiplicity of considerations, such as the object and purpose of the treaty, the provisions involved, the state of relations between the parties and their constitutional procedures for concluding treaties.[48] Ultimately, the decision will be as much one of policy and politics as of law.

[46] Cf. Arts. 2 and 13 of the *Draft Articles on Responsibility of States for Internationally Wrongful Acts* of the International Law Commission.

[47] For the text of the unsuccessful Austrian proposal, see Conference on Disarmament doc. CD/NTB/WP.242, dated 16 June 1995. See also M. Asada, 'CTBT: Legal Questions Arising from its Non Entry into Force', *Journal of Conflict and Security Law*, 7 (2002), 85, 118.

[48] While international law *permits* all states to apply their treaties provisionally, domestic law determines whether the representatives of a particular state can agree to do so in a particular case. See A. Michie, 'The Provisional Application of Treaties in South African Law and Practice', *South African Yearbook of International Law*, 30 (2005), 1, 2.

V. Provisional application where the treaty itself so provides

The following section will provide a summary overview of those instances of provisional application pursuant to a term of a non-proliferation treaty or a protocol or annex forming part of the treaty. The treaties in question, which are all bilateral instruments between the USA and the USSR or the Russian Federation, are the three strategic arms reduction treaties, namely START I of 1991, START II of 1993 and the New START of 2010, as well as the Plutonium Management and Disposition Agreement of 2000, which is representative of a number of subsidiary non-proliferation agreements containing substantially similar clauses on provisional application.

i. The Strategic Arms Reduction Treaty (START I)

The Strategic Arms Reduction Treaty between the USA and the USSR was signed in Moscow on 31 July 1991.[49] The treaty, which included six protocols and a memorandum of understanding, entered into force on 5 December 1994 and expired, in accordance with its terms, on 5 December 2009. Article II of the treaty – containing its core provisions – set numerical limits for each party's deployed delivery systems (1,600) and deployed nuclear warheads (6,000), which had to be reached within seven years of its entry into force.[50] Two protocols to START I and the memorandum of understanding provided for the provisional application upon signature of selected technical and institutional clauses of the treaty. The clauses provisionally applied included provisions governing:

- in terms of the protocol on the Joint Compliance and Inspection Commission, the mandate and procedures of the commission;
- in terms of the protocol on telemetric information,[51] procedures for the acquisition of equipment to play back telemetric information and related matters;
- in terms of the memorandum of understanding, procedures for the exchange of site diagrams and photographs.[52]

[49] Pursuant to a Protocol concluded at Lisbon on 23 May 1992, the former Soviet republics of Belarus, Kazakhstan and Ukraine also became parties to the Treaty.

[50] See J. Goldblat, *Arms Control* (London: Sage, 2002), pp. 88–92.

[51] The Definitions Annex to START I defines the expression 'telemetric information' as information that originates on board a missile during its flight tests that is broadcast or recorded for subsequent recovery.

[52] See US Department of State, 'Article by Article Legal Analysis of the START Treaty and its Associated Documents (Part 3)', available at www.state.gov.

In each case, the provisional application was evidently intended to assist the parties in preparing for the effective implementation and verification of the treaty following its entry into force. By establishing the Joint Compliance and Inspection Commission, the parties created a forum to settle the many technical implementing details which remained to be resolved before the treaty entered into force.[53] All three clauses on provisional application stipulated that the provisional application was to take place 'in light of and in conformity with the other provisions of the Treaty'. The duration of the provisional application was set at twelve months but would end beforehand if the treaty entered into force or if a party communicated to the other its decision to terminate the provisional application. Subject to the same conditions, the parties could extend the provisional application for additional periods. According to the US State Department, the twelve-month limit was necessary to ensure that the provisional application did not continue 'in perpetuity'.[54]

An interesting feature of the three provisions is the condition they set for terminating the provisional application, which modifies slightly the default rule under paragraph 2 of Article 25 of the Vienna Convention. In accordance with paragraph 2 of Article 25, a negotiating state may terminate the provisional application of a treaty with respect to itself by notification 'of its intention not to become a party to the treaty', unless the treaty provides otherwise or the parties otherwise agree. Under START I, however, the parties gave themselves the right to terminate the provisional application without necessarily having to opt out of the treaty altogether. It was hence possible, if only theoretically, for a party to terminate one or more of the three provisional arrangements under START I but for the treaty nevertheless to enter into force thereafter.

ii. The Treaty between the United States of America and the Russian Federation on Further Reduction and Limitation of Strategic Offensive Arms (START II)

The Treaty between the United States of America and the Russian Federation on Further Reduction and Limitation of Strategic Offensive Arms was signed in Moscow on 3 January 1993. As its name suggests,

[53] The agreements and joint statements of the joint compliance and inspection commission are published at www.dod.gov.

[54] US Department of State, 'Article by Article Legal Analysis of the START Treaty and its Associated Documents (Part 3)'.

START II provided for further cutbacks in the number of nuclear missiles deployed by the parties over and above those in START I. Under the terms of the treaty, each party was required to reduce the number of its deployed warheads to 3,000 from 3,500 by 1 January 2003. Following an unexpected delay in the entry into force of the treaty, this deadline was extended to 31 December 2007 by means of an extension protocol,[55] which was concluded in 1997 along with several agreements related to the anti-ballistic missile treaty of 1972.

Paragraph 8 of Article II of the treaty committed both parties not to transfer heavy intercontinental ballistic missiles to any recipient whatsoever. In accordance with paragraph 2 of Article VI, this non-proliferation obligation was provisionally applied from the date of signature of the treaty. At the time, the US Secretary of State explained that the provisional application of paragraph 8 of Article II:

> provides a useful collateral constraint since there are [ballistic missile] SS-18 silo launchers located outside Russia, and such transfers by Russia to the other Parties to the START Treaty – Belarus, Kazakhstan, and Ukraine – are not prohibited by the START Treaty.[56]

Events following the signature of START II provide an intriguing insight into the sensitivity of the interim period pending ratification of a non-proliferation treaty and of the risks inherent in that process. In the USA, the senate gave its advice and consent to START II in January 1996.[57] In the Russian Federation, however, the treaty was only submitted to the Duma in 1998. Thereafter, a series of international crises led Russian legislators to defer consideration of the treaty on more than one occasion.[58] The Russian parliament eventually passed a federal law on ratification of the treaty in April 2000,[59] and President Putin signed the

55 Goldblat, *Arms Control*, p. 95.

56 M. Nash, 'Contemporary Practice of the United States Relating to International Law', *American Journal of International Law*, 87 (1993), 258, 267.

57 M. Nash, 'Contemporary Practice of the United States Relating to International Law', *American Journal of International Law*, 90 (1993), 263, 270.

58 'Duma Postpones START II Ratification Decision', 27 *Disarmament Diplomacy* (June 1998) and 'START Vote Delayed Over Iraq', 33 *Disarmament Diplomacy* (December 1998/January 1999), both available at www.acronym.org.uk. See also C. Cerniello, 'Duma Drafts Resolution then Postpones Vote on START II', 28 *Arms Control Today* (November/December 1998) and 'Russia Postpones START II Vote Again', 29 *Arms Control Today* (December 1999), available at www.armscontrol.org.

59 Federal Law on Ratification of the Treaty between the Russian Federation and the United States of America on Further Reduction and Limitation of Strategic Offensive Arms.

requisite resolution of ratification shortly thereafter.[60] In terms of the federal law, the exchange of instruments of ratification was made conditional upon the completion by the USA of its domestic procedures with respect to the extension protocol and the anti-ballistic missile (ABM) related agreements signed in 1997. The federal law also listed certain extraordinary events which would give rise to a right on the part of the Russian Federation to withdraw from the treaty, including the USA's infringement of, or withdrawal from, the ABM Treaty of 1972. The latter event was expressly mentioned in the federal law in view of controversial US proposals to construct a national missile defence system, which was prohibited under the ABM Treaty and which, it was feared, would disrupt strategic stability to the detriment of Russian interests.[61]

Although both parties had now completed their internal ratification procedures with respect to the original START II, instruments of ratification were not exchanged. For its part, the USA had yet to ratify the extension protocol of 1997, while the Russian side was still uncertain of American intentions concerning the ABM Treaty. These eventually became apparent when, on 13 December 2001, the USA issued the necessary six-month notification to withdraw from the treaty.[62] The withdrawal took effect at midnight on 13 June 2002.[63] The very next day, President Putin declared that the Russian Federation would not become a party to START II. According to a statement issued by the Russian ministry of foreign affairs,[64]

> Taking into account the aforesaid actions of the USA and proceeding from the provisions of the Federal Law on ratification of the START-2 Treaty, the Russian Federation notes the absence of any prerequisites for the entry of the START-2 Treaty into force, and does not consider itself

[60] P. C. Bleek, 'Russia Ratifies START II, Extension Protocol; ABM-Related Agreements also Approved', 30 *Arms Control Today* (May 2000), available at www.armscontrol.org.

[61] Russian concerns were reflected in several statements issued by the foreign ministry, including statements 1094 (18 October 2000) and 1098 (19 October 2000).

[62] On the legal issues involved, see R. Müllerson, 'The ABM Treaty: Changed Circumstances, Extraordinary Events, Supreme Interests and International Law', *International and Comparative Law Quarterly*, 50 (2001), 509; J. B. Rhinelander, 'The ABM Treaty – Past, Present and Future (Part II)', *Journal of Conflict and Security Law*, 6 (2001), 225.

[63] 'Statement by the President', White House, Office of the Press Secretary, 13 June 2002.

[64] Statement 1221 'On Legal Status of the Treaty between Russia and the USA on Further Reduction and Limitation of Strategic Offensive Arms' (14 June 2002).

> bound any longer by the obligation under international law to refrain from any actions which could deprive this Treaty of its object and goal.

The Russian decision not to ratify START II had a further juridical consequence. In so far as paragraph 8 of Article II of the treaty was still being applied provisionally between the parties, Russia's notification of its decision to the USA would have terminated the provisional application of that paragraph in accordance with the customary rules on provisional application governing their relations.[65]

Shortly before the USA's withdrawal from the ABM Treaty took effect, the parties concluded the Strategic Offensive Reductions Treaty (SORT) of 24 May 2002.[66] In terms of SORT, the parties could each deploy no more than 1,700 to 2,200 strategic warheads by the end of 2012. Although SORT mitigated the effects of the collapse of START II, the latter's failure illustrates the considerable political challenges which a non-proliferation treaty may face before it enters into force. Above all, it illustrates that entry into force is an eventuality which cannot be taken for granted.

iii. Treaty between the United States of America and the Russian Federation on Measures for the Further Reduction and Limitation of Strategic Offensive Arms (New START)

The Treaty between the United States of America and the Russian Federation on Measures for the Further Reduction and Limitation of Strategic Offensive Arms was signed at Prague on 8 April 2010 and entered into force just ten months later on 5 February 2011, following exchange of instruments of ratification between the parties. The New START replaces both START I, which expired in December 2009, and the SORT Treaty, which would have expired in 2012.

The New START consists of sixteen articles and a protocol. The treaty establishes numerical limits for each party's deployed and non-deployed delivery systems (800) and deployed nuclear warheads (1,550), which must be achieved by 2018. In terms of section I of part 8 of the protocol, various provisions of the treaty and the protocol, which are listed in

[65] The termination would appear to have had no practical consequence inasmuch as Belarus, Kazakhstan and Ukraine (to whom the Russian Federation was not permitted to transfer certain silo launchers in terms of Art. II(8) of START II) had acceded to the NPT as non-nuclear-weapon states and were therefore bound by the non-proliferation obligations of that Treaty.

[66] 2350 UNTS 415; entered into force 1 June 2003.

sections II and III of part 8, were provisionally applied between the dates of signature and entry into force.[67] The provisional application extended, *inter alia*, to: the definitions used in the treaty; the list of types of ballistic missiles and launchers; the rules governing the treaty database and the exchange and release of information and data; the list of facilities subject to inspection activities; the measures to address an ambiguous situation; the principles governing the use of national technical means of verification; the procedures for converting and eliminating strategic offensive arms and facilities; and the arrangements for the bilateral consultative committee under the treaty.

Although none of the key limitations under the treaty or its verification procedures was provisionally applied, it is apparent that New START made far more extensive use of the technique of provisional application for preparatory and confidence-building purposes than either of its predecessors.

iv. The Plutonium Management and Disposition Agreement

The Plutonium Management and Disposition Agreement, or, to give it its full title, the Agreement between the Government of the United States of America and the Government of the Russian Federation Concerning the Management and Disposition of Plutonium Designated as No Longer Required for Defense Purposes and Related Cooperation,[68] was signed in Washington and Moscow on 29 August and 1 September 2000, respectively. In terms of the Agreement, each party undertakes to dispose of no less than 34 million tons of surplus weapons grade plutonium – said to be enough for 17,000 nuclear weapons – thereby preventing its re-use for military purposes and reducing the risk of theft or diversion.[69] The Agreement also provides for mutual monitoring and inspection of disposition activities, which are expected to commence in 2018,[70] and for the establishment of a joint consultative commission for the Agreement. A protocol to the Agreement was signed on 15 September 2006 and another on 13 April 2010,[71] the latter amending

[67] Section II of part eight lists thirteen articles and paragraphs of the Treaty, while section III lists ten parts, paragraphs and groups of paragraphs of the Protocol.

[68] See www.state.gov/documents/organization/18557.pdf.

[69] See State Department Fact Sheet, '2000 Plutonium Management and Disposition Agreement', 13 April 2000, available at www.state.gov.

[70] *Ibid.*

[71] D. Horner, 'Russia, US Sign Plutonium Pact' (May 2010), published at www.armscontrol.org.

provisions of the Agreement concerning the methods of disposition, the verification procedures, and the amount of potential US financial assistance to the Russian disposition programme.

The Agreement and its two protocols have not yet entered into force. In the meantime, all three instruments are being provisionally applied in accordance with substantially similar clauses. The Agreement, for example, provides in paragraph 1 of Article XIII that

> *This Agreement shall be applied provisionally from the date of signature* and shall enter into force on the date of the last written notification that the Parties have fulfilled the national procedures required for its entry into force. (emphasis added)

The simple opening clause of paragraph 1 of Article XIII, making the *entire* agreement provisionally applicable upon signature, is unusual in a non-proliferation treaty. Although clauses of this kind are found in countless other international agreements, they are restricted in non-proliferation practice to what may be termed subsidiary agreements, of which the Plutonium Management and Disposition Agreement is an example.[72] In such agreements, a simplified form of provisional application may be appropriate, as they contain no new basic norms or merely implement existing treaty obligations. Another factor facilitating their provisional application, at least by the USA, is that they are considered to be executive agreements as opposed to treaties under US law.[73] Since they do not require the advice and consent of the Senate, the government of the USA may agree to provisional application in full without running the risk of infringing on the Senate's constitutional prerogatives.

The extent to which the signatories are currently giving effect to the Agreement and its protocols is as yet unclear. The joint consultative commission is, however, operational and has reportedly reached agreement on a range of issues relating to monitoring and inspections under the Agreement.[74]

[72] Other relevant bilateral agreements between the USA and the Russian Federation containing simplified clauses on provisional application include the Protocol to the Agreement Concerning the Safe and Secure Transportation, Storage and Destruction of Weapons and Weapons Proliferation of 1999, and the Agreement Regarding Cooperation in the Area of Nuclear Material Physical Protection, Control and Accounting of 1999. Such clauses are also occasionally found in bilateral agreements concluded by the International Atomic Energy Agency (IAEA) and the Preparatory Commission for the CTBT Organization.

[73] Horner, 'Russia, US Sign Plutonium Pact'.

[74] State Department Fact Sheet, '2000 Plutonium Management and Disposition Agreement'.

VI. Provisional application agreed in some other manner

The second mode of provisional application foreseen in Article 25 of the Vienna Convention is, as we have seen, that in which the negotiating states agree to the provisional application in some manner other than the treaty itself. The two non-proliferation treaties which have made use of this procedure are the most important multilateral non-proliferation treaties concluded since 1990, namely the Chemical Weapons Convention and the Comprehensive Nuclear-Test-Ban Treaty.

i. Chemical Weapons Convention

The Convention on the Prohibition of the Development, Production, Stockpiling and Use of Chemical Weapons and on their Destruction (i.e., the Chemical Weapons Convention – CWC)[75] was opened for signature in Paris on 13 January 1993 and entered into force on 29 April 1997. The Convention is celebrated for being the first multilateral non-proliferation treaty to provide for the eradication of an entire class of weapons of mass destruction under a universal system of international inspection and control. The establishment and implementation of the elaborate system of monitoring and verification foreseen in the Convention naturally required equally elaborate preparations. To generate confidence in the system and to guarantee mutual compliance from the outset, it was necessary to ensure that the system was by and large functional as soon as the Convention entered into force and the Organization for the Prohibition of Chemical Weapons (OPCW) came into being. As is customary when founding a new international agency, the signatories decided to set up a preparatory body to complete the requisite groundwork. A resolution establishing the Preparatory Commission for the OPCW was accordingly adopted by the states signatories on 13 January 1993 at the signing ceremony in Paris. Annexed to the resolution was the constituent instrument of the Commission, the Text on the Establishment of a Preparatory Commission for the OPCW.[76]

In terms of the Text, the principal organs of the Preparatory Commission were a plenary of states signatories and a provisional technical secretariat. The Commission held its first session at The Hague in February 1993, altogether holding sixteen sessions before the

[75] 1974 UNTS 45; opened for signature 13 January 1993; entered into force 29 April 1997.

[76] L. W. Tabassi (ed.), *OPCW: The Legal Texts* (The Hague: T. M. C. Asser Press, 1999), p. 523.

CWC entered into force. In accordance with paragraph 1 of the Text, the Commission was responsible for carrying out the necessary preparations for the effective implementation of the CWC and for preparing for the first session of the conference of the states parties to the Convention following its entry into force. Besides specifying the tasks of the Commission relating to its own functioning, the Text lists the Commission's preparatory responsibilities in considerable detail, with frequent cross-references to clauses of the CWC and its annexes.

Among many other tasks, the Commission's responsibilities included the elaboration of a detailed staffing pattern for the future technical secretariat; the recruitment and training of staff; the preparation of financial and staff regulations and rules; the compilation of the programme of work and budget for the first year of activities of the OPCW; the development of arrangements to facilitate the election of twenty members of the Executive Council; the negotiation of draft agreements between the future OPCW and its member states on privileges and immunities; the preparation of draft guidelines on the inspection of chemical production facilities and on the handling of confidential data and information; and the elaboration of a draft headquarters agreement between the OPCW and the host country. Had the Preparatory Commission not been set up, its various substantive responsibilities would, of necessity, have been performed by the OPCW itself. Viewed from this perspective, the conclusion is inescapable that the text establishing the Commission amounted to an implied agreement on the provisional application, for preparatory purposes, of parts of the CWC dealing with certain functions and responsibilities of the future OPCW.[77] This interim preparatory regime lasted just over four years, from the time of adoption of the Paris resolution until the CWC entered into force in April 1997.

ii. Comprehensive Nuclear-Test-Ban Treaty

The Comprehensive Nuclear-Test-Ban Treaty (CTBT)[78] was opened for signature in New York on 24 September 1996. Article I of the Treaty

[77] Cf. 'Examples of Precedents of Provisional Application'. The provisional application of the constituent instruments considered in that report was mostly inferred from the mandate of the commission or similar body established to prepare the way for the organization or regime in question.

[78] UN doc. A/50/1027 (see also www.ctbto.org); opened for signature 24 September 1996; not yet in force.

prohibits all nuclear test explosions in all environments and for all purposes. The Treaty also provides for the establishment of the Comprehensive Nuclear-Test-Ban Treaty Organization (CTBTO), as well as for a sophisticated system for verifying compliance, which includes a global network of sensors known as the International Monitoring System (IMS). Confidence in the effectiveness of the verification regime naturally has an influence on whether or not states adhere to the treaty. An important aspect of this confidence is the functional readiness and reliability of the regime from the moment the treaty enters into force. Paragraph 1 of Article IV of the CTBT therefore provides, *inter alia*, that 'At entry into force of this Treaty, the verification regime shall be capable of meeting the verification requirements of this Treaty.'

The CTBT does not expressly state what is meant by the phrase 'capable of meeting the verification requirements of this Treaty' or how this objective is to be achieved. The treaty does, however, refer in several places to 'the Preparatory Commission',[79] assuming the Commission's existence as a matter of fact. The method chosen to establish the Preparatory Commission for the CTBTO replicated that used in the case of the Preparatory Commission for the OPCW. Shortly after the treaty was opened for signature, the depositary convened a meeting in New York on 19 November 1996, at which the signatories adopted a resolution establishing the Preparatory Commission for the CTBTO, to which was attached the Text on the Establishment of a Preparatory Commission for the CTBTO.[80]

As with the Preparatory Commission for the OPCW, the mandate of the Preparatory Commission for the CTBTO is to carry out the necessary preparations for the effective implementation of the CTBT and to prepare for the first session of the conference of the states parties to the treaty. In particular, the Preparatory Commission is tasked with undertaking 'all necessary preparations to ensure the operationalization of the Treaty's verification regime at entry into force pursuant to article IV, paragraph 1' (paragraph 13 of the Text). It must also 'supervise and coordinate, in fulfilling the requirements of the Treaty and its Protocol, the development, preparation, technical testing and, pending their formal commissioning,

[79] See Art. II, paras. 10, 26(h) and 49.

[80] UN doc. CTBT/MSS/L.1, 17 October 1996; 1999 *UK Treaty Series* 46. Aust cites the Text as an example of (1) a supplemental treaty with an unusual name, (2) a treaty not requiring signature and (3) a treaty entering into force *instantly* for all adopting states. See Aust, *Modern Treaty Law and Practice*, pp. 22, 24, 90.

provisional operation as necessary' of the International Data Centre (IDC) and International Monitoring System (paragraph 14). Several other paragraphs of the Text contain references to provisions of the CTBT, implying implementation, at least in part, of those provisions before entry into force. These include provisions on the funding of the IMS; the principles for appointing the staff of the organization; the preparation of IMS facility agreements;[81] and the development, in accordance with the Treaty and Protocol, of operational manuals for the various components of the verification regime. Thus, although not actually mandated to verify compliance with the CTBT, the Commission must build up an advanced stage of operational readiness that will enable it to do so in practice. Indeed, by the end of 2010, 85 percent of monitoring stations had been installed and the IMS was providing near global coverage.[82] This ongoing preparatory work has been achieved, in great part, through the implied provisional application of certain terms of the CTBT in accordance with the Text on the Establishment of the Preparatory Commission and as reinforced by the practice of the Commission.

The CTBT has now been signed by 183 states and ratified by 157, including thirty-six of the forty-four states whose ratification is required for its entry into force.[83] Despite this impressive progress towards universality, prospects for the entry into force of the treaty remain uncertain. A major setback occurred in 1999 when the US Senate declined to give its advice and consent to the ratification of the treaty.[84] Although there have been recent signals that the USA may again seek to ratify the treaty, it is not known when this might occur.[85] Furthermore, three other states whose adherence is a prerequisite for entry into force – North Korea, India and Pakistan – have actually carried out nuclear test

[81] Paragraph 12 of the Text foresees that such agreements will be in *draft* form for the approval of the future conference of the states parties. The practice of the Commission, however, is to conclude binding agreements in its own name (see, for example, the series of agreements published in vol. 2123 of UNTS). Since they are not drafts, the legal basis for the agreements cannot be the Text. Rather, it seems to be the provisional application, in practice, of paragraph 4 of part I of the Protocol to the CTBT, which stipulates that host states and the technical secretariat shall agree and cooperate in establishing, upgrading, financing and maintaining monitoring facilities in accordance with appropriate agreements or arrangements.

[82] CTBTO PrepCom document CTBT/ES/2010/4, dated 25 January 2011, para. 8.

[83] See www.ctbto.org.

[84] T. L. Deibel, 'The Death of a Treaty', *Foreign Affairs*, 81 (2002), 142; Asada, 'CTBT: Legal Questions Arising from its Non Entry into Force', 95.

[85] J. Lewis, 'The CTBT: Prospects for Entry into Force', *VERTIC Occasional Papers*, 4 (June 2010).

explosions since the treaty was opened for signature. Notwithstanding subsequent moratoriums announced by India and Pakistan, these three states have yet to sign the treaty let alone ratify it.

These and other political obstacles to the entry into force of the CTBT underscore the value of the treaty's provisional application over and above its purely preparatory function. As the arms control and disarmament committee of the International Law Association has observed,

> The provisional application, as a confidence-building mechanism, reinforces the legal standing of the CTBT, encourages further ratifications, and *deters any State from conducting nuclear tests in the future.*[86]

The committee's view raises an important question. What, some fifteen years after the CTBT was opened for signature, is the status under international law of the ban on nuclear test explosions in Article I of the treaty? The longer the provisional regime for the CTBT lasts, the more pertinent this question becomes. On the one hand, the basic obligations of the treaty as set out in Article I are not among those referred to in the Text on the Establishment of the Preparatory Commission for the CTBTO and therefore do not appear to be provisionally applied as such. On the other hand, it could reasonably be argued that the observance of Article I is assumed under the Text. It hardly seems likely that 182 signatory states would intend to construct an elaborate and costly system to verify compliance with that article while simultaneously permitting violations of it. Still, such an interpretation, based as it is on implied agreement, could be challenged by a nuclear-weapon state determined to resume testing.

Alternatively, it could be argued that a signatory's obligation not to conduct nuclear test explosions derives from its obligation of good faith towards the treaty. Such an obligation would include the general obligation of good faith that a signatory owes towards a treaty it is applying provisionally in whole or in part. It would also include the duty, under Article 18 of the Vienna Convention, to refrain from conduct which would defeat the object and purpose of the treaty until the signatory has made its intention clear not to become a party to the treaty.[87] However, reliance on a duty of good faith as a source of a prohibition of nuclear test explosions may also be problematic. First and foremost, a signatory

[86] Final Report of the Committee on Arms Control and Disarmament Law (2004), published at www.ila-hq.org (emphasis added).

[87] Dekker, *The Law of Arms Control*, pp. 677–678 concludes that 'the object and purpose of the CTBT comprises at least the prevention of the carrying out of nuclear test explosions anywhere'.

could lawfully terminate that duty by making its intention clear not to become a party to the CTBT. A signatory might also argue, however implausibly, that the duty of good faith does not prevent it from carrying out nuclear test explosions,[88] or, in the absence of an express stipulation, that the treaty is being applied provisionally at all. Furthermore, in accordance with the provisions of Article 18, a signatory which has ratified a treaty is under a duty to refrain from acts which would defeat the object and purpose of the treaty before it enters into force 'provided that such entry into force is not unduly delayed'. The obvious question, therefore, is whether the entry into force of the CTBT, which has been open for signature since September 1996, can be considered to have been unduly delayed. If so, its many ratifying states, which include three nuclear powers, could arguably have been released from the duty of good faith reflected in Article 18. As things stand, the requirements for the treaty's entry into force and the fact that the verification system is not yet complete suggest that the answer to that question is 'no'. But what if the current state of affairs were to persist for another fifteen years or longer?[89] Can the duty of good faith based on Article 18 continue indefinitely in respect of the CTBT?

In view of this uncertainty, it would seem desirable to consider whether there is another, non-treaty norm prohibiting nuclear test explosions that restrains signatories and non-signatories alike. Specifically, it would be useful to explore whether there is an emerging rule of customary international law prohibiting all nuclear-test explosions in all environments and for all purposes.[90] Such a supplementary customary norm, whether applying to all states equally or only to those not persistently objecting to it, would reinforce the provisional arrangements for the CTBT and counterbalance its failure to enter into force.

[88] One high official in the United States has asserted, albeit in a private capacity, that the object and purpose of the CTBT is extremely vague and that the obligation of good faith under Art. 18 of the Vienna Convention would not prevent the USA from conducting 'all nuclear testing for all purposes'. See D. S. Jonas, 'The Comprehensive Nuclear-Test-Ban Treaty: Current Legal Status in the United States and the Implications of a Nuclear Test Explosion', *NYU Journal of International Law and Politics*, 39 (2007), 1007, 1034, 1046.

[89] The General Agreement on Tariffs and Trade (GATT) of 1947 famously operated for nearly half a century on a 'provisional' basis pursuant to a Protocol of Provisional Application concluded in 1948 (55 UNTS 308). The US–Cuban Maritime Boundary Agreement of 1977 is still being provisionally applied after some thirty-five years. These examples, though rare, are by no means unique.

[90] Art. 38 of the Vienna Convention of 1969 recognizes that a rule set forth in a treaty may become binding upon a third state as a customary rule of international law, recognized as such.

While a few of important players maintain their distance, it is noteworthy that the treaty has been signed by nearly all states and ratified by the vast majority. It is not unreasonable to conclude that the states adhering to the treaty and subsidizing the work of the Preparatory Commission – most of which, as Asada points out,[91] are not permitted to possess nuclear devices much less test them – support a general norm prohibiting all nuclear test explosions in all environments. After all, the basic obligations of the CTBT complement and reaffirm existing treaty prohibitions which have themselves in all probability achieved customary status. These include the ban on test explosions in the atmosphere, under water and in outer space (the Partial Test-Ban Treaty); the prohibition of tests on celestial bodies (the Outer Space Treaty); the prohibition on tests exceeding 150 megatons (the Threshold Test-Ban Treaty); as well as the rules of the nuclear non-proliferation regime (the NPT and numerous other instruments[92]). As far as customary international law is concerned, therefore, it seems to be only the prohibition of *underground* nuclear test explosions below 150 megatons that remains in doubt.

When underground tests were conducted by India and Pakistan in 1998, the United Nations Security Council passed a resolution demanding that they refrain from further nuclear tests and calling upon all states not to carry out any nuclear weapon test explosion or any other nuclear explosion 'in accordance with the provisions of the CTBT'.[93] In condemning North Korea's underground nuclear test in 2009 in the strongest possible terms, the Security Council demanded that the country discontinue such tests and called upon it to join the CTBT.[94] Thus, although the evidence of the necessary *opinio iuris* is perhaps still incomplete, the longer the provisional arrangements for the CTBT persist, the more likely it is that a new customary norm will emerge encompassing a ban on underground tests.[95] Even if the entry into force provisions of the CTBT prevent it from ever coming into force, the

[91] Asada, 'CTBT: Legal Questions Arising from its Non Entry into Force', p. 87.

[92] On the link between the CTBT and the NPT, see T. Graham, Jr. and D. Hafemeister, 'Nuclear Testing and Proliferation – An Inextricable Connection', *Disarmament Diplomacy*, 91 (Summer 2009), available at www.acronym.org.uk.

[93] UN Security Council resolution S/RES/1172, dated 6 June 1998.

[94] UN Security Council resolution S/RES/1874, dated 12 June 2009.

[95] Writing in 2002, Asada concluded that a customary rule not to conduct nuclear tests in all environments was yet to be established; 'CTBT: Legal Questions Arising from its Non Entry into Force', 92–94.

establishment of the Preparatory Commission for the CTBTO, with its *de facto* verification capabilities, has, by and large, enabled states to circumvent this obstacle and to demonstrate their support for a norm prohibiting all nuclear test explosions for all time. Any state wishing to resort to testing in future will in all likelihood have to establish itself as a 'persistent objector' with respect to that norm and accept the universal condemnation which this will undoubtedly entail.

VII. Non-proliferation practice as *lex specialis*

It was briefly mentioned in the introduction to this chapter (section I, above) that state practice has given rise to special systems or 'regimes' of provisional application in certain functional areas of international law. Prominent special systems or regimes of provisional application include bilateral air transport agreements and multilateral commodity agreements, although there are a number of other examples as well. In general, a special system or regime of provisional application may be said to exist where there is a category of similar treaties containing similar clauses on provisional application serving a similar purpose. The clauses on which a special system or regime of provisional application are based are not necessarily innovative: they may in fact be no different from the clauses customarily included in other treaties and need not derogate from the fallback rules contained in Article 25 of the Vienna Convention. Nor is it necessary that each and every treaty in a particular field provide for provisional application. What constitutes a special system or regime of provisional application is the regular recourse to an essentially standardized form of provisional application in a specific thematic and purposive setting. As a particular manifestation of the general rule on provisional application reflected in Article 25, each special system or regime is arguably its own *lex specialis* on the subject.[96]

The obvious question, then, is whether the emergent practice of provisional application in the area of non-proliferation, which spans two decades, is sufficiently harmonious or uniform to qualify as a special

[96] Cf. M. Koskenniemi, 'Fragmentation of International Law: Difficulties Arising from the Diversification and Expansion of International Law', UN doc. A/CN.4/L.682, dated 13 April 2006, at 54 (on '*Lex specialis* as an application or elaboration of *lege generali*') and 68 (on the term *self-contained regime* as a reference to 'interrelated wholes of primary and secondary rules, sometimes also referred to as "systems" or "subsystems" of rules that cover some particular problem differently from the way it would be covered under general law').

system or regime of provisional application in the same way as the practice regarding, say, air transport or commodity agreements. If so, this may suggest that the law of non-proliferation as a whole is a special regime under international law. At first sight, however, non-proliferation practice is nowhere near as homogeneous as that which underpins most other special systems or regimes of provisional application. On the contrary, the various provisional arrangements tend to vary considerably from one non-proliferation treaty to another, as do the treaties themselves. Given these divergences, it could be concluded that there is no coherent system or regime of provisional application like those existing in other specialized domains.

Yet the picture emerging from non-proliferation practice is more nuanced than that. While the practice may not have coalesced into a *single*, cohesive special system or regime, a number of separate modalities or 'subsystems' of provisional application can be identified instead, each of which comprises a more or less similar class of non-proliferation treaties reflecting a more or less similar treatment of provisional application. Three such subsystems seem to exist. These are (1) the bilateral US–Russian START treaties (i.e., limited provisional application, mainly for institutional, preparatory and confidence-building purposes, in terms of the treaty or a protocol forming part of the treaty, with the possible exclusion of default rules under Article 25 of the Vienna Convention); (2) the global non-proliferation conventions represented by the CWC and the CTBT (i.e., limited provisional application, for preparatory and confidence-building purposes, implied under a separate agreement establishing a preparatory commission); and (3) subsidiary non-proliferation agreements such as the Plutonium Management and Disposition Agreement and its Protocols (i.e., provisional application in full pursuant to a simplified clause with the default rules under Article 25 maintained). It is, of course, possible that with time these subsystems will develop in different directions, as the needs of states may dictate. Right now, however, they each represent a reasonably consistent special usage of provisional application adapted to the circumstances at hand.

Although non-proliferation practice encompasses a number of subsystems of provisional application rather than a single special system or regime, the three subsystems still share several distinctive normative features that indicate that the practice may be more coherent than it at first seems. Six features will be mentioned here. The *first* is the extent to which provisional application serves a preparatory function. As we have seen, the need to monitor and to verify non-proliferation treaties from the moment they enter into force may require the establishment of a dedicated mechanism to oversee the necessary preparations. In the case of bilateral treaties, that mechanism is typically a joint consultative commission or similar treaty body, which is established by provisionally applying relevant treaty provisions upon signature. In global multilateral treaties, on the other hand, a separate entity with international legal personality, known as a preparatory commission, is set up to perform these tasks. While the device of an interim or preparatory commission is a familiar one in the law of international organization, the Preparatory Commissions for the OPCW and the CTBTO take preceding practice to a new level. With one possible exception,[97] the functions and responsibilities of these two preparatory commissions considerably exceed those of earlier preparatory bodies. Instead of the modest preparatory arrangements of the past, the exigencies of non-proliferation law may require the formation of complex provisional regimes which entail the *de facto* implementation of numerous substantive provisions of the treaty in question.

The *second* distinctive feature of non-proliferation practice is the unique role played by provisional application as a means of confidence-building among the signatories. In the case of the CTBT, to highlight one example, the provisional application of certain provisions has demonstrated their effectiveness, promoted a climate of mutual trust and cooperation, and encouraged the challenging process of signature and ratification of the treaty. Given the innate sensitivity of non-proliferation instruments and the difficulties associated with their entry into force, the value of such a confidence-building function should not be underrated.

A *third* distinctive feature of provisional application in this context is its reciprocal, contractual quality, in keeping with the character of the treaties themselves. As a rule, obligations assumed during the provisional period bind all signatories equally in both bilateral and multilateral instruments. There seems to be no place, in non-proliferation practice, for 'limiting' provisions which make the provisional application subject to national law or regulations.[98] Nor for any opt-in or opt-out clauses, which are frequently added to multilateral treaties in the interests of their universality, but which may have the undesirable

[97] i.e. the Interim Commission for the International Trade Organization, the body responsible for the provisional application of GATT. See n. 89, above.

[98] See n. 27, above and the associated text.

consequence – at least from a non-proliferation perspective – of uneven and asymmetrical commitments among the signatories.[99]

A *fourth* distinctive feature of provisional application in non-proliferation treaties is the limited number and scope of clauses which are provisionally applied. In view, perhaps, of its preparatory function, provisional application tends to be used more sparingly than elsewhere, with most non-proliferation treaties being provisionally applied in limited part only. Whereas it is usual in general practice to provide for the provisional application of the entire treaty pending its entry into force, in the area of non-proliferation such a procedure it seems is reserved for subsidiary agreements only.

A related, *fifth* distinctive feature is that core non-proliferation prohibitions and restrictions are not provisionally applied.[100] The focus is instead on technical implementing details, institutional provisions and subordinate commitments. Even the obligations under subsidiary non-proliferation agreements, which are provisionally applied in whole, are supplemental or reinforcing in character and are not fundamental to non-proliferation law in general. While it is possible that certain prohibitions (such as the ban on nuclear tests) may have to be observed as a matter of good faith during the provisional period, it seems that negotiating states consciously avoid giving express legal force to such commitments prior to entry into force.

Even though core non-proliferation norms are never provisionally applied, it is still possible – and this brings us to the *sixth* distinctive feature – for provisional application to play an ancillary role in the process by which primary treaty-based non-proliferation norms become part of general customary international law, binding on all states. In the case of the CTBT, especially, the implied provisional application of certain parts of the treaty has contributed to the establishment of a robust interim regime which deters further nuclear explosive tests, stigmatizes those that conduct such tests, and facilitates the emergence of a customary prohibition identical in scope to Article 1 of the Treaty. Though exceptional, such a role is nevertheless entirely compatible with the time-honoured function of provisional application as a temporary

[99] See nn. 19–21, above and the associated text.

[100] In this respect, non-proliferation treaties differ from humanitarian law-inspired arms-control treaties – in particular, the Convention on the Prohibition of Anti-Personnel Mines of 1997 and the Convention on Cluster Munitions of 2008, which provide for the provisional application of their basic obligations *only*.

expedient to ensure that the implementation of urgent or beneficial provisions is not delayed pending entry into force.

Most of these distinctive features are present, in varying degrees, in all three modalities or subsystems of provisional application into which non-proliferation practice may be divided. Despite a superficially diverse appearance, therefore, non-proliferation practice is united by features which, while perhaps not unique in themselves, have an individual weight and a combined impact which is certainly unique to non-proliferation law. As adaptations of pre-existing practice, these features reflect an approach to provisional application which is barely reminiscent of the customary procedure or of the other special systems or regimes under international law. Just as Article 25 of the Vienna Convention grants negotiating states extensive freedom of choice in shaping their provisional engagements, so the nature and particular requirements of non-proliferation treaties have ensured that they exercise that discretion to the full.[101] In the process, provisional arrangements have evolved which are not only tailored to the particularities of the treaties in question but which begin to alter the character of provisional application as an institution of the law of treaties. After two decades of practice, we can thus distinguish the clear contours of a *lex specialis* of provisional application exclusive to the law of non-proliferation.[102] That this *lex specialis* bears no resemblance to any other *lex specialis* on the subject only serves to emphasize its speciality. Indeed, on what has been called the 'sliding scale of specialness', non-proliferation practice may well be the strongest and most special in all of international law.[103]

VIII. Concluding remarks

In retrospect, the 1990s was a remarkable decade in the history of non-proliferation. The end of the Cold War facilitated not only the conclusion of numerous new non-proliferation treaties, but the inclusion, for the first time, of clauses on provisional application in several of them. Presenting a useful supplement to the interim obligation of good faith, the procedure of provisional application is now a regular component of

[101] See Koskenniemi, 'Fragmentation of International Law', 250.

[102] Cf. B. Simma and D. Pulkowski, 'Of Planets and the Universe: Self-contained Regimes in International Law', *European Journal of International Law*, 17 (2006), 483, 488.

[103] *Ibid.* 490.

both bilateral and multilateral non-proliferation treaties, where it serves the twin functions of confidence building and preparation for the full implementation and verification of the treaty upon entry into force. Taken as a whole, the various provisional arrangements in this field suggest an institution which is increasingly detached from customary practice and which is being incrementally adapted to suit the particular requirements of non-proliferation law. The resulting *lex specialis* of provisional application should, it is submitted, feature prominently in any conclusion that non-proliferation law is its own special regime under international law.

This conclusion does not, of course, mean that Article 25 of the Vienna Convention and the corresponding custom have no relevance to non-proliferation law. Quite the opposite: conventional and customary rules continue to operate in the background, determining the existence and legal effect of agreements on provisional application as well as parameters which signatories may, but need not, regulate among themselves, such as the duration and termination of the provisional period. But, overall, provisional arrangements in this area fulfil a normative function which is unquestionably unique. Moreover, so long as non-proliferation treaties are subject to ratification, the procedure will provide a flexible means by which states can mitigate some of the disadvantages inherent in this uncertain but unavoidable process. In view of obstacles to the entry into force of important treaties such as the CTBT, the significance of provisional application is difficult to overstate. Indeed, provisional application has the potential to contribute in no small measure to maintaining the utility, and therefore the primacy, of treaties in this field.

3

Interpretation of non-proliferation treaties

NIGEL D. WHITE

I. Introduction

The basic rules on interpretation contained in the Vienna Convention on the Law of Treaties (VCLT) are both universal and particular. They provide a 'toolbox' or, more accurately, a 'list of ingredients' of interpretative techniques – textual, purposive and subjective. The blending of these ingredients and the balance between them is not context-specific, although the peculiarities of a particular treaty cannot be ruled out when solving interpretive issues; nor do they depend on the subject matter of the treaty: rather, they depend on the *type* of treaty. The argument in this chapter is that there is no fragmentation to the extent that non-proliferation treaties are subject to different interpretive techniques when compared to, say, trade treaties or human rights treaties. Rather, any variation in interpretive technique is explicable on the basis of the different nature of treaty being considered: whether they are contractual, lawmaking or constitutional – categories that are not the product of fragmentation but can be found in most legal systems and are a reflection of different normative functions. In general terms, the contention in this chapter is that the more constitutional a treaty is the more contextual (in terms of purpose and practice) and less textual the interpretive method becomes.

After establishing these principles *in abstracto*, the analysis in the chapter turns to non-proliferation treaties, where the nature of the three key conventions – the Treaty on the Non-Proliferation of Nuclear Weapons (Nuclear Non-Proliferation Treaty – NPT), the Biological Weapons Convention (BWC) and the Chemical Weapons Convention (CWC) – is considered. For instance, the NPT is often stated to be a 'grand bargain' between nuclear-weapon states (NWSs) and non-nuclear weapon states (NNWSs), but this terminology does not indicate whether the NPT is a bargain in a bilateral contractual sense or in a social contractual or constitutional sense. The argument is that the NPT is constitutional, because, in general terms, the prevention of the destruction of humankind by nuclear war or nuclear holocaust is something that underpins the post-1945 international political and legal order. In contrast, the BWC and CWC are lawmaking in nature, though there are significant variations in structure between the two leading to more dynamic interpretation and development in the CWC. Together, the analysis of these three conventions, with comparisons to contractual arms-control treaties such as the Anti-Ballistic Missile Treaty (ABMT) and the Strategic Arms Reduction Treaty (START), illustrate that there is a sliding scale of interpretative methods, from the fully constitutional at the one end, to the purely contractual at the other. The consequences of this for particular provisions of the three treaties are reviewed in the penultimate section before some concluding remarks are made.

II. The rules of interpretation

Interpretation, which has been defined as an activity 'designed to clarify the text of a written manifestation of law and to recognize its sense with a view to its application to the realities of daily life and practice',[1] is the key that unlocks the opaque language so often prevalent in international conventions. However, despite the best attempts of lawyers and legal doctrine, interpretation as a method of gaining a 'right' answer is not always possible. Language is inherently ambiguous and there are many different actors with different agendas interpreting and applying the law. In some treaty regimes – human rights, for instance – authoritative interpretations given by treaty bodies are plentiful, but in the area of non-proliferation law, apart from an opinion of the International Court of Justice and some development by the Organization for the Prohibition of Chemical Weapons (OPCW) in the case of the CWC, we only have the text, the understandings and practice of the states parties (in conference or otherwise), and debates surrounding it. In the absence of developed secondary rules of adjudication, allowing courts or other authoritative bodies to give the final and bindings answers,[2] the quest for 'objective meaning' is a daunting one.[3]

1 M. Bos, 'Theory and Practice of Treaty Interpretation', *Netherlands International Law Review*, 27 (1980), 1, 15.

2 H. L. A. Hart, *The Concept of Law* (Oxford University Press, 1961), p. 92.

3 M. Koskenniemi, *From Apology to Utopia: The Structure of International Legal Argument* (Cambridge University Press, 2005), p. 475.

The rules of interpretation are contained in Articles 31 and 32 of the VCLT. Article 31 states:

> 1. A treaty shall be interpreted in good faith in accordance with the ordinary meaning to be given to the terms of the treaty in their context and in the light of its object and purpose.
> 2. The context for the purpose of the interpretation of a treaty shall comprise, in addition to the text, including its preamble and annexes:
>   (a) any agreement relating to the treaty which was made between all the parties in connexion with the conclusion of the treaty;
>   (b) any instrument which was made by one or more parties in connexion with the conclusion of the treaty and accepted by the other parties as an instrument related to the treaty.
> 3. There shall be taken into account, together with the context:
>   (a) any subsequent agreement between the parties regarding the interpretation of the treaty or the application of its provisions;
>   (b) any subsequent practice in the application of the treaty which establishes the agreement of the parties regarding its interpretation;
>   (c) any relevant rules of international law applicable in the relations between the parties.
> 4. A special meaning shall be given to a term if it is established that the parties so intended.

While Article 32 states:

> Recourse may be had to supplementary means of interpretation, including the preparatory work of the treaty and the circumstances of its conclusion, in order to confirm the meaning resulting from the application of article 31, or to determine the meaning when the interpretation according to article 31:
>
> (a) leaves the meaning ambiguous or obscure; or
> (b) leads to a result which is manifestly absurd or unreasonable.

It is normal to distil from these provisions the three approaches or what Fitzmaurice, writing before the VCLT, called the 'three main schools of thought on the subject': the 'intention of the parties or founding fathers school'; the 'textual or ordinary meaning of the words school'; and the 'teleological or aims and objects school'. Fitzmaurice paints a picture of these three schools of thought operating independently, often at loggerheads, and producing 'radically divergent results'.[4] However, in principle, an interpreter should not be a textualist

[4] G. G. Fitzmaurice, 'The Law and Procedure of the International Court of Justice: Treaty Interpretation and Certain other Treaty Points', *British Yearbook of International Law*, 28 (1951), 1. But see H. Waldock, *Yearbook of the International Law Commission*, 1964,

or a teleologist or a subjectivist, but should weigh up the application of all these principles in order to produce a coherent and consistent interpretation of a treaty. While by no means an argument for the 'right answer' thesis,[5] the weighted-principles approach of Dworkin is applicable since it is an approach that at least seeks a legitimate and acceptable answer.[6] The interpreter should weigh up the rules, principles, object and purposes found in the treaty, practice that amounts to interpretation, and the principles and norms of wider international legal order, to produce such an acceptable answer.[7] The question is acceptable to whom – states parties, jurists or some form of interpretive/judicial body? In the absence of the last, the answer must be that the interpretation should be acceptable to the states parties, on the basis that what is being interpreted are the rights and duties of those states. Treaty law is premised on *pacta sunt servanda*,[8] and, furthermore, in the absence of an independent interpretative body, more broadly reflects the horizontal nature of international law whereby states are both creators and subjects of international law.

An overview of the history of Western schools of thought regarding interpretation reveals that there has been a general move away from the text as the sole source of information. This development culminated in the 1969 Vienna Convention, where the different approaches are all (equally) represented, reflecting a (post)modernist approach to interpretation. In the period of absolute state sovereignty, the dominant positivist philosophy of the nineteenth century, clear and concise rules were identified and distilled by empirical observation of texts or state behaviour. The text was the beginning and the end of discovering meaning, though the intention of the

vol. 2, p. 53, where he states that different writers give 'relative weight' to the three approaches. Bos's analysis of writers and tribunals reveals evidence of all three approaches but states that the textual method of interpretation dominates. Bos, 'Theory and Practice of Treaty Interpretation', 136.

[5] See F. V. Kratochwil, *Rules, Norms and Decisions: On the Conditions of Practical and Legal Reasoning in International Relations* (Cambridge University Press, 1989), pp. 32–33, 40–42.

[6] R. Dworkin, *Taking Rights Seriously* (Cambridge, Mass.: Harvard University Press, 1978), pp. 110–123. Dworkin would probably agree with Amerasinghe's statement that 'interpretation of texts in international law is an art and not a science'. C. F. Amerasinghe, 'Interpretation of Texts in Open International Organizations', *British Yearbook of International Law*, 45 (1994), 175, 182.

[7] R. Dworkin, *Law's Empire* (Cambridge, Mass.: Harvard University Press, 1986), pp. 338–339.

[8] Art. 26 of the VCLT 1969.

parties behind the making of the treaty was utilized in case of doubt. Prior to the Vienna Convention, the increasing number of multilateral treaties meant greater ambiguity was creeping in, requiring a modification of formalism to the extent that although the text was still paramount other methods could be used to supplement the text, first the *travaux préparatoires* and then the object and purposes.[9] This approach still finds favour with some writers,[10] though they concede that a purely grammatical approach is no longer appropriate.[11] This approach is also reflected to a large degree in the decisions of the International Court of Justice, where the meaning that is drawn from the text is supported by the other approaches.[12] While this modified textual approach is not supported in this chapter as constituting the general approach to interpretation, it will be argued that the closer a treaty comes to being 'contractual' the more textual the method of interpretation.

Although Jacobs argues that the Vienna Convention preserves the 'primacy of the text' in the interests of certainty and to uphold the fundamental norm of treaty law – *pacta sunt servanda*[13] – the only hierarchy to be found in the provisions appears to be between the preparatory work (which is reduced to being supplemental by Article 32 – in itself a major break from tradition) and the other methods. The textual approach is mentioned first, reflecting the International Law Commission's Commentary on the draft articles that the text must be

9 M. S. McDougal, H. D. Lasswell and J. C. Millar, *The Interpretation of International Agreements and World Public Order: Principles of Content and Procedure* (New Haven, Conn.: Yale University Press, 1967), pp. 78–79.

10 I. M. Sinclair, *The Vienna Convention on the Law of Treaties*, 2nd edn (Manchester University Press, 1984), pp. 115–116, 141; R. Jennings and A. Watts, *Oppenheim's International Law*, 9th edn (Oxford University Press, 2006), p. 1271. But see A. Aust, *Modern Treaty Law and Practice*, 2nd edn (Cambridge University Press, 2007), p. 231.

11 Sinclair, *The Vienna Convention on the Law of Treaties*, p. 121; Jennings and Watts, *Oppenheim's International Law*, p. 1267.

12 Jennings and Watts, *Oppenheim's International Law*, p. 1273. See, for example, *Territorial Dispute Case* (*Libya* v. *Chad*), ICJ Reports 1994 6, 20–27. See, further, S. Engel, 'Living International Constitutions and the World Court (The Subsequent Practice of International Organs under their Constituent Instruments)', *International and Comparative Law Quarterly*, 16 (1967), 865, 905–910.

13 F. G. Jacobs, 'Varieties of Approach to Treaty Interpretation: With Special Reference to the Draft Convention on the Law of Treaties before the Vienna Diplomatic Conference', *International and Comparative Law Quarterly*, 18 (1969), 318, 340, 343.

the starting point for any attempted interpretation,[14] but in ascertaining the final meaning of a treaty provision due (arguably, equal) weight must be given to the purposive and subjective (current intent) approaches.[15] Indeed, the closer a treaty comes to a constitutional form, the more the move towards parity between the approaches. In the drafting process that led to the Vienna Convention it is noticeable that both subsequent practice and the objects and purposes were promoted from being simply supplemental to being primary means of interpretation, marking a considerable departure from previous orthodoxy.[16] The Vienna Convention thus embodied a further development in the evolution of treaty interpretation by giving potentially equal value to all three approaches and by downgrading the *travaux* (original intent) in favour of subsequent practice and agreement (current intent). The equality of treatment of the means of interpretation does not necessarily lead to chaos or uncertainty, but can potentially produce a fair and balanced interpretation that reflects the current agreed meaning, one which allows the treaty to develop but which does not undermine the principle of *pacta sunt servanda*. Indeed, in constitutional texts it is only by evaluating all three approaches that the rights and duties of the parties can be ascertained. This approach to interpretation is supported to some extent by McDougal, who argues against the orthodox presumption that the text holds the answer. However, he argues that the Vienna Convention is still too pro-textual in that it does not widen the context sufficiently to include not only the practice of the parties and the purposes of the treaty but the nature of the treaty and its fit into the international legal and political system.[17] McDougal's position is too broad and ultimately driven by policy considerations, though a legitimate extension of context beyond the dictates of Articles 31 and 32 of the Vienna Convention may allow for a treaty to be interpreted in the light of other treaties and customs operating in the same area, for example, non-proliferation. It is worthwhile examining the three interpretative components in a little more detail, before discussing their applicability to non-proliferation treaties.

[14] Commentary of the International Law Commission on the Draft Convention on the Law of Treaties, Report of the ILC, 18th Sess., 4 May–19 July 1966, 51.

[15] A. Aust, *Modern Treaty Law and Practice*, 2nd edn (Cambridge University Press, 2007), p. 231.

[16] Jacobs, 'Varieties of Approach to Treaty Interpretation', 327, 329, 337.

[17] M. S. McDougal, 'The International Law Commission's Draft Articles upon Interpretation: Textuality Redivivus', *American Journal of International Law*, 61 (1967), 992.

i. Textual

This approach is stated first of all in Article 31(1) of the Vienna Convention. Interpretation shall be 'in accordance with the ordinary meaning to be given to the terms of the treaty in their context'. The context is explained in Article 31(2) as including any agreements or memoranda made by all the parties, or, indeed, by one or more of them, at the time of the conclusion of the treaty. The textual approach concentrates on the text and emphasises an examination of the words used. The ILC explained that 'the text must be presumed to be the authentic expression of the intention of the parties, the starting point of interpretation is the elucidation of the meaning of the text, not an investigation *ab initio* into the intentions of the parties'.[18] Thus, the textual approach is predicated on the basis that this is the surest way of ascertaining the parties' intention, not the *travaux*, which are relegated to subsidiary means in Article 32.[19] Although the Vienna Convention prioritizes intent, as embodied in the text, over intent, evidenced in negotiations prior to the treaty, intent manifested after the treaty, found in practice or agreement of the states parties, is recognized alongside the text.

Prior to the adoption of the Vienna Convention, textualism or formalism prevailed, though the dominance of this approach does seem to have waned after the Convention. Formalism is superficially attractive, for it appears to produce certainty and continuity. The 'proper' meaning of a word or a phrase does not really change over time if the text is divorced from context, purpose and practice. The fear is that the introduction of these variables will produce uncertainty and will lead to subjective, politicized interpretations. Nevertheless, even legal systems that are based on formalism recognize that the text is not enough by itself.[20] The English canons of statutory interpretation recognize that the 'literal rule' must be supplemented by the 'golden rule', to avoid manifest absurdity, and the 'mischief rule' so that the purposes of the legislation are achieved.[21] Even the greatest English positivist, H. L. A. Hart, recognized that language was ambiguous and that words only had a core

[18] *Yearbook of the International Law Commission, 1966*, vol. 2, p. 220.

[19] Bos, 'Theory and Practice of Treaty Interpretation', 145.

[20] Kelsen, the pure positivist, himself recognized that there may be no one single correct textual interpretation. H. Kelsen, *Pure Theory of Law*, 2nd edn (Berkeley, Calif.: University of California Press, 1967), p. 351.

[21] R. Cross, J. Bell and G. Engle, *Cross: Statutory Interpretation*, 3rd edn (London: Butterworths, 1995).

meaning of certainty, thus allowing the interpreter some discretion.[22] However, these views still seemed to be based on the assumption that the text is paramount and that other approaches are supplementary. While this may be the case with contractual documents, it is not the case with evolutionary and social documents, such as constitutions.

ii. Purposive

A treaty is interpreted in the light of its object and purpose. The preamble and any specific provisions outlining the purposes of the treaty or organization are examined in order to aid an understanding of the particular provisions. It can be combined with the principle of effectiveness[23] in order to allow an organization or conference to act constitutionally, even though the text may be silent. Furthermore, if a purposive interpretation is supported by a subjective interpretation, for instance, based on subsequent agreement or practice, then there appears to be no reason why the non-textual approaches in combination should not prevail.

In a different sense, the objects and purposes of the treaty can be said to define the framework of the constitutional treaty, a framework which is filled in by the practice of organs of an organization consisting of member states, or, in the absence of such, by states (meeting in conference or separately).[24] In essence, the object and purposes of a treaty define the maximum extent within which practice can develop and are, therefore, in the case of constitutional treaties, which are highly evolutionary, of fundamental importance.

iii. Subjective (current intent)

Searching for the meaning of a treaty in the *travaux* may be quite common in practice, but such a subjective approach would, according to the VCLT, only be a supplementary means of interpretation and would not take precedence over the other approaches. More significant

[22] Hart, *The Concept of Law*, pp. 140–150.

[23] See T. Sato, *Evolving Constitutions of International Organizations* (The Hague: Kluwer, 1996), pp. 25–30; G. Fitzmaurice, *The Law and Procedure of the International Court of Justice* (Cambridge University Press, 1986), p. 345. See, further, H. Lauterpacht, 'Restrictive Interpretation and the Principle of Effectiveness in the Law of Treaties', *British Yearbook of International Law*, 26 (1949), 48.

[24] Pollux [i.e., Edward Hambro], 'The Interpretation of the Charter', *British Yearbook of International Law*, 23 (1946), 54.

for understanding treaty texts is the current intent of states parties. What the parties believe to be the meaning of a term today is much more important than what (often a minority of) the parties thought it meant when the treaty was drafted.[25] Indeed, as time passes, subsequent practice and agreement of states parties become much more important than original intent. This is particularly evident in a constitutional treaty, where the text is applied and developed on a regular basis. Judge Alvarez in the *Second Admissions* case stated that it is

> necessary, when interpreting treaties – in particular, the Charter of the United Nations – to look ahead, that is, to have regard to the new conditions, and not to look back, or to have recourse to *travaux préparatoires*. A treaty or a text that has once been established acquires a life of its own. Consequently, in interpreting it we must have regard to the exigencies of contemporary life, rather than to the intentions of those who framed it.[26]

While a perfectly valid argument for playing down the role of the *travaux* in interpreting constitutional texts, Judge Alvarez's judicial rhetoric is unclear on the meaning of the 'exigencies of contemporary life', and there is a danger here that this will lead to policy arguments along the lines advocated by McDougal.[27] It seems to be a more legitimate and accepted method to rely on subsequent practice and agreement as evidence of intent in the case of constitutional texts. Current intent by itself is not sufficient to establish meaning, but it must be given equal weight alongside the text and the purposes.

Article 31(3) of the Vienna Convention mentions subsequent agreement and subsequent practice as methods of interpretation. For instance, the declarations of states during review conferences of the non-proliferation treaties can be viewed as subsequent practice or subsequent agreement. Subsequent agreement and practice as a means of interpreting, modifying and possibly amending a treaty is still an under-examined area of the law of treaties,[28] and yet it is an issue of fundamental

[25] McDougal, Laswell and Miller, *The Interpretation of International Agreements and World Public Order*, p. 135.

[26] ICJ Reports 1950 18.

[27] McDougal, 'The International Law Commission's Draft Articles upon Interpretation'.

[28] But see O. Corten and P. Klein (eds.), *The Vienna Convention on the Law of Treaties: A Commentary* (Oxford University Press, 2011), pp. 826–829; R. Gardiner, *Treaty Interpretation* (Oxford University Press, 2008), pp. 216–249.

importance, particularly for constitutional treaties,[29] or for any treaty which is a living instrument. There is considerable disagreement as to the role of subsequent practice in treaty interpretation. For instance, Judge Spender, in the *Expenses* case, although not an advocate of the narrow textual approach, was against using subsequent practice when it operated against the sovereign will of a minority of states, preferring instead to give greater weight to the purposive approach.[30]

As well as the level of support needed, there is the potential incompatibility of a consistent line of subsequent practice with the object and purpose of the treaty. A subjective interpretation which looks at the intention of the parties based on their subsequent conduct (agreement or practice) may be incompatible with a 'teleological' interpretation based on the object and purpose of the treaty. Although practice and the teleological approach both encourage expansion from the express words, they do not necessarily encourage parallel expansion. What if practice is contrary to the object and purpose? Do the object and purposes constitute a limitation on the development of the treaty by subsequent practice? Similarly, if practice indicates an interpretation which is directly contrary to the text then is this practice valid? If equal weight is given to all three approaches – the subjective, purposive and textual, then the answer to these questions depends on how they balance out. However, in the posited case where practice and purposes are at loggerheads, the text may not provide the solution, and so there is, unsurprisingly, no clear answer. When it stated in the *Expenses* case that '[w]hen the Organization takes action which warrants the assertion that it was appropriate for the fulfilment of one of the stated purposes of the United Nations, the presumption is that such an action is not *ultra vires* the Organization',[31] the International Court implicitly accepted that the main limitation on the practice of the UN is the object and purposes of the organization.

It is recognized that practice may not only interpret and perhaps modify the language of a constitutional treaty, but it also, in certain cases, can lead to an amendment of the textual meaning.[32] It is self-evident

[29] H. Waldock, 'Third Report on the Law of Treaties', *Yearbook of the International Law Commission*, 2 (1964), 59–60; Sato, *Evolving Constitutions of International Organizations*, p. 232.

[30] ICJ Reports 1962 184–185. See also S. Rosenne, *Developments in the Law of Treaties* (Cambridge University Press, 1989), p. 237.

[31] *Expenses* Case, ICJ Reports 1962 168.

[32] Jacobs, 'Varieties of Approach to Treaty Interpretation', 332.

that this event will be a rarity, but it remains a possibility, particularly when formal amendment procedures are rarely used. Modification of the treaty by subsequent practice or agreement can occur to develop the text, to fill lacunae, and to provide concrete definitions of ambiguous terms, but it can also, in some cases, amend or revise the text – maybe even radically revising the plain meaning of the text. However, if this revision produces a result that is directly contrary to the text of the treaty, then the presumption must be that it unlawful, unless there is overwhelming and consistent support for the revision among the parties, at least to a level required for a formal amendment of the treaty. The line between interpretation and revision is inevitably blurred,[33] and it seems that because of this blurring it is impossible in normal cases to apply separate rules concerning levels of support to each, except in the clear case of what would normally (if undertaken by one state, or a minority of states) amount to a clear violation of the core meaning of an express term. This requires the higher level of support required for amendment.

As regards the type and level of practice required within a constitutional treaty, Amerasinghe provides us with some useful criteria. First, he is rightly careful to identify that a practical interpretation of a treaty must be based on a consistent line of conduct by parties, which is regarded as normative by those parties.[34] Secondly, where a practice does not amend a text, but fills lacunae or removes ambiguities, practice unanimously supported by the membership is clearly sufficient. Amerasinghe further states that 'where there is a *large* majority in favour of the practice . . . it is arguable that a small obstinate minority, whether it is always the same minority or not, cannot obstruct an interpretation given by the membership of the organ.'[35] However, when there is a substantial minority opposing the interpretation, such practice has limited effect. 'This position may change with time and repetition, as members adjust themselves

[33] Sato, *Evolving Constitutions of International Organizations*, p. 31. See, further, comments by Lachs, Summary Records of the 766th Meeting of the ILC, *Yearbook of the International Law Commission*, 1 (1964), 286, para. 46. This confusion was enhanced by the deletion at the UN Conference on the Law of Treaties of a draft article on amendment of treaties by subsequent practice. First Session, Vienna, 26 March–24 May 1968, UNOR 207–15, 215, para. 60 (1969).

[34] C. F. Amerasinghe, *Principles of the Institutional Law of International Organizations*, 2nd edn (Cambridge University Press, 2005), p. 51.

[35] *Ibid.* 52.

to a new practice but the mere fact of a majority vote, irrespective of its size, cannot be sufficient to establish a practice.'[36]

The justification for these reasoned and practical guidelines seems to be the achievement of a compromise between two extremes. A narrow view subjects any development to the express consent of all parties, while the wider view relies on implied consent. As Amerasinghe states,

> while a practice may not 'change' a constitutional provision in the sense of amending it, a substantial minority may be entitled to maintain that it did not implicitly agree to 'development' of the text against its will. The same argument may not be applied to a small minority. There is an element of implied agreement in the case of the latter, to the extent that it cannot obstruct the functioning [of the treaty].[37]

Although Amerasinghe is analysing the constituent documents of organizations, there is no reason not to apply his provisions to other constitutional treaties, since his criteria concern practice by states parties to a treaty, whether in the organs of an organization or, more generally, within the framework of the treaty. Other writers are a little more cautious, as illustrated by Gardiner's view that 'when searching for practice relating to interpretation of a particular treaty provision, the defining test is that the practice must establish the agreement of the parties',[38] though that agreement can be manifest or imputable.[39]

As has been stated above, subsequent practice may amend the treaty. Here, however, a much greater weight of practice must be present for amendment to occur. According to Amerasinghe, 'even if every party might not itself have actively participated in the practice, [the practice] must be such as to establish the agreement of the parties as a whole to the modification in question'.[40] Thus, when practice has allegedly modified the text, express consent, though still not in an absolute sense, prevails. Amerasinghe seems to classify as practical amendments only those which are directly contrary to the text. This seems an unduly narrow view of amendment and ignores the fact that interpretation slides into amendment without there being a clear distinction. Interpretations

[36] *Ibid.*

[37] *Ibid.* 53. See also Sato, *Evolving Constitutions of International Organizations*, p. 32; ILC Report [1966], *Yearbook of the International Law Commission*, 2 (1967), 222, para. 15; E. Lauterpacht, 'The Development of the Law of International Organization by the Decisions of International Tribunals', *Hague Recueil*, 152 (1976), 460.

[38] Gardiner, *Treaty Interpretation*, p. 227.

[39] *Ibid.* 236. See also Aust, *Modern Treaty Law and Practice*, p. 243.

[40] Amerasinghe, *Principles of the Institutional Law of International Organizations*, p. 53.

which modify the meaning of words, for instance, can equally be seen as amendments. Furthermore, any interpretation that modifies the meaning of a text should be supported by states parties to the level required for the formal amendment of the treaty, or, in the absence of any provision allowing for amendment, support should illustrate the agreement of the parties as a whole to the interpretation.[41]

III. Different types of treaty

In the modern era, treaty law purports to cover a range of different types of conventions. At the one end of the spectrum there is the bilateral, contractual treaty. In the area of arms control this is embodied by the now defunct Anti-Ballistic Missile (ABM) Treaty, and the Strategic Arms Reduction Treaties (STARTs) between the USA and the USSR/Russia. In these treaties there is greater certainty in the text as the terms were hammered out on a take-it-or-leave-it basis by the two parties. The rights and duties are relatively clear and, therefore, the text dominates the life of the treaty unless both parties agree on changes, or, as with the 1972 ABM Treaty between the USA and USSR/Russia, one party withdraws. This is not to say that the ABM Treaty was not an important treaty, it was the 'cornerstone of strategic stability' during the Cold War,[42] but it reflected the bilateral and bipolar nature of the Cold War.[43] At the other end of the spectrum there is a multiparty constitutional treaty that is both conventional and institutional, laying down rules, but also creating institutions and organs. Those organs are political, consisting of states parties, though they may also be legal, consisting of committees of experts or judicial bodies. In international law, the UN Charter is such a document, and, at the regional level, there are the treaties establishing the European Union.

Attempts have been made, mainly since the adoption of the Covenant of the League of Nations, in 1919, to suggest that there is a significant distinction to be drawn between ordinary 'contractual' bilateral or

[41] See L. Gross, 'The International Court of Justice and the United Nations', *Hague Recueil*, 109 (1963), 313, 428; M. Akehurst, 'The Hierarchy of the Sources of International Law', *British Yearbook of International Law*, 47 (1974–1975), 273, 278.

[42] J. Rhinelander, 'The ABM Treaty – Past, Present and Future (Part I)', *Journal of Conflict and Security Law*, 6 (2001), 91, 92.

[43] R. Mullerson, 'The ABM Treaty: Changed Circumstances, Extraordinary Events, Supreme Interests and International Law', *International and Comparative Law Quarterly*, 50 (2001), 509, 509.

multilateral treaties, and 'constitutional' multilateral treaties.[44] Such a suggestion was quite a radical departure from the view dominant in the nineteenth century that international law was in essence private (contractual) law between consenting states acting as equals, rather than any form of public law. The fine balance in the debate can be seen as far back as 1919 when Huber depicted the legal character of the League of Nations Covenant as 'neither contractual nor constitutional'.[45] Huber was clearly of the view that the Covenant had a different legal character to the mainly contractual exchanges and agreements that preceded it.

McNair, writing in 1930, was less cautious, stating that 'the society of States has not yet got a complete Constitution, but it has a great deal of Constitutional Law', including not only the Covenant but also other foundational treaties. He concluded by stating that 'it seems to me that these constitutional treaties . . . create a kind of public law transcending in kind and not merely in degree the ordinary agreements between States'.[46] While the meaning of a bilateral or multilateral contractual arrangement, whereby all the 'contracting parties concur in the purpose of creating identical rules binding upon all of them',[47] is relatively clear, what exactly is meant by a 'constitution' or 'constitutional law' is much more complicated, especially in the international context. McNair alludes to a form of international law that transcends the normal legal relations of states, which is suggestive of a move away from the purely horizontal consensual system epitomized by a contract.

A more detailed distinction between contract and constitution is developed by Abromeit and Hitzel-Cassagnes. For them, the essence of a contract is a pact based on the mutual consent or agreement of all the partners, it is a product of bargaining and exchange and its purpose is to achieve mutual advantage. In such a treaty regime the partners are 'masters of the treaty'[48] in that 'every change of the contractual terms calls for the consent of all the parties',[49] any disagreement will result in either the continuation of the original contract, or the creation of a new contract or contracts with

[44] N. D. White, *Law of International Organizations*, 2nd edn (Manchester University Press, 2005), pp. 14–23.

[45] Cited in A. Zimmern, *The League of Nations and the Rule of Law, 1918–1935* (New York: Russell and Russell, 1969), pp. 290–291.

[46] A. D. McNair, 'The Functions and Different Legal Character of Treaties', *British Yearbook of International Law*, 11 (1930), 100, 112.

[47] *Ibid.* 105.

[48] H. Abromeit and T. Hitzel-Cassagnes, 'Constitutional Change and Contractual Revision: Principles and Procedures', *European Law Journal*, 5 (1999), 23, 34.

[49] *Ibid.* 25.

different partners. 'The decisive quality' of a contract 'is that of unanimity, combined with notions of common or shared interests and reciprocity'.[50] While constitutions have their foundation in an original or more fundamental contractual agreement between partners, the partners thereafter cease to be masters of the treaty but are the subjects of it.[51] 'A constitution typically sets out the fundamental rules of a political order and establishes the basic political institutions.'[52] Once constitutions are established they can take on a life of their own through a combination of 'usage', 'authoritative interpretation' (by political and legal organs) and by 'formal amendment'.[53] If the development is by a political process, by usage, interpretation or modification, then various majorities are permissible. In the case of interpretation by a judicial body, then development occurs through institutions that are beyond the control of states (even acting as a majority).[54]

There are various strengths of constitutions; some may command more respect and loyalty than others.[55] Some may simply be constitutions in a formal sense of 'establish[ing] and regulat[ing] the main organs of government, their constitution and powers'.[56] Others may be constitutions in a more fundamental sense. Raz defined these as having the elements of being not only constitutive, but also stable, written, superior, justiciable, entrenched, and an expression of a common ideology.[57] In this sense, the fundamental constitutive treaties, such as the UN Charter, can be seen as constitutions, but also, following McNair, can treaties that lay down the basic rules of the international legal order and are not simply an exchange of rights and duties between states parties.

i. *Interpreting different types of treaty*

When applying interpretive techniques, treaties that are constitutional or 'living instruments'[58] require a different emphasis from a static

[50] *Ibid.* 31. [51] *Ibid.* 30. [52] *Ibid.* 28. [53] *Ibid.* 32. [54] *Ibid.* 34.

[55] J. Crawford, 'The Charter of the United Nations as Constitution', in H. Fox (ed.), *The Changing Constitution of the United Nations* (London: British Institute of International Law, 1997), 1.

[56] P. Craig, 'Constitutions, Constitutionalism, and the European Union', *European Law Journal*, 7 (2001), 125, 126.

[57] J. Raz, 'On Authority and Interpretation of Constitutions: Some Preliminaries', in L. Alexander (ed.), *Constitutionalism* (Cambridge University Press, 1998), pp. 152–153.

[58] See, generally, P.-M. Dupuy, 'The Constitutional Dimension of the Charter of the United Nations Revisited', *Max Planck Yearbook of United Nations Law* (1998), 1; M. Reisman, 'Constitutional Crisis at the UN', *American Journal of International Law*, 87 (1993), 83; Sato, *Evolving Constitutions of International Organizations*, pp. 229–231.

bilateral or multilateral contractual treaty that is not the subject of continuous application by an organization, treaty organ or conference of the parties.[59] To interpret contractual treaties, use is made of textual and purposive techniques, as, in the absence of subsequent practice or agreement by the parties, the interpreter mainly has the text (whether in the form of the operative provisions, the preamble or other purposive provisions) at his or her disposal. The preparatory work may be used as a supplementary means, but the only evidence of current intent, as opposed to original intent, is to be found in unilateral statements of some of the parties to the treaty on the meaning of a particular provision.

Constitutional treaties evolve in order to keep pace with developments in their areas of competence. Subsequent agreement or practice is therefore a significant means of interpreting and developing such treaties. Nevertheless, sole reliance on practice as the test of legality is not acceptable, although it has become increasingly common; as Rosenne notes, it is as though the international lawyer is becoming 'the computerized collective memory or historian of the organisation'.[60] Practice is not the only means of interpretation that should be applied to constitutional documents; equal weight should also be given to the other methods of interpretation, as outlined in the VCLT. The basic proposition is that of equal weight, as each method of interpretation is equally valid. There are no meta-arguments which would justify a hierarchy of approaches.

The question remains, however, as to how to apply these rules consistently and fairly without producing contradictory results (for instance, if the text states one thing and practice another). Melanczuk seems to suggest that meaning lies in the eye of the interpreter when he writes that 'there are no rules of interpretation, only presumptions; and the presumptions very often conflict with one another. The choice between conflicting presumptions is almost bound to be influenced by political factors, however hard one tries to exclude them.'[61] It is true to say that a particular method of interpretation will be chosen by a state for political reasons. It is noticeable that the West's purposive and practical understanding of the powers of the UN General Assembly in the first decade of the UN was soon replaced by a textual analysis in later years when they ceased to dominate that organ.[62] States

[59] Bos, 'Theory and Practice of Treaty Interpretation', pp. 156–161.

[60] Rosenne, *Developments in the Law of Treaties*, p. 244.

[61] P. Melanczuk, *Akehurst's Introduction to International Law*, 7th edn (London: Routledge, 1996), p. 365.

[62] N. D. White, *Keeping the Peace: The United Nations and the Maintenance of International Peace and Security*, 2nd edn (Manchester University Press, 1997), p. 148.

parties obviously have freedom to interpret the treaty. However, this should not prevent a dispassionate judge or observer from applying the rules of interpretation with reasonable consistency, for, as Bos states, 'interpretation and all other forms of ascertainment . . . are subject to the requirements of reason (absence of prejudice, objectivity, consistency, and clarity), order, and efficiency'.[63] This includes an examination of the member states' views of the meaning of particular provisions when exercising their freedom of interpretation.[64]

Unfortunately, non-proliferation law is not overstocked with courts sitting in judgment and applying the rules of interpretation in a consistent and coherent manner. In such circumstances, the analysis of interpretation offered by deconstructionists seems more attractive. Like the Marxist theorists before them who claimed that international law was not based on a community consensus but emerged out of the struggle between East and West, resulting in many 'political' treaties (such as the NPT) containing deliberately ambiguous norms which could equally be used to support the Western and Socialist positions,[65] deconstructionism's position is that 'interpretation creates meaning rather than discovers it'.[66] However, to claim that this is always the case is an exaggeration. Some phrases and terms may be so ambiguous as to lead to subjective interpretation, but once there is a body of consensual practice on the term then it has a definite meaning. Other terms or phrases may have a plain meaning, or may be clearly explicable in the light of the objects and purposes of the treaty. There may still remain controversial provisions of treaties, which have no settled meaning, but these instances should not be used as an excuse for the dismissal of all law as simply politics.

Contractual treaties are generally narrowly interpreted by relying primarily on a textual approach, while in constitutional texts the purposes and practice are given equal weight to the text. Although the VCLT gives no indication of the weight to be given to the various approaches contained in Article 31, it is submitted here that the weight given to each does vary with the type of treaty.

[63] Bos, 'Theory and Practice of Treaty Interpretation', p. 19. [64] *Ibid.* 27–28.

[65] G. I. Tunkin, *Theory of International Law* (Cambridge, Mass.: Harvard University Press, 1974), p. xx; V. Kartashkin, 'The Marxist–Leninist Approach: The Theory of Class Struggle and Contemporary International Law', in R. J. MacDonald and D. M. Johnston (eds.), *Structure and Processes of International Law* (The Hague: Martinus Nijhoff, 1983), p. 84.

[66] Koskenniemi, *From Apology to Utopia*, p. 475.

IV. The nature of non-proliferation treaties

The three non-proliferation treaties to be considered in this analysis are the 1968 Treaty on the Non-Proliferation of Nuclear Weapons (Nuclear Non-Proliferation Treaty – NPT), the 1972 Biological Weapons Convention (BWC) and the 1993 Chemical Weapons Convention (CWC). They are all multilateral treaties, but only the CWC is institutional as well as conventional, establishing the Organization for the Prohibition of Chemical Weapons (OPCW). This does not necessarily mean that only the CWC is constitutional; we have to go deeper to try and understand the nature of these treaties. In general terms, the overall purpose of these treaties is to address the 'horizontal proliferation of WMD' with provisions:

> proscribing possession, development, and transfer of both single-use WMD-related materials (i.e. those items and technologies primarily suited for use in WMD development programs) as well as dual-use WMD-related materials (i.e. items and technologies which have both civilian and military applications).[67]

As well as aiming to prevent the proliferation of WMDs among a wider group of states, the treaties also aim to prevent the proliferation of weapons within states already possessing them ('vertical proliferation').[68]

Given that the regulation of violence and the means of violence is endemic in any society (at least one not proclaiming to be a 'suicide club'),[69] these agreements are clearly foundational in that they purport to regulate the most dangerous forms of weapons capable of facilitating the most violent and destructive international acts and causing the most egregious harm against populations and their environment. The three treaties are by no means without numerous weaknesses, the NPT in particular was not meant to be the final say in the regulation of nuclear weapons.[70] However, together they represent the building blocks upon which non-proliferation law is built.[71]

[67] D. H. Joyner, *International Law and the Proliferation of Weapons of Mass Destruction* (Oxford University Press, 2009), p. xv.

[68] *Ibid.* [69] Hart, *The Concept of Law*, p. 189.

[70] Mohamed ElBaradei, the Director-General of the IAEA, has written that the NPT was the 'best that could be achieved' in the Cold War, and the 'asymmetry it endorsed was never intended to be permanent'. M. ElBaradei, 'Towards a Safer World', *The Economist*, 16 Oct 2003, in Joyner, *International Law and the Proliferation of Weapons of Mass Destruction*, p. 68.

[71] Joyner, *International Law and the Proliferation of Weapons of Mass Destruction*, p. xv.

In the seminal article written at the time of the NPT, Mason Willrich is in no doubt about the significance of the treaty for achieving the 'goal of overriding importance in the nuclear era ... the avoidance of nuclear war'.[72] The NPT was agreed in the Cold War period, when both superpowers desired to draw back from mutually assured destruction, and should be seen in the context of other treaty developments, such as the Outer Space Treaty (OST) of 1967; which not only constituted a bargain between the superpowers on the usage and development (and demilitarisation) of outer space, but also was lawmaking for the rest of the international community.

In a sense, the UN Charter is similar to the NPT and the OST, having at its heart a bargain between the Great Powers (the five permanent members, or P5), but also binding the wider community of states and establishing a new world order. Just as McNair in the 1930s described the Covenant of the League as being at the centre of the emerging constitutionalization of international law, so the UN Charter is at the heart of the post-1945 legal order, alongside numerous other foundational treaties, some of which may be viewed as constitutional (such as the Charter) and others lawmaking (such as the Genocide Convention of 1948, the Geneva Conventions of 1949, the Antarctic Treaty of 1959, the International Covenants on Human Rights of the 1960s, the Law of the Sea Convention of 1982, and the Rome Statute on the International Criminal Court of 1998). These constitutional and lawmaking treaties together establish basic regimes governing different parts of the planet and outer space, as well as establishing the basic requirements of humanity in the treatment of individuals or groups, whether in wartime or in peacetime. They also establish the basic requirements of security for states and for individuals within them. The question is whether the non-proliferation treaties fit into this type of treaty (and, if so, whether they are constitutional as well as just lawmaking) or whether they are, like the ABM Treaty or the NATO Treaty of 1949, primarily contractual arrangements. Non-proliferation law may be a mixture of contractual, lawmaking and constitutional treaties, just as collective security treaties include contractual, lawmaking and constitutional types.

It is common to describe the NPT of 1968 as a 'grand bargain' between nuclear-weapon states (NWSs) and non-nuclear-weapon states

[72] M. Willrich, 'The Treaty on Non-Proliferation of Nuclear Weapons: Nuclear Technology Confronts World Politics', *Yale Law Journal*, 77 (1968), 1447, 1449.

(NNWSs). This suggests some sort of exchange of rights and duties between these two different groupings of states. Essentially, NWSs were obliged not to provide WMDs to NNWSs, and not to proliferate their own; indeed, the obligation is 'to eventually disarm themselves of nuclear weapons'.[73] NNWSs, on their side, agreed not to acquire nuclear weapons or to develop them themselves. 'In exchange for their commitment to forgo what would otherwise be their right, equal to that' of NWSs, NNWSs insisted on the recognition of their right not only to acquire 'nuclear technologies for the purpose of civilian power generation', but also to an obligation on NWSs to help in the development of their civilian nuclear programmes.[74] In crude terms, the deal was for NWSs to retain their right to nuclear weapons while NNWSs gave up any right to have them. In exchange for this deviation from sovereign equality, NWSs promised to disarm gradually and to help develop peaceful uses of nuclear technology in NNWSs. This bargain, according to Joyner, distinguishes the NPT as a contractual treaty from 'most other large multilateral treaties', for example, the Genocide Convention and the Law of the Sea Convention, which are lawmaking treaties where 'there is no consideration given between the states in exchange for the undertaking of obligations'.[75] He likens these lawmaking treaties to 'legislation under domestic law, binding each member equally to their rules without consideration'.[76]

While an understandable argument, Joyner may be failing to distinguish between different forms of contract. There are those contracts that represent an agreement upon which a society is built, for instance, by limiting the rights and freedoms for members in exchange for strong government and security (in Hobbesian terms), or stronger freedoms and rights of members in exchange for a more liberal form of government and less security (in Lockean terms). These 'social contracts' are socially much more profound than a contractual transaction whereby one party agrees to give up weapons if the other party does (as in the strategic arms reduction treaties); or whereby one party agrees to come to the aid of another if attacked, as long as other parties will come to their aid if they are attacked (as in the NATO treaty). Such social contracts at the domestic level are embodied in constitutional documents, such as the Magna Carta of 1215 or the Bill of Rights 1689, when the English monarchy agreed to certain limitations upon their powers in exchange for loyalty; while at the international level they can be found in the UN

[73] Joyner, *International Law and the Proliferation of Weapons of Mass Destruction*, p. 8.
[74] *Ibid.* 9. [75] *Ibid.* [76] *Ibid.*

Charter, whereby the five Great Powers agreed to act as the world's police force in exchange for voting rights that no other member would possess. It is no coincidence that those five permanent members are the NWSs at the heart of the NPT grand bargain, thus suggesting that the NPT is something more profound than an ordinary *traité-contrat*; indeed, it may be more constitutional than a *traité-loi* since it develops the grand bargain found in the UN Charter by extending the inequality between the P5 and other members of the UN to the possession of nuclear weapons. Maybe the difference is between grand bargains, meaning social contracts, and mere bargains, meaning transactional contracts.

Of the five nuclear-weapons states at the time of the NPT, three were original parties in 1968 (USA, USSR, UK), while two only became parties in 1992 (China and France). Further, though the treaty was originally adopted for twenty-five years, it was renewed indefinitely by consensus at the Review Conference in New York in 1995. This indicates that, despite the presence of a right of withdrawal (in Article X),[77] in one sense the grand bargain has become even stronger over the decades, though the spread of nuclear weapons to states outside the five – to India, Pakistan and Israel (not parties to the NPT) and North Korea (withdrew in 2003) – indicates the strain it is under.[78] The essence of the NPT is that a handful of states have the right to nuclear weapons, while others do not. Despite that inequality, the grand bargain, taken as a whole, is a constitutional treaty. Furthermore, the NPT, like the CWC, has an institutional element (in the form of the IAEA) which assists in the development of the treaty by interpreting and applying them (especially Article III). As Williamson states, the potential 'dual-use' capability of both nuclear material and chemicals requires a 'high degree of intrusiveness' by the OPCW and the IAEA.[79]

Just as in the UN Charter, there is an inbuilt premise that the P5 are to be trusted with such privileges in exchange for the security they can provide. The grand bargain in the NPT is premised on NWSs being responsible members of international society, members who would not use these weapons unjustifiably, distinguishing them from other states

[77] ElBaradei argued in 2004 that the right of withdrawal should be removed from the NPT, given the importance of the treaty to international security. Cited in M. Glennon, *The Fog of Law: Pragmatism, Security and International Law* (Palo Alto, Calif.: Stanford University Press, 2010), p. 132.

[78] E. Louka, *Nuclear Weapons, Justice and the Law* (Cheltenham: Elgar, 2011), pp. 98–122.

[79] R. L. Williamson, 'Hard Law, Soft Law, and Non-Law in Multilateral Arms Control: Some Compliance Hypotheses', *Chinese Journal of International Law*, 4 (2003), 59, 72.

unable, or deemed unable, to bear this burden. This inequality in a sense provides the basis for governance in that it distinguishes between those who wield power and those who are subject to it, and, no matter how unfair it is or appears to be, it has represented the basis of the international legal order since 1945. In a sense, all lawmaking treaties, although more often based on the equality of states parties, are subject to the more profound inequalities found in the international legal and political orders, so that while the Genocide Convention establishes that genocide is a crime under international law and applies to all states parties equally, there is no question that the United Nations Security Council (UNSC) would make a determination that genocide was being committed by a permanent member given that any such determination, let alone proposal to take action, would be vetoed. Other lawmaking treaties are more obviously tied to this inequality: the Rome Statute establishing the International Criminal Court empowers the UNSC both to refer cases to the Court and to defer cases, perpetuating the grand bargain at the heart of the United Nations.

Thus, it is contended that the NPT forms part of the grand bargain or social contract at the heart of the international legal and political order, alongside the UN Charter, and should be interpreted as a constitutional text not a contractual one,[80] thereby placing equal emphasis on the purposes of the treaty, the practice of parties, as well as the words of the provisions themselves. This is not the orthodox position, which portrays the grand bargain in the NPT being a relatively straightforward exchange between two groups of states.[81] The consequences of this for the different provisions of the NPT are reviewed in the next section, but before then the nature of the BWC and CWC will be considered.

While Joyner argues that the NPT is contractual, he states that the BWC and CWC are 'unquestionably lawmaking treaties, providing a blanket prohibition upon development and possession, as well as proliferation, of their subject weapons technologies, binding upon all states parties'.[82] While disagreeing with Joyner's classification of the NPT, his analysis of the BWC and CWC seems sound. Just as some domestic legislation may be seen to develop the constitution of a country, other pieces are more accurately viewed as lawmaking, laying down rules for

80 But see Glennon, *The Fog of Law*, pp. 136–139 who argued strongly against 'entrenchment' of the NPT and instead urged a more coercive counterproliferation regime.

81 Joyner, *International Law and the Proliferation of Weapons of Mass Destruction*, pp. 10–11.

82 *Ibid.* 69.

all members of society, the validity of which is derived from the constitution.[83] The same can be applied to the international scene, contrasting those treaties that continue the grand bargain of the UN Charter and those that develop rules for all states. Of course, the line is not always that clear – the UN Charter is both constitutional and lawmaking, while treaties such as the Genocide Convention are lawmaking but of a very fundamental nature, and should be seen as very high up the constitutional hierarchy. The prevention of intentional eradication of whole groups of people from the international community can also be seen as a matter of basic survival. However, the very nature of such a hierarchy in international law is hugely controversial, signifying that the limited analysis of such matters in this chapter is incomplete and debatable.

In these terms, it is argued that while the NPT is constitutional, the BWC and CWC are lawmaking treaties – though we still have to consider whether the presence of the OPCW makes a difference to the latter. The NPT is 'elevated' above the other non-proliferation treaties for two reasons: the presence of the grand bargain and the fact that nuclear weapons are the most destructive and, paradoxically, are seen as the most legitimate of the WMDs – a legitimacy enhanced by the NPT itself,[84] which, unlike the other treaties, does not prohibit the WMDs in question, it just limits their proliferation. Nuclear weapons are allowed, but only in the hands of the Great Powers, thereby recognizing their central role in the international legal order.[85]

The BWC is a lawmaking treaty establishing a universal prohibition on the possession of such weapons, but, because of the absence of institutional machinery, its implementation and its development have stagnated.[86] This is not untypical of lawmaking treaties agreed during the Cold War era, and can be contrasted with the CWC agreed in 1993, which, as well as containing a clear ban on chemical weapons, constituted the OPCW. Undoubtedly, it is important to have a ban on these invidious weapons, but, in the absence of such machinery, there is an obvious problem that non-proliferation of biological weapons depends solely on each state party accepting and implementing its obligations. Even under the later CWC, where there is oversight machinery, the lack

[83] Kelsen, *Pure Theory of Law*, pp. 221–222.

[84] Joyner, *International Law and the Proliferation of Weapons of Mass Destruction*, p. 69.

[85] See, further, G. Simpson, *Great Powers and Outlaw States* (Cambridge University Press, 2004).

[86] Joyner, *International Law and the Proliferation of Weapons of Mass Destruction*, p. 123.

of usage of the system that allows one state to challenge another[87] suggests that states are not always willing to look behind the veil of *pacta sunt servanda*.[88] The OPCW is confined to carrying out inspections in states parties' territories on the basis of agreement between the organization and state party. The fact that it has carried out over 4,000 inspections in eighty-one states parties since the coming into force of the CWC in 1997[89] is a cause for both celebration (that verification is occurring) and concern (given that there are 188 states parties to the CWC). Having said all of that, Joyner confidently reports that only seven states maintain a clandestine biological weapons programme (China, Egypt, Iran, Israel, North Korea, Russia and Syria), while six have chemical weapons programmes (China, Egypt, Iran, Israel, North Korea and Syria).[90] It is noteworthy that these lists include two out of the five states which form the core of Great Powers at the heart of the grand bargains in the UN Charter and the NPT.

The CWC cannot be viewed as constitutional in a profound sense in that it is not part of the grand bargain underlying the international legal order, though it is more of a living instrument than the BWC, evolving by means of interpretation and application to meet the changing needs of society. In this regard, there has been some interpretation of the CWC by the OPCW – for instance, the OPCW has 'developed an internationally unique, peer-reviewed, and certified analytical database, containing information on over 3,400 chemical weapons-related compounds. This database is essential for on-site verification activities of OPCW inspection teams, and is also made available to States Parties'.[91] This might suggest that for lawmaking treaties we can have regard to the text, purposes and, where applicable, the practice of the parties and of treaty institutions, such as the OPCW, whose interpretation has been accepted by the states parties.

Thus, we have a complex, arguably fragmented, system of interpretation within non-proliferation treaties in that by looking at the nature of each treaty we can see that one (the NPT) is constitutional, another (the BWC) is lawmaking but largely stagnant, and one (the CWC) is lawmaking and living, but less than constitutional. On this basis it is argued

[87] Art. IX(9) CWC.
[88] Joyner, *International Law and the Proliferation of Weapons of Mass Destruction*, p. 115.
[89] Available at www.opcw.org/news-publications/publications/facts-and-figures/.
[90] Joyner, *International Law and the Proliferation of Weapons of Mass Destruction*, p. 79.
[91] *Ibid.*

that fragmentation is not necessarily a result of the development of special regimes (such as non-proliferation) but is, if anything, a result of having different types of legal instruments. Having said that, any legal system has different legal documents, different forms of agreement – constitutional, lawmaking and contractual – so why should the international legal order differ in this respect? Thus, we are not concerned with fragmentation but with distinguishing different forms of law. This is not unheard of in non-proliferation law: Joyner, for instance, distinguishes between contractual and lawmaking treaties, although, it is argued here, he misapplies this distinction. More relevant to the argument in this chapter is Williamson's identification that in international law:

> Treaties may function as constitutions that set the basic framework of the legal order, statutes that set forth norms of conduct, and contracts that govern the relations between two parties but rarely anyone else. In keeping with that analogy, treaties setting forth arms control provisions between the US and the Soviet Union were more clearly analogous to contacts than to statutes ... Multilateral arms control treaties, in contrast, are more closely analogous to statutes in domestic law, creating (or codifying) norms of general applicability.[92]

The classification of treaties in a general sense is the one used in this chapter, but while Williamson (in contrast to Joyner) views the NPT as lawmaking,[93] the argument in this chapter is that the NPT is a treaty that helps set the basic framework of the legal order as a constitutional document, while the BWC and CWC are lawmaking.

V. Interpretation of non-proliferation treaties

It is not possible here to undertake a detailed analysis of the NPT, BWC and CWC, or even to undertake a thorough review of the most controversial provisions of those treaties. Instead, this section will consider some of the controversies surrounding interpretation in general terms, and point to some of the implications of the above findings regarding the nature of these non-proliferation treaties and the consequences for interpretation.

As regards the NPT, Joyner argues that the treaty should be interpreted in a contractual manner, meaning, in effect, that the original intent of the contracting parties, combined with the text, should provide our framework for interpretation. Although Joyner does not fully

[92] Williamson, 'Hard Law, Soft Law', 65–66. [93] *Ibid.* 66–67.

develop the consequences of this,[94] it has been argued above that under a contractual paradigm the treaty represents a precise bargain at the time of its making and so should be interpreted accordingly. Joyner analyses the diplomatic history behind the NPT and concludes that it clearly establishes that the treaty was 'not fundamentally about regulating nuclear weapons proliferation, as it is often summarily described to be'. It was, and, he states, still is, 'fundamentally about regulating nuclear energy in its full dual-use nature and range of applications'.[95] Thus, under this analysis, all the elements of the bargain remain in place and in full force – that is, the obligations on NWSs not to proliferate to NNWSs (in Article I) and to negotiate nuclear disarmament (in Article VI), and in return the obligations on NNWSs not to acquire nuclear weapons (in Article II), to develop peaceful uses of nuclear weapons in accordance with Articles I and II (in Article IV), and to submit to safeguard agreements negotiated with the IAEA to prevent peaceful uses of nuclear energy being diverted to nuclear weapons programmes (in Article III).

Joyner argues that this balance cannot be disturbed by subsequent interpretation; in fact, he argues that subsequent statements (after 1998, more vociferously after 9/11 in 2001) by some NWSs (especially the USA) emphasizing non-proliferation obligations, and playing down or eroding their disarmament obligations,[96] are incompatible with the NPT.[97] However, while it may be argued that in 1968 all the elements of the grand bargain carried equal weight, as that was what was necessary to achieve the bargain, it is much more difficult to sustain that original understanding if that bargain is part of the constitutional international order, which must be allowed to be developed by the subsequent agreement and practice of states parties in accordance with changes in international relations. The avoidance of nuclear war by limiting the spread of nuclear weapons can be seen as the bottom line for the NPT, and this in itself would permit the prioritization of non-proliferation over disarmament. However, the interpretation of constitutional treaties is not driven by a pragmatic understanding of the changing nature of international relations but by the changing understanding of states parties. Subsequent practice as a means of interpretation means that changes in emphasis within a constitutional regime must be supported by states parties. There

[94] D.H. Joyner, *Interpreting the Nuclear Non-Proliferation Treaty* (Oxford University Press, 2011), p. 20.

[95] *Ibid.* 28. [96] *Ibid.* 37–45 [97] *Ibid.* 108.

is little indication from the five-yearly NPT Review Conferences that NNWSs agree with NWS interpretations,[98] hence overall practice does not point to a changed understanding of the NPT. In fact, as Joyner points out, a purposive analysis of the NPT supports the original grand bargain under which equal weight was to be given to all the elements,[99] including non-proliferation and disarmament. Thus, a constitutional approach to interpretation, which has regard to subsequent practice of the parties as well as the purposes of the treaty rather than just the text, produces a stronger reaffirmation of the 'grand bargain' than a textual approach.

Indeed, under a textual approach it is possible to read the non-proliferation provisions of Articles I and II of the NPT as embodying much firmer obligations on states parties (each NWS and NNWS 'undertakes not to . . .') than the disarmament obligation in Article VI (in which states parties 'undertake to pursue negotiations in good faith on effective measures relating to the cessation of the nuclear arms race at an early date and to nuclear disarmament . . .'). The latter provision has been interpreted very narrowly indeed by one US representative on nuclear non-proliferation to mean that it contains no legal requirement to conclude negotiations,[100] disagreeing with the International Court of Justice in its 1996 advisory opinion, which stated that 'there exists an obligation to pursue in good faith and bring to a conclusion negotiations leading to nuclear disarmament in all its aspects under strict and effective international control'.[101]

Thus, applying a constitutional approach to interpretation opens the NPT up to subsequent (re)interpretation by the parties. In fact, the consistent statements by NNWS (which are the vast majority of states parties to the NPT) that the different components of the grand bargain have equal weight in the treaty[102] is the key element in maintaining that interpretation. Focus has been on the states parties coming together in review conferences, differentiating the NPT from other constitutional treaties, such as the UN Charter, where subsequent interpretation is undertaken by the political organs of the UN – both the United Nations General Assembly (UNGA) (where all members are present)

[98] *Ibid.* 45–46. [99] *Ibid.* 31–32, 34.

[100] C. A. Ford, 'Debating Disarmament: Interpreting Art. VI of the Treaty on Non-Proliferation of Nuclear Weapons', *Non-proliferation Review*, 14(3) (2007), 403, 408.

[101] *Threat or Use of Nuclear Weapons*, ICJ Reports 1996 26, para. 99.

[102] Joyner, *Interpreting the Nuclear Non-Proliferation Treaty*, p. 73.

and the United Nations Security Council (UNSC) (where only fifteen members are present, including the P5). A difficult question in relation to the NPT is whether a constitutional approach to interpretation opens up the NPT for (re)interpretation by institutions which have responsibilities towards it. The IAEA can undoubtedly have an influence on the development of the obligation on NNWSs to develop peaceful uses of nuclear power through the development of safeguard agreements with NNWSs under Article III of the NPT;[103] but can the UNSC have an influence on the non-proliferation elements in the exercise of its security functions? To admit this could be seen as allowing the NWSs under the NPT (via their position as the P5 in the UNSC) to have an undue influence on the understanding of the obligations under the NPT.

It is not possible to undertake an in-depth study of the UNSC and its responses to proliferation generally and in specific instances (North Korea and Iran).[104] However, a brief review of UNSC Resolution 1887 on nuclear non-proliferation and nuclear disarmament, adopted unanimously in September 2009, shows, as the title suggests, an emphasis on both non-proliferation and disarmament. The only equivocation in this regard is that while the resolution potentially regards violation of the non-proliferation provisions as a threat to international peace and security (and subject to UNSC competence and, presumably, measures), the obligation to disarm on NWSs is not such a matter, though the resolution does call upon states to negotiate in good faith under Article VI of the NPT. But this simply reflects the very nature of the inequality at the heart of the post-1945 international legal order, whereby the Great Powers (as NWSs and as P5 members) are not subject to UNSC censure or measures. The Resolution calls upon 'all States Parties to the NPT to cooperate so that the 2010 NPT Review Conference can successfully strengthen the Treaty and set realistic and achievable goals in all the Treaty's three pillars: non-proliferation, the peaceful uses of nuclear energy, and disarmament'.

Equal emphasis on the three pillars of the NPT is also found in the final document of the 2010 NPT Review Conference,[105] which witnessed a return to consensus under the influence of President Obama and in

[103] *Ibid.* 92–93 on IAEA's role under Art. III of the NPT. See, further, L. Rockwood, 'The IAEA's Strengthened Safeguard System', *Journal of Conflict and Security Law*, 7 (2002), 123.

[104] On this Glennon suggests that the USA and the EU may be enforcing a different set of rules to the NPT against Iran, but does not include the UNSC in this. Glennon, *The Fog of Law*, p. 137.

[105] Joyner, *Interpreting the Nuclear Non-Proliferation Treaty*, pp. 121–122.

light of a new START agreement between the USA and Russia. Thus, in 2009–2010, there was strong subsequent practice to support the continuation of the grand bargain of the NPT, understood in a constitutional sense. But times change. In April 2004, only five years before Resolution 1887, the UNSC adopted Resolution 1540, which legislated against proliferation of all WMDs (nuclear, biological and chemical), especially to non-state actors, but only referred generally to disarmament obligations and treaties. While it might be possible to argue that UNSC Resolution 1887 was specifically commenting on the obligations of states under the NPT, and therefore can be seen as part of the constitutional understanding of the NPT, Resolution 1540 was not so focused, and hence could not be seen as a constitutional interpretation of the NPT. However, as with many aspects of interpretation of international obligations, the boundary between valid and invalid subsequent practice is unclear.

Moving on to the interpretation of the CWC and BWC, being lawmaking treaties rather than constitutional ones, a few general comments will be made. Interpretation, in the context of lawmaking treaties, aims to facilitate an understanding of the laws being set down in order for the intended purposes of the legislation to be achieved so that the behaviour to be prohibited or modified is properly addressed. Multilateral lawmaking treaties are unlikely to be precise and detailed at the point of adoption given the amount of compromise necessary to achieve agreement;[106] thus, interpretation serves the purpose of clarifying those obligations.

In the case of Article I of the BWC of 1972, states parties commit 'never in any circumstances to develop, produce, stockpile or otherwise acquire or retain' biological agents or toxins that are not justified for peaceful purposes. The level of development by subsequent practice of this obligation under the BWC has been limited. Review conferences have not managed to agree a list of prohibited material, or a verification process that would not only help supervise the obligation but also deepen and develop it.[107] The lack of institutional mechanism (though a state may refer breaches of the BWC to the UNSC under Article VI) within the treaty are a severe drawback in this regard and can be contrasted with the CWC. Despite the limitation in the structure of the BWC, Review Conferences of the parties have succeeded in providing some

[106] Aust, *Modern Treaty Law and Practice*, p. 230.

[107] See, generally, Joyner, *International Law and the Proliferation of Weapons of Mass Destruction*, pp. 91–100.

clarification. For instance, the Second Review Conference of 1986 did affirm that the BWC covered 'all natural or artificially created microbial or other biological agents or toxins whatever their origin or method of production'. It was not until the Fourth Review Conference of 1996, however, that states parties confirmed that the prohibition in Article I covered the use of biological weapons, something that was not explicit in the text of the provision.[108]

In contrast, the CWC of 1992 is a much more detailed and dynamic lawmaking treaty. The obligations on states parties in Article I are much more detailed (and include non-use and destruction of existing weapons as well as non-production, non-development and non-transfer)[109] and precise, with definitions (Article II) as well as amendable (Article XV) schedules listing prohibited categories of chemicals.[110] Furthermore, the treaty creates the OPCW, consisting of political and technical organs to ensure implementation of the treaty and to verify compliance (Article VIII). All of this provides for clarification and updating of the obligations and definitions provided in the text by formal amendment but also, to a lesser extent, by interpretive practice, including by the PrepCom that preceded the establishment of the OPCW in 1997 as well as other organs of the OPCW – particularly the conference of the states parties.[111] While consensus is normally sought in the plenary organ, a two-thirds majority is permitted (Article VIII (18)). The Convention is far too detailed and technical to allow for significant interpretive development by the OPCW and can be contrasted with the much vaguer and open-ended phrases of the BWC. As den Dekker points out, the 'adaptation of existing technical norms (primarily to the demands of scientific development) and the drawing up of new ones is relatively uncomplicated'. The 'potential need for interpretation' of the CWC is further obviated by Article II, which contains definitions and criteria specifically applicable to the CWC. Having said that, den Dekker does recognize the subsequent practice of the organs of OPCW in the shape of the issuance of a 'considerable number of understandings and decisions on the interpretation and clarification of specific treaty provisions'.[112]

[108] *Ibid.* 92.

[109] See E. P. J. Myjer (ed.), *Issues of Arms Control Law and the Chemical Weapons Convention* (The Hague: Martinus Nijhoff, 2001), p. 78.

[110] Joyner, *International Law and the Proliferation of Weapons of Mass Destruction*, p. 104.

[111] Myjer, *Issues of Arms Control Law*, pp. 89–90, 93.

[112] G. den Dekker, *The Law of Arms Control: International Supervision and Enforcement* (The Hague: Martinus Nijhoff, 2001), p. 269.

The end of the Cold War, and the use of chemical weapons by Iraq in the Iran–Iraq War of 1980–1988, and against its own people, allowed for a much more profound level of agreement in the CWC of 1993 than was achievable in the Cold War-dominated BWC of 1972. This was reflected in the clear object and purposes of the CWC – 'banning chemical weapons',[113] the clear obligations, definitions, as well as effective processes for amendment of the treaty and institutional verification of it. The effect is a lawmaking treaty with a legislative and interpretive dynamic built in, but operating within a reasonably tightly drawn framework. Thus, while the CWC can be said to be a living instrument, it falls short of the constitutional nature of the NPT.

VI. Conclusion

This chapter has argued against fragmentation in the area of interpretation of non-proliferation treaties. There is no special regime that should be applied to these treaties because of their subject matter. Rather, it has been argued that the distinction that should be applied is between different types of treaties – constitutional, lawmaking and contractual – a distinction which applies across all substantive areas of international law. The chapter is premised on the VCLT being sufficiently flexible to accommodate interpretative approaches that reflect the differing nature of international treaties. The existence of constitutional, lawmaking and contractual treaties within the international legal order generally, and within non-proliferation law in particular, should not come as a surprise, though the development of lawmaking and constitutional instruments at the international level has been slower and made more difficult by the essentially contractual foundations of international law.

Furthermore, the identification of treaties as constitutional does not signify that the author of this chapter has an idealistic vision of world order, for at their heart instruments such as the UN Charter and the NPT are profoundly unfair, at least in the sense of being unequal. Indeed, it is the presence of this inequality that, for this author, signifies that they are part of the constitutional order of post-1945 international relations. It is the acceptance of that inequality by other states (by becoming members of the UN or parties to the NPT), and by the fact that those instruments contain the rules and institutions necessary to try to ensure the survival of the planet, that give them their legitimacy as constitutional

[113] Myjer, *Issues of Arms Control Law*, p. 89.

instruments. It also means that, as with any constitution, there is potentially a fair degree of flexibility within them, allowing for constitutional development by usage. However, despite attempts by NWSs, the NPT's provisions remain largely untouched by subsequent agreement or practice, though the IAEA has developed NNWS obligations on peaceful uses of nuclear power.

In contrast in some ways to the NPT, the CWC, though not constitutional, is a dynamic lawmaking treaty, in comparison to its more stagnant older relative, the BWC. The presence of contractual treaties in the area of non-proliferation and arms control serves to show that it is the nature of the treaty that is important for issues of interpretation, not the subject matter; but the fact that the CWC is more dynamic in some ways than the NPT illustrates that a search for hard and fast rules about precise scientific methods of interpretation is not only wasteful but probably also undesirable. Basic constitutional norms concerning the non-use of force (found in the UN Charter) and the possession and non-proliferation of the most destructive weapons ever known to mankind (found in the NPT) should not be subject to regular change – any change must reflect a new social contract. However, subsequent agreement or practice that helps to clarify some of the unclear obligations in the NPT – such as those on disarmament – would be welcome.

4

Violation of non-proliferation treaties and related verification treaties

ERIC MYJER AND JONATHAN HERBACH

I. Introduction

i. General: the national security component

As is the case with any other treaty, a non-proliferation treaty can be violated. Non-proliferation treaties, however, are of a special character, since they concern states parties' national security. Under the law of treaties, this does not make the commitment to get rid of a complete category of weapons – like chemical weapons – or not to seek to develop a certain category of weapons – like nuclear weapons – a commitment of a higher order. States are free to possess weapons, unless they have decided to commit themselves otherwise.[1] This, of course, is notwithstanding a possible decision by the Security Council under Chapter VII, that they would regard any such breach as giving rise to an Article 39 UN Charter situation which might lead to a binding decision, as in the case of the North Korean (DPRK) withdrawal from the Nuclear Non-Proliferation Treaty,[2] in which the Security Council demanded not only that the DPRK immediately retract its announcement of withdrawal from the NPT but also 'that the DPRK return to the Treaty on the Non-Proliferation of Nuclear Weapons and International Atomic Energy Agency (IAEA) safeguards'.[3] This reaction of the Security Council follows its earlier resolutions whereby it stated that proliferation of nuclear, chemical or biological weapons, as well as their means of delivery, constitute a threat to the peace.[4] However, the national security dimension of weapons will, as a rule, ensure that a state party will

[1] *Nicaragua* v. *United States*, ICJ Reports 1986 135, para. 269.
[2] Cf. S/RES 1695 (2006) of 15 July 2006, juncto. S/RES/1718 (2006).
[3] S/RES/1718 (2006).
[4] Compare, for instance, S/RES 1540 (2004), of 28 April 2004, or S/RES 1695 (2006).

only accept limitations on its freedom to posses weapons if a possible breach by other contracting state(s) can always be detected if it were to occur, for states do not want to allow other states to gain a military, tactical or strategic advantage that could be used either politically or militarily to their detriment.

In other words, serious non-proliferation commitments demand strict supervision. It will be understandable that this is more so the case with respect to arms control or disarmament commitments concerning weapons of mass destruction with the potentially large-scale destructive consequences of such weapons. That is why, especially with regard to the conclusion of treaties containing any meaningful commitment concerning the non-proliferation of weapons of mass destruction, an elaborate system of supervision tends to be a condition *sine qua non*. This is what gives these arms control, or non-proliferation, treaties their special character. Of course, general public international law concerning the law of treaties also contains the necessary correction mechanisms in case of (a material) breach, including the termination and suspension of the operation of treaties,[5] as well as the rules on state responsibility. These rules may contribute to deterrence of possible breaches. However, since non-proliferation treaties impact on the national security of a state, any breach of the treaty also amounts to a breach of the national security of that state. National security is about 'here and now' and does not lend itself to the more elaborate, often time-consuming, procedures that general public international law may offer. Therefore, a specific supervisory regime that takes the national security component into consideration is necessary. A comprehensive system of supervision needs not only to allow for the early detection of a breach, it also needs to provide for an effective correction mechanism. An additional complication is that WMD-related substances are inherently dual-use, namely viable both for military use as a weapon or for civilian use – for instance, for energy or industrial purposes. Effective supervision is, in other words, about ensuring compliance with non-proliferation commitments, either by deterring any possible breach or by detecting and correcting in case a breach occurs.

Applying the supervisory model described in the next section, with its four functions, we will look in this chapter at the treaty-specific model of supervision as applied under WMD treaties with a non-proliferation

[5] Cf. the Vienna Convention on the Law of Treaties (1969), section 3.

component and, where relevant, at related specific verification treaties. In so doing, we will examine the Treaty on the Non-Proliferation of Nuclear Weapons (Non-Proliferation Treaty – NPT), with its system of safeguards agreements, the Chemical Weapons Convention (CWC), and the Biological Weapons Convention (BWC). We will also look at the Comprehensive Nuclear-Test-Ban Treaty (CTBT), which does not primarily deal with the non-proliferation of nuclear weapons, but instead establishes an absolute ban on the testing of nuclear explosive devices. It shows, however, that within the area of non-proliferation law exists a fairly detailed, comprehensive system of supervision comprised of far-reaching commitments.

ii. The supervisory model and its different functions

With regard to supervision, four functions can be distinguished, namely (1) the *collection function* (collection of the relevant information); (2) the *review function* (judging state behaviour for its conformity with an agreed rule of international law); (3) the *creative function* (interpretation or clarification of the rules); and (4) the *correction function* (the correction of state behaviour, when it is established that a state has violated an international obligation).[6] Collection, review and the creative function could be referred to collectively as the verification process. Also included in the verification process are on-site inspections (OSI) with the objective of collecting information. What the system of supervision aims to do, of course, is to verify whether a state party fulfils its obligations under the relevant treaty, and therefore is complying with its commitments. Subsequently, if a state party is not complying, is there a treaty-specific correction mechanism, is the mechanism treaty-external but still of a specific regime character, or does one have to fall back on the general rules of international law regarding breach of treaty commitments?

This chapter will pay less attention to the creative function of supervision, for that also deals with the interpretation of the non-proliferation treaties, which is dealt with in Chapter 3.

[6] See, more generally, E. P. J. Myjer, 'The Organization for the Prohibition of Chemical Weapons: Moving Closer towards an International Arms Control Organization? A Quantum Leap in the Institutional Law of Arms Control Law', in E. P. J. Myjer (ed.), *Issues of Arms Control Law and the Chemical Weapons Convention* (The Hague: Martinus Nijhoff, 2001), pp. 104–107.

II. IAEA safeguards and supervision of nuclear non-proliferation

Opened for signature in 1968 and having entered into force on 5 March 1970, the NPT is the flagship instrument of the nuclear non-proliferation regime and has, at this point, achieved near-universal application,[7] with more parties having ratified the NPT than any other non-proliferation treaty. In 1995, the Review and Extension Conference of the Parties to the NPT agreed to extend the treaty indefinitely, meaning that, for the foreseeable future, the NPT will remain the centrepiece of efforts to stanch the spread of nuclear weapons.[8]

A comprehensive discussion of all NPT elements is outside the scope of the present chapter.[9] It will suffice here to give a short overview of the relevant non-proliferation provisions of the NPT necessary to set the stage for examining the supervisory mechanisms. Article II of the NPT requires non-nuclear-weapon states (NNWSs) to undertake not to receive the transfer of nuclear weapons or nuclear explosive devices, or direct or indirect control over such weapons or devices, not to manufacture or otherwise acquire such weapons or devices and not to receive assistance in the manufacture of such weapons or devices. The function of supervising the fulfilment of NNWS obligations under the NPT is given to the IAEA:

> Each non-nuclear-weapon State Party to the Treaty undertakes to accept safeguards, as set forth in an agreement to be negotiated and concluded with the International Atomic Energy Agency in accordance with the Statute of the International Atomic Energy Agency and the Agency's safeguards system, for the exclusive purpose of verification of the fulfilment of its obligations assumed under this Treaty with a view to preventing diversion of nuclear energy from peaceful uses to nuclear weapons or other nuclear explosive devices. Procedures for the safeguards required by this Article shall be followed with respect to source or special fissionable material whether it is being produced, processed or used in any principal nuclear facility or is outside any such facility. The safeguards required by this Article shall be applied on all source or special fissionable material in all peaceful nuclear activities within the territory of such State, under its jurisdiction, or carried out under its control anywhere.[10]

7 The most recent figures place the number of states parties at 191.

8 NPT/CONF.1995/32 (Part I), Decision 3.

9 For a recent study on the interpretation of the NPT, see D. H. Joyner, *Interpreting the Nuclear Non-Proliferation Treaty* (Oxford University Press, 2011).

10 Art. III.1 NPT.

In other words, the IAEA is the recognized competent organ to verify and ensure compliance with safeguards agreements that are enacted in order for states parties to fulfil their obligations under the aforementioned article of the NPT. The IAEA was the first specialized international organization tasked directly with supervising compliance with multilateral non-proliferation obligations.[11] However, the Agency's competencies are broader in scope and, therefore, it cannot be considered a strict non-proliferation organization.

Founded in 1957 as an autonomous international organization, the IAEA's general objective is to accelerate and enlarge the contribution of atomic energy globally to peace, health and prosperity and, at the same time, ensure that atomic energy will not be misused for military purposes.[12] The IAEA is composed of three organs: the General Conference, the Board of Governors, and the Staff or Secretariat. For the purposes of the present study, it is sufficient at this point to describe the three organs in broad strokes.[13] The General Conference, which is the plenary body of the organization, is made up of all member states of the IAEA and has the authority to take decisions on any matter specifically referred to it for this purpose by the Board of Governors, to propose matters for consideration by the Board and to request reports from the Board on any matter relating to the functions of the IAEA.[14] The Board of Governors is the executive body of the organization having thirty members, ten designated by the outgoing board and twenty elected by the General Conference in accordance with equitable geographical representation.[15] The Staff is the permanent administrative, scientific and technical body, headed by the Director General, whose functioning is to a large extent overseen by the Board.[16]

It differs from other supervisory bodies considered in this chapter in that its establishment pre-dates and is separate from the entry into force of the norm-setting non-proliferation treaty[17] – the NPT – with respect to which it has been tasked with supervisory responsibilities. This, along

[11] J. Goldblat, *Arms Control: A Guide to Negotiations and Agreements* (London: Sage, 1994), p. 227.

[12] IAEA Statute, Art. II.

[13] For a more detailed explanation of roles and responsibilities of the IAEA organs, see G. den Dekker, *The Law of Arms Control: International Supervision and Enforcement* (The Hague: Martinus Nijhoff, 2001), chap. 6, part II.

[14] IAEA Statute, Art. V(F). [15] IAEA Statute, Art. VI. [16] IAEA Statute, Art. VII.

[17] The safeguards system is also applied to Nuclear-Weapon-Free Zone (NWFZ) treaties.

with its other competencies not strictly pertaining to nuclear non-proliferation, including activities related to fostering efficient and safe use of nuclear energy, promoting sustainable development with nuclear techniques and assisting states in furthering their capabilities with respect to the peaceful use of nuclear energy, means that the IAEA cannot be considered a 'single-purpose organization' in the mould of the Organization for the Prohibition of Chemical Weapons (OPCW).[18] With respect to the nuclear non-proliferation regime, the IAEA makes use of a unique supervisory system based on bilateral compliance agreements between the Agency and individual states and safeguards agreements, as opposed to one established in a single treaty.

i. Supervisory functions within the safeguards system

The supervision of compliance with the legal obligations of NNWSs parties to the NPT is carried out in accordance with the provisions of the IAEA Statute and safeguards agreements modelled on INFCIRC/153 (corrected),[19] which together form the safeguards system. The objective of the safeguards system is to detect and deter the diversion of significant quantities of nuclear material from peaceful nuclear activities to the production of nuclear weapons or of other nuclear explosive devices or for purposes unknown.[20] As such, the safeguards system is fundamental to the nuclear non-proliferation regime.[21] Within the safeguards system, then, it is possible to identify the various supervisory functions, characteristic of the supervision of WMD-related non-proliferation law regimes, performed by the IAEA in controlling compliance with the safeguards obligations.

a. Treaty-specific verification: the collection and review functions

Nuclear material accountancy forms the basis of the safeguards system. When any nuclear material that has, as part of the nuclear fuel cycle,

[18] Cf. Myjer, 'The Organization for the Prohibition of Chemical Weapons', p. 88.

[19] 'The Structure and Content of Agreements Between the Agency and States Required in Connection with the Treaty on the Non-Proliferation of Nuclear Weapons', also referred to as Comprehensive Safeguards Agreements (CSAs). How these instruments – safeguards agreements and the IAEA Statute – are used together is key to understanding and applying the full scope of the supervisory function. An Additional Protocol, discussed more below, if in force can also be considered part of the safeguards system.

[20] INFCIRC/153 (corrected), para. 28. 'Significant quantity' refers to the amount of material a state needs to produce its first nuclear explosive device.

[21] NPT/CONF.2010/50 (vol. 1).

become suitable for fuel fabrication or isotopic enrichment leaves the plant or process stage in which it has been produced, or is imported into the state, the nuclear material must be made subject to safeguards procedures.[22] The state must also inform the IAEA when material containing uranium or thorium, although not having reached the aforementioned stage of the nuclear fuel cycle, is exported to a NNWS or is imported, unless it has been exported or imported for specifically non-nuclear purposes.[23] Based on these thresholds, the safeguards agreement should stipulate that reports regarding nuclear material that is subject to safeguards be provided to the IAEA by the state, the initial one being submitted within thirty days of the last day of the calendar month in which the agreement enters into force.[24] Initial accounting will be supplemented by inventory change reports and material balance reports in order to determine the amount of and changes to the amount of nuclear material within defined areas.[25] This duty to report supports the collection function of the IAEA. Based on the information collected by the Agency by way of these declarations, the Agency creates a unified inventory of all the nuclear material in the state that is subject to safeguards. This inventory is initially established upon reception of the initial report and is updated according to information provided in subsequent submissions from the states. Additional information is gathered via monitoring of open sources, such as news reports, internet sites and relevant publications, as well as received from third parties. The Agency can also, pursuant to concluded safeguards agreements, request and must be provided with amplifications or clarifications of any reports if relevant for the purposes of safeguards.[26]

[22] INFCIRC/153 (corrected), para. 34(c). 'Nuclear material' refers to any source or any fissionable material as defined in Art. XX of the IAEA Statute. 'Source material', according to Art. XX(3) of the Statute, means uranium containing the mixture of isotopes occurring in nature; uranium depleted in the isotope 235; thorium; and any of the foregoing in the form of metal, alloy, chemical compound, or concentrate. 'Special fissionable material', as defined in Art. XX(1) of the Statute, means plutonium-239; uranium-233; uranium enriched in the isotopes 235 or 233 (meaning 'uranium containing the isotopes 235 or 233 or both in an amount such that the abundance ratio of the sum of these isotopes to the isotope 238 is greater than the ratio of the isotope 235 to the isotope 238 occurring in nature'); and any material containing one or more of the foregoing.

[23] INFCIRC/153 (corrected), para. 34(a) and (b).

[24] INFCIRC/153 (corrected), para. 62.

[25] See INFCIRC/153 (corrected), para. 63 and the definition of 'material balance area' in para. 110.

[26] INFCIRC/153 (corrected), para. 69.

The implementation of national systems for accountancy and control provide the foundation for the verification process – collection and review activities conducted by the Agency. In order to check the validity and accuracy of the information collected through national reporting so as to provide clear and convincing evidence of compliance or non-compliance with legal obligations in timely fashion,[27] on-site inspections (OSIs) are foreseen. The OSIs are limited in purpose, scope, access rights for inspectors, frequency and intensity according to the provisions laid out in the safeguards agreements.

CSAs set out three types of inspections: ad hoc, routine and special.[28] Ad hoc inspections are carried out in order to verify the information contained in the initial reports, to identify and verify changes in the situation that have taken place following the initial report and to identify, and if possible verify the quantity and composition of, nuclear material prior to transfer into or out of the state. The term 'identify' in these provisions suggests that supplemental information is collected in addition to being verified, though still based on original declarations. Routine inspections are then meant to verify that the reports are consistent with records, to verify the location identity, quantity and composition of the nuclear material subject to safeguards and to verify information regarding discrepancies – material unaccounted for, shipper/receiver differences and uncertainties in the book inventory.[29] In the course of these two types of inspections, inspectors are tasked with conducting a variety of information-gathering, monitoring and surveillance activities, though they are limited to declared facilities, and the number of inspections allowed depends in great measure on the amount of nuclear material present in the declared facilities.[30] If the IAEA deems the information provided by the state (including explanations and information gathered

[27] See 'Review of the Implementation of the Recommendations and Decisions Adopted by the General Assembly at its Tenth Special Session: Report of the Disarmament Commission', A/51/182, part II (G).

[28] INFCIRC/153 (corrected), paras. 70–82.

[29] 'Book inventory' refers to the sum formula of the most recent physical inventory and all inventory changes that have taken place since the physical inventory was taken.

[30] See, further, Dekker, *The Law of Arms Control*, p. 288; R. J. S. Harry, 'IAEA Safeguards and Non-Proliferation', in M. van Leeuwen (ed.), *The Future of the International Nuclear Non-Proliferation Regime* (The Hague: Martinus Nijhoff, 1995); A. von Baeckmann, 'The Treaty on the Non-Proliferation of Nuclear Weapons (NPT) (1968)', in S. Sur (ed.), *Verification of Current Disarmament and Arms Limitation Agreements: Ways, Means and Practices* (Aldershot: United Nations Institute for Disarmament Research, 1991).

from routine inspections) is inadequate, or in order to verify information contained in special reports, the Agency may make special inspections. Such inspections require consultation with the state if, for example, inspection of separate locations is to be carried out. Special inspections are implicitly adversarial and undoubtedly of high political sensitivity, thus such measures have only been invoked on two occasions. In 1992, after 470 grams of plutonium was found in a secret laboratory in Romania that had been active under the Ceauşescu regime, Romania itself requested a special inspection by the IAEA. Then, in 1993, the Director General initiated the special inspections procedure with respect to North Korea following discrepancies between the North Korean initial declaration and IAEA findings that suggested the existence of undeclared plutonium. In this latter case, however, the request for the special inspection was denied by North Korea, leading to the conclusion of non-compliance with its safeguards agreement and a subsequent report on the matter from the Agency to the Security Council under Article XII(C) of the IAEA Statute (see below).

This common, declaration-based model of verification prescribed under the CSA leaves the potential for states to keep certain activities outside the purview of IAEA supervision. As a measure supplemental to the CSA featuring, to a certain extent, strengthened verification provisions, the Model Additional Protocol was adopted by the Board of Governors in 1997.[31] At this point, roughly half of the NNWSs parties to the NPT have additional protocols in force. The Model Additional Protocol extends the power of the IAEA with respect to gathering information and having site access, including providing for the right of the Agency to conduct environmental sampling at locations outside of declared sites,[32] primarily with the aim of ruling out the existence of undeclared nuclear material. Whether or not the additional protocol is an integral part of the safeguards system is being debated.[33] It is worth noting that the Treaty of Semipalatinsk, which entered into force in March 2009 and establishes the Central Asian NWFZ, actually requires states parties to conclude an additional protocol side by side with a CSA.[34]

[31] INFCIRC/540 (corrected). For a strong analysis of the Model Addition Protocol, see M. Asada, 'The Treaty on the Non-Proliferation of Nuclear Weapons and the Universalization of the Additional Protocol', *Journal of Conflict and Security Law*, 16 (2011), 3–34. See also L. Rockwood, 'The IAEA's Strengthened Safeguards System', *Journal of Conflict and Security Law*, 7 (2002), 123–136.

[32] INFCIRC/540 (corrected), Arts. 4, 5 and 9. [33] See NPT/CONF.2010/50 (vol. 1).

[34] Treaty on a Nuclear-Weapon-Free Zone in Central Asia, Art. 8.

In carrying out the review function, it is up to the IAEA to determine, based on the results of information collection, and related verification activities, the conformity of state behaviour with the relevant legal obligations undertaken pursuant to the CSA, and, if applicable, the additional protocol. The Staff and the Board of Directors each has a role in the review process. Inspectors are first responsible for obtaining and verifying information and reporting any case of non-compliance to the Director General. The Director General is then tasked with relaying a report from the inspectors of non-compliance to the Board of Governors, which in turn has the ability to determine whether or not the Agency is able to verify that no diversion of nuclear material has occurred.[35] To be sure, such a finding does not necessarily mean that a diversion to the manufacture of nuclear weapons or other nuclear explosive devices has taken place. It could be, for example, that state behaviour has prevented the inspectors from effectively performing their verification tasks. In other words, the Agency makes the assessment not that the material has been diverted for non-peaceful activities, but instead that it cannot verify whether such a violation has or has not occurred. In taking any subsequent action, the Agency 'shall afford the State every reasonable opportunity to furnish the Board with any necessary reassurance'.[36] The specific form and content of such reassurance is not further elaborated, though one could envision providing clarification or allowing for additional inspection. This appears to be an instance in which the creative function is involved in that the determination of the adequacy of reassurances lies with the Agency. It does seem that a measure such as the request for clarification could be enacted in order to prevent the need for further corrective action. The comprehensive evaluation of a state's nuclear programme is conducted annually based on, among other things, updated declarations made by states and results of ongoing inspection activities.

b. Creative function

Paragraph 21 of INFCIRC/153 gives the Board the ability to consider questions arising out of the interpretation or application of the Agreement. In other words, this gives the Board the power of shaping and clarifying legal rules pursuant to said agreements. Any contention that persists[37] after consideration by the Board should be subject to

[35] INFCIRC/153 (corrected), para. 19. [36] *Ibid.*
[37] See INFCIRC/153 (corrected), para. 22.

negotiation or another procedure agreed to by the parties[38] (the state and the Agency). If no settlement is reached, the dispute should, if so requested by either party, be submitted to an arbitral tribunal. Unlike in the case of the OPCW under the CWC, the creative function here extends only to the bilateral safeguards agreements, not directly to the NPT. Perhaps the most obvious example of the IAEA's creative function is that the Agency itself formulated the structure and content of the CSA, which, after being concluded, must be adhered to by NNWSs.

ii. Violations, the correction function and the role of the UN Security Council

A violation, or non-compliance, in this context refers to the specific agreements concluded within the safeguards system – in other words, non-compliance with a safeguards agreement. The question is how and to what extent this is linked to related obligations under the NPT? As mentioned before, a finding of non-compliance with the obligations under a CSA is not necessarily equivalent to a determination that nuclear material has been diverted to nuclear weapons or other nuclear explosive devices.[39] Article III of the NPT specifically establishes the rationale of having to conclude a safeguards agreement with the IAEA as being to verify compliance with the prime NNWS obligation contained in Article II of the NPT. The language of Article III sets forth the obligation to 'accept safeguards', meaning in effect that concluding such an agreement with the IAEA in and of itself fulfils the requirements of that article.[40] This wording establishes the concrete connection between safeguards agreements – the supervisory mechanism – and the NPT proper in terms of demonstrating compliance with obligations.

One would expect an effective system of supervision as a rule to be able to conclude that a state either is in full compliance with or has breached its primary commitments. In the case of the IAEA safeguards system, even if there appears to be reason to determine that a state is

[38] See dispute settlement techniques as listed in Art. 33 of the UN Charter.

[39] See, for example, IAEA Media Advisory 2003/48: 'the Agency is not able to verify that there has been no diversion of nuclear material subject to safeguards to nuclear weapons or other nuclear explosive devices.'

[40] See NPT/CONF.2010/50 (vol. 1), 2010 Review Conference of the Parties to the Treaty on the Non-Proliferation of Nuclear Weapons, Final Document, para. 14, which seems to equate the bringing into force of a CSA with compliance with Art. III of the NPT.

non-compliant with the central NPT obligations, the Agency will only find that the state is non-compliant with its safeguards agreement. This determination does not in fact concern the material component of the NPT, but rather only the procedural component contained in the safeguards agreement, such as declaring a relevant facility. It appears, therefore, that there is no direct link between non-compliance with a safeguards agreement and a violation of Article III of the NPT.[41] Illustrative of this point is the wording of the relevant provision in the CSA, paragraph 19, which connects the possible corrective measures to a finding by the Agency that it is 'not able to verify that there has been no diversion of *nuclear* material required to be safeguarded under the Agreement to nuclear weapons or other nuclear explosive devices'. This inability to verify again relates to the procedural component of the safeguards system, such as the finding by the Board that Syria was non-compliant owing to the undeclared construction of a nuclear reactor at Dair Alzour and the failure to provide design information for the facility,[42] as opposed to a finding of a breach of the prime obligation contained in Article II of the NPT. The IAEA makes the determination of non-compliance with a safeguards agreement, and thereafter it is up to the states parties to the NPT to establish a breach of the treaty.

In terms of correction, paragraph 19 of INFCIRC/153 provides the Board recourse to Article XII(C) of the IAEA Statute. According to the paragraph, the Board 'may' make reports as envisioned in Article XII and 'may also take, where applicable, the other measures provided for in that paragraph'. This seems to indicate that the Board is able to take such action if and when it deems necessary, in the absence of sufficient reassurance from the state involved. The report referred to is one detailing the non-compliance with the safeguards agreement, submitted by the Board to all members of the IAEA and to the UN Security Council and General Assembly.

Article XII(C) goes on to set forth corrective measures that may be taken by the Board if the non-compliant state or states fail to take corrective action within a reasonable period of time. Again, the corrective action required to remedy any non-compliance that has been found

[41] See, for example, J. Action, 'Deterring Safeguards Violations', *Carnegie Endowment for International Peace* (2009), p. 5: '[S]tates party to the NPT should clarify and emphasize at the 2010 Review Conference that, in the future, non-compliance with safeguards agreements will violate article III of the NPT.'

[42] GOV/2011/41.

to have occurred is left undefined, most probably as necessary action would need to be determined on a case-by-case basis. As with most other non-proliferation treaties, one of the corrective steps that may be taken against a violator is the suspension of the exercise of privileges and rights of membership, or an internal sanction, which would only apply to the 151 member states of the IAEA.[43] The Board is also given the ability to take one or both of the following measures: curtail or suspend the assistance being provided by a member of the Agency or by the Agency itself, and call for the return of material and equipment made available to the non-compliant state or group of states. This correction procedure applies to any non-compliance with the agreement, or agreements, between the IAEA and the state, and, from an actual enforcement perspective, seems quite weak.[44]

In accordance with the aforementioned paragraph 19 of INFCIRC/153 and Article XII(C) of the IAEA Statute, the Board is the organ tasked with determining and taking follow-up steps with respect to instances of non-compliance. A recent example of this is action undertaken having made a finding of non-compliance, and pursuant to Article XII(C) of the Statute, with respect to Syria.[45] As seen in the series of resolutions adopted by the Board with respect to the situation in Iran, however, failure adequately to demonstrate adherence to safeguards obligations does not automatically trigger the corrective measures, as the state is given time to remedy the situation itself. Having assessed Iranian nuclear activities and adopted numerous resolutions on the topic following from verification of Iranian declarations since 2002, the Board only invoked the Article XII non-compliance procedure for the first time in 2005, though it did not take the aforementioned corrective steps, other than transmitting reports to the Security Council.[46] This latter action appears

[43] Art. XII(C) of the IAEA Statute. See also Dekker, *The Law of Arms Control*, pp. 295–296. North Korea withdrew its membership on 13 June 1994.

[44] See Myjer, 'The Organization for the Prohibition of Chemical Weapons', pp. 122–125. For further examples of commentators assessing the relative strength of the corrective, or enforcement, mechanisms available to the IAEA, see Goldblat, *Arms Control*, pp. 236–237 and Rockwood, 'The IAEA's Strengthened Safeguards System', p. 125.

[45] GOV/2011/41, 'Implementation of the NPT Safeguards Agreement in the Syrian Arab Republic', Resolution adopted by the Board of Governors on 9 June 2011.

[46] GOV/2005/77, 'Implementation of the NPT Safeguards Agreement in the Islamic Republic of Iran', Resolution adopted by the Board of Governors on 24 September 2005. See, similarly, GOV/2011/41, 'Implementation of the NPT Safeguards Agreement in the Syrian Arab Republic', containing a determination of non-compliance with Syria's safeguards agreement.

to be the preferred corrective option for the Agency as it has been taken on numerous previous occasions.[47]

Perhaps because of the weakness of the enforcement element available to the Agency, and as with the other treaties examined in this chapter, the Security Council plays a clear role in the supervision of nuclear non-proliferation. The Council is not given any additional competencies, outside of its UN Charter-mandated functions, under the safeguards system and is not formally part of the correction process besides receiving reports of non-compliance if the Board of Governors of the IAEA so decides. The Security Council may undertake its own investigation and come to its own conclusions on matters of compliance, whether or not it is part of a non-proliferation treaty's supervisory mechanism.[48] Determining that activities involving non-compliance with safeguards agreements, and non-proliferation of WMD in general,[49] constitute a threat to international peace and security allows the Council, under the system of collective security, to take corrective action in the form of military or non-military measures under Chapter VII of the UN Charter. The ongoing case of potential illicit nuclear activities in Iran is illustrative of the enforcement function of the Council within the nuclear non-proliferation regime, as well as of the relationship to the IAEA safeguards system, supporting and augmenting the Agency's correction function.[50] It is worth noting that the Resolutions adopted by the Security Council with respect to non-proliferation issues in Iran not only include the imposition of sanctions but also demand adherence with the safeguards requirements of the IAEA, clearly establishing the role of the Security Council in the reinforcement of the Agency's supervisory functions.

This system of verification treaties (safeguards agreements), being separate from the non-proliferation treaty pursuant to which they are applied, ensures that the safeguards system is applicable to other instances and also gives the safeguards system under the IAEA a special character compared to the following instruments.

[47] Examples of reports made to the Security Council pursuant to Art. XII(C) of the Statute include: Israel (1981), Iraq (1991), Romania (1992), North Korea (1993, 1994 and 2003), Libya (2004) and Syria (2011).

[48] See Dekker, *The Law of Arms Control*, pp. 115–116. The Security Council, in this way, can independently carry out the various functions of supervision.

[49] See S/RES/1540 (2004), n. 3.

[50] See S/RES/1969 (2006); S/RES/1737 (2006); S/RES/1747 (2007); S/RES/1803 (2008); S/RES/1835 (2008); S/RES/1887 (2009); S/RES/1929 (2010).

III. The Chemical Weapons Convention

In the aftermath of the fall of the 'iron curtain', one of the positive developments was the conclusion of the Chemical Weapons Convention (CWC). It was signed in January 1993 and entered into force in April 1997. This non-proliferation treaty is a milestone in the law of non-proliferation not only because it bans a complete category of weapons[51] but also because it created the institutional framework for a comprehensive system of supervision. This institutional framework is the Organization for the Prohibition of Chemical Weapons (OPCW). The OPCW was established exclusively for the purpose of the CWC, unlike as was the case at the time of concluding the NPT, which used the institutional framework of the already existing IAEA to ensure supervision of NNWSs' commitments under the treaty. The OPCW is an international organization that provides (and steers) all the different elements for the supervision of state parties' commitments under the CWC. It also provides for the necessary framework to 'run' this international organization and to maintain the CWC by organizing the review conferences. For our purposes, however, a concise description of the special characteristics of the supervisory system will suffice.

i. The system of supervision

a. Treaty-specific verification: the collection and review functions

Collecting the necessary information to be able to verify compliance is done in a dual way. On the one hand, states parties will provide comprehensive information, both initially and annually thereafter, if applicable for the particular state, on the existence of chemical weapons, chemical weapon production facilities (CWPFs), on old and abandoned weapons and on their destruction or on their possible conversion, as well as information focused on the industry with respect to the production, import/export or consumption of chemical that are listed in the three schedules in the Convention's Annex on Chemicals. These schedules point to the dual character of chemical substances and their use in the chemical industry and thereby to the important role of the chemical industry under the CWC. In addition, the related facilities will have to be

[51] Art. I CWC.

reported. Next to this information obtained from states parties, there is the information that the OPCW collects and has collected over the years – via its inspections and via the combined reporting processes of all individual states, from older inspection reports, or by following scientific and political developments.

The proof of the pudding, though, is obviously in the eating. The information obtained from states parties needs to be verified. This will be done via an initial inspection and thereafter by routine inspections. For this purpose the OPCW has an international inspectorate consisting of highly trained specialist inspectors. In general, four types of inspections can be distinguished: the initial inspection, the routine inspection, the challenge inspection and the inspection in case of alleged use of chemical weapons. Both the initial and the routine inspections take place at the initiative of the OPCW and deal with data control. The challenge inspection takes place at the request of states parties. For each declared facility a Facility Agreement will have to be concluded with the OPCW.

The initial inspection takes place after states parties have made their declarations. This may concern chemical weapons and the place they are stored, chemical weapons production facilities and chemicals that fulfil the criteria of the CWC and its annexes, and chemical production facilities. These are, for instance, the chemicals used by the chemical industries to make pharmaceuticals, pesticides or other commercial products. Routine inspections will take place in the years after the initial inspections and centre on states parties annual declarations. It will be clear that, given the fact that the CWC is a near universal non-proliferation treaty, budgetary restraints mean that routine inspections of all the declared facilities cannot take place each year, but will take place selectively. Therefore, the ultimate check on this system is the challenge inspection that a state party may request 'for the sole purpose of clarifying and resolving any questions concerning possible non compliance with the provisions of this Convention'.[52] To this point, no challenge inspection has been requested.

The actual review function is about judging state behaviour for its conformity with an agreed rule of law – in other words, with the obligations under the CWC. In this case, this means that an assessment needs to take place whereby the declarations will be compared with the inspection results and the treaty obligations. This review function may involve the three organs of the OPCW, namely the Technical Secretariat,

[52] Art. IX, para. 8, CWC.

the Executive Council and the Conference. When the information confirms a state party's compliance with the CWC, the review will be concluded at the level of the Technical Secretariat. This is the first (and most often only) stage of the review process. Only if ambiguities cannot be solved by the Technical Secretariat will the Executive Council be involved. In order to solve ambiguities, the Technical Secretariat will use dispute settlement techniques.[53] If uncertainties cannot be resolved in this way, 'or the facts established are of a nature to suggest that obligations under the Convention have not been met',[54] the Director General of the OPCW shall inform the Executive Council, thereby entering the second stage of the review process. This will also be the case when a challenge inspection has been asked for. Also, the Executive Council will be involved in cases in which states parties request its assistance in the clarification of 'any situation which may be considered ambiguous or which gives rise to a concern about the possible non-compliance of another State Party'.[55] The Executive Council then shall consult with the states parties involved and, as appropriate, request the state party 'to take measures to redress the situation within a specified period'.[56] Depending on the resulting action by the state party, and if the Executive Council considers further action to be necessary, it may decide to inform all states parties to bring the matter to the attention of the Conference, or make recommendations to the Conference regarding measures to redress the situation to ensure compliance.[57] By involving the Conference, the third stage of the review process is entered. This is logical because the Conference is the central organ of the OPCW and the principal organ to take decisions on 'any questions, matters or issues related to this Convention raised by a State Party or brought to its attention by the Executive Council'.[58]

Besides possibly involving the Conference, in a case of particular gravity and urgency, the Executive Council might bring issues of non-compliance directly to the attention of the UN General Assembly or the Security Council.[59] Although this is a course of action foreseen under the Convention, it shows the restrictions inherent in the Convention's system of supervision. Such an appeal to the UN General Assembly or

[53] See Myjer, 'The Organization for the Prohibition of Chemical Weapons', pp. 117–118.
[54] Verification Annex, Part II, para. 65.
[55] Art. IX, para. 3. See Myjer, 'The Organization for the Prohibition of Chemical Weapons', p. 119.
[56] See Art. VIII, para. 36. [57] *Ibid.* [58] Art. VIII, para. 19. [59] Art. VIII, para. 6.

to the Security Council clearly indicates non-compliance by a state party that the Executive Council considers to be of a dimension that endangers, or is likely to endanger, the maintenance of international peace and security that apparently cannot be fixed within the compliance regime of the CWC. This is the ultimate last resort in issues of peace and security, for it is only the Security Council that can take the necessary binding measures under Chapter VII of the UN Charter.

b. The correction function

With the involvement of the Conference or, especially, of the Security Council we are right in the middle of the correction function, for it concerns the question of what actually can be done if there is a breach of compliance. Article XII of the Convention deals with 'measures to redress a situation and to ensure compliance including sanctions'. It is important to realize that depriving a state party of its membership of the OPCW is not allowed as a sanction,[60] thereby attempting to preserve the universality of the Convention.[61] However, in cases whereby a state party has been asked to redress a situation by the Executive Council and such a state party fails to act, the Conference could restrict or suspend the state party's right and privileges[62] until it complies. The Conference could also recommend collective measures to states parties in conformity with international law.[63] It also could bring the issue to the attention of the UN General Assembly or the UN Security Council in cases of particular gravity.[64]

c. The creative function

The creative function essentially concerns the clarification of the applicable rules under the CWC and of the rules adopted within the OPCW. The special character of this international organization, where there is a constant referral back and forth between states parties and the OPCW,

[60] Art. VIII, para. 2.

[61] This is not withstanding a state party's right to withdrawal under Art. XVI CWC.

[62] These could be the right to participate in the exchange of chemicals, equipment and scientific and technical information relating to the development and application of chemistry for purposes not prohibited under the CWC (para. 2b, Art. XI). Also it could recommend member states' restrictions in trade concerning chemicals, equipment and know-how (para. 2c, Art. XI). Another sanction would be the suspension of the right to assistance and protection against chemical weapons under Art. X. Another possibility is treating such a state party as a non-treaty party as far as the transfer of chemicals is concerned.

[63] Art. XII, para. 3. [64] Art. XII, para. 4.

ensures an organic process where to a large extent dispute settlement techniques like consultation and clarification are also being used.

IV. The Comprehensive Nuclear-Test-Ban Treaty

The Comprehensive Nuclear-Test-Ban Treaty (CTBT) is not a non-proliferation treaty in the classic sense. However, it is clear that there is a relationship between the CTBT and the nuclear non-proliferation regime. UN Secretary General Ban Ki-moon, in a message released in recognition of the then forthcoming International Day against Nuclear Tests, called for the timely entry into force of the CTBT as an essential feature of the international disarmament and non-proliferation regime.[65] This reference to the role of the CTBT in the area of nuclear non-proliferation reiterates a connection made explicit in the Preamble to the CTBT, in which nuclear proliferation or non-proliferation 'in all its aspects' is mentioned five times, as well as in numerous other documents.[66] By obliging parties not to carry out any nuclear weapon test explosion or any other nuclear explosion, to prohibit and prevent any nuclear explosion anywhere under its jurisdiction or control, and not to cause, encourage or participate in the carrying out of any such explosion,[67] the improvement of existing and the development of new advanced types of nuclear weapons is inhibited. Therefore, the thinking goes, NWSs will be constrained in modernizing and maintaining their stockpiles (vertical proliferation) and NNWSs will be unable to obtain and prove the capabilities of nuclear weapons. As a caveat, it must be pointed out that neither subcritical tests nor computer simulations are prohibited, thus calling into question the comprehensiveness of the

[65] 'On International Day against Nuclear Tests, Secretary-General Seeks Test Ban Treaty Ratification for "Safer, Saner World for All"', press release, 12 August 2011.

[66] CTBT Preamble, para. 5: '*Recognizing* that the cessation of all nuclear weapon test explosions and all other nuclear explosions, by constraining the development and qualitative improvement of nuclear weapons and ending the development of advanced new types of nuclear weapons, constitutes an effective measure of nuclear disarmament and non-proliferation in all its aspects'; CTBT Preamble, para. 10: '*Affirming* the purpose of attracting the adherence of all States to this Treaty and its objective to contribute effectively to the prevention of the proliferation of nuclear weapons in all its aspects.' See also, for example, Security Council Resolutions S/RES/1172 (1998), S/RES/1718 (2006), S/RES/1874 (2009) and General Assembly Resolutions A/RES/63/87 and A/RES/64/69. For the reference to non-proliferation in the Preamble as indicative of the Treaty's object and purpose, see L. Tabassi, 'The Nuclear Test Ban: *Lex Lata* or *de Lege Ferenda*?', *Journal of Conflict and Security Law*, 14 (2009), 317–318.

[67] Art. I CTBT.

ban.[68] The debate persists as to the potential effect of the CTBT on nuclear non-proliferation. However, based on its object and purpose and the officially recognized relationship between the treaty and non-proliferation, the CTBT can be seen, and will be viewed, in the context of the present chapter, as a nuclear non-proliferation-related instrument.

The CTBT was negotiated between 1993 and 1996, by which time the states recognized as NWSs under the NPT had all implemented a voluntary moratorium on nuclear weapon testing. Currently, 182 states have signed the CTBT, of which 154 have ratified. In order to enter into force, the CTBT requires ratification from forty-four states listed in Annex 2 to the Treaty. This has proved to be an insurmountable obstacle to entry into force as, to date, only thirty-five of these states have ratified and there is no indication that the rest will soon follow suit.[69] Though the CTBT is not yet in force, Article 18 of the 1969 Vienna Convention on the Law of Treaties obliges signatories and states that have consented to be bound by the Treaty not to defeat its object and purpose prior to its entry into force.[70] The lack of prospects for entry into force[71] in the near future has resulted in the Security Council taking an active role in the correction element, a supervisory construction which will be discussed further below.

i. *The role of the Preparatory Commission*

What is perhaps most unique about the status of the CTBT is the fact that the institutional supervisory structure, the Comprehensive Nuclear-Test-Ban Treaty Organization, modelled on the OPCW,[72] has

[68] See M. Asada, 'CTBT: Legal Questions Arising from its Non-Entry-Into-Force', *Journal of Conflict and Security Law*, 7 (2002), 85–122 and G. den Dekker, 'Forbearance is no Acquittance: The Legal Status of the Comprehensive Nuclear-Test-Ban Treaty', *Leiden Journal of International Law*, 13 (2000), 673.

[69] Three have yet to sign: North Korea, India and Pakistan. Each of these states has conducted nuclear weapons tests since 1996, breaking the *de facto* moratorium.

[70] For a strong analysis of what this means in the case of the CTBT, see L. Tabassi, 'The Nuclear Test Ban'. Regarding obligations *inter se*, see J. Klabbers, 'Strange Bedfellows: The "Interim Obligation" and the 1993 Chemical Weapons Convention', in E. P. J. Myjer (ed.), *Issues of Arms Control Law and the Chemical Weapons Convention* (The Hague: Martinus Nijhoff, 2001), pp. 11–29, as well as related commentaries by E. W. Vierdag, T. Marauhn and J. Sztucki.

[71] Though see Chapter 2 of this volume on provisional application.

[72] Art. II CTBT. 'The Organization shall be comprised of a Conference of States Parties (overseeing implementation of and reviewing compliance with the Treaty), and Executive Council (bearing primary responsibility for the functioning of the supervision

provisionally been activated in the form of a Preparatory Commission (which will be referred to here as the PrepCom). The PrepCom was established in 1996 by means of a Resolution by states signatories,[73] has the legal standing of an international organization, able, for example, to negotiate and to enter into agreements, and is composed of representatives of all states that have signed the treaty. The PrepCom has two main functions: supporting and advancing the steps necessary to achieve entry into force, and ensuring that the verification measures envisioned in the CTBT are operational as of the entry into force.[74] The organs of the PrepCom consist of a plenary body, which includes all signatories, and a provisional Technical Secretariat (PTS) that is tasked with assisting the Commission in its activities and conducting such functions as may be determined by the Commission.[75] In practice, the PTS functions have included (in addition to verification-related activities such as supervising the establishment of the International Monitoring System (IMS) and developing the necessary infrastructure and operational manuals for use in conducting on-site inspections) organizing capacity-building sessions and conducting various outreach activities aimed at raising awareness about the CTBT, and promoting its universality and entry into force.[76] There is also an Executive Secretary who heads the PTS and reports directly to the Commission on PTS activities. The PrepCom has its seat in Vienna, which was strategically chosen owing to its proximity particularly to the IAEA, allowing for cooperation and utilization of relevant expertise and resources.[77]

The verification regime envisioned in the CTBT to ensure compliance is four-pronged, comprised of an IMS, consultation and clarification, on-site inspections and confidence-building measures.[78] Underlining the importance of strict supervision of the central treaty obligations to the

mechanism ensuring compliance with the Treaty) and the Technical Secretariat (carrying out verification functions entrusted to it by the Treaty, including supervising and coordinating the IMS).' For a detailed description of the CTBTO, see Dekker, *The Law of Arms Control*, chap. 6, part III.

73 CTBT/MSS/RES/1, 'Resolution Establishing the Preparatory Commission for the Comprehensive Nuclear-Test-Ban Treaty Organization'.

74 Art. IV(1) CTBT. 75 CTBT/MSS/Res.1, para. 8(c).

76 See Art. XIV/2011/3 CTBT.

77 The IAEA originally attempted to extend its responsibilities to the implementation and verification of the CTBT. See R. Johnson, *Unfinished Business: The Negotiation of the CTBT and the End of Nuclear Testing* (United Nations Institute for Disarmament Research, 2009), pp. 172–173.

78 Asada categorizes the four elements into major verification measures (the IMS and OSI) and supplementary mechanisms (consultation and clarification and confidence-

overall effectiveness of the Treaty, and in order to abide by the terms of Article IV of the Treaty, the PTS has as its primary task the establishment of the verification mechanisms. A special working group of the plenary body – Working Group B – is set up to deal exclusively with the examination of verification issues. The PrepCom has made significant progress in the development and preparation of the technical infrastructure and implementation guidelines for the CTBT verification mechanisms, thus providing the foundation for treaty supervision, particularly with respect to the collection function, namely in the form of the IMS. According to Asada, this mechanism is, unlike the other verification elements, already becoming available owing to the *sui generis* nature of the relevant provision of the Treaty.[79] It is also the collection function that can be foreseen to make an immediate impact on nuclear non-proliferation, even pending the treaty's entry into force as the network is already delivering data, by considerably diminishing the chance that clandestine activities go undetected and by potentially providing information applicable to nuclear forensic analysis that could attribute the source of the nuclear material used in a detonation.[80]

ii. Treaty-specific verification: the IMS, IDC and NTM

The collection function as contained in the CTBT is fulfilled via a combination of the IMS, along with the central role of the International Data Center (IDC), both of which are currently overseen by the PTS, and national technical means (NTM). Not only is there a network of stations collecting information under the auspices of the CTBTO (or at this time the PrepCom), but each state party is also encouraged to make use of its own national monitoring techniques and therewith cooperate, through arrangement made with the CTBTO,[81] in the international exchange of data to assist in compliance verification.

building measures). See Asada, 'CTBT: Legal Questions Arising from its Non-Entry-Into-Force', p. 89.

79 See *ibid.* 103. As on-site inspections, whose sole purpose according to Art. IV(35) is to clarify whether a nuclear weapon test explosion or any other nuclear explosion has taken place, cannot be used until entry into force, the procedure for conducting the inspections will not be covered in great detail in this chapter.

80 This is something that could eventually further be supported by on-site inspections, which are meant, 'to the extent possible, to gather any facts which might assist in identifying any possible violator' (Art. IV(35)). See W. Dunlop and H. Smith, 'Who Did It? Using International Forensics to Detect and Deter Nuclear Terrorism', *Arms Control Today*, 36 (October 2006).

81 Art. IV(27) CTBT.

The technological data-gathering structure comprising the IMS is unique in the verification of non-proliferation treaties in that it collects data objectively by means of off-site measurement rather than through the 'subjective' method of declarations, thereby further reducing the potential for cheating.[82] Pursuant to Article IV(16), the IMS shall be comprised of facilities dedicated to seismological monitoring, radionuclide monitoring, hydroacoustic monitoring and infrasound monitoring,[83] which are meant to work in tandem to detect prohibited behaviour. It is envisioned that, when complete, the IMS will consist of 337 monitoring facilities – of which roughly 80 percent are now operational – in some eighty-nine countries.[84] The PTS is responsible for concluding monitoring station agreements with states.

It is subsequently for the IDC to receive, collect, process, analyse, report on and archive data from the IMS, including analysis results from certified labs.[85] Furthermore, the IDC is tasked with continuously monitoring and reporting on the operational status of IMS facilities, communications links and its own processing systems.[86] In processing and analysing raw data from the IMS, the IDC partially fulfils the review function. In part, the IDC will apply standard event screening criteria, as specified in Annex II to the Protocol to the CTBT, to highlight in an event bulletin events that are considered consistent with natural phenomena or non-nuclear, man-made phenomena.[87] Prior to the entry into force, these tasks too are placed under the authority of the PTS, which also distributes the data to members of the PrepCom. Judgement on the nature of any event, however, is ultimately left up to the states parties.

Also unique in terms of non-proliferation law verification, NTM are explicitly included as an integral source, separate from the IMS, of data collection under the treaty. NTM may be used under Article IV(5), in a manner consistent with generally recognized principles of international law,[88] as a means of verification regarding compliance of states parties

[82] Dekker, 'Forbearance is no Acquittance', p. 678.

[83] Seismological monitoring measures movements in the Earth's crust; radionuclide monitoring, which will include certified laboratories, measures radioactive particles and gases in the atmosphere; hydroacoustic monitoring refers to the movement of sounds under water; and infrasound monitoring looks at the movement of sounds in the atmosphere.

[84] See www.ctbto.org.

[85] Protocol to the Comprehensive Nuclear-Test-Ban Treaty, Part I, para. 16.

[86] *Ibid.*, para. 23. [87] *Ibid.*, para. 18(b).

[88] One can think here of such principles as non-interference in the internal affairs of a state and territorial integrity.

with the treaty. NTM can be comprised of methods and mechanisms such as photographic satellite reconnaissance, electromagnetic satellite surveillance, electronic intercepts, radar surveillance and seismic instrumentation.[89] Pursuant to Article IV(37), data obtained through NTM can serve as the basis, on its own or in combination with information collected by the IMS, for on-site inspection requests.

iii. Violations of the CTBT and the role of the Security Council

Notwithstanding the obligations under the Vienna Convention on the Law of Treaties of signatories and states that have ratified the treaty pending entry into force, one cannot talk of a violation of the CTBT itself unless the prohibitions contained therein have become customary international law. Once the treaty is in force, though, the CTBTO will be able to take corrective actions to redress a violation of the provisions of the treaty.[90] Again, similar to supervision under other non-proliferation law treaties, the relevant Article provides for the Conference of States Parties to decide on internal sanctions, which include the restriction or suspension of rights and privileges under the treaty or, in cases where non-compliance with the basic obligations of the treaty as set forth in Article I has damaged the object and purpose, the Conference may recommend collective measures in conformity with international law. If the case is urgent, the Conference can bring the issue to the attention of the United Nations under Article V, though to which specific organ is not explicitly mentioned. With regard to the settlement of disputes concerning the application or interpretation of the treaty, the CTBT in Article VI contains procedures nearly identical to those laid out in Article XIV of the CWC. The decision as to whether there has been a violation of the Treaty is ultimately left up the states parties.

The nuclear weapons tests conducted by North Korea in 2006 and 2009 provide examples of how certain aspects of CTBT verification can work in practice and an indication of the state of development of the CTBT verification system. In 2006,[91] members of the PrepCom received from the PTS a preliminary analysis of the event, with information on time, magnitude and location, within two hours of the blast. The PTS

[89] For a longer list of techniques, see Goldblat, *Arms Control*, pp. 213–215.
[90] Art. V CTBT.
[91] CTBT/PC-28/1/Annex IV. See also Johnson, *Unfinished Business*, pp. 209–212.

subsequently organized three technical briefings with a more detailed analysis, using data from both seismic and radionuclide monitoring stations, confirming the preliminary information, which was followed by a plenary session as a forum for members of the PrepCom to discuss the event. What was also notable was that the fission yield produced by the blast and detected by the monitors was below the system's baseline of one kiloton, showing the system to be more sensitive than originally planned. In this case, the IMS data played an essential role in definitively identifying the event as a nuclear explosion.[92] The 2009 nuclear weapon test explosion served to indicate how the capacity of the monitoring system had increased.[93] Again, data were made available to the PrepCom members within two hours, and the PTS produced an IDC-reviewed bulletin in accordance with the timeline envisioned after entry into force. Both of these events serve to demonstrate the capacity of the verification system of the CTBT promptly to detect and identify the occurrence of an activity prohibited under the terms of the treaty.

Another interesting aspect of the monitoring system being established by the PrepCom is that the IMS is not border sensitive. In other words, the system at least of raw data collection operates indiscriminately, meaning detection of an illicit activity would in practice not be limited to states parties. Though the treaty's correction mechanism would not be applicable in such cases and is in any case, of course, not officially in use pending entry of the treaty into force, evidence of a nuclear weapon explosion or any other nuclear explosion obtained by the CTBT verification system could serve to inform actions by the UN Security Council under Chapter VII.[94] With respect to the nuclear weapon tests in North Korea, the Security Council recognized the inherent challenge to non-proliferation in general and the NPT in particular constituted by such tests, and the Council made the requisite determination of a threat to international peace and security in order to take action under Chapter VII.[95] Here again, the link between the ban on nuclear testing and non-proliferation is made explicit. The verification system of the CTBT, namely monitoring under the auspices of the IMS, could as such be

[92] Johnson, *Unfinished Business*, p. 211.

[93] CTBT/ES/2009/2: 'Twenty-three primary seismic stations detected the 2009 event compared to the 13 primary seismic stations that detected the 2006 event.'

[94] See L. Tabassi, 'The Nuclear Test Ban', p. 337 and P. Szasz, 'The Security Council Starts Legislating', *American Journal of International Law*, 96 (2002), 904–905.

[95] S/RES/1874 (2009), S/RES/1718 (2006).

used more generally to check compliance with non-proliferation obligations even absent the entry into force of the CTBT.

V. Verification of the Biological Weapons Convention

The Convention on the Prohibition of the Development, Production and Stockpiling of Bacteriological (Biological) and Toxin Weapons and on their Destruction (the Biological and Toxin Weapons Convention – BTWC *also known as* the Biological Weapons Convention – BWC), which entered into force on 26 March 1975, was 'an arms control landmark because it was the first treaty to outlaw an entire class of weapons and to require actual disarmament through destruction of stockpiles'.[96] However, the BWC is reflective of a compromise between the great powers during a lull in Cold War hostilities, a belief in the limited battlefield utility of biological weapons, and a need to account for the inherently dual-use nature of the agents and toxins covered. Therefore, it is composed of indeterminate language founded on the intent-based definition of prohibited items in Article I,[97] essentially meaning that the prohibition covers all biological agents and toxins unless they are justified for peaceful purposes. Furthermore, it became apparent almost immediately after the entry into force of the BWC that developments in genetic engineering and other aspects of biotechnology would serve as major challenges to the regime.[98]

i. Relevant provisions, processes and attempts at enhancement

The above-mentioned issues pertain also to the non-proliferation obligation contained in the Convention,[99] and have certainly impacted

[96] D. Fidler and L. Gostin, *Biosecurity in the Global Age: Biological Weapons, Public Health, and the Rule of Law* (Palo Alto, Calif.: Stanford University Press, 2008), p. 47.

[97] 'Each State Party to this Convention undertakes never in any circumstances to develop, produce, stockpile or otherwise acquire or retain: (1) Microbial or other biological agents, or toxins whatever their origin or method of production, of types and in quantities that have no justification for prophylactic, protective or other peaceful purposes; (2) Weapons, equipment or means of delivery designed to use such agents or toxins for hostile purposes in armed conflict.'

[98] See N. Sims, *The Evolution of Biological Disarmament, SIPRI Chemical and Biological Warfare Studies* (Oxford University Press, 2001), p. vii.

[99] Art. III BWC: 'Each State Party to this Convention undertakes not to transfer to any recipient whatsoever, directly or indirectly, and not in any way to assist, encourage, or induce any State, group of States or international organizations to manufacture or

attempts to ensure compliance with the BWC through the implementation of verification mechanisms. As a result, verification of BWC obligations is notoriously weak. Unlike for nuclear weapons (the IAEA) and chemical weapons (the OPCW), there is no international supervisory organization overseeing obligations under the BWC. This institutional deficit of the BWC regime was one of the primary focus areas of the Ad Hoc Group, established in 1994 by a Special Conference of States Parties and tasked with considering 'appropriate measures, including possible verification measures, and draft proposals to strengthen the convention, to be included, as appropriate, in a legally binding instrument, to be submitted for the consideration of the States Parties'.[100] The work of the Ad Hoc Group culminated in the text of a Draft Protocol, presented in 2001, containing institutional legal provisions for the establishment of a specialized, autonomous international supervisory organization in the image of the OPCW, the so-called Organization for the Prohibition of Biological Weapons (OPBW), with similar legal personality and the legal capacity necessary to fulfil its objectives.[101] However, the Draft Protocol was ultimately rejected,[102] and resurrection in the form of similar supervisory initiatives is not to be expected.

The main text of the BWC, for its part, does not contain specific detailed verification provisions, though certain articles are relevant to compliance with the treaty's obligations. Article V provides for consultation and cooperation among states parties to solve problems related to the objective or application of the Convention, and was invoked, for example, to deal with the allegations of a BWC violation made by Cuba with respect to the *Thrips palmi* plague in 1996.[103] The scope of this Article has historically been viewed in fairly broad terms by the states parties as a catch-all for undertaking initiatives aimed at further developing the regime. For example, pursuant to Article V, the Second Review Conference laid the groundwork for consultative meetings, which can be

otherwise acquire any of the agents, toxins, weapons, equipment or means of delivery specified in article I of the Convention.' Obligations set forth in Art. III, for example, have been deemed sufficiently comprehensive to cover prohibited transfer to any recipient, though they require appropriate action on the national level with respect to biosecurity, biosafety and export controls in order effectively to implement the provision. See BWC/CONF.VI/6, p. 10.

100 BWC/SPCONF/1, p. 10, para. 36. 101 BWC/AD HOC GROUP/CRP.8

102 For an in-depth assessment of the negotiations and impact of the Protocol's collapse on international efforts to control biological weapons, see J. Littlewood, *The Biological Weapons Convention: A Failed Revolution* (Aldershot: Ashgate Publishing, 2005).

103 See BWC/AD HOC GROUP/WP.417.

requested by any state, recognizing the need for 'all states to deal seriously with compliance issues and [emphasizing] that the failure to do so undermines the Convention and the arms control process in general'.[104] The Third Review Conference went further by using Article V as a springboard for the creation of an Ad Hoc Group of Governmental Experts (referred to as verification experts or VEREX) tasked with identifying and examining 'potential verification measures from a scientific and technical standpoint',[105] which resulted in the submission of a list of twenty-one potential verification measures, considered at a Special Conference of states parties in 1994, leading to the establishment of the aforementioned Ad Hoc Group. It is up to the states parties themselves to initiate procedures under Article V.

Article VI, similar to the other instruments examined in this chapter, makes available the option for any state party to bring a complaint to the UN Security Council if it finds that another state party is acting in breach of its obligations under the Convention. Again, though, it is up to the state party or states parties to provide 'all possible evidence confirming [the complaint's] validity' in requesting the consideration of such a complaint by the Security Council. Therefore, states parties, by way of national technical means, are made responsible for identifying and establishing the existence of a violation. To date, the Article VI procedure has not been invoked and, owing to the veto-wielding power of the permanent members of the Security Council, is thought of as a weak compliance measure.

Security Council Resolution 1540, adopted in 2004 and aimed at enhancing non-proliferation efforts with a focus on non-state actors and the threat of WMD terrorism, has, in part, supported the relevant provisions of the BWC. It has also extended the scope of related prohibitions, owing to the fact that Resolution 1540 is binding on all member states of the United Nations, whereas the BWC falls far short of universality.[106] Under the terms of the Resolution, UN member states are obliged not to provide support to non-state actors attempting to develop, acquire, manufacture, possess, transport, transfer or use biological weapons and must adopt domestic legislation prohibiting non-state actors from conducting these activities. States are also required to enact domestic controls over related material in order to prevent proliferation. Resolution 1540, thereby, adds additional prohibited activities with

[104] BWC/CONF.II/13/II, 1986, p. 5. [105] BWC/CONF.III/23 (Part II).

[106] There are currently 164 states parties.

respect to transport, transfer and use to those included under the BWC.[107] States parties to the BWC, furthermore, have recognized that information required to be provided by states to the 1540 Committee on steps taken, or intended to be taken, to implement the Resolution may serve as a useful resource for states in similarly fulfilling national implementation obligations under the BWC.[108]

ii. Treaty-specific compliance monitoring: role of the Review Conferences

Absent agreement on legally binding measures to augment the monitoring of compliance, the process for dealing with potential breaches of the BWC has been established in the political setting of the periodic review conferences.[109] Owing to the institutional deficit, the review conferences, as well as the related meetings of experts, represent the sole forum for the development of the BWC regime. At the Second Review Conference in 1986, the process was first established, and later expanded at the Third Review Conference in 1991, for consultation and cooperation in solving any problems, including compliance issues, which may arise with respect 'to the objective of, or in the application of the provisions of'[110] the BWC. Under the procedure, a consultative meeting to consider any such matters – preceded by bilateral or other consultations among the states involved in the problem and an informal meeting of the states parties interested to discuss the arrangements for the formal meeting – shall be convened within sixty days of the receipt of request of any state party and open to all states parties. Within this process, the distinction is made but the close relationship is established between the convening of a meeting within the BWC framework and the initiation of a treaty-external procedure within the framework of the UN.

At this moment, however, annual data exchange under the programme of confidence-building measures (CBMs) serves as the primary

[107] See S/2008/493. The relevant article, Art. III of the BWC, only refers to transfers from the state, not to transfers among non-state actors, as well as to assistance from the state to other states and international organizations, as opposed to assistance to non-state actors.

[108] See BWC/CONF.VI/6. The 1540 Committee is established in S/RES/1540 (2004), para. 4.

[109] Review conferences are convened pursuant to Art. XII BWC 'with a view to assuring that the purposes of the preamble and the provisions of the Convention . . . are being realized'.

[110] Art. V BWC.

component to assess compliance with BWC obligations. Agreed to during the Second Review Conference, and expanded following the Third Review Conference, CBMs are aimed at enhancing compliance through transparency. These measures include: exchange of information on research centres and laboratories, national biodefence research and development programmes and on outbreaks of infections diseases and similar occurrences caused by toxins; encouragement of publication of results of biological research related to the Convention, and promotion of the use of knowledge; active promotion of contacts between scientists, other experts and facilities engaged in biological research directly related to the Convention; and declarations of legislation, regulations and other measures, including exports and/or imports of pathogenic microorganisms, of past activities in offensive and/or defensive biological research and development programmes since 1 January 1946, and on vaccine production facilities.[111] CBMs are voluntary, politically binding commitments and, as such, cannot be considered as adequate replacements for legally binding verification measures. Reliance is essentially placed on national oversight and willingness to provide and pool information under the auspices of the UN to ensure the absence of prohibited activities. From a verification perspective, therefore, the BWC is almost entirely reliant on national action.[112]

VI. Some concluding observations

We have looked at the supervisory mechanisms of the core non-proliferation treaties and especially at the mechanisms that are in place to control compliance when it has been alleged and/or established that a state is not complying. This is, in other words, about the correction function of the supervisory system of the particular non-proliferation instrument. Given that we are looking at branches of international law[113] that can be regarded as special regimes – of which arms control law is the

[111] BWC/CONF.III/23, Part II, Annex to Final Declaration on Confidence-building measures.

[112] For an overview of technical means available for national verification activities related to biological weapons, see K. Nixdorff, 'Biological Weapons Convention', in Rudolf Avenhaus, Nicholas Kyriakopoulos, Michel Richard and Gotthard Stein (eds.), *Verifying Treaty Compliance: Limiting Weapons of Mass Destruction and Monitoring Kyoto Protocol Provisions* (Berlin: Springer, 2006), pp. 114–126.

[113] 'Fragmentation of International Law: Difficulties Arising from the Diversification and Expansion of International Law', Report of the Study Group of the International Law Commission, finalized by M. Koskenniemi, Helsinki, 2007, p. 81.

wider and non-proliferation law is the narrower[114] – we can distinguish three levels at which correction is possible. The first level is the correction function of the particular non-proliferation instrument or treaty-specific correction. The second level is within the regime of the UN (that of collective security), be it via the Security Council (BWC), the Security Council or General Assembly (IAEA Statute, CWC), or the United Nations in general (CTBTO). With the Security Council acting in a binding fashion in a concrete case, it is acting within its competence and enforces Charter obligations.[115] The third level would be applying general rules of public international law, in our case the law of treaties and the rules relating to material breach.

We have seen that, in the case of the NPT linked with the IAEA's safeguards system, there is a strict verification system contained, in the first instance, in safeguards agreements made with individual states, and stricter still if the Additional Protocol is applicable, allowing for collection and subsequent review of information. However, even though the IAEA has the possibility to take corrective measures, initially it shall call on the state to remedy any non-compliance it finds to have occurred. The Statute-mandated corrective measures follow the report that shall be made to the UN Security Council and General Assembly, as well as to the other member states, thus in the first instance placing the correction function outside the special regime. These referral cases are made upon detected non-compliance with the safeguards agreement and not specifically with reference to the NPT. The CWC, for its part, has a comprehensive system of supervision that allows for an effective review of states parties' commitments. With respect to the corrective function, however, it is weak. There are a number of soft sanctions foreseen, but for hard, binding sanctions the Executive Council or the Conference of the OPCW will also here have to address the Security Council. The same would be the case with the CTBT under which, upon its entry into force, the UN collective security regime would also be the last resort in case of non-compliance. The BWC is a special case, devoid of treaty-specific supervision. It is reliant in the first instance on consultation either within the BWC framework itself or initiated within the UN framework. The BWC is, however, entirely reliant on the UN for corrective measures in case of

[114] D. H. Joyner, *International Law and the Proliferation of Weapons of Mass Destruction* (Oxford University Press, 2009), pp. xvi–xvii.

[115] See *ibid.* 180. See also Joyner discussing when the Security Council acts outside its competence when it acts as a legislator. *Ibid.* 176 ff. (esp. pp. 181 ff.).

non-compliance (Article VI). The BWC – states parties now more or less having given up on the potential for further legally binding verification measures – is, in effect, a special regime of a different character, with politically binding decisions adopted at Review Conferences allowing for diplomatic procedures, such as the system of CBMs. Here the Security Council is not only the last resort, but the primary corrective mechanism.

The security dimension of possible WMD proliferation is what has led to the special regime in the first place. Security, however, is also what has prevented the creation of effective correction mechanisms in the respective non-proliferation instruments. This same security dimension steers towards the Security Council for ultimate sanctions and will prevent states from possible cumbersome sanction procedures under the law of treaties, which we have identified as the third level. Perhaps the exception is the CWC supervisory system, which is a transparent system where compliance is primarily being controlled within the system more by making use of methods of dispute settlement[116] (like information exchange and clarification) and less by making use of the more traditional coercive methods to enforce compliance. This compliance control model corresponds to the management model of Chayes and Chayes.[117]

It appears that the special regime embodied by these non-proliferation treaties is developing into a system where there is greatest emphasis on transparency and information exchange. This, in general, has resulted in supervision comprised of treaty-specific verification and treaty-external correction, where the ultimate binding corrective measures could be initiated at the level of the UN Security Council. Such UN involvement is less threatening, since the system is in place anyway and is always controlled by the veto of the five permanent members of the Security Council.

[116] Cf. Art 33 of the UN Charter.

[117] A. Chayes and A. H. Chayes, *The New Sovereignty: Compliance with International Regulatory Agreements* (Cambridge, Mass.: Harvard University Press, 1995). See Myjer, 'The Organization for the Prohibition of Chemical Weapons', pp. 127–132. Also see E. P. J. Myjer, 'A Reporting System on International Humanitarian Law: An Arms Control Law Experience', in M. Bothe (ed.), *Towards a Better Implementation of International Humanitarian Law* (Berlin: Bochumer Schriften, 2001), pp. 38–54.

5

Withdrawal from non-proliferation treaties

DANIEL H. JOYNER AND MARCO ROSCINI

Our first task in this chapter is to consider whether there exist (and if so to what extent there exist) within the law and legal practice related to WMD non-proliferation treaties, specific and specialized rules on the subject of withdrawal from treaties that differ from the general rules of international law on the subject of treaty withdrawal (and/or from specialized rules on treaty withdrawal in other substantive areas of international law).

To the extent that such specialized rules are found to exist, our second task will be to consider whether these specialized rules present in non-proliferation treaties can be considered as evidence partially supporting the conclusion that non-proliferation law is a special regime explainable by fragmentation and special regime theory. We will begin by considering the general rules of international law regarding withdrawal from treaties, which are to be found in the 1969 Vienna Convention on the Law of Treaties (VCLT) and in related customary international law. We will then proceed to consider the specific rules regarding treaty withdrawal that are commonly found in non-proliferation treaties. Having described both general and specific rules on treaty withdrawal, we will proceed to consider whether and to what extent these general and specific rules overlap with each other in scope, and whether and to what extent there are conflicts, specialized priorities or exclusionary dynamics existing as between the general rules of international law and specific rules in non-proliferation treaties.

We will next consider whether and to what extent the specific rules on treaty withdrawal found in non-proliferation treaties differ from the specific rules on treaty withdrawal found in other substantive areas of international law. We will discuss the reasons for differences found, and consider the question of whether these reasons evidence specialized interstitial norms present in the area of non-proliferation law. Finally, we will consider whether there are legal rules emanating from sources external to non-proliferation treaties that constitute special rules regarding withdrawal from non-proliferation treaties, differing from the general rules of those legal sources and/or general rules of international law. Specifically, we will consider the dealings of the United Nations Security Council with the Democratic People's Republic of North Korea, relative to North Korea's withdrawal from the 1968 Treaty on the Non-Proliferation of Nuclear Weapons (Nuclear Non-Proliferation Treaty – NPT).

I. General rules on withdrawal from treaties

The general rules of international law regarding withdrawal from treaties are to be found in the VCLT, in Articles 54–64. Article 54 provides that, generally, 'The termination of a treaty or the withdrawal of a party may take place: (a) in conformity with the provisions of the treaty; or (b) at any time by consent of all the parties after consultation with the other contracting States.' Article 56 provides that if a treaty does not within its terms contain a specific provision on withdrawal, a state party may not withdraw its membership from the treaty, absent contrary implications determined to exist in the treaty. However, for the purposes of the current examination of non-proliferation treaties, most of which do contain provisions specifying terms for withdrawal, the more relevant general rule is to be found in Article 54(a) quoted above.

In addition to these textually dependent rules on withdrawal in Articles 54 and 56, Articles 60–62 of the VCLT contain general rules for withdrawal from all treaties upon the occurrence of certain defined events: material breach, supervening impossibility of performance and fundamental change of circumstances. It is worth noting that nothing within the provisions of Articles 54–64 of the VCLT, or in their context within the treaty, would appear to indicate that these three general rules for withdrawal in Articles 60–62 apply with any less force to treaties that do contain provisions specifying terms for withdrawal than to treaties that do not.[1]

II. Specific rules on withdrawal in non-proliferation treaties

For ease of reference, we include in an Annex to this chapter a number of examples of withdrawal clauses found in non-proliferation treaties,

[1] See Art. 31 VCLT.

including those found in the Treaty Banning Nuclear Weapon Tests in the Atmosphere, in Outer Space and Under Water; the Treaty on the Non-Proliferation of Nuclear Weapons; the Treaty for the Prohibition of Nuclear Weapons in Latin America and the Caribbean (Treaty of Tlatelolco); the Treaty between the United States of America and the Union of Soviet Socialist Republics on the Limitation of Anti-Ballistic Missile Systems (Anti-Ballistic Missile Treaty); the Convention on the Prohibition of the Development, Production and Stockpiling of Bacteriological (Biological) and Toxin Weapons and on their Destruction (Biological Weapons Convention); the Treaty between the United States of America and the Union of Soviet Socialist Republics on the Reduction and Limitation of Strategic Offensive Arms (Strategic Arms Reduction Treaty); and the Convention on the Prohibition of the Development, Production, Stockpiling and Use of Chemical Weapons and on their Destruction (Chemical Weapons Convention). Readers will quickly note the striking similarity of the terms of these provisions. Indeed, a review of withdrawal clauses in non-proliferation treaties reveals that the language negotiated in 1963 for the withdrawal clause of the multilateral Treaty Banning Nuclear Weapon Tests in the Atmosphere, in Outer Space and Under Water, afterwards served as the template (with only occasional minor alterations) in essentially all non-proliferation treaties that followed up to the present day. As it appears in Article X of the 1968 NPT, this common provision reads:

> Each party shall in exercising its national sovereignty have the right to withdraw from the Treaty if it decides that extraordinary events, related to the subject matter of this Treaty, have jeopardized the supreme interests of its country. It shall give notice of such withdrawal to all other parties to the Treaty and to the United Nations Security Council three months in advance. Such notice shall include a statement of the extraordinary events it regards as having jeopardized its supreme interests.

i. Comparison to the general rules of international law on treaty withdrawal

The first question to be considered is how this common specific rule on withdrawal in non-proliferation treaties, often referred to as the 'extraordinary events' clause, compares to the general rules on treaty withdrawal in international law, which as noted above are to be found in the VCLT. Again, Article 54 of the VCLT provides that 'The termination of a treaty or the withdrawal of a party may take place: (a) in conformity with the provisions of the treaty.' Thus, the general rules of the VCLT explicitly conceive of and allow for the existence of lawful withdrawal clauses within the provisions of treaties. Article X of the NPT, and the other withdrawal clauses in non-proliferation treaties excerpted in the Annex, fit squarely within this provision of Article 54 VCLT, and are thus in complete harmony with this VCLT general rule on treaty withdrawal.

As noted above, Articles 60–62 of the VCLT contain additional general rules providing for withdrawal from treaties in certain discrete circumstances: material breach, supervening impossibility of performance and fundamental change of circumstances. One question which arises is whether, in light of the specific withdrawal clause present in non-proliferation treaties, these three general rules for withdrawal in certain discrete circumstances may still be claimed by treaty parties as separate grounds for withdrawal, or whether the special rules on withdrawal contained in non-proliferation treaties exclude any resort to the general grounds for terminating a treaty.

The rules of the VCLT are generally written as presumptive rules of treaty law, codifying in most cases pre-existing rules of customary international law, which may be altered or specified by the parties to a treaty in a particular treaty text. In such a case of specification or alteration in a particular treaty text, the treaty provision becomes the *lex specialis*, and will govern the relations between the parties. However, to the extent that the general rules of the VCLT are not contradicted or altered in a treaty text, the general rules are still applicable to the relations between the treaty parties as rules of VCLT treaty law and customary international law.[2] Thus, we must begin with the proposition that the general rules of the VCLT, including Articles 60–62 on withdrawal in discrete circumstances, are applicable to the parties to non-proliferation treaties, to the extent that those general rules are not explicitly or implicitly modified or contradicted (i.e., made mutually exclusive) by the treaty parties in a particular treaty instrument.[3]

[2] See R. Müllerson, 'The ABM Treaty: Changed Circumstances, Extraordinary Events, Supreme Interests and International Law', *International and Comparative Law Quarterly*, 50 (2001), 530. 'Express provisions providing for the possibility of the denunciation of a treaty do not exclude the use of another concept available for treaty termination.'

[3] See N. Ronzitti, 'Problems of Arms Control Treaty Interpretation', in J. Dahlitz and D. Dicke (eds.), *The International Law of Arms Control and Disarmament, Proceedings of the Symposium, Geneva 28 February–2 March 1991* (New York: United Nations, 1991), 121. See also the ILC Commentary to Article 55 of the Articles on State Responsibility:

So, we must look to see to what extent the 'extraordinary events' withdrawal clause in non-proliferation treaties overlaps with, modifies, and therefore pre-empts, the general withdrawal rules in Articles 60–62 VCLT. Of the three general rules on withdrawal contained in Articles 60–62 VCLT, the rules on material breach (*inadimplenti non est adimplendum*) and fundamental change of circumstances (*rebus sic stantibus*) present possibilities of overlap with the 'extraordinary events' clause in non-proliferation treaties.

With regard first to Article 60 VCLT and material breach, Article 60 defines material breach of a treaty as consisting of either '(a) a repudiation of the treaty not sanctioned by the present Convention'; or '(b) the violation of a provision essential to the accomplishment of the object or purpose of the treaty.' Under both definitions, the behaviour to which the withdrawing party is responding will implicate the liability of a breaching treaty party for an internationally wrongful act.[4] By contrast, the withdrawal provision in non-proliferation treaties requires only that the condition to which the withdrawing party is responding consist in 'extraordinary events, related to the subject matter of this Treaty, [which] have jeopardized the supreme interests of its country'.[5]

In a number of ways, therefore, the concept of material breach in Article 60 VCLT covers a much more narrow and limited subset of occurrences in international relations as compared to the set of occurrences covered by the 'extraordinary events' clause in non-proliferation

'For the *lex specialis* principle to apply it is not enough that the same subject matter is dealt with by two provisions; there must be some actual inconsistency between them, or else a discernable intention that one provision is to exclude the other.' J. Crawford, *The International Law Commission's Articles on State Responsibility. Introduction, Text and Commentaries* (Cambridge University Press, 2002), p. 307. G. Fitzmaurice, Special Rapporteur of the ILC, Third Report of the Law of Treaties, A/CN.4/115 and Corr. 1 (1958), 44: 'The whole question of what inconsistency or conflict between two treaties means is a difficult one. Two treaties may be inconsistent in the sense that they set up mutually discordant systems, but so long as these do not have to be applied to or between the same parties, it may be quite possible to apply both. Thus, even though with some difficulty or at some inconvenience, State A may be able to apply one system in regard to State B under treaty X and another in regard to State C under treaty Y. In short, there may be a conflict between the treaties concerned, without this necessarily resulting in any conflict of *obligation* for any of the parties.'

4 See Ronzitti, 'Problems of Arms Control Treaty Interpretation', 121.

5 It might be recalled that, in the context of the NPT, Germany proposed the conclusion of an agreement clarifying, among other things, what constitutes an 'extraordinary event'. Preparatory Committee for the 2005 Review Conference of the Parties to the Treaty on the Non-Proliferation of Nuclear Weapons, Working Paper No. 15, NPT/CONF.2005/PC.III/WP.15, 29 April 2004. Available at www.un.org/en/conf/npt/2005/npt-conf2005-wp56e.pdf.

treaties.[6] First, while material breach requires an internationally wrongful act by another party to the same treaty, the 'extraordinary events' clause can be satisfied by events not caused or effected by the actions of any of the parties to the treaty. The extraordinary events mentioned in the provision must merely be 'related to the subject matter' of the treaty, and have 'jeopardized the supreme interests' of the withdrawing party. These extraordinary events may thus be caused by perfectly lawful actions of parties to the same treaty, or by the actions of non-parties to the treaty, or by non-state actors, or by no actors.

Secondly, the extraordinary events conceived of in non-proliferation treaty withdrawal clauses can consist in a vastly wider range of actions, circumstances and developments in international politics than are conceived of by the narrow material breach events of treaty repudiation or essential treaty provision violation by a treaty party.

Pursuant to this analysis, the extraordinary events clause in non-proliferation treaties should be seen not to modify or preclude the general rule on material breach found in Article 60 VCLT, but simply to add to the possible actions of treaty parties, and provide for further events in international relations, which may justify treaty withdrawal by an affected party, over and above that which is contained in the principle of material breach. Material breach is thus essentially a lesser included concept within the concept of extraordinary events in non-proliferation treaty withdrawal clauses. The only sense in which this is not true is the fact that material breach can be grounds both for withdrawal from treaties and for suspension of treaties, whereas extraordinary events clauses only conceive of treaty withdrawal.[7] However, this is not a point on which extraordinary events clauses in any way modify or make mutually exclusive the material breach principle, and so the result is the same – that the material breach principle is unchanged by extraordinary events clauses and remains in full effect with regard to non-proliferation treaty parties.

With regard to Article 62 VCLT and *rebus sic stantibus*, the principle that a treaty party may suspend or terminate its treaty obligations in light of a fundamental change in circumstances that was unforeseen to the treaty parties, changes facts or conditions which were an essential basis for the original consent of the parties to the treaty and would radically change the dynamics of relations between treaty parties has been long recognized as a principle of customary international law and finds

[6] See Ronzitti, 'Problems of Arms Control Treaty Interpretation', 121. [7] *Ibid.*

analogues in some domestic contract law principles.[8] It was codified in Article 62 of the VCLT, along with a specification of a number of prerequisite criteria, the purposes of which are clearly to circumscribe this potential basis for treaty withdrawal to make it more objectively determinable and limited in its applicability.[9]

The doctrine of *rebus sic stantibus* has been invoked many times by states. However, it has been considered only rarely by international tribunals, and there is still some considerable debate regarding the scope of the principle and justifiable factual bases for its valid invocation.[10] From state practice and from the few instances in which international tribunals have considered the scope of *rebus sic stantibus* as a justification for treaty withdrawal, one can, however, draw a few persuasive conclusions regarding its scope and application.

The factual context for the valid invocation of *rebus sic stantibus* as a basis for treaty withdrawal is generally held to be limited to significant events in international relations, such as war, the coming into existence of new states, the dissolution of a state or secession of a part of a state, or internal revolution within a state resulting in a fundamental change in the character of the government.[11] Anthony Aust further observes that, in drafting VCLT Article 62, the International Law Commission took notice of the modern trend of the inclusion of explicit withdrawal clauses in most treaties, and thus prescribed an even more limited scope for the doctrine of *rebus sic stantibus* than had existed previously.[12]

Again, the significant events in international relations which may form the factual context for valid invocation of *rebus sic stantibus* as a basis for treaty withdrawal must, according to Article 62 VCLT, additionally be events which (1) were unforeseen by the parties; (2) change facts or conditions which were an essential basis for the original consent to the treaty by the parties; *and* (3) have the effect of radically transforming the extent of obligations still to be performed under the treaty. The valid invocation of the doctrine of *rebus sic stantibus* as a basis for treaty withdrawal is thus, understandably and prudently, only possible in extreme cases.

[8] See A. Aust, *Modern Treaty Law and Practice*, 2nd edn (Cambridge University Press, 2007), pp. 297–301.

[9] See *ibid.* [10] See *ibid.*

[11] See C. Cohn, 'Interpreting the Withdrawal Clause in Arms Control Treaties', *Michigan Journal of International Law*, 10 (1989), 849, 854–864.

[12] Aust, *Modern Treaty Law and Practice*, pp. 297–298.

How, then, does the doctrine of *rebus sic stantibus* compare to the concept of 'extraordinary events' in non-proliferation treaty withdrawal clauses? First, the concept of extraordinary events would appear to encompass a significantly broader variety of events occurring in international relations than does the doctrine of *rebus sic stantibus*. Again, there is very little in either state practice or international judicial opinion which can serve to limit the types or nature of events includable within the legal concept of extraordinary events.[13] Textually, the only guide to meaning seems to be the invalidity of ordinary events for this purpose, which is of little interpretive assistance.[14]

[13] With regard to state practice, North Korea qualified the US hostile policy against North Korea as 'extraordinary events' jeopardizing North Korean security when announcing its intention to withdraw from the NPT on 10 January 2003. See R. Winters, 'Preventing Repeat Offenders: North Korea's Withdrawal and the Need for Revisions to the Nuclear Non-Proliferation Treaty', *Vanderbilt Journal of Transnational Law*, 38 (2005), 1513. In order to justify its withdrawal from the ABM Treaty, the United States seems to have qualified the September 11 attacks and the possible missile attacks with weapons of mass destruction and without warning against the USA by terrorists or 'rogue states' as extraordinary events related to the subject matter of the treaty and jeopardizing US security (13 December 2001). See text at www.acronym.org.uk/docs/0112/doc01.htm#text. The Russian Federation also listed the 'exceptional circumstances affecting the security of the Russian Federation' and justifying the decision to suspend its participation in the CFE Treaty. The list includes the failure of Eastern European countries to make the necessary changes to the treaty regime in order to take their NATO membership into account; the increased number of NATO states and the 'exclusive group' character of the alliance; the US plan to deploy conventional forces in Bulgaria and Romania; the failure to ratify early the Adaptation Agreement and to comply with the Istanbul Agreements by certain CFE parties; and the non-participation of the Baltic states in the CFE Treaty. Information on the decree 'On Suspending the Russian Federation's Participation in the Treaty on Conventional Armed Forces in Europe and Related International Agreements', 14 July 2007, available at www.cdi.org/russia/johnson/2007-161-32.cfm.

[14] See, generally, M. Roscini, 'Something Old, Something New: The 2006 Semipalatinsk Treaty on a Nuclear Weapon Free Zone in Central Asia', *Chinese Journal of International Law*, 7 (2008), 593; E. Schwelb, 'The Nuclear-Test-Ban Treaty and International Law', *American Journal of International Law*, 58 (1964), 663; J. Goldblat and P. G. Alves, 'Responses to Violations of Arms Control Agreements' in S. Sur (ed.), *Disarmament and Arms Limitation Obligations: Problems of Compliance and Enforcement* (Aldershot: United Nations Institute for Disarmament Research, 1991), p. 284; F. M. Menéndez, 'Zonas libres de armas nucleares en el derecho internacional', in *Cursos de derecho internacional de Vitoria-Gasteiz 1983* (Universidad del País Vasco, 1985), 162. Göran Lysén argues that 'extraordinary events' would be a breach of the treaty, the supervening impossibility of performance, the fundamental change of circumstances and the outbreak of war or armed conflict, and that to be 'extraordinary' the event should 'either be unforeseeable or, though foreseeable, thought by the parties as highly unlikely to occur'. G. Lysén, *The International Regulation of Armaments: The Law of Disarmament* (Uppsala: Iustus, 1990), pp. 176–177.

Second, the standard clause in extraordinary events provisions requiring that the subject events be 'related to the subject matter of this Treaty', due to its lack of specification, would seem to be presumptively significantly broader than the three specified treaty-relating criteria which Article 62 VCLT imposes upon events that would form the basis for a *rebus sic stantibus* claim. Indeed, the latter would appear to be lesser inclusive criteria within the former.

Third, unlike the doctrine of *rebus sic stantibus*, extraordinary events provisions do not require that the events in question have been unforeseen by the treaty parties. Nor do extraordinary events provisions disqualify events on the basis that they are the full or partial result of a breach of international law by the party invoking the principle; unlike the doctrine of *rebus sic stantibus* as codified in Article 62 VCLT. In both of these ways as well, therefore, extraordinary events provisions would appear to be broader and more inclusive of events in international relations than is the doctrine of *rebus sic stantibus*.

It would appear, therefore, that those events which would satisfy the *rebus sic stantibus* doctrine, inclusive of the three treaty-relation criteria outlined above, would also satisfy the extraordinary events concept and its broader 'related to the subject matter of this treaty' standard clause. Like the general material breach rule, therefore, the doctrine of *rebus sic stantibus* as a general rule of treaty withdrawal would appear to be a lesser included legal doctrine within the scope of the broader extraordinary events withdrawal provision found in non-proliferation treaties. And again, similarly, since there is no modifying, preclusive or mutually exclusive effect as between the two rules, both are fully applicable to the parties to non-proliferation treaties.

In conclusion, therefore, there is no conflict between the general rules on treaty withdrawal contained in Articles 60–62 VCLT and the specific rule contained in the withdrawal clause common to non-proliferation treaties.

ii. Comparison to withdrawal rules in other treaties

As observed previously, the modern trend in treaty-making is to include an explicit withdrawal clause in the text of a treaty. Such clauses are therefore quite common in treaties in many substantive areas of international law. The next question to be considered is whether and to what extent the specific 'exceptional circumstances' withdrawal clause common to non-proliferation treaties differs from the specific withdrawal clauses contained in treaties in other substantive areas of international law.

The answer appears to be that the formulation of the withdrawal clause common to non-proliferation treaties is indeed quite unique, and differs markedly from withdrawal clauses in most other treaties, particularly with regard to the requirement in the 'exceptional circumstances' provision for the withdrawing state to provide a justification for its decision to withdraw. In his comprehensive study of withdrawal clauses in treaties, Laurence Helfer notes this uniqueness when he observes:

> The overwhelming majority of the denunciation and withdrawal clauses listed in these exemplary documents do not require a state to provide any justification for its decision to quit a treaty. To the contrary, notices of denunciation are generally short, stylized letters of two or three paragraphs that simply inform the treaty depository that a state is withdrawing from a particular agreement as of a specified date.
>
> In a small number of agreements, however, a withdrawing state must explain its actions. Such explanations are particularly prevalent in arms control treaties. Most arms control agreements also restrict withdrawal to particular factual contexts, although they leave it to the denouncing state to determine whether such facts exist.[15]

This uniqueness of the 'exceptional circumstances' provision, and its difference from withdrawal provisions in other treaties, raises the question of whether there are particular or even unique concerns, values or principles underlying the sources of international law in the non-proliferation area that explain this difference in the formulation of withdrawal clauses as between non-proliferation treaties and treaties in other substantive areas of international law. In fragmentation theory literature, Vaughan Lowe has very usefully identified these extra-legal principles that underlie special regimes as 'interstitial norms'.[16] Pursuant to fragmentation theory, by reference to these interstitial norms reflecting the values specific to an issue area, specialized substantive rules can emerge through both formal (hard law) and informal (soft law) legal sources.[17]

While all explicit withdrawal clauses in treaties may be said to be motivated by the parties' values in preserving their sovereign rights not only to enter into obligations but also to withdraw from them (thus

[15] L. Helfer, 'Exiting Treaties', *Virginia Law Review*, 91 (2005), 1579, 1597–1598.

[16] V. Lowe, 'The Politics of Law-Making: Are the Method and Character of Norm Creation Changing?', in M. Byers (ed.), *The Role of Law in International Politics* (Oxford University Press, 2000), pp. 207, 216.

[17] See G. Teubner and A. Fischer-Lescano, 'Regime Collisions: The Vain Search for Legal Unity in the Fragmentation of Global Law', *Michigan Journal of International Law*, 25 (2004), 1999.

preserving the consensual basis of the sources of international law), in the non-proliferation area there are particular concerns and values that underlie both the presence of withdrawal clauses and the particular formulation of those clauses.

The particular political, military and technological contexts in which non-proliferation treaties exist and perform their functions have the most influence in this regard. Reasons for having a withdrawal clause in non-proliferation treaties that flow from these contexts include the following. The issue area of horizontal and vertical proliferation of weapons of mass destruction involves national security concerns second to none in terms of their sensitivity and importance to national governments. This issue area is further characterized by an international relations environment of dynamic political/security change and by an environment of dynamic technological change. This dynamic technological environment is further complicated by the dual-use nature of many WMD-related technologies, meaning that they have both civilian and military uses, and technological change is constantly occurring in both aspects of their use.

In this issue area of high security sensitivity and dynamic political and technological change and complexity, withdrawal clauses in non-proliferation treaties are a political necessity in order to assure national officials, including military planners and legislators who must give their consent to ratification, that entry into a non-proliferation treaty does not permanently limit their flexibility to deal with new circumstances occurring in any of these areas of concern. This is to assure them that whatever policy options they forego (or whatever positive obligations they assume) in non-proliferation treaties are not set in stone, but can be re-evaluated if necessary.[18] Without such an assurance, the adoption of non-proliferation treaties would be much more difficult in the first instance.

In addition to these reasons for having withdrawal clauses that are particular to the issue area of WMD non-proliferation, there are also reasons particular to this issue area which explain the specific formulation of those withdrawal clauses – that is, the formulation of the common 'exceptional circumstances' withdrawal clause. These are reasons why non-proliferation treaty drafters desire particularly to stress in the treaty text, as much as is possible without impinging unduly upon the need for flexible withdrawal criteria, the importance of preserving

[18] See N. Sims, 'Withdrawal Clauses in Disarmament Treaties: A Questionable Logic?', *Disarmament Diplomacy*, 42 (December 1999).

non-proliferation treaty commitments and of maintaining membership in non-proliferation treaties once they are established. These reasons include the following.

Security relationships involving WMD stockpiles and operational fielding are highly sensitive to sudden changes that unbalance a previously balanced and understood set of security relationships. Maintaining treaty relationships, except in cases of real national security need, fosters an atmosphere of predictability in WMD-related security relationships, and this in turn facilitates the maintenance of positive security relationships between states. Unpredictability in those security relationships puts both political and military leaders on edge, which is generally retrograde to international peace and security.

Further, a number of non-proliferation treaties are of a contract treaty nature, in the sense that they specify different obligations for different parties to the treaty, establishing at some level a quid pro quo arrangement of agreed commitments (e.g., the NPT). Other non-proliferation treaties, if not containing quid pro quo obligations, contain obligations the implementation of which are similarly asynchronous, or staggered in time (e.g., START). In all such treaties, the asynchronous nature of treaty implementation creates a particular need for trust and predictability as between treaty parties so that no one party will fear that their efforts at compliance will go unreciprocated. Along the same lines, a number of non-proliferation treaties provide for positive assistance from developed states parties to developing states parties in the areas of civilian technology uses (e.g., NPT, BWC, CWC). Withdrawal from such treaties by a party after such assistance has been provided to that party can create a similar feeling of windfall through cheating in the minds of those parties remaining in the treaty.

Thus, when viewed as a whole, the particular interstitial norms at work in the non-proliferation issue area explain both the presence of withdrawal clauses in non-proliferation treaties as well as the specific and unique formulation of the common 'exceptional circumstances' withdrawal provision in non-proliferation treaties, which provide more specified and more demanding criteria for withdrawal than are provided for in most other treaties.

iii. The Security Council and non-proliferation treaty withdrawal

As noted in the introductory paragraphs of this chapter, our task herein is to consider whether and to what extent there exist within the law and legal practice related to non-proliferation treaties, specific and specialized rules on the subject of withdrawal from treaties that differ from the general rules of international law on the subject of treaty withdrawal, and/or from specialized rules on treaty withdrawal in other substantive areas of international law.

We have thus far considered the possibility of the existence of such specialized rules in non-proliferation treaties in comparison with both the general rules on treaty withdrawal in international law and rules on treaty withdrawal contained in other treaties. Lastly, we will turn our consideration to the question of whether there are legal rules emanating from sources of law external to non-proliferation treaties that constitute special rules regarding withdrawal from non-proliferation treaties, as differing from the general rules of those legal sources and/or general rules of international law. Specifically, we will consider whether such special rules can be found in the practice of the United Nations Security Council and its legal decisions regarding non-proliferation treaty withdrawal.

Inasmuch as the United Nations Charter provides in Article 25 that all states parties 'agree to accept and carry out the decisions of the Security Council in accordance with the present Charter', the decisions of the Security Council are legally binding upon all UN members and thus are, in essence, sources of international legal obligation. The Security Council has had many occasions to consider, and to adopt binding decisions regarding issues of WMD proliferation. Most of these decisions have related to the WMD programmes of a relatively few states, including Iraq, Iran, Libya, Syria and North Korea. In only one context, however, has the Security Council considered the withdrawal of a state from a non-proliferation treaty. This of course is the case of North Korea's withdrawal from the NPT in 2003.[19]

Security Council Resolution 1874 was adopted on 12 June 2009 in response to the nuclear weapon test which had been conducted by North Korea on 25 May 2009. This was the second nuclear weapon test conducted by North Korea, its first having been held on 9 October 2006. The Security Council had responded to the first nuclear test by the adoption of Resolution 1718 on 14 October 2006. Resolution 1874 essentially reiterates the Security Council's condemnatory position on North Korea's nuclear tests, and it further builds upon and supplements the

[19] See, generally, the excellent article by M. Asada on this subject: 'Arms Control Law in Crisis? A Study of the North Korean Nuclear Issue', *Journal of Conflict and Security Law*, 9(3) (2004), 331–355.

sanctions imposed upon North Korea in Resolution 1718. Resolution 1874 represented the latest in a long line of Security Council resolutions focused on the problem of North Korea's nuclear weapons programme.[20] Longstanding international concern about North Korea's nuclear weapons programme had been aggravated by three principal events: the first was North Korea's announcement on 10 January 2003 that it would withdraw from the NPT, and the second and third were the 2006 and 2009 nuclear weapon tests.

North Korea's withdrawal from the NPT was of course significant on a number of levels. It represented the first and only time that a state had withdrawn its membership from the NPT, which is the cornerstone legal instrument in the nuclear non-proliferation normative regime. It also effectively removed from North Korea any obligation of either conventional or customary international law prohibiting it from developing or possessing, or even proliferating, nuclear weapons.[21] It is within this context of North Korea's withdrawal from the NPT, and its evidencing to the world its possession of nuclear weapons through its tests, that Resolution 1874 must be understood.

In Resolution 1874, acting under Article 41 of its Chapter VII authority, the Council first condemns, 'in the strongest terms', the 25 May 2009 nuclear test. It then demands that North Korea not conduct any further nuclear weapon tests, or launch any ballistic missile technology. These injunctions are clearly aimed at reiterating the prohibitions placed upon North Korea by Resolution 1718 and at addressing the immediate symptoms of the problem of its nuclear weapons programme. The Council then goes on to address the more fundamental legal problem relating to North Korea's nuclear weapons programme – the absence of international law prohibiting North Korea from development, possession and proliferation of nuclear weapons in light of North Korea's withdrawal from the NPT. In operative paragraphs 5 and 6, the Council demands that North Korea retract its statement of withdrawal from the NPT and return 'at an early date' to membership in the NPT and to a safeguards agreement with the International Atomic Energy Agency (IAEA).

Following its demand that North Korea rejoin the NPT, the Council proceeds in operative paragraph 8 to 'decide' that North Korea shall abandon its nuclear weapons and related development programme and shall submit itself to the terms of a safeguards agreement administered

[20] E.g., Resolution 825 (1993); Resolution 1695 (2006); Resolution 1718 (2006).
[21] Asada, 'Arms Control Law in Crisis?', 331–355.

by the IAEA. North Korea concluded a safeguards agreement with the IAEA on 30 January 1992 (INFCIRC/403). However, pursuant to Article 26 of the safeguards agreement, its continuance in force was limited to the term of North Korea's membership in the NPT.[22] Thus, North Korea's withdrawal from the NPT simultaneously worked a withdrawal from its safeguards agreement with the IAEA.[23] Operative paragraph 8 of Resolution 1874 thus purports to reverse North Korea's withdrawal from the NPT, and its withdrawal from its IAEA safeguards agreement, by commanding the state to abide by one of the central obligations of the NPT – that is, the obligation of non-nuclear-weapon states not to develop or possess nuclear weapons – and to abide by the terms of its IAEA safeguards agreement.

As far as we have been able to determine, Resolution 1874 is the first and only instance of the UN Security Council condemning a state's withdrawal from a treaty. This is the case notwithstanding the occurrence of numerous high-profile instances of treaty withdrawal in a number of substantive areas of international law within the past sixty-five years.[24] These cases include at least one high-profile instance of withdrawal from a non-proliferation treaty: the US withdrawal from the Anti-Ballistic Missile Treaty in 2002. It is unquestionably the first instance of the Security Council using its binding legal authority under Article 25 of the UN Charter to order a state to re-accede to a treaty from which it had withdrawn in accordance with an explicit treaty withdrawal clause written into the treaty text. The first observation one could therefore make about this decision of the Security Council is that it is in apparent disharmony with its prior record of a lack of condemnations of, and legal decisions regarding, states' withdrawal from treaties.

[22] Art. 26 of the Democratic People's Republic of Korea's safeguards agreement provides, 'This Agreement shall remain in force as long as the Democratic People's Republic of Korea is party to the Treaty [the NPT].'

[23] See F. Kirgis, 'North Korea's Withdrawal from the Nuclear Non-proliferation Treaty', *ASIL Insights*, January 2003. Available at www.asil.org/insigh96.cfm.

[24] See, generally, Helfer, 'Exiting Treaties'; Helfer, 'Overlegalizing Human Rights: International Relations Theory and the Commonwealth Caribbean Backlash against Human Rights Regimes', *Columbia Law Review*, 102 (2002), 1832; A. Chayes, 'Nicaragua, the United States, and the World Court', *Columbia Law Review*, 85 (1985), 1445; E. T. Swaine, 'Unsigning', *Stanford Law Review*, 55 (2003), 2061; D. D. Caron, 'The International Whaling Commission and the North Atlantic Marine Mammal Commission: The Institutional Risks of Coercion in Consensual Structures', *American Journal of International Law*, 89 (1995), 154.

However, this observation would not appear to have much probative value when considering whether there is, in Security Council legal practice, a special rule regarding treaty withdrawal in the context of non-proliferation treaties. The Security Council's primary role under the UN Charter, as codified in Article 39, is to act in situations which it determines to comprise a threat to international peace and security. Such a determination, and such actions, are inherently the product of discretionary decision-making by the Security Council, and will be intensely tied to the specific facts of each situation presented, and to political, economic and other factors. Thus, the absence of the Security Council's condemnation of other cases of treaty withdrawal cannot be clearly said to constitute a general rule or pattern of Security Council practice, with which its decision in Resolution 1874 regarding North Korea stands as disharmonious in a legally relevant sense.

The second observation one could make is that Resolution 1874 appears to be in disharmony with the general rules on treaty withdrawal contained in the VCLT and in customary international law. As noted above, Article 54 of the VCLT provides that treaty withdrawal may be lawfully accomplished by states by reference to an explicit withdrawal provision in the treaty text. In adopting Resolution 1874 as a decision legally requiring North Korea to re-accede to the NPT, and by so doing to undo its withdrawal from the treaty, the Security Council effectively nullified North Korea's entitlement under general international law, codified in Article 54 VCLT and reflecting customary international law, lawfully to withdraw from the NPT pursuant to an explicit withdrawal provision in the treaty text.

To be clear, we are not here saying that Resolution 1874 is unlawful, or *ultra vires* the Security Council's authority, because of this disharmony with the general rules of international law on treaty withdrawal. Articles 25 and 103 of the UN Charter, read together, make clear that obligations arising under the UN Charter, including UN Security Council Resolutions, are generally superior to other international legal rights and obligations. Rather, what we are observing is that, while Resolution 1874 is only one data point, it may be a point of evidence for the emerging creation of a special rule in the legal practice of the Security Council regarding withdrawal from non-proliferation treaties that differs from the rules on treaty withdrawal in general international law.

This observation raises interesting questions about the content of such an emerging special rule. Is it a rule generally prohibiting withdrawal from the NPT, notwithstanding the presence of an explicit withdrawal clause in Article X? Again, North Korea is the first state to withdraw from the NPT, so we have no other data point for how the Security Council will treat other cases of NPT withdrawal. Alternatively, is this special rule an even broader rule prohibiting withdrawal from any non-proliferation treaty, notwithstanding the presence of common 'extraordinary circumstances' clauses? This formulation of the rule would appear to be belied by the case of the US withdrawal from the ABM treaty. However, one obvious explanation for this exception is the fact of US permanent membership on the Security Council, and the veto power that it derives from this status.

Or, as yet another alternative was Resolution 1874, and the command to re-accede to the NPT, a decision limited to the specific facts of the case of North Korea, and a determination that those particular facts constituted a threat to international peace that had to be dealt with in this particular way? Under this theory, future withdrawals by other states from the NPT, or from other non-proliferation treaties, might not be blocked and reversed by the Security Council. We simply do not have enough data points of Security Council practice in this area to reach any conclusion as to which of these three alternatives provides the best explanation for the content of an emerging special rule evidenced by Resolution 1874.

Even without more data points, however, this one data point does seem to indicate at a minimum that, at least in some cases, the Security Council will use its legal power, operating under some concept of a special rule or practice with regard to withdrawal from non-proliferation treaties, to issue legally binding decisions requiring re-accession to treaties from which a state has withdrawn pursuant to a textual withdrawal clause, and in so doing nullify the withdrawing state's entitlement to treaty withdrawal under general international law.

iv. Conclusions

In summary, then, in this chapter we have compared the specific rules on treaty withdrawal in non-proliferation treaties with general international law on treaty withdrawal and with withdrawal provisions in treaties in other substantive areas of international law. We have also compared the legal practice of the UN Security Council in the area of non-proliferation treaty withdrawal, with general international law on treaty withdrawal. The purpose of these comparisons has been to determine whether and to what extent there can be said to be special rules regarding withdrawal from non-proliferation treaties that differ from the general rules of international law on the subject of treaty withdrawal and/or from specialized rules on treaty withdrawal in other substantive areas of international law.

The results of this study are as follows. We have determined that the specific rules on treaty withdrawal in non-proliferation treaties do not differ from the general rules on treaty withdrawal in international law. We have further determined that the specific rules on treaty withdrawal in non-proliferation treaties do differ significantly from withdrawal provisions in treaties in other substantive areas of international law, and that interstitial norms present in the area of WMD non-proliferation effectively explain these differences. Finally, we have determined that there is evidence, in Resolution 1874, of the emerging creation of a special rule in the legal practice of the UN Security Council regarding withdrawal from non-proliferation treaties that departs from the rules on treaty withdrawal in general international law.

The last question to consider is whether and to what extent the evidence of special rules on non-proliferation treaty withdrawal that we have found through this study can be considered to constitute evidence partially supporting the conclusion that non-proliferation law is a special regime explainable by fragmentation and special regime theory.

We have determined herein that not only are there special rules regarding treaty withdrawal present in non-proliferation treaties and in the legal practice of the UN Security Council but that there are also specialized interstitial norms present in the issue area of WMD proliferation that explain these rules, which differ from the general rules of international law and from specialized rules in other substantive areas of international law. This rule specialization is precisely what fragmentation theory predicts will happen in special regimes that 'emerge from the informal activity of lawyers, diplomats, pressure groups, more through shifts in legal culture and in response to practical needs of specialization than as conscious acts of regime-creation'.[25]

We conclude therefore that, while certainly not definitive of the question, and applying directly only to a finding of specialness with regard to treaty withdrawal rules, the evidence of special rules on non-proliferation treaty

[25] 'Fragmentation of International Law: Difficulties Arising from the Diversification and Expansion of International Law', Report of the Study Group of the International Law Commission, A/CN.4/L.682, 13 April 2006, 84.

withdrawal that we have found herein does constitute probative evidence supporting the conclusion that non-proliferation law is a special regime from at least this perspective, and explainable by fragmentation theory.

Annex: examples of withdrawal provisions in non-proliferation treaties

Treaty Banning Nuclear Weapon Tests in the Atmosphere, in Outer Space and Under Water (1963)

Article IV

This Treaty shall be of unlimited duration.

Each party shall in exercising its national sovereignty have the right to withdraw from the Treaty if it decides that extraordinary events, related to the subject matter of this Treaty, have jeopardized the supreme interests of its country. It shall give notice of such withdrawal to all other parties to the Treaty three months in advance.

Treaty on the Non-Proliferation of Nuclear Weapons (1968) (NPT)

Article X

1. Each Party shall in exercising its national sovereignty have the right to withdraw from the Treaty if it decides that extraordinary events, related to the subject matter of this Treaty, have jeopardized the supreme interests of its country. It shall give notice of such withdrawal to all other Parties to the Treaty and to the United Nations Security Council three months in advance. Such notice shall include a statement of the extraordinary events it regards as having jeopardized its supreme interests.

Treaty for the Prohibition of Nuclear Weapons in Latin America and the Caribbean (1968) (Treaty of Tlatelolco)

Article 31: Duration and denunciation

1. This Treaty shall be of a permanent nature and shall remain in force indefinitely, but any Party may denounce it by notifying the Secretary General of the Agency if, in the opinion of the denouncing State, there have arisen or may arise circumstances connected with the content of

this Treaty or of the annexed Additional Protocols I and II which affect its supreme interests or the peace and security of one or more Contracting Parties.

2. The denunciation shall take effect three months after the delivery to the Secretary General of the Agency of the notification by the Government of the Signatory State concerned. The Secretary General shall immediately communicate such notification to the other Contracting Parties and to the Secretary General of the United Nations for the information of the United Nations Security Council and the General Assembly. He shall also communicate it to the Secretary General of the Organization of American States.

Treaty between the United States of America and the Union of Soviet Socialist Republics on the Limitation of Anti-Ballistic Missile Systems (1972) (ABM)

Article XV

1. This Treaty shall be of unlimited duration.
2. Each Party shall, in exercising its national sovereignty, have the right to withdraw from this Treaty if it decides that extraordinary events related to the subject matter of this Treaty have jeopardized its supreme interests. It shall give notice of its decision to the other Party six months prior to withdrawal from the Treaty. Such notice shall include a statement of the extraordinary events the notifying Party regards as having jeopardized its supreme interests.

The Convention on the Prohibition of the Development, Production and Stockpiling of Bacteriological (Biological) and Toxin Weapons and on their Destruction (1972) (BWC)

Article XIII

(1) This Convention shall be of unlimited duration.
(2) Each State Party to this Convention shall in exercising its national sovereignty have the right to withdraw from the Convention if it decides that extraordinary events, related to the subject matter of the Convention, have jeopardized the supreme interests of its country. It shall give notice of such withdrawal to all other States Parties to the Convention and to the United Nations Security Council three months

in advance. Such notice shall include a statement of the extraordinary events it regards as having jeopardized its supreme interests.

Treaty between the United States of America and the Union of Soviet Socialist Republics on the Reduction and Limitation of Strategic Offensive Arms (1991) (START I)

Article XVII

3. Each Party shall, in exercising its national sovereignty, have the right to withdraw from this Treaty if it decides that extraordinary events related to the subject matter of this Treaty have jeopardized its supreme interests. It shall give notice of its decision to the other Party six months prior to withdrawal from this Treaty. Such notice shall include a statement of the extraordinary events the notifying Party regards as having jeopardized its supreme interests.

Convention on the Prohibition of the Development, Production, Stockpiling and Use of Chemical Weapons and on their Destruction (1993) (CWC)

Article XVI. Duration and Withdrawal

1. This Convention shall be of unlimited duration.
2. Each State Party shall, in exercising its national sovereignty, have the right to withdraw from this Convention if it decides that extraordinary events, related to the subject matter of this Convention, have jeopardized the supreme interests of its country. It shall give notice of such withdrawal 90 days in advance to all other States Parties, the Executive Council, the Depositary and the United Nations Security Council. Such notice shall include a statement of the extraordinary events it regards as having jeopardized its supreme interests.
3. The withdrawal of a State Party from this Convention shall not in any way affect the duty of States to continue fulfilling the obligations assumed under any relevant rules of international law, particularly the Geneva Protocol of 1925.

11

The law of state responsibility

6

The 'injured state' in the case of breach of a non-proliferation treaty and the legal consequences of such a breach

MATTHEW HAPPOLD

Traditionally, state responsibility has been viewed from a bilateralist perspective, with states owing obligations to each other individually, so that international law could be reduced to a network of, often reciprocal, bilateral relations. However, with an increasing belief that states share certain common interests and the multiplication of the number of multilateral treaties aimed at their protection, perceptions have changed. It is now widely accepted that states can owe obligations not only to other states individually but also to groups of states and even to the international community as a whole (whatever that might be).

Non-proliferation treaties are outstanding examples of the type of treaty where breach by one party of the treaty can radically change the position of every other party to it.[1] If a party to a non-proliferation treaty begins, in breach of the obligations it has undertaken, to construct an arsenal of weapons prohibited under the treaty, it becomes a potential threat to the all other parties,[2] which may then, in turn, consider it necessary to abandon their treaty commitments in order to safeguard themselves against their erstwhile treaty partner. An arms race thus ensues which the treaty was specifically designed to avoid. Another chapter in this volume (Chapter 8) deals with issues of the law of treaties and the consequences of breaches of the provisions of non-proliferation

[1] Art. 60(2)(c), Vienna Convention on the Law of Treaties, 1155 UNTS 331 (1969) (hereinafter VCLT).

[2] Not only because it might use those weapons against other states but also because it might transfer them, or the 'know-how' acquired in developing them, to other states, or even simply incite other states, themselves feeling threatened by the first state's behaviour, to develop such weapons for themselves.

treaties for their continued existence and operation.[3] This chapter, instead, covers issues of state responsibility for such breaches. It examines first which states can react to which breaches of non-proliferation treaties; in particular, which states parties should be considered to be 'injured states' and in what circumstances states parties which are not 'injured states' can nevertheless advance claims for breach. Second, it considers the legal consequences of such internationally wrongful acts, in particular the secondary obligations placed on wrongdoing states as a consequence of their breach of their primary obligations under non-proliferation treaties. It will be demonstrated that the particularities of non-proliferation agreements as regards the question of who is an injured state are already recognized in the international law of state responsibility and that, in this respect, they cannot be described as an aspect of a 'special regime'. However, in most cases, the traditional emphasis placed on the obligation to make reparation as the consequence of breach of an international engagement has little importance in relation to non-proliferation agreements. Obligations of cessation and non-repetition have a more important place.

Finally, it will be recalled that the term 'self-contained regime' was used by the International Court of Justice in the *Tehran Hostages* Case specifically to refer to the consequences of breach. Accordingly, the chapter will examine whether non-proliferation agreements permit states parties to act unilaterally to invoke their treaty partners' international responsibility, or whether they are restricted to utilizing any relevant treaty compliance mechanisms. Again, it will be argued that non-proliferation agreements do not establish 'special regimes', albeit that in practice the law of state responsibility does not play a major role in ensuring observance of the commitments undertaken by states parties to them.

I. Injured states in non-proliferation treaties

Under international law, a state is internationally responsible for its internationally wrongful acts:[4] that is, all conduct which is attributable to the state

[3] D. Fleck, 'State responsibility consequences of termination of or withdrawal from non-proliferation treaties'.

[4] Art. 1, International Law Commission's Articles on the Responsibility of States for Internationally Wrongful Acts (hereinafter ILC Articles), Annex, GA res. 56/83: Responsibility of states for internationally wrongful acts (12 December 2001).

under international law and constitutes a breach of its international obligations.[5] Who, however, is entitled to invoke the responsibility of a state: to demand cessation of the offending conduct (if the breach is a continuing one), to seek assurances and guarantees of non-repetition; to bring a claim for reparation; and, if necessary, to institute countermeasures?[6] Here the rule, as codified in the International Law Commission's Articles on State Responsibility (ILC Articles), is that 'only the party to whom an international obligation is due can bring a claim in respect of its breach.'[7] In other words, the wrongdoing state must be in breach of an obligation which it owes to the state invoking responsibility, which the ILC Articles refer to as the 'injured state'.

A distinction, however, must be made between invocation of a state's international responsibility and simple criticism of a state's conduct, even if the latter is made on avowedly legal grounds (i.e., on the basis that the state criticized is in breach of its treaty obligations). Protest at a state's actions, even calls that the state brings itself back into conformity with its international obligations, do not necessarily amount to invocation of that state's international responsibility, which requires the 'taking [of] measures of a relatively formal character'.[8] Such measures need not involve the initiation of proceedings before an international court or tribunal but do require the assertion of specific claims, the prerequisite to which is that the state invoking responsibility has a legal right to bring such claims. In other words, even when one state asserts that another has acted in breach of its legal obligations and informs that other state that it needs to bring its conduct back into conformity with them, this is not necessarily an invocation of the second state's international responsibility by the first. Close attention needs to be paid to the context and content of the first state's statements. This is important because, except in limited and, at present, unclear circumstances,[9] only an injured state is entitled to institute countermeasures against a wrongdoing state and the

[5] *Ibid.*, Art. 2.

[6] Questions concerning countermeasures are examined in Chapter 7 of this book: S. Singh, 'Non-proliferation law and countermeasures'.

[7] *Barcelona Traction, Light and Power Company Limited* (*Belgium* v. *Spain*), ICJ Reports 1970 3, 32.

[8] International Law Commission, Report on the work of its fifty-third session (23 April–1 June and 2 July–10 August 2001), Official Records of the General Assembly, Fifty-sixth Session, Supplement No. 10, UN doc. A/56/210, Commentary to Art. 42 of the Draft Articles on the Responsibility of States for Internationally Wrongful Acts, p. 117.

[9] On measures taken by states other than an injured state, see Art. 54, ILC Articles. The term 'lawful measures' is, of course, entirely question-begging. But see C. J. Tams,

situations when a non-injured state can bring an international claim are extremely limited, as are the demands that non-injured states can make (although this, as will be seen, is less of an issue in the non-proliferation context).

So who is an injured state? Article 42 of the ILC Articles provides that:

> A State is entitled as an injured State to invoke the responsibility of another State if the obligation breached is owed to:
>
> (a) that State individually; or
> (b) a group of States including that State, or the international community as a whole, and the breach of the obligation:
>   (i) specially affects that State; or
>   (ii) is of such a character as radically to change the position of all the other States to which the obligation is owed with respect to the further performance of the obligation.

It can immediately be seen that Article 42 covers three separate situations, of ascending degrees of importance. Indeed, examination of the work of the ILC indicates that the different definitions of an injured state in Article 42(b)(i) and (ii) were motivated, at least in part, by a concern to limit the possible range of responses to breaches of multilateral obligations by reference to the seriousness of the infringement.[10]

- The first is when an obligation is owed by one state to another. This can be the case even in the context of a multilateral treaty; the situation being that each party owes the obligations it assumes under the treaty to each other party individually, so that the treaty regime is best analysed as a network of bilateral relationships.
- The second is when an obligation is owed by one state to a group of states (which can amount to all states in the world) and one of that group is 'specially affected' by its breach.[11] Such obligations are usually described as *erga omnes* or (if treaty-based) *erga omnes partes* obligations.[12] It should be noted, however, that in such situations it is not enough simply that a state is a member of the group to which the obligation is owed, it must also be 'specially affected' by the breach. A distinction is made between states which have suffered particular

Enforcing Obligations Erga Omnes in International Law (Cambridge University Press, 2005).

[10] See International Law Commission, Third Report on State Responsibility, by Mr. James Crawford, Special Rapporteur, UN Doc. A/CN.4/507, 15 March 2000, para. 71.

[11] This would appear to be the situation in *Ahamadou Sadio Diallo* (*Guinea* v. *DRC*) (preliminary objections), judgment of 24 May 2007, in particular paras. 28–29 and 31.

[12] See *Barcelona Traction*.

adverse effects as a result of the internationally wrongful act and those which have merely a legal interest in the wrongdoing state's performance of its obligation.[13]

- The third situation also covers obligations owed to groups of states. However, it applies when the breach of the obligation 'is of such a character as radically to change the position of all the other states to which the obligation is owed with respect to the further performance of the obligation'. Obligations, breach of which can give rise to such consequences, are often referred to as 'integral obligations'; a term current in both the law of state responsibility and the law of treaties.[14] Formally, it is the nature of breach, not of the obligation *per se*, which is crucial in the law of state responsibility, but one might consider that only breaches of integral obligations are likely to give rise to such serious consequences. In such cases, all states which are members of the group of states to which the obligation is owed are considered to be injured states and are entitled to invoke the responsibility of the wrongdoing state.

Certain breaches of certain provisions of non-proliferation treaties fall squarely within this third category. Breaches of other provisions of such treaties, however, cannot be said to partake of such a quality and fall instead within the situations described in Article 42(a) and Article 42(b)(i). What is consequently required in any particular situation is an analysis of the relevant treaty provision[15] and of the specific breach alleged; that is, the principal questions are treaty- and fact-specific. Nevertheless, certain general comments can usefully be made with regards to the various different categories of obligations encountered in non-proliferation treaties.

i. Obligations owed to other states parties individually (Article 42(a))

Examples of such obligations do appear in non-proliferation treaties. This is unsurprising, as they are the paradigmatic form of legal obligation in international law. However, in the non-proliferation context,

[13] For an explanation of what 'specially affects' was intended to mean, see ILC commentary to Art. 42, p. 119: 'For a State to be considered injured, it must be affected by the breach in a way which distinguishes it from the generality of other States to which the obligation is owed.' The term itself was taken from Art. 60(2)(b) VCLT.

[14] See International Law Commission, Third Report on the Law of Treaties, by Mr. G. G. Fitzmaurice, Special Rapporteur, UN doc. A/CN.4.107, 15 March 1957, p. 57.

[15] Through the prism of the principles set out in Arts. 31 and 32 VCLT.

such obligations are generally of secondary importance in the scheme of the treaties in which they appear.

In particular, such obligations take the form of duties to notify and consult before undertaking particular forms of activities likely to affect neighbouring states parties. An example of such an obligation is found in the Treaty on the Southeast Asia Nuclear-Weapon-Free Zone (the Bangkok Treaty).[16] Article 4 of the treaty provides that none of its provisions should be taken to prejudice states parties' right to use nuclear energy for peaceful purposes. However, prior to embarking on any peaceful nuclear energy programmes, a state party must undertake 'rigorous nuclear safety assessment conforming to guidelines and standards recommended by the IAEA for the protection of health and minimization of danger to life and property'. Moreover, the party agrees:

> upon request, to make available *to another State Party* the assessment except information relating to personal data, information protected by intellectual property rights or by industrial or commercial confidentiality, and information relating to national security.[17]

Given that the requirement that the obligation to provide the assessment only arises following a request by another party, it is difficult to see that the obligation is owed to anybody other than the requesting state.[18] This conclusion is strengthened when one considers the likely purpose of the provision: to ensure that states parties neighbouring those contemplating peaceful nuclear energy programmes can obtain the information necessary to determine whether such developments will have a deleterious impact on their nationals' life, health and property.[19] The obligation can consequently be seen as supplementing the verification mechanisms established under the treaty.

[16] Treaty on the Southeast Asia Nuclear-Weapon-Free Zone, 35 *ILM* 356 (1995) (hereinafter Bangkok Treaty).

[17] *Ibid.*, Art. 4(2)(c) (emphasis added).

[18] This type of 'information duty' is specifically mentioned as an example of a form of bilateral relationship in multilateral treaties in K. Sachariew, 'State Responsibility for Multilateral Treaty Violations: Identifying the "Injured State" and its Legal Status', *Netherlands International Law Review*, 35 (1988), 273, 278.

[19] Art. 4(2)(e) also provides that states parties undertake to dispose of 'radioactive wastes and other radioactive material in accordance with IAEA standards and procedures . . . on land within the territory of another State which has consented to such disposal'. This would also seem to be an obligation owed to that state individually, although given that the term used is 'state', not, as elsewhere in the treaty, 'state party', the obligation might even be owed to third parties to the treaty. See Art. 36 VCLT.

Another type of obligation in non-proliferation treaties which might also be considered to be essentially bilateral are those prohibiting attacks on other parties. Certainly, it would seem natural (and, indeed, correct, so far as it goes) to see the aggressor as having breached a duty owed to its victim. As will be shown in the next section, however, these are better seen as obligations of an *inter omnes partes* nature, as the other states parties to such treaties also have a legal interest in their observance.

ii. Obligations owed to all states parties, breach of which specifically affects one such state (Article 42(b)(i))

Protocols to the various regional nuclear-free-weapon zone treaties designed for ratification by the nuclear-weapon states parties to the Treaty on the Non-Proliferation of Nuclear Weapons contain what are known as 'negative security assurances', obliging parties not to use or threaten to use nuclear weapons against the contracting parties to those treaties.[20] For example, Article 3 of Additional Protocol II to the Treaty of Tlatelolco[21] provides that

> The Governments represented by the undersigned Plenipotentiaries ... undertake not to use or threaten to use nuclear weapons against the Contracting Parties to the Treaty for the Prohibition of Nuclear Weapons in Latin America.

Similarly, Article 2 of the Protocol to the Bangkok Treaty states that

> Each State Party undertakes not to use or threaten to use nuclear weapons against any State Party to the Treaty. It further undertakes not to use or threaten to use nuclear weapons within the Southeast Asia Nuclear-Weapon-Free Zone.

Leaving aside questions of the conformity of any such use or threat of use of nuclear weapons with the United Nations Charter[22] or, indeed, with other

[20] See GA res. 3472 (XXX)B: Comprehensive study of the question of nuclear-weapon-free zones in all its aspects, para. 2 (11 December 1975). For further details, see M. Roscini, 'Negative Security Assurances in the Protocols Additional to the Treaties Establishing Nuclear Weapon Free Zones', in H. Gartner (ed.), *Obama and the Bomb: The Vision of a World Free of Nuclear Weapons* (Frankfurt: Peter Lang, 2011).

[21] Treaty for the Prohibition of Nuclear Weapons in Latin America and the Caribbean, 634 UNTS 281 (1967) (hereinafter Treaty of Tlatelolco).

[22] Art. 2(4), Charter of the United Nations, 1 UNTS XVI (1945).

international law standards,[23] it might be thought that such obligations are obligations *erga omnes partes*, that is that they are owed to all parties to the relevant treaty. An argument can be made for this on the basis of the provisions' wording – note the use of the term 'the Contracting Parties' in the first provision and the reference to the relevant nuclear-weapon-free zone in the second[24] – and also from the object and purpose of the agreements.[25] Certainly, the general prohibition on the use or threat of force is viewed in such a manner;[26] maintaining international peace and security and ensuring that the rules on the non-use of force are not eroded are viewed as interests which all states (should) share. One might also consider that breach of such a provision would most immediately affect the state targeted in such an attack,[27] but given the indiscriminate effects of nuclear weapons, other states might suffer possibly very substantial, albeit lesser, material impacts.[28]

However, in contradistinction with Article 42(b)(ii), breach of such an obligation would not immediately seem radically to change the position of all other states to whom the obligation is owed with respect to the further performance of the obligation.[29] For these reasons, therefore, breach of such obligations are best classified as falling within Article 42(b)(i).

[23] See *Legality of the Threat or Use of Nuclear Weapons*, Advisory Opinion, ICJ Reports 1996 226, 266, where the International Court of Justice stated that the threat or use of nuclear weapons must be consistent with 'the requirements of the international law applicable in armed conflict, particularly those of the principles and rules of international humanitarian law'.

[24] Although it might also be noted that the 'Southeast Asia Nuclear-Weapon-Free Zone' as defined in Art. 1(a) of the Bangkok Treaty goes beyond the parties' territories to include their continental shelves and exclusive economic zones.

[25] Which would appear to be to further the purpose of the treaties to which they are protocols, which is to assure the total absence of nuclear weapons in territories covered by them and thereby promote general disarmament.

[26] See J. Crawford, Third Report on State Responsibility, pp. 48–49: 'The obligation not to use force against the territorial integrity or political independence of other State is an obligation *erga omnes*, but the particular victim is the State against which the armed force is used.'

[27] Which, given the wording of the Protocol to the Bangkok Treaty, need not necessarily be a party to that treaty.

[28] Indeed, one would imagine them to be potentially extremely serious, whether arising out of radiation, refugee flows, financial impacts or material damage to the possessions, as well as the death and injury, of other such states' nationals within the targeted state's territory.

[29] In the first place, it would not affect their obligations under the underlying treaty. Moreover, the states parties to both treaties owe no obligations under either of them to the parties to their protocols, and they are not themselves parties to them.

iii. Obligations owed to all states parties, breach of which radically changes the position of all other states to which the obligation is owed with respect to the further performance of the obligation (Article 42(b)(ii))

The wording of Article 42(b)(ii)) of the ILC Articles derives from and largely mirrors Article 60(2)(c) of the Vienna Convention on the Law of Treaties.[30] However, the latter provision applies more narrowly. It refers only to situations when a 'material breach' 'radically changes the position of every party with respect to the further performance of its obligations under the treaty'. This difference is justified on the basis that Article 60(2)(c) of the Vienna Convention permits a party acting in response to such a breach to suspend the operation of the treaty in part or in whole, whereas the ILC Articles deal with a distinct (and, indeed, wider) question: that of the wrongdoing state's secondary obligations consequence upon a breach of its primary obligations, and the extent of other states' rights to take measures to induce the wrongdoing state to comply with its obligations.

In each case, however, the reference is to what are referred to as integral obligations.[31] Examination of the *travaux préparatoires* of the ILC Articles show clearly that non-proliferation agreements were considered by the drafters squarely to fall within the category of treaties containing such obligations. Crawford in his third report on state responsibility referred to disarmament treaties (in particular, regional nuclear-free-zone treaties and test-ban treaties) as establishing legal regimes, in the maintenance of which all the states parties have a common legal interest:

> In such cases, though it is conceivable that one or other states might be specially affected by a breach, this is unlikely, and is anyway without prejudice to the general interest in the subject matter which is shared by all the states parties collectively.[32]

In his fourth report Crawford instanced obligations in non-proliferation and disarmament treaties as 'integral' insofar as breach of such obligations threatens the treaty structure as a whole.[33] Finally, the ILC commentary on the draft articles, discussing draft Article 42(b)(ii), states that

[30] See n. 1, above. [31] See text accompanying n. 14, above.

[32] Crawford, Third Report on State Responsibility, p. 47.

[33] International Law Commission, Fourth Report on State Responsibility by Mr. James Crawford, Special Rapporteur, UN doc. A/CN.4/517, 2 April 2001, p. 15.

> Examples of Treaties [falling within the scope of the provision] include a disarmament treaty, a nuclear free-zone treaty, or any other treaty where each parties' [*sic*] performance is effectively conditioned on and requires the performance of each of the others.[34]

In this respect, the Treaty on the Non-Proliferation of Nuclear Weapons (NPT)[35] is exemplary. The NPT embodies a grand bargain.[36] On one side, the non-nuclear-weapon states agreed to renounce the acquisition of nuclear weapons but had their 'inalienable right' to acquire and use nuclear technology for peaceful purposes confirmed, albeit subject to international supervision.[37] On the other, the nuclear-weapon states (China, France, Russia, the UK and the USA) retained their nuclear arsenals but were required to pursue negotiations 'in good faith' towards general nuclear disarmament.[38] Indeed, the failure of the nuclear-weapon states to pursue such a goal has proved to be a major source of tensions within the NPT regime.[39] However, it can immediately be seen, as is made express in the Treaty's preamble, that one of the premises on which the NPT is based is that 'the proliferation of nuclear weapons would seriously enhance the danger of nuclear war'.[40] In consequence, the bedrock provisions of the NPT can be seen as Articles I and II, in which, on the one hand, the nuclear-weapon states parties to the treaty agree not to transfer nuclear weapons or assist in their manufacture or acquisition; and, on the other, the non-nuclear-weapon states parties agree not to receive the transfer of nuclear weapons or to acquire or manufacture such devices. These provisions must be seen as integral, as any state party's failure to comply with them serves to undermine the treaty regime.

Moreover, Article III on safeguards can also be seen as having the same status. The provision requires non-nuclear-weapon states parties to accept IAEA safeguards to verify their obligations arising under the treaty and, in particular, to prevent the 'diversion of nuclear energy from

[34] ILC Commentary to Art. 42, p. 119.

[35] Treaty on the Non-Proliferation of Nuclear Weapons, 729 UNTS 161 (1968).

[36] See D. H. Joyner, *Interpreting the Nuclear Non-Proliferation Treaty* (Oxford University Press, 2011).

[37] Treaty on the Non-Proliferation of Nuclear Weapons, Arts. I–IV. [38] *Ibid.*, Art. VI.

[39] This was particularly an issue at the 1995 Review and Extension Conference, convened to decide whether the NPT should continue in force indefinitely or simply be extended for an additional fixed period or periods. In the event, indefinite extension was agreed as part of a 'package deal'. See J. Dahapale, *Multilateral Diplomacy and the NPT: An Insider's Account* (New York: United Nations, 2005), pp. 41–59.

[40] Treaty on the Non-Proliferation of Nuclear Weapons, Preamble.

peaceful uses to nuclear weapons or other nuclear explosive devices'. Absent Article III (given, in particular, Article IV of the Treaty's recognition of parties' 'inalienable right' to develop nuclear energy for peaceful purposes), the extent of a state's compliance with their Article I and II obligations could not be assumed, leading to a loss of trust in and possible erosion of the treaty regime. Indeed, one might go further: as Article III of the NPT exists in order to prevent states parties being able to breach Articles I and II of the treaty, ultimately the provisions all serve the same purpose and should, therefore, be seen as partaking in the same quality of integral provisions.

Similar provisions can be seen in other non-proliferation treaties. Article I of the Sea-Bed Treaty[41] commits states parties not to place weapons of mass destruction on the seabed. To that end, Article III(1) provides that: 'each State Party to the Treaty shall have the right to verify through observations the activities of other State Parties to the Treaty.' That each (i.e., every) state party has such a right would seem to indicate that Article I gives rise to an integral obligation as it shows that each party has a legal interest in its observance by all the other parties. However, the two provisions also show the close linkage between non-proliferation obligations and obligations regarding verification. Although it might be argued that the Sea-Bed Treaty should be seen as exceptional, because of its small number of parties and because its prohibitions relate to the use of areas outside of states' territory (and, consequently, potentially accessible to all states),[42] other non-proliferation treaties also permit any party to require verification of other parties' commitments or complain about their breach.

In the Biological Weapons Convention,[43] Article I contains an absolute prohibition on the development, production, stockpiling, acquisition or retention of biological agents, toxins, weapons, equipment and means of delivery. Article VI then provides that 'Any State Party to this Convention which finds that any other State Party is acting in breach of

[41] Treaty on the Prohibition of the Emplacement of Nuclear Weapons and other Weapons of Mass Destruction on the Sea-Bed and the Ocean Floor and in the Subsoil Thereof, 955 UNTS 115 (1971) (hereinafter Sea-Bed Treaty).

[42] Art. II of the Sea-Bed Treaty includes in the areas where the parties undertake not to place nuclear or other weapons of mass destruction on the seabed and subsoil beyond states' territorial seas, parts of which are outside of any state's jurisdiction.

[43] Convention on the Prohibition of the Development, Production, and Stockpiling of Bacteriological (Biological) and Toxin Weapons and on their Destruction, 1015 UNTS 163 (1972).

obligations deriving from the provisions of the Convention may lodge a complaint with the Security Council of the United Nations.' Again, the implication seems to be that each party has a legal interest in the compliance of all other parties with their obligations under the Convention.

As regards the regional nuclear-weapon-free-zone treaties, the Treaty of Tlatelolco simply allows any signatory state to request the convocation of a meeting of all the signatories 'to consider questions which may affect the very essence' of the treaty.[44] However, the Treaty of Rarotonga permits any party which considers that another party is in breach of its obligations under the treaty to draw the issue to the attention of the party complained of and, if the matter is not resolved, to bring a complaint to the Director of the South Pacific Bureau for Economic-Co-operation.[45] Upon receipt of a complaint, the Director is obliged to convene the Consultative Committee established under the treaty[46] 'as quickly as possible to consider it'.[47] Similarly, the Bangkok Treaty gives each state party the right to request any other state party to provide clarification 'concerning any situation which may be considered ambiguous or which may give rise to doubts about the compliance of that State Party' with the treaty.[48] In such circumstances, states parties also have the right to request the Executive Committee of the Commission for the Southeast Asia Nuclear-Weapon-Free Zone to send a fact-finding mission to the other party.[49] Such requests may only be refused by the Executive Committee if they are 'frivolous, abusive or clearly beyond the scope of [the] Treaty'.[50] The Pelindaba Treaty also provides that a state party, having drawn the subject-matter of a complaint that another party is in breach of its obligations under the treaty to the attention of the party complained about, and having failed to receive satisfaction, has the right to take its complaint to the African Commission on Nuclear Energy.[51] The Semipalatinsk Treaty, however, contains no such similar provisions.[52]

[44] Treaty of Tlatelolco, Art. 6.

[45] Art. 2, Annex 4, South Pacific Nuclear-Free-Zone Treaty, 24 *ILM* 1140 (1985) (hereinafter Treaty of Rarotonga). Art. 1 of the Annex requires that the complainant consults with the other party first.

[46] *Ibid.*, Annex 3. [47] *Ibid.*, Art. 2, Annex 4. [48] Bangkok Treaty, Art. 12(1).

[49] *Ibid.*, Art. 13. [50] *Ibid.*, Art. 2(a), Annex.

[51] African Nuclear-Weapon-Free-Zone Treaty, 35 *ILM* 698 (1996) (hereinafter Pelindaba Treaty).

[52] Treaty on a Nuclear-Free Zone in Central Asia, opened for signature 8 September 2006 (hereinafter Semipalatinsk Treaty). The Semipalantinsk Treaty is particularly weak in compliance mechanisms. See M. Roscini, 'Something Old, Something New: The 2006

It might be argued that these provisions simply indicate that a state party to one of these treaties is given the right to make a complaint against another state party when the latter has acted (or is considered to have acted) in breach of an obligation owed to the former. This, however, is not how the provisions are worded. When they refer to obligations, they refer simply to obligations 'under' the relevant treaty (the Rarotonga and Pelindaba Treaties) or they talk of situations which are ambiguous or which give rise to doubts about parties' compliance with the treaty (the Bangkok Treaty) or (a weak formula, which rather begs the question) questions affecting the essence of the treaty (the Treaty of Tlatelolco). There is nothing in any of these treaties which suggests a requirement of standing before a party can raise an issue or make a compliant.

A perhaps more substantial objection would be that these provisions say nothing about state responsibility at all. They simply establish compliance mechanisms for the purposes of the treaties and say nothing about issues of state responsibility for breach of the treaties' provisions. This argument can also be countered, at least in part, by referring to the treaty texts. Both the Bangkok and Pelindaba Treaties include provisions for the settlement of disputes arising from, or out of, the interpretation of the treaty,[53] but in each case there is no mention about disputes concerning its 'application', suggesting perhaps that such disputes are covered by other provisions, that is, those already mentioned. The Treaty of Tlatelolco does refer to the settlement of disputes 'concerning the interpretation or application of this Treaty'.[54] However, the Tlatelolco Treaty was the first regional nuclear-free-weapon-zone treaty to be adopted, and its compliance procedures (as already shown) are weak, so that the argument that the existence of a specific dispute settlement provision covering the interpretation *and* application of the Treaty shows that its compliance provisions are unconcerned with issues of state responsibility cannot be said to be particularly strong. It seems better to view the two procedures as complimentary.[55]

Semipalatinsk Treaty on a Nuclear Free Zone in Central Asia', *Chinese Journal of International Law*, 7 (2008), 593.

53 Bangkok Treaty, Art. 21 (Settlement of Disputes) and Pelindaba Treaty, Art. 15 (Interpretation of the Treaty).

54 Treaty of Tlatelolco, Art. 24 (Settlement of Disputes).

55 There are no provisions on the settlement of disputes in the Rarotonga and Semipalantinsk Treaties.

More recent treaties have even more sophisticated procedures. The Chemical Weapons Convention[56] gives all states parties the right to request the Executive Committee of the Organization for the Prohibition of Chemical Weapons to:

> Obtain clarification from another State Party on any situation which may be considered ambiguous or which gives rise to a concern about the possible non-compliance of another State Party with this Convention.[57]

In addition, in particular when requests for clarifications have proved unavailing,[58] states parties have the right to request:

> An on-site challenge inspection of any facility or location in the territory or in any place under the jurisdiction or control of any other State Party for the sole purpose of clarifying or resolving any questions concerning possible non-compliance with the provisions of this Convention.[59]

The Executive Committee may only refuse an inspection request if it considers it to be 'frivolous, abusive or clearly beyond the scope' of the Chemical Weapons Convention.[60] Recommendations based on the results of a challenge inspection can be made by the Executive Committee to the OPCW Conference,[61] which 'shall take the necessary measures . . . to ensure compliance with this Convention and *to redress and remedy* any situation which contravenes the provisions of this Convention'.[62] These latter provisions make clear that questions of state responsibility for breach of the Convention are involved.

The Comprehensive Nuclear-Test-Ban Treaty[63] (not yet in force[64]) operates in a similar manner. The treaty provides that 'All States Parties . . . shall enjoy the equal right of verification and assume the equal obligation to accept verification.'[65] States parties may request clarification of 'any matter which causes concern about possible non-compliance with the basic obligations of this treaty';[66] request the Director-General of the Comprehensive Nuclear-Test-Ban Organization

[56] Convention on the Prohibition of the Development, Production, Stockpiling and Use of Chemical Weapons and on their Destruction, 32 *ILM* 800 (1993) (hereinafter CWC).

[57] *Ibid.*, Art. IX (4). [58] *Ibid.* See Art. IX (7), which links the two procedures.

[59] *Ibid.*, Art. IX (8). [60] *Ibid.*, Art. IX (17). [61] *Ibid.*, Art. IX (23) and (25).

[62] *Ibid.*, Art. XII (1) (emphasis added).

[63] Comprehensive Nuclear-Test-Ban Treaty, 35 *ILM* 1439 (1996).

[64] Although some 155 states have ratified the Comprehensive Nuclear-Test-Ban Treaty, only thirty-five of the forty-four Annex 2 States, whose ratification is necessary in order for the Treaty to come into force, have done so.

[65] Comprehensive Nuclear-Test-Ban Treaty, Art. IV(1). [66] *Ibid.*, Art. IV (29).

(CTBTO) to assist in clarifying any such matter;[67] request the CTBTO Executive Council to obtain clarification on any such matter;[68] and, if it considers the clarifications obtained in the last case unsatisfactory, request a meeting of the Council to consider the matter and make recommendations to the CTBTO Conference.[69] States parties also have the right to request an on-site inspection:[70]

> To clarify whether a nuclear weapon test explosion or any other nuclear explosion has been carried out in violation of Article I [*imposing a comprehensive nuclear test ban*] and, to the extent possible, to gather any facts which might assist in identifying any possible perpetrator.[71]

An inspection having been undertaken, the Executive Council can make recommendations to CTBTO Conference. In responding to Council recommendations arising out of requests both for clarifications and on-site inspections, the Conference 'shall take the necessary measures . . . to ensure compliance with this Treaty and to redress and remedy any situation which contravenes the provisions of this Treaty'.[72] Again, it seems clear that the Conference is intended to take measures concerning states parties' international responsibility.

What then can be concluded from this survey? The evidence adduced is necessarily indirect. However, it does seem to show that every party to the treaties examined is viewed as having a legal interest in the performance by every other party of their treaty obligations, or, at least (as the Comprehensive Nuclear-Test-Ban Treaty puts it), of their 'basic obligations'. It might be argued that the fact that a party has a legal interest in other parties' performance of a treaty obligation does not, of itself, mean that the obligation is integral in character; it is necessary to show that breach of the obligation can change radically the position of all other states to which the obligation is owed with respect to the further performance of the obligation. But the question can be reversed to ask why all parties to such treaties are considered to have a legal interest in the performance of their 'basic obligations' vis-à-vis all other parties. The answer must be that it is because the effectiveness of such obligations is

[67] *Ibid.*, Art. IV (31). [68] *Ibid.*, Art. IV (32). [69] *Ibid.*, Art. IV (33).

[70] *Ibid.*, Art. IV (34).

[71] It remains at the discretion of the Executive Council, however, whether an on-site inspection is undertaken. *Ibid.*, Art. IV(46). See also Art. IV(67), which indicates that the Executive Council can refuse to approve an on-site inspection on the basis that the request was 'frivolous or abusive' but does not seem to limit the reasons for refusal to those two grounds alone.

[72] *Ibid.*, Art. V(1).

founded upon their observance by all parties to the treaty, that is, because they are integral obligations.

Indeed, it does not seem they can be categorized otherwise. It might be perhaps possible to class them as *erga omnes partes* obligations, at least in some cases, but a failure to verify one's commitments does not seem easily to fit into that category. All parties are affected equally and none of them is specifically affected, still less suffers any material damage. The compliance provisions of non-proliferation treaties must, in consequence, be seen to argue strongly for the classification of at least those treaties' 'basic obligations' (which would seem to include those relating to disarmament, non-proliferation and verification) as obligations of such a character that their breach entitles all states parties to invoke the responsibility of the wrongdoing party.

II. Legal consequences of breaches of provisions of non-proliferation treaties

As already mentioned, the harm arising out of many breaches of non-proliferation treaties is that they serve to undermine the treaty regime. A party's breach of its verification obligations does not necessarily mean that it is also in breach of non-proliferation or disarmament obligations, but it can give rise to suspicions that it is, and such suspicions alone can result in other parties failing to comply with their obligations under the treaty. Article 60(2)(c) of the Vienna Convention on the Law of Treaties permits the suspension of the operation of a treaty, in part or in whole, by any party other than the defaulting state 'if the treaty is of such a character that a material breach of its provisions by one party radically changes the position of every party with respect to the further performance of its obligations under the treaty'. However, this is often the least desirable result. In most cases what is wanted is to bring the defaulting state (i.e., in the terminology of the law of state responsibility, the wrongdoing state) back into compliance with its obligations, so that the conditions threatening the integrity of the treaty regime are removed.

Such concerns are addressed in the ILC Articles. Article 29 of the ILC Articles on State Responsibility provides that:

> The legal consequences of an internationally wrongful act under this Part [Part Two: Content of the International Responsibility of a State] does not affect the continued duty of the responsible State to perform the obligation breached.

Similarly, Article 30 of the ILC Articles states that:

> The State responsible for the internationally wrongful act is under an obligation:
>
> (a) To cease that act, if it is continuing;
> (b) To offer appropriate assurances and guarantees of non-repetition, if circumstances so require.

Article 30(a) would simply appear to be the obverse of Article 29 in relation to continuing acts, as it seems obvious that a state cannot perform an obligation if at the same time it continues to breach it. And breaches of many obligations under non-proliferation agreements, in particular those concerning the verification of commitments and the non-possession of prohibited weapons, would appear to be continuing acts. Finally, Article 31 of the ILC Articles provides that:

> 1. The responsible state is under an obligation to make full reparation for the injury caused by the internationally wrongful act.
> 2. Injury includes any damage, whether material or moral, caused by the internationally wrongful act of a state.

Article 33 of the ILC Articles makes it clear that the aforementioned obligations may be owed not only to another (single) state but to several states, that is, that they apply in the case of breaches of integral obligations.

It might be thought, however, that this latter obligation is, in the non-proliferation context, the least significant. The obligation to make reparation has been said to be 'the indispensible complement of a failure to apply a convention';[73] however, in making the remark the Permanent Court of International Justice was speaking extremely generally. In a later phase of the same proceedings, it specified that 'reparation must, so far as possible, wipe out the consequences of the illegal act and re-establish the situation which would, in all probability, have existed it that act had not been committed'.[74] The obligation to make reparation only applies in cases of injury. And injury 'includes' (and, indeed, would appear to be synonymous with) damage, whether material or moral, caused by the internationally wrongful act, which definition, according to the ILC Commentary:

> is intended both as inclusive, covering both material and moral damage broadly understood, and as limitative, excluding merely abstract

[73] *Factory at Chorzów, Jurisdiction* (1927) PCIJ Series A, No. 9, p. 21.
[74] *Factory at Chorzów, Merits* (1928) PCIJ Series A, No. 17, p. 47.

> concerns or general interests of a state which is individually unaffected by the breach. 'Material' damage here refers to damage to property or other interests of the state and its nationals which are assessable in financial terms. 'Moral' damage includes such things are individual pain and suffering, loss of loved ones or personal affront associated with an intrusion on one's home or private life.[75]

The concept of 'injury' would appear to be a wide one, but although it does not seem apt to describe states' concerns arising out of a breach of a non-proliferation agreement as 'abstract', the breach itself would not necessarily cause either material or moral damage. As always, whether reparation is warranted depends on the nature of the breach. However, whereas breach of a negative security assurance not to use nuclear weapons would plainly cause injury, breach of an undertaking to permit verification of a state's disarmament or non-proliferation obligations would not seem to. In such situations, cessation of the internationally wrongful act (accompanied, if necessary, by appropriate assurances and guarantees) would suffice to restore the *status quo ante*.

III. The relevance of the law of state responsibility in the non-proliferation context

The foregoing discussion has indicated that the law of state responsibility does accommodate non-proliferation agreements, at least in theory. A problem, however, immediately arises insofar as states parties to non-proliferation agreements have not, in practice, sought to enforce other parties' treaty obligations through the invocation of state responsibility and the bringing of international claims. Instead, non-proliferation agreements have included more and more institutionalized compliance control procedures.[76]

The term 'self-contained regime' came into prominence as a result of its use by the International Court of Justice in its judgment in the *United States Diplomatic and Consular Staff in Tehran* Case,[77] where the Court stated that:

75 ILC commentary to Art. 31, pp. 91–92.

76 For analysis of this development, see T. Marauhn, 'Dispute Resolution, Compliance Control and Enforcement of International Arms Control Law', in G. Ulfsein (ed.), *Making Treaties Work: Human Rights, Environment and Arms Control* (Cambridge University Press, 2007).

77 The term 'self-contained', referring to the provisions on the Kiel Canal in the Treaty of Versailles, had previously been used by the Permanent Court of International Justice in *The S.S. Wimbledon*, Judgment, PCIJ, Series A, No. 1, pp. 23–24.

> The rules of diplomatic law, in short, constitute a self-contained régime which, on the one hand, lays down the receiving state's obligations regarding the facilities, privileges and immunities to be accorded to diplomatic missions and, on the other, foresees their possible abuse by members of the mission and specifies the means at the disposal of the receiving state to counter any such abuse. These means are, by their nature, entirely efficacious.[78]

Breach of a sending state's obligations in diplomatic law can be countered by means specified in that body of law itself: that is, by the receiving state's withdrawal of its recognition of the offending members of the mission as such. Given that these methods were, in the Court's view, 'entirely efficacious', their existence precluded recourse to other remedies generally permitted by the international law of state responsibility. The Court's opinion on the existence of such regimes was reflected in Article 55 (*lex specialis*) of the ILC Articles, which, *inter alia*, provides that:

> These articles do not apply where and to the extent that . . . the content *or implementation* of the international responsibility of a state are governed by special rules of international law.[79]

The question consequently arises whether the compliance mechanisms found in various non-proliferation agreements provide exclusive remedies; whether they amount to dispute settlement procedures which must be utilized by parties to those treaties in cases of alleged breach; or whether they have no effect on the applicability of the general rules of the law of state responsibility, simply applying alongside them.[80]

On consideration, the latter would appear correct. The ILC commentary to Article 55 provides that:

> For the *lex specialis* principle to apply it is not enough that the same subject matter is dealt with by two provisions; there must be some actual

[78] *United States Diplomatic and Consular Staff in Tehran* (*USA* v. *Iran*), Judgment, ICJ Reports 1980 3, 40.

[79] Emphasis added.

[80] This issue is also relevant as regards the availability of countermeasures as a response to breaches of non-proliferation treaties. Art. 50(2) of the ILC Articles states that 'A State taking countermeasures is not relieved from fulfilling its obligations: (a) Under any dispute settlement procedure applicable between it and the responsible State.' For discussion, see Chapter 7, below: Sahib Singh, 'Non-proliferation law and countermeasures'.

> inconsistency between them, or else a discernable intention that one provision is to exclude the other. Thus the question is essentially one of interpretation.[81]

In the first instance, it might be argued that no actual inconsistency exists, as compliance mechanisms cover different ground from dispute settlement mechanisms. However, it has already been argued that compliance control procedures in non-proliferation agreements often have a dual function, both preventive and curative.[82] Rather, it would be better to say that questions of cure are subsidiary to questions of prevention.[83] In the second instance, however, none of the non-proliferation agreements analysed includes any provision which seeks to exclude states parties from bringing international claims outside of any mechanisms established by the treaty, either explicitly or implicitly (i.e., by providing that specified methods of dispute settlement are to be used exclusively to enforce obligations under the relevant treaty). Indeed, the fact that most such mechanisms provide for settlement by a political body, either by some conference of states parties or by reference of the matter to the United Nations Security Council, might also be thought to argue against any such conclusion.

Subsequent state practice (or, rather, the lack of it) when it comes to seeking to enforce obligations under non-proliferation agreements might be thought to argue the contrary.[84] However, it is difficult to see states' abstention as arising out of any legal scruples. Rather, it would appear to be based on reasons which it is hoped should appear obvious from the discussion above.

The move away from dispute resolution to compliance control is a development that has occurred more widely than just in the non-proliferation context.[85] International claims, even if brought to protect obligations *erga omnes partes*, are by nature unilateral rather than multilateral reactions to treaty breach. Non-proliferation agreements have consequently increasingly sought to provide institutionalized

[81] ILC commentary to Art. 55, p. 140.
[82] See the discussions, above, of the Bangkok and Pelindaba Treaties, the Chemical Weapons Convention and the Comprehensive Nuclear-Test-Ban Treaty.
[83] See Art. XII(I) CWC and Art. V(1) Comprehensive Nuclear-Test-Ban Treaty, considered above.
[84] Relevant, in the context of the interpretation of treaties, by virtue of the rule codified in Art. 31(2)(b) VCLT.
[85] See Ulfstein, *Making Treaties Work*.

mechanisms for the determination of non-compliance and collective responses thereto. Although the law of state responsibility is well adapted to fit the peculiarities of non-proliferation agreements, it does not provide an adequate means either to prevent or to cure their breach. As a consequence, although applicable in theory, in practice it has little relevance.

7

Non-proliferation law and countermeasures

SAHIB SINGH

I. Introduction

> Under the rules of present-day international law, *and unless the contrary results from special obligations arising from particular treaties, notably from mechanisms created within the framework of international organisations*, each state establishes for itself its legal situation vis-à-vis other States. If a situation arises which, in one State's view, results in the violation of an international obligation by another State, the first State is entitled … to affirm its rights through 'countermeasures'.[1]

Since this 1978 dictum by the arbitral tribunal in the *Case Concerning the Air Services Agreement*, there has been a concerted focus on the relationship between special treaty regimes and the taking of countermeasures as provided by customary international law. This chapter focuses on a particular aspect of this general enquiry: namely the extent to which non-proliferation law, and the special obligations and institutional mechanisms created by the governing treaties, enables, limits or otherwise modifies the right to resort to countermeasures under general international law.[2] This examination permits a determination

1 *Case Concerning the Air Services Agreement of 27 March 1946 between the United States of America and France*, 9 December 1978, XVII RIAA, 443, para. 81.

2 The general enquiry, which this chapter applies specifically to non-proliferation law, was stated by the ILC and Special Rapporteur Arangio-Ruiz in 1992, Fourth Report on State Responsibility, by Mr. Gaetano Arangio-Ruiz, Special Rapporteur, A/CN.4/444 and Adds. 1–3, *ILC Yearbook* (1992), vol. 2(1), p. 35, para. 97 (hereinafter Arangio-Ruiz, Fourth Report); J. Crawford, *The International Law Commission's Articles on State Responsibility: Introduction, Text and Commentaries* (Cambridge University Press, 2002), p. 283 (hereinafter Crawford, *ILC Commentaries*).

of the extent to which non-proliferation law is a special regime[3] (as distinct from the notion of self-contained regimes[4]).

The need for the present enquiry derives from both a scholastic lacuna and its relevance for contemporary non-proliferation practice. The former is rooted in the extensive institutional mechanisms contained in most major non-proliferation treaties. Such mechanisms enable verification and supervision of compliance, determinations of non-compliance and collective reactions to non-compliance. Is this what the *Air Services Agreement* arbitration was referring to when the tribunal carved out 'mechanisms created within the framework of international organisations' from the capability to resort unimpeded to the general international law right of countermeasures?[5] Even presuming that one could answer this question in the affirmative, doctrinal arguments have been made indicating the insufficiency of such institutional mechanisms in dealing with cases of non-compliance. This, in turn, renders resort to unilateral measures 'more likely'.[6]

The second rationale for this chapter, that of practical relevance, is rooted in state practice indicating non-compliance with non-proliferation obligations, the (mal-)functioning of relevant treaty-specific institutional mechanisms and resort by actors to unilateral measures. A recent example is Iran's arguable continuing non-compliance with its Safeguards Agreement and obligations contained in subsidiary agreements,[7] as related to the Nuclear Non-Proliferation

[3] The term 'special regime' has been intertwined with the term 'subsystems' by Special Rapporteur Riphagen. See Third Report on Content, Degrees and Forms of International Responsibility (Part 2 of the Draft Articles), by Mr. Willem Riphagen, Special Rapporteur, A/CN.4/354 and Corr. 1 and Adds. 1–2, *ILC Yearbook* (1982), vol. 2(1), p. 28, para. 38 and Fourth Report on Content, Degrees and Forms of International Responsibility (Part 2 of the Draft Articles), by Mr. Willem Riphagen, Special Rapporteur, A/CN.4/344 and Add. 1 and Add. 1/Corr. 1, *ILC Yearbook* (1983), vol. 2(1), p. 23, para. 127. See also the distinction made by Joyner and Roscini in the Introduction to this book (p. 4).

[4] See, B. Simma, 'Self-Contained Regimes', *Netherlands Yearbook of International Law*, 16 (1985), 117; B. Simma and D. Pulkowski, 'Of Planets and the Universe: Self-Contained Regimes in International Law', *European Journal of International Law*, 17 (2006), 483; 'Fragmentation of International Law: Difficulties Arising from the Diversification and Expansion of International Law', Report of the Study Group of the International Law Commission, Finalized by Martti Koskenniemi, A/CN.4/L.682, 13 April 2006, 65–101 (hereinafter ILC Report on Fragmentation).

[5] G. den Dekker, *The Law of Arms Control: International Supervision and Enforcement* (The Hague: Martinus Nijhoff, 2001), p. 334.

[6] *Ibid.* 333.

[7] Outlining the case for Iranian non-compliance, see IAEA, *Implementation of the NPT Safeguards Agreement and Relevant Provisions of Security Council Resolutions 1737 (2006),*

Treaty (NPT),[8] as well as the subsequent resort to unilateral measures (alongside but independent from obligations imposed by Security Council Resolutions 1737 (2006) and 1929 (2010)), to ensure compliance by the USA,[9] European States[10] and Japan.[11] At this purely pragmatic level, with enforcement clearly being integral to the non-proliferation system and recent practice demonstrating substantive recourse to unilateral self-help measures, the legal regime of countermeasures as specifically applied alongside established institutional mechanisms (such as the IAEA) is in need of delimitation and clarification.

Given this apparent need for clarification, the specific enquiry being undertaken by this chapter will be subject to the following structure. First, the contours of the present enquiry will be defined in a methodological section. This section (section II) will make important distinctions that are integral to reaching a conclusion on the pivotal question posed by this chapter and the book: does the non-proliferation regime *stricto sensu* comprise a special regime within international law? Second, section III will examine *who* may take countermeasures in non-proliferation law, special regard being given to the character of

1747 (2007), 1803 (2008) and 1835 (2008) in the Islamic Republic of Iran: Report of the Director General, IAEA Doc. GOV/2009/8, 19 February 2009, paras. 15–22; IAEA, *Implementation of the NPT Safeguards Agreement and Relevant Provisions of Security Council Resolutions 1737 (2006), 1747 (2007), 1803 (2008) and 1835 (2008) in the Islamic Republic of Iran: Report of the Director General*, IAEA Doc. GOV/2009/35, 5 June 2009. Most recently and damningly, see IAEA, *Implementation of the NPT Safeguards Agreement and Relevant Provisions of Security Council Resolutions in the Islamic Republic of Iran*, IAEA Doc. GOV/2011/65, 8 November 2011 (hereinafter IAEA, Iran Report).

8 Treaty on the Non-Proliferation of Nuclear Weapons, 729 UNTS 161 (hereinafter NPT).

9 See, e.g., Executive Order 12959, 9 May 1995, 60 Fed. Reg. 24757. See also subsequent notices which annually renew the ban on investment in Iran and imports from the country, which are effected pursuant to the International Emergency Powers Act, 50 USC 1701–1706, and the National Emergencies Act, 50 USC 1622(d). An example of such a notice is Notice of 11 March 2009, 74 Fed. Reg. 10999.

10 See, e.g., Freezing of Bank Assets: BBC News, 'EU Imposes New Sanctions on Iran', 23 June 2008, http://news.bbc.co.uk/1/hi/world/middle_east/7469283.stm and, despite Iran arguing their illegality, BBC News, 'EU Expands Iran Nuclear Sanctions', 8 August 2008, http://news.bbc.co.uk/1/hi/world/middle_east/7549879.stm. See, further, the broader freezing of assets of persons and entities not listed by the Security Council: Council Common Position (EC) No. 2007/140/CFSP, 27 February 2007, Preamble, para. 10 and Art. 3, 2007 OJ (L61) 50; Council Regulation 423/2007, Preamble, para. 6 and Art. 7(2), 2007 OJ (L103) 1, 4. For a general discussion of the EU Common Position, see N. J. Calamita, 'Sanctions, Countermeasures, and the Iranian Nuclear Issue', *Vanderbilt Journal of Transnational Law*, 42 (2009), 1407–1408.

11 See, e.g., BBC News, 'Japan Imposes New Iran Sanctions over Nuclear Programme', 3 September 2010, www.bbc.co.uk/news/world-asia-pacific-11173774.

non-proliferation obligations. Third, and finally, the paper will examine the range of rights, obligations and mechanisms that exist across the different rules of non-proliferation law, with a view to whether these limit or otherwise modify the ability to resort to countermeasures under general international law. This section will examine three main sources for such rules, rights, obligations and mechanisms: (a) the main non-proliferation treaties, including the NPT, the Chemical Weapons Convention (CWC)[12] and the Biological Weapons Convention (BWC),[13] among others; (b) those obligations imposed by relevant United Nations Security Council Resolutions (UNSC Res.) and the relevant consequences thereof; and (c) those primary rules governing non-proliferation, exceptions to these rules and the secondary rules implementing these within the World Trade Organization (WTO). Having examined *when* and *how* recourse is made to the general law of countermeasures, section IV will further examine the limitations and expansions of *what* countermeasures are permissible/impermissible in non-proliferation law.

The chapter will conclude, after the above review of non-proliferation provisions and the ambiguity of the present enquiry, that non-proliferation law cannot be considered a special regime with regard to countermeasures within the meaning intended by Joyner and Roscini.

II. Clarifications and limitations to the present enquiry

Essential to doctrinal enquiry is the need to define its scope and limitations. This objectivization demarcates a value for the resulting work, independent of the inevitable subjective conclusions reached in the same: managing the expectations of the reader and grounding the author from reaching far-fetched conclusions.

In order to address the question of whether non-proliferation law is a special regime with regards to the taking of countermeasures, two issues require clarification. First, the present book (and consequently this chapter) has chosen to examine non-proliferation law as a special regime. Choosing non-proliferation law as a point of functional differentiation

[12] Convention on the Prohibition of the Development, Production, Stockpiling and Use of Chemical Weapons and their Destruction 32 *ILM* 800 (hereinafter CWC).

[13] Convention on the Prohibition of the Development, Production, and Stockpiling of Bacteriological (Biological) and Toxin Weapons and their Destruction, 1015 UNTS 163 (hereinafter BWC).

has specific consequences and numerous limitations when considering diversities that may arise from different specific treaties (II. i). Second, determining the relationship between the procedures, rules, mechanisms and obligations contained in non-proliferation law and the general international law of countermeasures is necessarily a question of interpretation and bias-based presumptions (II. ii). Drawing attention to these presumptions and the uncertain nature of interpretation in the absence of application will, in turn, highlight the ambiguities of identifying the extent to which non-proliferation law is a special regime. Each issue will be addressed in turn.

i. A question of non-proliferation law as a special regime or treaties as special regimes?

Joyner and Roscini have chosen to examine the extent to which specifically non-proliferation law is a special regime. This deliberate choice begs two questions: (a) what falls within the definition of 'non-proliferation law' for the purposes of the present enquiry, and (b) what are the consequences of choosing to evaluate specifically non-proliferation law, and not say a specific treaty and its related agreements,[14] as a special regime?

For the purposes of the present book, Joyner and Roscini have drawn on an extremely broad definition of non-proliferation law:

> 'non-proliferation law' is defined herein to include all weapons of mass destruction (WMD) related treaties (i.e., chemical, biological, radiological and nuclear (CBRN) weapons-related treaties and missile-related treaties, due to their CBRN delivery relevance). Essentially, this term is intended to include WMD-related arms control treaties (treaties by which states agree to limit or reduce the amount and kinds of weapons they are entitled to possess); WMD-related disarmament treaties (treaties by which states agree to renounce entirely the possession of certain weapons and relinquish entirely existing stockpiles); WMD-related non-proliferation treaties (treaties that aim to prevent the spread of weapons); as well as WMD-related treaties limiting certain specific conduct, such as those banning weapon testing.[15]

[14] e.g., evaluating the non-proliferation of biological weapons through examining specific treaty regimes such as the BWC and the 1925 Geneva Protocol. See Protocol for the Prohibition of the Use in War of Asphyxiating, Poisonous or Other Gases, and of Bacteriological Methods of Warfare, 94 LNTS 65.

[15] Joyner and Roscini, Introduction, p. 11.

Such a wide definition may be challenged.[16] However, the present purpose of drawing attention to it is to highlight the diversity of the types of treaties contained under the umbrella term 'non-proliferation'. This multiplicity of treaties is consequentially reflected in a multitude of rights, procedures and institutional mechanisms that are established by particular treaties. The right to resort to countermeasures in relation to non-proliferation obligations is dependent on relevant treaties and the specific obligations and types of institutional mechanisms created therein. The obvious danger is of extrapolating the special rule that is likely to be treaty specific to being one that could demonstrate the special nature of non-proliferation law. Such an extrapolation is unjustified and of little practical relevance. This problem is one that has been highlighted by the International Law Commission (ILC), in its Report on Fragmentation,[17] and by academics:[18] both have noted that differentiation along the lines of topical areas such as 'international human rights law' and 'international environmental law' 'may perhaps seem altogether too abstract to be of much relevance'.[19] In seeking to demonstrate the special nature of non-proliferation law any identified special rules or mechanisms related to countermeasures *may* be over-extended and taken out of their immediate, treaty-specific context.[20] The present

[16] e.g., Robinson has elsewhere argued that classifying the BWC and CWC under the rubric of non-proliferation, as Joyner and Roscini do, is reductive and inaccurate. J. Robinson, 'Chemical and Biological Weapons', in N. Busch and D. H. Joyner (eds.), *Combating Weapons of Mass Destruction: The Future of International Nonproliferation Policy* (Athens, Ga.: University of Georgia Press, 2009), p. 86. From a policy perspective, Joyner has also been sympathetic to the arguments made by Robinson. See D. H. Joyner, *International Law and Proliferation of Weapons of Mass Destruction* (Oxford University Press, 2009), pp. 83–84. Furthermore, there is the argument that this definition does not do justice to the valid distinction between non-proliferation law and counter-proliferation law. See *ibid.* 246 and 250 (also, generally, Chapter 6, above).

[17] ILC Report on Fragmentation, p. 17, para. 21. For a view on the ILC's approach, see S. Singh, 'The Potential of International Law: Fragmentation and Ethics', *Leiden Journal of International Law*, 24 (2011), 28–29.

[18] See a critique of placing too much emphasis on the speciality of 'international human rights law', in A. Pellet, '"Droits de l'Hommisme" et droit international', *Gilberto Amado Memorial Lecture*, 18 July 2000 (New York: United Nations, 2000).

[19] ILC Report on Fragmentation, p. 70, para. 133.

[20] The arbitrariness of classifying a specific rule on countermeasures as one of 'non-proliferation law' is best highlighted by Arts. 22 and 23 of the Dispute Settlement Understanding (DSU) under the WTO, which permits countermeasures for breach of WTO obligations (see section IV. i. c, below). The necessity to maintain a treaty-specific context has been highlighted by Ago. See Fifth Report on State Responsibility, by Mr. Robert Ago, Special Rapporteur – the Internationally Wrongful Act of the State, Source

author counsels against this. The discovery of any specialized rules modifying, limiting or otherwise impacting on the right to take countermeasures should only be stated to be truly reflective of a particular treaty regime – and must be considered given this context.[21]

ii. The danger of presumptions in examining the specialness of the non-proliferation legal regime

Evaluating whether non-proliferation law contains (or whether, more specifically, particular non-proliferation treaties contain) specialized rules on the taking of countermeasures, or such specific legal rules or institutional mechanisms which may affect the application of the general law of countermeasures, necessarily requires an analysis of the relationship between the former and the latter.[22] In turn, analysis of this relationship is an exercise in treaty interpretation.[23] The only possible exception to this would be when a specific treaty *explicitly excludes*[24] the application of the general law of countermeasures; a scenario entirely inapplicable to non-proliferation law and treaties.[25] Even in cases of explicit *modification of or derogation from* the general law of countermeasures, interpretation retains its necessity to determine the *extent* to which the special rule modifies or derogates from the general rule. For example, does the special rule only affect one specific part of the general law on countermeasures (i.e., invocation based on determination of breach, invocation based only in response to a specific type of breach,[26]

of International Responsibility (continued), A/CN.4/291 and Adds. 1 and 2 and Corr. 1 (1976), vol. 2 (1) 6, para. 14.

21 ILC Report on Fragmentation, 72, para. 135.

22 For clarification and deriving from the analysis in section IV. i. a, below, the specific legal rule in this regard should also include any non-proliferation obligations and not merely non-proliferation treaties. The author has countermeasures under the DSU in mind, where the underlying substantive obligation may govern WMD.

23 Third Report on State Responsibility, by Mr. James Crawford, Special Rapporteur, A/CN.4/507, paras. 343 and 420 (hereinafter Crawford, Third Report); Crawford, 'The ILC's Articles on Responsibility of States for Internally Wrongful Acts: A Retrospect', *American Journal of International Law*, 96 (2002), 880; Crawford, *ILC Commentaries*, p. 291; ILC Report on Fragmentation, p. 73, para. 137.

24 Requirement of express or explicit derogation or exclusion found in Arangio-Ruiz, Fourth Report, para. 125(b); and *Elettronica Sicula S.p.A. (ELSI)*, Judgment, ICJ Reports 1989 42, para. 50.

25 Dekker, *The Law of Arms Control*, p. 347 and Calamita, 'Sanctions, Countermeasures, and the Iranian Nuclear Issue', 1435.

26 e.g., Art. 2019 of the North American Agreement of Free Trade, 33 *ILM* 605 (1993); Art. 6, Annex of the Protocol of Ouro Preto, 17 December 1994 and Art. 23, Protocol of Brasilia for the Solution of Controversies, 17 December 1991.

standing to bring countermeasures etc.) while leaving all other requirements to which it does not speak to general international law?

It is precisely this endemic reliance on interpretation in the context of the fragmentation discourse that allows the introduction of presumptions and bias in analysing whether non-proliferation law is a special regime. Interpretation of particular non-proliferation provisions and determining the *extent* to which they interact with (modify, apply, derogate from, exclude etc.) the general international law of countermeasures depends on one's perspective. Particularists, non-proliferation law specialists, are likely to approach the question with the presumption in favour of limiting the role of general international law. Universalists, general international lawyers, are likely to favour the presumptive and broad application of general international law.[27] Therefore the extent to which this chapter can yield an answer to the question of whether non-proliferation law is a special regime (and to what extent) depends 'on whether we choose a universalistic or a particularistic perspective, whether we first see the universe or the planets ... [since each] tends to yield different results.'[28] This second methodological clarification should therefore highlight the inherent ambiguity that accompanies what this chapter sets out to achieve. However, that is not to diminish its overall resolve and purpose.

Therefore, when digesting the next three sections, the reader should be aware of (a) taking any special rules limiting or modifying the resort to countermeasures out of its treaty-specific context and extrapolating it to a generalization about non-proliferation law, and (b) the inherent ambiguity of presumptuous perspectives that come with determining the *extent of the interrelationship and separateness* of non-proliferation law (the particular) and the general law of countermeasures (the universal). Both these points are essential to understanding non-proliferation

[27] See, e.g., Crawford, Third Report, para. 147. It is arguable that the ILC Articles on State Responsibility are *in toto* premised on a universalist perspective.

[28] Simma and Pulkowski, 'Self-Contained Regimes', 506. The article is the source of this second methodological clarification, although the article's authors apply their analysis to the case of arguable self-contained regimes. The present chapter's analysis is more susceptible to the presumption highlighted above, since it is more dependent on analysing the *extent of interaction* between special law and general law, which is tangential to Simma and Pulkowski's enquiry, which sought to analyse the binary distinction of application/non-application of general international law in relation to specific self-contained regimes. For further analysis of the continuous oscillation between universal and particular perspectives in fragmentation discourse, see Singh, 'The Potential of International Law'.

law as a special regime, the nature of that regime and the limitations of developing such an understanding.

III. Non-proliferation law and standing to take countermeasures

This section will address the question of *who* may take countermeasures. This question is premised on the understanding that most non-proliferation treaties are multilateral, and such treaties largely contain collective obligations. The present author does not consider such treaties to contain bundles of bilateral rights (with the possible exception to those identified in section IV). Furthermore, this question does not seek to prejudge either (a) whether general non-proliferation treaties, which contain no specific rules governing countermeasures, permit resort to countermeasures, or (b) those specific rules regulating countermeasures found in some treaties – both of which will be addressed in section IV, below.[29] This question of standing to take countermeasures can be regulated by specific treaty provisions[30] or, in their absence, residual general rules of standing.[31] Given that non-proliferation law lacks the former (except, arguably, four such provisions highlighted in section IV. i. b–c, below), one is required to examine the manner in which the residual general rules on standing apply, given the identifiable special characteristics of non-proliferation obligations.

Reverted deductive logic determines that a consequence of asking *who* may take countermeasures is the antecedent question far more specific to the current enquiry: *Are collective non-proliferation obligations predominantly possessive of a specific character (self-existent, interdependent etc.), enabling dominant resort to a particular rule within the general rules of standing to take countermeasures*? This question also begs its own, namely what classification of obligations enables the resort to countermeasures, what type of countermeasures are permitted and which particular rules of the general rules on standing to take countermeasures are utilized and what

[29] See section IV. i. b–c. This relates in particular to those special rules such as Arts. 22 and 23 DSU and specific UNSC Resolutions, as well as Art. XII(3) CWC and Art. V(3) CTBT.

[30] e.g., Art. 35 Universal Postal Convention, 364 UNTS 3; Art. 4(4) Multilateral Agreement on Non-Scheduled Air Services in Europe, 310 UNTS 229; Art. 8, State of the International Regime of Maritime Ports, 58 LNTS 301 (each of which provides the right to take certain countermeasures to *all parties* of the treaty).

[31] See C. Tams, *Enforcing Obligations Erga Omnes in International Law* (Cambridge University Press, 2005), p. 36.

are its effects? However, should the italicized question above be answered in the positive, then this would certainly go some way towards identifying a special characteristic of the non-proliferation regime. This should not be equated with the conclusion that it may contribute to determining non-proliferation law as a special regime.

In accordance with the ILC Articles on State Responsibility,[32] a state only has unequivocal standing to take countermeasures where it is an 'injured state'.[33] A state may be so considered if it sustains an injury as envisaged by the three situations delineated in Article 42 ILC Articles. The definitional delineations made by Article 42, and therefore the right to invoke responsibility and resort to countermeasures, are *dependent on the nature of the underlying obligation and its breach*. A fundamental differentiation made by Article 42 is that it gives standing to breaches of both bilateral obligations and specific types of collective obligations (Article 42(a) and (b), respectively). The key point to note is that Article 42 *does not* provide standing to invoke a breach of *all* collective obligations. Rather, there exists a certain subset of collective obligations, whose breach can only be invoked in a limited manner and not through countermeasures – these are contained in Article 48.[34] For the purposes of the present section, we are only concerned with multilateral treaties containing collective obligations, falling within the scope of Article 42(b) ILC Articles. So two key questions arise for the purposes of the present enquiry:

(A) In accordance with general international law, which collective obligations contained in multilateral treaties, upon their breach, permit resort to countermeasures and what are the attributes of such obligations?
(B) Do non-proliferation treaties contain those type of collective obligations whose breach enables a resort to countermeasures (identified in A), and if such obligations are generally predominant in such treaties, is this indicative of a degree of specialness of non-proliferation law?

Each will be considered in turn.

[32] Report of the International Law Commission on the Work of its Fifty-third Session, A/56/10, *ILC Yearbook* (2001), vol. 2(2), p. 1 (hereinafter ILC Articles on State Responsibility).

[33] *Ibid.*, Art. 49. The articles leave open the question of whether a state not defined as such may take countermeasures in relation to certain types of multilateral obligations. See *ibid.*, Arts. 48 and 54.

[34] It should be noted that focus on multilateral treaties containing collective obligations is deliberate. Countermeasures in bilateral treaties are necessarily bilateral; countermeasures in multilateral treaties with collective obligations may enable countermeasures by all states parties to that treaty.

i. Classification of obligations contained in multilateral treaties and their attributes

a. Ancestry of the classification of multilateral obligations: Fitzmaurice and the law of treaties

The classification and sub-categorization of obligations that is undertaken by the ILC Articles on State Responsibility finds its ancestry in the ILC's work on the law of treaties, and in particular the work of Special Rapporteur Sir Gerald Fitzmaurice. Drawing upon previous work regarding the distinction between contract and lawmaking treaties to establish the foundational concept of reciprocity,[35] he considered three classifications of multilateral obligations: (a) reciprocal; (b) self-existent and; (c) interdependent. This classification of obligations had legal consequences upon the termination/suspension of treaties and conflicts between treaties.[36]

Reciprocal obligations were those that provided 'for a mutual interchange of benefits between the parties, with rights and obligations for each involving specific treatment at the hands of and towards each of the others individually'.[37] In contrast, Fitzmaurice's 'self-existent'[38] and

[35] Fitzmaurice drew upon the work of H. Triepel, *Volkerrecht und Landesrecht* (Leipzig: C. L. Herschfeld Verlag, 1899), p. 46.

[36] For a brief analysis, see J. Pauwelyn, 'The Typology of Multilateral Treaty Obligations: Are WTO Obligations Bilateral or Collective in Nature?', *European Journal of International Law*, 14 (2003), 911–915.

[37] Third Report on the Law of Treaties, by Mr. G. G. Fitzmaurice, Special Rapporteur, A/CN.4/115 and Corr. 1, *ILC Yearbook* (1958), vol. 2, p. 27 (hereinafter Fitzmaurice, Third Report). See also for other references, Second Report on the Law of Treaties, by Mr. G. G. Fitzmaurice, Special Rapporteur, A/CN.4/107, *ILC Yearbook* (1957), vol. 2, pp. 30, 54, para. 124, and p. 68, para. 209 (hereinafter Fitzmaurice, Second Report); Fitzmaurice, Third Report, p. 41, para. 78; Fourth Report on the Law of Treaties, by Mr. G. G. Fitzmaurice, Special Rapporteur, A/CN.4/120, *ILC Yearbook* (1959), vol. 2, p. 66, para. 82, and p. 70, para. 102 (hereinafter Fitzmaurice, Fourth Report). For commentary, see K. Sachariew, 'State Responsibility for Multilateral Treaty Violations: Identifying the Injured State and its Legal Status', *Netherlands International Law Review*, 35 (1988), 277–278.

[38] The term 'self-existent obligations' will be used in this chapter. Fitzmaurice, confusingly, addressed such obligations as requiring 'integral performance'. Cf. Fitzmaurice, Second Report, p. 31 (draft Article 19(1)(iv)). He also used to contrast 'integral obligations' with interdependent obligations. Cf. Fitzmaurice, Third Report, pp. 27–28. The term 'self-existent' has therefore been used alongside 'integral' obligations to describe this category. Cf. Pauwelyn, 'The Typology of Multilateral Treaty Obligations', 911 and Sachariew, 'State Responsibility for Multilateral Treaty Violations', 276–277. Other terms have been used to describe this type of obligation. Cf. Tams, *Enforcing Obligations*, p. 55 ('absolute obligations'); B. Simma, 'From Bilateralism to Community Interest in International Law', *Recueil des Cours*, 250 (1994), 217, 364–369 ('objective obligation'); R. Provost, *International*

'interdependent'[39] obligations are devoid of reciprocity since all states concerned with such obligations had the same interest in observing them.[40] In common, these two types of obligations constitute mutually exclusive subsets of collective obligations. Yet, the fundamental difference between them is that interdependent obligations have to be performed between the parties, while self-existent obligations can be applied independently, by each of the parties to the collective obligation.

Fitzmaurice defined self-existent obligations as follows:

> Neither juridically, nor from the practical point of view is the obligation of any party dependent on a corresponding performance by the others. The obligation has an absolute rather than reciprocal character – it is, so to speak, and obligation owed to the world rather than towards particular parties. Such obligations may be called self-existent.[41]

It has been uncontroversially understood that this definition extends to include human rights treaties and broadly 'those of the social or humanitarian kind, the principal object of which is the benefit of individuals' and standard-setting environmental obligations.[42] Almost certainly, treaties and obligations of such a type (e.g., humanitarian, environmental etc.) are not exhaustive of the matter. Indeed, when classifying an obligation as self-existent, one must be guided by the definitional foundations of this subcategory: namely that guiding characteristic that goes to the heart of defining 'self-existent' obligations. This guiding characteristic is undoubtedly that such obligations must be performed independently, irrespective and in total disregard of corresponding performance by other parties. Upon this reasoning, to delimit self-existent obligations on the basis of their functional content (i.e., humanitarian etc.) is unnecessarily narrow. Rather, 'the category comprises *all* obligations that are to be performed

Human Rights and Humanitarian Law (Cambridge University Press, 2002), pp. 133–134 ('internal obligation').

39 The term 'integral' has also been used to describe this category of obligation. As under the ILC Articles on State Responsibility, this article shall avoid this classification. Cf. Crawford, *ILC Commentaries*, p. 257 n. 706; Crawford, Third Report, paras. 91 and 106 (b) n. 195. The term interdependent obligation is also in conformity with Fitzmaurice's classification and terminology. Fitzmaurice, Third Report, p. 27.

40 Tams, *Enforcing Obligations*, pp. 55–56.

41 Fitzmaurice, Third Report, p. 54, para. 126.

42 Fitzmaurice, Fourth Report, p. 46 n. 12. Fitzmaurice also broadly saw as applicable the following: 'obligation of any country to maintain certain standards of working conditions or to prohibit certain practices in consequence of the conventions of the International Labour Organisation; or again under maritime conventions as regards standards of safety at sea.' Fitzmaurice, Second Report, para. 125. Cf. Fitzmaurice, Third Report, p. 44, para. 92.

independently, irrespective of their content. This is notably the case for all obligations requiring States to adopt a uniform conduct. This includes, for example, the duty to harmonise national laws'.[43]

In direct contrast, interdependent obligations are defined by their ability to establish a performance-related co-dependency between all parties to the obligations. The clearest introduction is provided by Fitzmaurice who distinguishes interdependent obligations from self-existent ones by working through the example of disarmament treaties, which is adopted and extrapolated in the final version of the draft articles in 1966:

> The difference between the self-existent type, and the rubric (b) type [interdependent obligations] ... can easily be seen by comparing the cases mentioned in paragraph 125 above with that of a treaty on disarmament. In the latter case, and unless the contrary is expressly provided by the treaty, the obligation of *each party to disarm*, or not to *exceed a certain level of armaments*, or *not to manufacture* or *possess* certain types of weapons, is necessarily dependent on a corresponding performance of the same thing by all the other parties, since it is of the essence of such a treaty that the undertaking of each party is given in return for a similar undertaking by the others.[44]
>
> ...
>
> [There are] [s]pecial types of treaty, e.g., disarmament treaties, where a breach by one party tends to undermine the whole regime of the treaty as between all the parties. In the case of a material breach of such a treaty ... it could not suspend the performance of its own obligations under the treaty vis-à-vis the defaulting State without at the same time violating its obligations to other parties. Yet, unless it does so, it may be unable to protect itself against the threat resulting from the arming of the defaulting State. In these cases, where a material breach of the treaty by one party radically changes the position of every party with respect to the further performance of its obligations.[45]

Interdependent obligations may therefore be defined as those in which 'performance by any party is necessarily dependent on an equal or corresponding performance by all other parties'.[46] Given the inextricable

[43] Approach taken by Tams, *Enforcing Obligations*, pp. 57–58 (emphasis in original). See also for rejection of a narrow categorization, Simma, 'From Bilateralism to Community Interest', 337.

[44] Fitzmaurice, Second Report, p. 54, para. 126 (emphasis added). He also provides other examples (*ibid.*, n. 73).

[45] Report of the International Law Commission to the General Assembly on the second part of its Seventeenth Session and Eighteenth Session, A/6309/Rev. 1, *ILC Yearbook* (1966), vol. 2, p. 255 (hereinafter Draft Articles on the Law of Treaties).

[46] Fitzmaurice, Second Report, p. 31 (Draft Art. 19.1(ii)(b)).

link between equal performance of such an obligation by all parties to it, any one state's non-compliance may put into question the very purpose of the obligation – and where it forms part of a larger regime, the purposive and effective functioning of that system.[47] The innate nature of interdependent obligations is that they are 'dominated by a sort of global reciprocity'[48] and must be confined to those obligations 'scrupulous performance of which by all states bound by them constitutes a condition *sine qua non* for the functioning of the system they set up'.[49]

The distinction between interdependent and self-existent obligations is important to maintain, for, as will be seen, they may mutually exclude specific obligations from the other category.[50] However, as will also be seen in the next section, interdependent obligations are not only central to the invocation of responsibility by all parties to the obligation, but are by their very nature obligations that attract decentralized responses to breaches (section III. i. b, below). For this reason, and for their overwhelming presence in non-proliferation treaties, they are central to determining the predominant application of certain rules (within the general rules) of standing to take countermeasures in this area of law (section III. ii, below).

b. ILC Articles on State Responsibility: using Fitzmaurice's classifications for standing to invoke responsibility

The ILC Articles on State Responsibility drew heavily from Fitzmaurice's typology of multilateral obligations.[51] However, the purpose of this importation was to allow the ILC to develop a functional methodology for determining which states (or group of states) were to be provided with the right to invoke the responsibility of the defaulting state and, for example, act by the taking of countermeasures.[52] In conjunction with

[47] Draft Articles on the Law of Treaties, p. 255. Cf. L.-A. Sicilianos, 'The Relationship between Reprisals and Denunciation or Suspension of a Treaty', *European Journal of International Law*, 4 (1993), 348.

[48] L-A. Sicilianos, 'The Classification of Obligations and the Multilateral Dimension of the Relations of International Responsibility', *European Journal of International Law*, 13 (2002), 1135.

[49] *Ibid.* 1134.

[50] Pauwelyn, 'The Typology of Multilateral Treaty Obligations', 923–924.

[51] See, e.g., Crawford, *ILC Commentaries*, p. 259; Crawford, Third Report, p. 40, para. 91 and n. 175.

[52] Previous to Crawford importing the distinction was the problematic draft Art. 40, which failed to cover breaches of all possible obligations and did not differentiate between different levels of legal interest of states. For a discussion of previous problems, see B. Simma, 'Bilateralism and Community Interest in the Law of State Responsibility', in Y. Dinstein and T. Tabory (eds.), *International Law at a Time of Perplexity: Essays in*

this the ILC distinguished invoking states between those who had protected legal interests ('injured states' – Article 42) and those whose collective interests (but not legal interests) may have been infringed ('a state other than an injured state' – Article 48).

These two methodological manoeuvres had two consequences. First, the ILC made a logical connection between interdependent obligations, breach of which allowed *all parties* to the obligation to be considered injured states, thereby identifying a broad range of states capable of taking countermeasures (as among all the other rights of recourse available upon invocation of responsibility). Second, the ILC introduced an element of uncertainty about which collective obligations would enable a state to resort to the full panoply of rights of recourse upon invocation of their breach. The line between interdependent obligations, as a subcategory of collective obligations, and obligations protecting the collective interest was blurred.[53] A ready example is that nuclear-weapon-free-zone treaties were considered an example of those containing interdependent obligations, protected by Article 42(b)(ii) ILC Articles, and also as an example of those within the collective interest obligations protected by Article 48(1)(a). The tension between Article 42(b)(ii) and Article 48(1)(a) ILC Articles is not a debate to be had here, but it should make the reader wary when classifying obligations contained in a particular treaty. Resort to first principles, the definition and core characteristics of different types of obligations (see section III. i. a, above), is a necessity.[54]

Article 42(b)(ii) ILC Articles articulates the relationship between standing to invoke responsibility and interdependent obligations. The latter is a 'special category of obligations, breach of which must be considered as affecting *per se* every other State to which the obligation is owed'.[55] Necessarily any breach of such an obligation radically changes the position of every other party in respect to the further performance of that obligation. Accordingly, every state to which the interdependent obligation is owed has

Honour of Shabtai Roseenne (The Hague: Martinus Nijhoff, 1989), 821; Crawford, Third Report, paras. 66 *et seq.*; Sicilianos, 'Reprisals and Suspension', 103, 116 and 136 *et seq.*

[53] Sicilianos, 'Classification of Obligations', 1135–1136; C. Yamdda, A/C.6/56/SR.12, para. 6; G. Gaja, 'The Concept of an Injured State', in J. Crawford, A. Pellet and S. Olleson (eds.), *The Law of International Responsibility* (Oxford University Press, 2011), 945.

[54] Calamita, 'Sanctions, Countermeasures, and the Iranian Nuclear Issue', 1424 (noting the overlap in treatment of nuclear-free-zone treaties in the different ILC Articles on State Responsibility, but not resorting to first principles and definitional characteristics of interdependent obligations moving forward).

[55] Crawford, *ILC Commentaries*, p. 259.

standing to invoke the responsibility of the defaulting state, including resort to countermeasures. Article 42(b)(ii) presumes that a diverse and broad decentralized response to such interdependent obligations arises from the nature of the obligations themselves. This is strongly rooted in a similar treatment under the law of treaties.[56]

Therefore, the nature of interdependent obligations permits a broad decentralized response, giving standing to *all parties* to the obligation to take countermeasures in the case of breach of a necessarily collective obligation. This contrasts with those special rules that only permit bilateral countermeasures and/or those obligations that are reciprocally bilateral in nature. The question is now whether non-proliferation treaties contain such interdependent obligations, and, if so, to what extent.

ii. A typology of non-proliferation obligations and the potential prevalence of interdependent obligations as indicative of a special regime

Fitzmaurice and Crawford have both provided disarmament and nuclear-weapon-free-zone treaties as clear-cut examples of agreements of an interdependent nature. This has led non-proliferation law specialists[57] to state, loosely, and incorrectly, that the character of non-proliferation treaties means that any breach of the obligations contained therein permits recourse to countermeasures through Article 42(b)(ii). This approach incorrectly collapses the fundamental distinction between treaties and obligations, and that of the law of treaties with the law of state responsibility. While it may be true that interdependent obligations 'usually arise under treaties establishing particular [treaty] regimes',[58] not all obligations under such regimes are innately of an interdependent nature nor can they be presumed to be. When examining a treaty to identify interdependent obligations, one must seek to determine the exact nature of the obligation in question and evaluate whether a breach of said obligation would affect *per se* every other party state's future performance of *that same specific obligation*.[59]

56 See Fitzmaurice, Second Report, p. 31; Draft Articles on the Law of Treaties, 255.

57 e.g., Calamita, 'Sanctions, Countermeasures, and the Iranian Nuclear Issue', 1426–1428 (referring to the NPT as 'the essence of an integrated agreement'); Dekker, *The Law of Arms Control*, p. 351.

58 Crawford, *ILC Commentaries*, p. 260.

59 This interpretation is consistent with the ILC's wish to keep this category of obligations and invocation under Art. 42(b)(ii) 'narrow in its scope'. Cf. *ibid.* The same

It is therefore necessary first to construct a rough typology of different types of specific obligations contained in non-proliferation treaties, before then examining whether from first principles they qualify as interdependent obligations. Should a prevalence of interdependent obligations be found to exist, it may be stated that non-proliferation law may be considered as containing special characteristics, inasmuch as it predominantly gives standing to *all* states parties to such treaties to take countermeasures. In short, it may be determined to be an area of law that permits broad, collective forms of decentralized enforcement.

a. A typology of non-proliferation obligations

The author considers that across the variety of non-proliferation treaties there exist four categories of obligations of relevance. This typology is far from exhaustive and should be considered quite crude, serving only the purpose of the present enquiry.

(i) *Substantive obligations* – these prohibit states, varyingly, to: develop, produce; acquire, retain, possess; use; receive transfer of, transfer to, provide; and assist, encourage or induce another state to some of those obligations previously mentioned. In addition to the obligation to destroy WMDs.[60]

(ii) *Substantive peaceful use obligations* – these are *positive* obligations, normally to undertake: to facilitate in the fullest exchange of equipment, materials and scientific information in the peaceful uses of

interpretation is adopted by Gaja, 'The Concept of an Injured State', p. 946: 'At issue in both texts [Draft Articles on the Law of Treaties and ILC Articles on State Responsibility] is the radical modification of a situation. However the envisaged modification does not have the same character in respect of both texts. For Articles on the Responsibility of States for Internationally Wrongful Acts (ARSIWA), at issue is a *modification which affects the future performance of the specific obligations in question.* The Vienna Convention, on the other hand, concerns a modification which affects the totality of obligations deriving from the treaty' (emphasis added).

60 Each of these obligations is contained in one or more of the following: Arts. I, II and III (2) NPT; Arts. I, II and III BWC; Arts. I, V(4), V(7) and V(8) CWC; Art. 1, The Comprehensive Nuclear-Test-Ban Treaty, 35 *ILM* 1439 (hereinafter CTBT); Art. 1, Treaty Banning Nuclear Weapon Tests in the Atmosphere, Outer Space and Underwater, 480 UNTS 43 (hereinafter PTBT); Arts. 3, 4(a), 5(1), 6 and 7, South Pacific Nuclear-Free-Zone Treaty, 1145 UNTS 177 (hereinafter South Pacific NFZT); Art. 1, Treaty for the Prohibition of Nuclear Weapons in Latin America, 634 UNTS 326 (hereinafter Latin America NFZT); Art. 3, Treaty on the Southeast Asia Nuclear-Weapon-Free Zone, 35 *ILM* 635 (hereinafter Southeast Asia NFZT) and Art. 2, Additional Protocol to Southeast Asia NFZT; Arts. 3, 4, 5, 6(b) and 6(c), African Nuclear-Weapon-Free-Zone Treaty, 35 *ILM* 698 (hereinafter African NFZT); Art. 1, Protocol I to African NFZT and Art. 1 Protocol II to African NFZT.

the relevant WMD;[61] and to make available the potential benefits of any peaceful application.[62]

(iii) *Verification/safeguard obligations* – these *procedural* obligations non-exhaustively include: reporting possession, location, intended transfers, new plants, access to facilities for inspection and clarification process.[63]

(iv) *National implementation obligations* – such obligations require states to establish domestic legislation or systems of law in accordance with domestic constitutional processes; ensuring accordance with specific obligations (both procedural and substantive) outlined in a non-proliferation treaty.[64] These will not be explored below.

These categories should not be considered as exhaustive nor mutually exclusive. It should not be surprising that a certain category of obligations have an inbuilt overlap with another: most predominantly between category (i) substantive obligations and category (iii) procedural obligations. Examples include Article III(2) NPT and substantive obligations relating to the destruction of chemical weapons contained in Article V(8) and the Verification Annex to the CWC, whereby rates and sequencing of destructions are clearly procedural obligations. In such cases, one can still delimit the procedural aspects and substantive aspects of particular obligations. Indeed, in evaluating the level or significance of a breach, it is stated that this is a necessity.

[61] e.g., Art. IV(2) NPT; Art. X(1) BWC; Art. 8(2) African NFZT. These positive obligations should be distinguished from the general right to use certain WMDs for peaceful purposes (e.g., Art. IV(1) NPT; Art. X(2) BWC; Arts. I and II(1)(a) CWC; Art. 17, Latin America NFZT; Art. 8(1) African NFZT).

[62] e.g., Art. V NPT.

[63] e.g., Art. III(1) NPT; IAEA, *The Structure and Content of Agreements between the Agency and States Required in Connection with the Treaty on the Nonproliferation of Nuclear Weapons*, Doc. No. INFIRC/153; Model Additional Protocol, Doc. No. INFCIRC/540; e.g., *Agreement between Iran and the Agency for the Application of Safeguards in Connect with the Treaty on the Non-Proliferation of Nuclear Weapons*, Doc. No. INFCIRC/214, 13 December 1974 (hereinafter Iran Safeguards Agreement); Arts. III(1), IV(4)–(7), V(6) and V(9) CWC; Arts. IV(3)–(4), IV(7), IV(11), IV(30), IV(43) and IV(53) CTBT; Part II(16) (18) (23), Protocol to the CTBT; Arts. 4(b), 8, 9, 10, Annex 2 and Annex 4, South Pacific NFZT; Arts. 12–16, Latin America NFZT; Arts. 5 and 10–13, Southeast Asia NFZT; Arts. 6(a), 6(d), 9 and 13, African NFZT.

[64] e.g., Art. III(1) read alongside Arts. 7(a) and 32 Iran Safeguards Agreement; Art. VII(1) CWC; Art. IV BWC; Art. III(1) CTBT. These can arguably qualify as absolute, although this is open to debate.

b. Character of non-proliferation obligations: determining the prevalence of interdependent obligations

Given the stated typology of non-proliferation obligations, it remains to be determined which of categories (i) to (iv) can be qualified, from first principles, as interdependent obligations. Namely, which categories of non-proliferation obligations, upon breach, will enable *all parties* to the relevant multilateral treaty recourse to take countermeasures?

This question will, of course, require the above-stated definitional foundations of interdependent obligations (section III. i. a) and avoid the pitfalls of other commentators. However, as also previously noted, the *core characteristic* of interdependent obligations differs when one considers if from a treaty-law-based perspective, in contrast to the law of state responsibility. From a treaty law perspective, the core characteristic is that a breach of a specific treaty obligation of an interdependent nature renders future performance of the treaty by all other parties to it impossible, indeed breach of a specific obligation threatens the entire structure of the treaty. However, from a state responsibility law and Article 42(b)(ii) perspective, the determining characteristic of an interdependent obligation is that a breach of specific obligation would *per se* affect and undermine every other state's future performance of *solely that same specific obligation*. The central problem is that Professor Crawford has directly imported the core characteristic of interdependent obligations under treaty law into the law of state responsibility.[65] Gaja notes that this should not 'create inconsistencies',[66] but as will be seen in this chapter's attempt to characterize the four categories of non-proliferation obligations, it creates confusion and logical anomalies.

Category (i) – substantive obligations Substantive non-proliferation obligations should be clear-cut examples of those classifiable as interdependent. Indeed, while exploring disarmament and nuclear-weapon-free zone treaties, Fitzmaurice envisaged certain substantive obligations, contained therein, as exemplary of his interdependent category. These

[65] Crawford, *ILC Commentaries*, pp. 41 and 260. For a similar view within the context of state responsibility, cf. Sicilianos, 'Classification of Obligations', 1134. In the context of treaty law for a similar conclusion, see Sicilanos, 'Reprisals and Suspension', 348. Also, see text accompanying nn. 47 and 48, above.

[66] Gaja, 'The Concept of an Injured State', p. 946 ('Still the partial reproduction of the text from the Vienna Convention in the ARSIWA seems the result of expediency, rather than logical coherence. The solution arrived at allows the use of an accepted formulation, to express what is in fact a relatively new concept'); Crawford, Third Report, para. 91.

included the obligation to disarm and the prohibitions on manufacturing and possession. His explanation of these particular obligations indicated that he believed that a breach of any one of them would result in necessary non-performance of the *same* obligation by other states parties to the obligation.[67] This cannot be said of *all* the substantive obligations contained in category (i) above: breach of a particular obligation would not necessarily undermine the future performance of *that particular obligation* by other parties.

A clear example is that of the obligations not to transfer WMDs,[68] nor to assist, encourage, or induce[69] other states in their acquiring or manufacturing of WMDs. Should state A breach its obligation not to transfer WMDs to state B, states C to Z, parties to the treaty, would not in turn feel that they are unable to perform the particular obligation prohibiting the transfer of WMDs to other states. Rather, states C to Z cannot remain arsenal free, and would seek to non-perform different obligations, seeking to possess or expand possession of WMDs through acquisition or manufacturing. Given the apparent asymmetry between those obligations being breached, and those obligations in danger of future non-performance, if one were to adopt a narrow approach then only certain substantive obligations may be qualified as interdependent (e.g., prohibitions to develop, produce, manufacture, acquire, retain, possess, use, destroy and receive). Again, it is the tension of the characteristics given to interdependent obligations under treaty law and the law of state responsibility that rears its head. The stated example, adopting a *narrow approach*, is reflective of a strict application of the law of state responsibility methodology (as contained in Article 42(b)(ii) and indicated by Gaja). A *broad approach*, based on the law of treaties, and incorporated into the law of state responsibility in a passing statement by Crawford,[70] would reach a different conclusion to the example cited above. While the narrow approach may exclude the prohibition on transfer as qualifying as an interdependent obligation, the broad approach would argue that

[67] Fitzmaurice, Second Report, p. 54, para. 126 ('the obligation of *each party to disarm*, or not to *exceed a certain level of armaments*, or *not to manufacture* or *possess* certain types of weapons, is necessarily dependent on a corresponding *performance of the same thing by all the other parties*, since it is of the essence of such a treaty that the undertaking of each party is given in return for a similar undertaking by the others') (emphasis added).

[68] e.g., Art. I NPT; Art. III BWC; Art. I(1)(a) CWC.

[69] e.g., Art. I NPT; Art. III BWC; Art. I(1)(d) CWC; Art. I(2) CTBT; Art. 1(2) PTBT; Art. 3(c) South Pacific NFZT; Art. 1(2) Latin America NFZT; Art. 3(4)(b) Southeast Asia NFZT; Arts. 3(c), 11 and Art. 2 Protocol I and Arts. 1 and 2 Protocol 2 African NFZT.

[70] See text accompanying n. 65, above.

irrespective of whether a breach of this obligation is likely to induce non-performance of the same obligation it would threaten the entire structure of the treaty and, therefore, undoubtedly qualify as interdependent in nature (see, e.g., Article XXII (3) CWC).[71]

So, that which appears clear is not.

Category (ii) – peaceful use obligations In direct contrast, positive peaceful use obligations, as defined in category a.(ii) above, certainly cannot be qualified as interdependent. This is merely a matter of logic. Should WMD possessive states not fulfil their obligation to help non-possessive states in developing peaceful uses and technology for the relevant WMD,[72] then the latter are hardly capable of reciprocal non-compliance of the same obligation (qualifying, perhaps, as synallagmatic obligations), let alone whether the positive peaceful use obligations is of such a nature that it will undoubtedly induce reciprocal non-performance. Furthermore, it is often argued that such peaceful use obligations were central to securing the conclusion of the main multi-lateral treaties.[73] This, however, is irrelevant for evaluating whether or not the obligation is interdependent,[74] and, even under the broad approach (treaty law based), breach of these provisions would not threaten the entire structure of the treaty.

Category (iii) – verification/safeguard obligations Given that most cases of non-compliance in the operation of non-proliferation treaties are those relating to procedural verification and safeguard obligations,[75] identifying whether they are of an interdependent nature takes on a specific practical importance. It should be abundantly clear that if one adopts the narrow approach, then one can certainly conclude that safeguard and verification obligations are not interdependent in nature, since non-compliance by one state will not undermine future performance by all other states parties to that obligation. There is also the

[71] Art. XII(3) CWC may not be strictly qualified as a rule governing countermeasures, since it governs lawful measures as recommended by an institutional body. The present author would disagree with such a reading. See also Art. V(3) CTBT and section IV. i. b, below.

[72] e.g., under Art. 5 NPT.

[73] For a discussion in the context of the NPT, cf. Joyner, *International Law and Proliferation of Weapons of Mass Destruction*, p. 44.

[74] Similar reasoning in the context of absolute obligations, cf. Tams, *Enforcing Obligations*, p. 56.

[75] Dekker, *The Law of Arms Control*, p. 338.

understanding that some procedural obligations can be purely bilateral in nature (see text accompanying n. 155, below). The question remains whether, under the broad approach, breach of such obligations would necessarily result in undermining the entire structure of the treaty? Other authors have answered yes.[76] In the present author's opinion, such a conclusion and its supporting arguments are at best vaguely argued and at worst arbitrary.

The stated supporters of the proposition that safeguards and verification obligations are interdependent have developed their argument in three steps: (a) the safeguards system was, in some cases, part of the basic bargain upon which the treaty was concluded – it was therefore intentionally central to the treaty's structure;[77] (b) because such obligations are extensively complemented by institutional frameworks, in most cases, they are part of a collective commitment which envisages verification and determination of non-compliance at its core;[78] and (c) breach of safeguard and verification obligations are a gateway to a breach of substantive obligations.[79]

With due respect to the proponents of these arguments, only argument (c) has the potential for argumentative merit, and, even then, only when developed properly. Argument (a), as similarly suggested above, is irrelevant to the determination of whether certain obligations are interdependent in nature.[80] Argument (b) seems an entirely arbitrary criterion upon which to evaluate a set of obligations' interdependent nature – rather than concentrating on the content and nature of the obligations *per se*, this approach looks at the supportive framework and context of such obligations. Ultimately, neither (a) nor (b) answers the central question of whether a breach of safeguard and verification

[76] See, generally, Calamita, 'Sanctions, Countermeasures, and the Iranian Nuclear Issue'; Dekker, *The Law of Arms Control*, p. 338.

[77] Calamita, 'Sanctions, Countermeasures, and the Iranian Nuclear Issue', 1427, citing J. S. Nye, 'Maintaining the Non-Proliferation Regime', *International Organizations*, 35 (1981), 17.

[78] Calamita, 'Sanctions, Countermeasures, and the Iranian Nuclear Issue', 1428, citing R. K. Smith, 'Explaining the Non-Proliferation Regime: Anomalies for Contemporary International Relations Theory', *International Organizations*, 41 (1987), 260.

[79] Dekker, *The Law of Arms Control*, p. 339: 'Clearly, violations of institutional law may deprive the States Parties of the possibility of establishing whether non-compliance with the substantive law of the arms control treaty has occurred. For that reason, this type of violation may lead to the frustration of the fulfillment of the object and purpose of arms control treaties, even if account is taken of the fact that supervision is not considered to be an end in itself.'

[80] See n. 74, above.

obligations would undermine the entire treaty structure. Argument (c) comes close; by linking verification obligations to substantive ones it should be understood that there may be specific verification obligations whose breach, if of *sufficient gravity*, may endanger the entire treaty regime by undermining knowledge of substantive breaches. This brings up two sub-issues: the type of verification obligation involved and the type of breach involved. First, one must differentiate those procedural verification obligations that have a distinct and direct connection to substantive obligations (e.g., the obligation to disclose and report and the existence of a facility utilizing WMDs for peaceful purposes[81]) and those that do not (e.g., reporting within a specific timeframe[82]). Second, one must consider that for the first type of obligation just submitted the *significance of the breach* involved is critical. Should it be a case of *technical non-compliance* which is manifest,[83] of a verification obligation that is strongly linked to substantive ones, then this is hardly sufficient to enable standing for all states parties to that obligation to take countermeasures. The significance of the breach is a point made by both Crawford and Gaja:

> In practice interdependent obligations covered by paragraph (b) (ii) will usually arise under treaties establishing particular regimes. Even under such treaties *it may not be the case that just any breach of the obligation* has the effect of undermining the performance of all the other states involved, and it is desirable that this subparagraph be narrow in its scope.[84]
>
> Where the breach is not significant, the states affected will still have legal entitlements, but only so far as provided by article 48 ARSIWA.[85]

From the preceding analysis it should be clear that the only case that exists for verification obligations being interdependent in nature is under the broad, treaty law based, approach. Even then only a specific subset of verification obligations, that is, those with a distinct link to substantive obligations, in cases of a significant breach, enable all states party to the obligation to take countermeasures.

[81] e.g., Art. 8(b)(ii) Iran Safeguards Agreement. [82] e.g., Art. V(9)(b) CWC.

[83] See examples in A. Kelle, 'NBC Arms Control Under Stress', *International Spectator*, 35(3) (2000), 85–86.

[84] Crawford, *ILC Commentaries*, p. 260 (emphasis added).

[85] Gaja, 'The Concept of an Injured State', p. 945.

iii. Conclusion on standing to take countermeasures

The preceding section aimed to examine the extent of any specialness of the non-proliferation legal regime in relation to standing to take countermeasures. The following conclusions can be drawn from the analysis of both general international law and non-proliferation law. First, only interdependent obligations enable a decentralized response upon breach, allowing all states parties to the obligation in question to take countermeasures upon invocation of responsibility of the defaulting state. Second, identification of obligations that qualify as interdependent is problematic owing to the practical implementation of the concept in treaty law and state responsibility law. This has led the present author to develop a narrow (state responsibility based) and broad (treaty law based) approach to identifying which non-proliferation obligations qualify. Third, the majority of substantive non-proliferation obligations qualify as interdependent under the narrow approach, while the rest would only qualify under the broad approach. Fourth, only a small minority of procedural verification obligations may qualify as interdependent based on a broad approach, and decentralized countermeasures may only then be taken upon a significant breach of such procedural non-proliferation obligations.

Given the above four conclusions, it can be stated that there is a predominance of interdependent obligations in non-proliferation treaties, at least comparative to *most* other treaties. Accordingly, within the limits identified in the above analysis, non-proliferation law is more inclined to enable a decentralized response, allowing all states parties to non-proliferation treaties to take countermeasures for the breach of certain obligations. Due regard must be had to this special characteristic. However, its significance in the context of identifying a special regime is limited, if not entirely doubtful.

IV. Diverse non-proliferation rules that affect when resort to countermeasures under general international law is made and what their content may be

This section will consider two further issues. First, *when* states parties to non-proliferation treaties may take recourse to countermeasures under general international law (IV. i). This will necessarily require an examination of particular rules contained across non-proliferation treaties. Second, *what* countermeasures can be taken should general international law be considered applicable (IV. ii). The premise of this section, and both sub-issues, is that the general international rules governing countermeasures are 'residual and may be excluded or modified';[86] a point identified in the *Case Concerning the Air Services Agreement*.[87] Yet, analysis and common sense dictate that the relationship between specific non-proliferation treaty provisions or mechanisms and general international law is one of gradation: different non-proliferation rules have varying degrees of specialness.[88] Each special rule may modify the application of the general law of countermeasures to a different degree. Yet, it is in determining the degree of modification, and therefore specialness of non-proliferation law, that one may fall fallible to the presumptions highlighted in section II. ii, below – for this is an essentially indeterminate exercise in interpretation. Some authors have attempted to phrase the same enquiry in terms of absolutes in order to remove the role of previously highlighted presumptions.[89] The present author does not consider this possible, especially given the categories of non-proliferation rules being examined in this section – each set with their own varying degrees of specialness.

Category 1: *Non-proliferation rules which are silent as to their compatibility with the application of the general law of countermeasures.*

Category 2: *Non-proliferation rules which expressly dictate their application alongside the general law of countermeasures.*

Category 3: *Non-proliferation rules which not only implicitly dictate, but also specifically exclude, the application of the general law of countermeasures.*

Each will be examined in turn in subsection i below. At this junction is should be noted that categories 1–3 are not mutually exclusive, in that a specific treaty may contain different provisions which are each identifiable under categories 1 and 2: the CWC and CTBT being relevant examples.

[86] Crawford, *ILC Commentaries*, p. 283. [87] See text accompanying n. 1, above.

[88] This is consistent with, but slightly more specific than, the approach the ILC adopted in Art. 55 of the ILC Articles on State Responsibility. Cf. Crawford, *ILC Commentaries*, p. 308. See, as more relevant, drawing on the normative strength of specific rules, ILC Report on Fragmentation, 80, para. 151.

[89] Dekker, *The Law of Arms Control*, p. 348. Similarly, see n. 25, above.

i. *When countermeasures may be taken: determination by categories of non-proliferation rules with varying degrees of specialness*[90]

a. Category 1: non-proliferation rules which are *silent* as to their compatibility with the application of the general law of countermeasures

The clear majority of non-proliferation treaties do not contain provisions that govern a state's ability to resort to countermeasures. Not only are category 1 rules the clear majority across non-proliferation law, but they are typified by the presence of an extensive institutional framework that governs both compliance and enforcement of relevant non-proliferation obligations. The central question is whether the existence of such treaty institutional frameworks may preclude or condition the resort to countermeasures under general international law. The arbitral tribunal's dictum in the *Case Concerning the Air Services Agreement* made precisely this point, and it bears repeating as well as closer scrutiny:

> Under the rules of present-day international law, *and unless the contrary results from special obligations arising from particular treaties, notably from mechanisms created within the framework of international organisations*, each State establishes for itself its legal situation vis-à-vis other States. If a situation arises which, in one State's view, results in the violation of an international obligation by another State, the first State is entitled . . . to affirm its rights through 'countermeasures'.[91]

Commentators have used this dictum to condition the resort to countermeasures under general international law (whether through imposing procedural or substantive prerequisites), owing to the mere presence of extensive institutional frameworks.[92] Such an approach has a certain appeal from a policy perspective: ad hoc machinery may be more

[90] The term *lex specialis* is deliberately avoided. The ILC states that '[f]or the *lex specialis* principle to apply it is not enough that the same subject matter is dealt with by two provisions; there must be some actual inconsistency between them, or else a discernable intention that one provision is to exclude the other.' Cf. Crawford, *ILC Commentaries*, p. 307. Here only categories 1 and 3 could be classifiable under this definition of the *lex specialis* principle, the former due to arguable intention and the latter through explicit exclusion. Category 2 may fall within this, but only to the extent that any inconsistency between the rules can be shown.

[91] *Case Concerning the Air Services Agreement of 27 March 1946* (emphasis added).

[92] Dekker, *The Law of Arms Control*, p. 344 (arguing in favour of certain procedural prerequisites); M. Koskenniemi, 'Breach of Treaty or Non-Compliance? Reflections on the Enforcement of the Montreal Protocol', *Yearbook of International Environmental*

organized, targeted and effective in monitoring violations of non-proliferation treaty obligations and organizing responses thereto.[93] However, it is contended that such a broad-brush approach is a misguided reading of the *Air Services Arbitration* dictum: a close reading reveals three points of note.

First, derogations from the general international law right to resort to countermeasures may be imposed by special *obligations* that may or may not derive from treaty-specific institutional frameworks. It is notable that the dictum refers to *obligations* and not rights: namely the rule in question must have a mandatory functionality. States must therefore be required to utilize an *institutionally mandated procedure*, upon instances of non-compliance, within a treaty. Second, to fall within the carve-out of the dictum, such special obligations have to be *contrary* to the rules governing countermeasures under general international law. This requirement indicates that there must be a degree of incompatibility between the general and special obligations.[94] What this degree of incompatibility is indiscernible from the dictum.[95] Third, the mere existence of a treaty-specific institutional framework for compliance and enforcement is not enough to ensure derogation from, modification of, or pre-conditioning of, the general international law of countermeasures – unless of course recourse to it is obligatory.[96] To this end, the degree of enforcement capability within the institutional framework is irrelevant.[97] Therefore, while the dictum does show a significant tendency towards upholding the

Law, 3 (1992), 136 (arguing that treaty mechanisms are provided a primary role, while general law becomes operational on the failure of the latter); S. Sur (ed.), *Verification of Current Disarmament and Arms Limitation Agreements: Ways, Means and Practices* (Aldershot: United Nations Institute for Disarmament Research, 1991), p. 28 (arguing for conditioning of resort to general international law based on treaty mechanisms); Arangio-Ruiz, Fourth Report, p. 40, para. 112.

93 See, generally, Simma, 'From Bilateralism to Community Interest', 104.

94 This is somewhat akin to the inconsistency requirement of the *lex specialis* principle. See n. 90, above.

95 It is unclear whether an obligation has specifically to exclude recourse to other rights under general international law (extreme incompatibility as used by the tribunal in *Eureko* v. *Slovak Republic*, PCA Case No. 2008-13, Award on Jurisdiction, Arbitrability and Suspension, 26 October 2010 (UNCITRAL), paras. 253–254, 273–274), or whether any inconsistency between two rules is enough. The former seems to be the position adopted by Dekker, *The Law of Arms Control*, p. 347.

96 This is close to the conclusion reached by Special Rapporteur Arangio-Ruiz. See Arangio-Ruiz, Fourth Report, p. 40, para. 114).

97 The tribunal considered the degree of enforcement of an institutional framework within the context of whether the initiation of judicial proceedings precludes resort to countermeasures under general international law. *Case Concerning the Air Services Agreement of 27 March 1946*, 445, para. 94).

relevance and functioning of a treaty-specific regime, this cannot be an overarching consideration when one considers whether the same treaty posits procedural or substantive prerequisites to the taking of countermeasures. Rather, the first two points established above are the relevant determining criteria for whether a treaty regime may establish derogations from, or pre-requisites to, the taking of countermeasures under general international law.

Relevance of extensive treaty-specific institutional frameworks Given the lessons learnt from the *Air Services Arbitration*, let us first consider, at a general level, whether the extensive treaty institutional frameworks, as a whole, may pre-condition resort to countermeasures under general international law. The majority of non-proliferation treaties are characterized by *reference to* extensive ad hoc institutional mechanisms. The nature of such references may differ considerably. Some treaties operate upon an internally established or internally cohesive institutional framework, such as the CWC, CTBT and NPT. Such treaties may also refer to the institutional framework of the United Nations (UN) as a supervisory mechanism.[98] Others only have a reference to UN organs,[99] while others still have taken reference to external systems such as the IAEA.[100] The most relevant treaties for the present subsection, the CWC, CTBT and NPT, all establish two tiers of institutional frameworks: the primary tier for monitoring and compliance falling to internally cohesive bodies, and, where the first tier is unable to, the secondary tier of UN organs for dealing with compliance issues. However, as a general rule, these non-proliferation treaties, and others, do *not make it obligatory* to remedy a breach of the treaty by resort to the established treaty-specific mechanism. More importantly, not one non-proliferation treaty mandates recourse to such ad hoc institutions to the exclusion of all other remedies. This non-obligatory nature derives from (a) the institutional

[98] E.g., Art. III(1) NPT; Art. XII(7)(c) Statute of the International Atomic Energy Agency, 276 UNTS 3 (hereinafter IAEA Statute); Art. VIII(c)(36) and Art. XII(2) and (3) CWC.

[99] Arts. VI and VII BWC; Art. V(3) Convention on the Prohibition of Military or Any Other Hostile Use of Environmental Modification Techniques, 1108 UNTS 151 (hereinafter ENMOD Convention).

[100] Art. 14(3) Southeast Asia NFZT. It should be noted that the IAEA was technically established outside the framework of the NPT and has broader functions, but has so effectively been made co-extensive with the NPT regime that it is for the purposes of this chapter treated as an 'internal' institutionalized framework.

machinery, as a general rule,[101] not being obligated to undertake measures in cases of non-compliance (as opposed to having discretion to choose which measures are undertaken) and (b) states not being obligated to take resort to such ad hoc institutions in the face of non-compliance[102] (as opposed to being required to follow the 'requests' or 'recommendations'[103] of the institutional treaty bodies, upon determination of breach and determination of response measures by body). Therefore, at a very general level, given that there is no identifiable obligation upon states *to initiate* treaty-specific institutional mechanisms, the latter cannot constitute (as a whole) a derogation from or precondition to the institution of countermeasures under general international law.[104] The lack of any specific obligation mandating recourse to treaty institutional frameworks upon non-compliance renders such frameworks foul of the first criterion of the test laid down in the *Air Services Arbitration*, manifesting its carve-out inapplicable. States are permitted to take recourse to unilateral countermeasures under general international law unimpeded.

The second point of consideration then becomes whether treaties containing such extensive ad hoc institutional frameworks, and even

[101] There is a notable exception (see text on following page); see Art. II(B)(26)(g) CTBT. See also Art. V(1) CTBT. The other exception is the relationship between the primary and secondary institutional machinery in the NPT-IAEA. The IAEA is obligated to report non-compliance to the UN Security Council ('shall') under Art. XII(7)(c) IAEA Statute. This does not prejudge the question of what the IAEA asks of the UN Security Council.

[102] See, for UN Organs, Art. VI(a) BWC (states 'may' lodge a complaint to the UN Security Council in cases of suspected non-compliance).

[103] The questionable obligatory character of institutional body 'requests' or 'recommendations' is important if a state wishes to undertake countermeasures under general international law while a treaty-specific institutional body is seized of the matter and has made recommendations or requests. The position of the present author of provisions such as: Art. VIII(c)(36) CWC (Executive Council may 'request' state action); Art. XII(2) and (3) CWC (Conference may 'recommend' collective measures); Art. II(c)(41) CTBT (Executive Council may 'request' state action); and Art. V(3) CTBT (Conference may 'recommend' collective measures) are that they are not necessarily obligatory, even if they carry a sanction.

[104] It should be noted that while this determination relates to the state's obligation to initiate institutional procedures, once such procedures have already begun there remains no bar to resorting to countermeasures. Indeed, should treaty-specific bodies seek to undertake measures against state members, in accordance with relevant treaty provisions, such measures are per se lawful and governed by the international law of responsibility for international organizations. See, in particular, ILC, *Draft Articles on the Responsibility of International Organization, with Commentaries*, 47–48 (Art. 22, Commentaries, paras. 3 and 5), *ILC Yearbook* (2011), vol. 2 (part 2).

those that do not, contain *specific provisions that may constitute procedural preconditions*. There are two types of provisions that are relevant: (a) provisions relating to a decentralized process for a determination of a breach of a non-proliferation treaty, and (b) provisions concerning consultation between states parties. Both will be considered in turn.

Determination of breach provisions A natural part of non-proliferation treaties that contain an extensive institutional framework are processes for assessing compliance and mechanisms for the determination of treaty breaches. As is well known, under general international law, countermeasures may only be taken against a state that is responsible for a breach of an international obligation. The central question that arises is as follows: if a state chooses to take countermeasures, may it undertake a unilateral assessment of the existence of breach (which is of course subject to objective determination)[105] as is its right under general international law, or must the state first take recourse to treaty mechanisms which will definitively determine the existence of a breach?

Non-proliferation treaties contain provisions that seek to clarify the existence of a breach through multilateral and bilateral procedures. The former include those where a treaty body is empowered to collect information and determine the existence of a breach, while the latter are primarily those such as challenge inspections – which while at the first instance may be a bilateral measure, are implemented through a collective treaty procedure. Clear examples include Articles IX (2), (3) and (8) CWC and Articles IV(c) and (d) CTBT – both of which exist among a sophisticated internally coherent treaty-specific institutional framework. However, similar procedures exist outside treaties with extensive institutional machinery, and in such cases constitute the only real teeth that such treaties may possess.[106]

However, again the central problem that arises is that such determination of breach procedures are not always mandatory, and, as such, do not impose an obligation upon states to take recourse to them.[107] Article IX(2) CWC states that 'States Parties *should, whenever possible*, first make every effort to clarify and resolve, through the exchange of

[105] Crawford, *ILC Commentaries*, p. 285; Crawford, Third Report, p. 5.

[106] See the elaborate procedure contained in Annex 4, South Pacific NFZT; Annex IV, African NFZT (determination of breach, complaints and challenge inspections procedure); Art. 13 and Annex, Southeast Asia NFZT.

[107] Supporting this, Dekker, *The Law of Arms Control*, p. 347.

information and consultations, any matter which may cause doubt about compliance with this Convention.' Article IV(c)(29) CTBT contains similar non-binding language. Challenge site inspections are also framed in terms of rights, and therefore optionally invokable by a state seeking to take countermeasures.[108] In contrast, the South Pacific and African NFZTs do contain limited mandatory requirements, extending only to bilateral measures of clarifying the breach with the alleged violating state.[109] All non-proliferation treaties are devoid of an obligation requiring a state to determine the existence of a breach through collective mechanisms such as treaty-specific institutions.[110] Even in cases such as the IAEA where non-compliance procedures are so utterly extensive,[111] one will still find it difficult to pinpoint a state party obligation to utilize the organization's extensive non-compliance determination procedures. Indeed, such an obligation is entirely absent despite considerable state involvement in the determination of breach procedures.

Therefore, given their non-obligatory nature, determination of breach procedures contained in non-proliferation treaties cannot constitute procedural prerequisites for a state seeking to take countermeasures under general international law.[112]

108 See, e.g., Art. IX(8) CWC: 'Each State Party has the *right* to request an on-site challenge inspection of any facility or location in the territory or in any other place under the jurisdiction or control of any other State Party'.

109 Art. 1, Annex 4, South Pacific NFZT: 'A Party which considers that there are grounds for a complaint that another Party is in breach of its obligations under this Treaty *shall*, before bringing such a complaint to the Director, bring the subject matter of the complaint to the attention of the Party complained of and shall allow the latter reasonable opportunity to provide it with an explanation and to resolve the matter' (emphasis added); Art. 1, Annex IV, African NFZT: 'A Party which considers that there are grounds for a complaint that another Party or a Party to Protocol II is in breach of its obligations under this Treaty *shall bring* the subject matter of the complaint to the attention of the Party complained of and *shall allow* the latter thirty days to provide it with an explanation and to resolve the matter' (emphasis added).

110 See, e.g., Art. 2, Annex 4, South Pacific NFZT; Art. 2, Annex IV, African NFZT; Art. IX(3) CWC; Art. 13 and Annex, Southeast Asia NFZT; Art. IV(c)(31) CTBT.

111 See, generally, A. von Baeckmann, 'The Treaty on the Non-Proliferation of Nuclear Weapons', in Sur, *Verification of Current Disarmament and Arms Limitation Agreements*, p. 167; L. Herron, 'A Lawyer's View of Safeguards and Non-Proliferation', *IAEA Bulletin* (September 1982), 32; Calamita, 'Sanctions, Countermeasures, and the Iranian Nuclear Issue', 1430–1432.

112 Contrary to the assertions of Dekker, *The Law of Arms Control*, p. 344 (arguing that a state's freedom to judge the existence of a breach should be limited by treaty mechanisms) and Calamita, 'Sanctions, Countermeasures, and the Iranian Nuclear Issue', 1430.

Consultation provisions Certain non-proliferation treaties, such as the BWC and ENMOD Convention, contain provisions mandating that states parties are *obligated* to undertake consultations if problems arise regarding application of the relevant treaty.[113] However, despite possessing an obligatory character and being arguably inconsistent with certain aspects of the general law countermeasures, such specific consultation provisions have been discarded as hampering the resort to countermeasures under the terms of general international law.[114] The tribunal in the *Air Services Arbitration* made this determination when it considered both a treaty-specific consultation obligation and the general international law obligation to negotiate.[115] Despite this, and equally applicable to the proceeding sections on the relevance of extensive treaty-specific institutional frameworks and determination of breach procedures, the relevance of such provisions may operate in the examining the proportionality of countermeasures taken. Therefore, while none qualifies as a strict procedural prerequisite to the taking of countermeasures under general international law, despite convincing policy arguments to the contrary, all such aspects of non-proliferation treaties may be instrumental in establishing extra criteria for adjudicating the proportionality of countermeasures taken.[116]

Indeed, given the above analysis, it is hard to see anything but a secondary role in relation to the taking of countermeasures for non-proliferation treaties that contain no specific rules on the latter, but contain extensive institutional mechanisms for compliance and verification.[117]

[113] See, e.g., Art. V BWC; Art. V(1) ENMOD Convention: 'The States Parties to this Convention *undertake to consult* one another and to cooperate in solving any problems which may arise in relation to the objectives of, or in the application of the provisions of, the Convention.'

[114] See Art. 52(1)(b) ILC Articles on State Responsibility, which require the *offer* to negotiate, but do not mandate actual negotiations or determine how they must be carried out (except of course under normal good faith requirements). Importantly, Art. 52(1)(b) does not preclude the taking of certain countermeasures during negotiations (see Art. 52(2)).

[115] *Case Concerning the Air Services Agreement of 27 March 1946*, paras. 87–93.

[116] This is consistent with the reasoning of the tribunal, *ibid.*, paras. 90–91. See, generally, on proportionality of countermeasures, E. Cannizzaro, 'The Role of Proportionality in the Law of International Countermeasures', *European Journal of International Law*, 12 (2001), 889; T. Franck, 'On Proportionality of Countermeasures in International Law', *American Journal of International Law*, 102 (2008), 715.

[117] *Contra* Koskenniemi, 'Breach of Treaty or Non-Compliance?', 136.

b. Category 2: non-proliferation rules which expressly dictate their application alongside the general law of countermeasures

In contrast with the majority of non-proliferation treaty regimes examined in the preceding subsection, there is a small minority of rules that expressly govern the taking of certain countermeasures. The identified rules are:

> **Article XII(3) CWC**
>
> In cases where serious damage to the object and purpose of this Convention may result from activities prohibited under the Convention, in particular by Article I, the Conference may recommend collective measures to State Parties in conformity with international law.

> **Article V(3) CTBT**
>
> In cases where damage to the object and purpose of this Treaty may result from non-compliance with the basic obligations of this Treaty, the Conference may recommend to State Parties collective measures which are in conformity with international law.

These provisions are relatively unique in that they not only affirm that some non-proliferation obligations contained in each are interdependent, but also institutionalize resort to third-party countermeasures.[118] Five points can be taken from these provisions. First, they only relate to a breach of obligations fundamental to the treaty (i.e., 'basic obligations' for the CTBT and Article 1 obligations for the CWC). Arguably they only relate to those obligations contained in the treaty that can be classified as interdependent.[119] Second, such a breach of fundamental treaty obligations must damage (or for the CWC, more restrictively, 'damage seriously') the object and purpose of the relevant treaty. This point is largely peripheral and superfluous, given that any breach of an interdependent or fundamental obligation will necessarily damage the object and purpose of the treaty. Third, the provisions dictate that a treaty-specific institution 'may recommend' resort to third-party countermeasures. This is a significant step towards institutionalizing and bringing into the multilateral fold a unilateral resort. This encouraging aspect of

[118] See n. 71, above and accompanying text. However, these feature may be somewhat subject to circular reasoning: namely the small number of obligations which may be classed as interdependent, only in part to the fact they are identified alongside the resort to collective countermeasures.

[119] See section III. ii .b, below for more on interdependent obligations in non-proliferation treaties.

bringing collective enforcement within the framework of international institutions[120] must be tempered by two observations: not only does the provision only enable a non-binding 'recommendation' by a treaty institution, but it does not prohibit states from taking actions independent of any treaty body determination of the issue. Fourth, the provisions relate to 'collective measures' – a misguided term that requires clarification. Such provisions relate to countermeasures that may be taken by third states, that is, states other than those directly injured, which by their definition are unilateral, even if taken for collective ends (i.e., upholding the central tenets of a non-proliferation treaty). Fifth, and finally, they require that any countermeasures taken pursuant to a treaty institution's recommendation be taken 'in conformity with international law'. Given that the international law governing third-party countermeasures is currently in a state of limbo,[121] this is a rather idiosyncratic criterion. A constructive interpretation would argue that the international law governing the *legality* of third-party countermeasures is in a state of limbo, but the substantive conditional requirements of such countermeasures (presuming valid *prima facie* legality) are determined in accordance with current customary international law.

All in all, taking into account the above points, both provisions are extremely narrow in their applicability to the law governing countermeasures. They could arguably be determinative of the procedure to be undertaken for third-party countermeasures: imposing the procedural pre-requisite of a treaty institution's 'recommendation' before resort to such measures is permitted. However, these provisions do not govern countermeasures taken in response to breaches of non-proliferation obligations that are not classifiable as interdependent (the vast majority of them). Nor do they govern those countermeasures taken by a directly injured state (i.e., within the scope of Article 42(a) and (b)(i) ILC Articles). Yet, in any case, they do constitute special rules for the purposes of the present inquiry – indicative of those which expressly govern their relationship with general international law.

[120] For similarly sympathetic literature to preferring third-party enforcement through countermeasures being conducted with international institutions, see J. Charney, 'Third State Remedies in International Law', *Michigan Journal of International Law*, 10 (1989), 91; O. Schachter, *International Law in Theory and Practice* (Dordrecht: Martinus Nijhoff, 1991), p. 197.

[121] Art. 54 ILC Articles on State Responsibility (savings clause); critique of the traditional position offered by Tams, *Enforcing Obligations*.

c. Category 3: non-proliferation rules which not only implicitly dictate, but also specifically *exclude*, the application of the general law of countermeasures

While categories 1 and 2 have been concerned with non-proliferation rules contained in non-proliferation treaties that impact on the taking of countermeasures, no category 3 rules are contained in treaties obviously classifiable as belonging to the regime of non-proliferation law.[122] Indeed, the two rules that will be examined are part of the World Trade Organization (WTO) and UN Security Council legal regimes. They are marked by a strong degree of specialness, in comparison to the previous rules considered, for they arguably expressly or implicitly exclude all resort to specific countermeasures taken under general international law. The following analysis will first consider the taking of countermeasures under the WTO Dispute Settlement Understanding (DSU), and then any prohibitions that arise through specific UN Security Council Chapter VII resolutions.

WTO rules on non-proliferation law and countermeasures The primary role of WTO rules in regard to non-proliferation law is its effect on national export mechanisms for weapons technologies. The export of WMDs is a particularly troubling issue given the dual-use problem that occurs with many components of such weapons.[123] As is well known, the WTO system, typified by Articles I and XI of the GATT, offers a wide system of protection to imports and exports prohibiting a large array of restraints and extending most-favoured-nation (MFN) treatment. These prohibitions on restraining the import and export of weapons-related technologies are problematic for dual-use items: namely those items that possess peaceful civilian uses alongside their weapons-related functions. Given pressing non-proliferation initiatives and concerns at the time of the drafting of the GATT, it does contain a security exception to the stated prohibition on export and import restraints – therefore, in limited circumstances, enabling states legally to prevent the export or import of

[122] Please take recourse to the clarifications provided in section IV.ii, below.

[123] See, generally, Michael D. Beck, Richard T. Cupitt, Seema Galhaut and Scott A. Jones, *To Supply or to Deny: Comparing Nonproliferation Export Controls in Five Key Countries* (New York: Kluwer, 2003); R. Cupitt, 'Multilateral Nonproliferation Export Control Arrangement in 2000: Achievements, Challenges and Reform', Centre for Strategic and International Studies, September 2000; D. Joyner (ed.), *Nonproliferation Export Controls: Origins, Challenges and Proposals for Strengthening* (Aldershot: Ashgate, 2006).

certain weapons-related technologies. Article XXI of the GATT, and in particular subsections (b)(i) and (ii) lay out the pertinent security exceptions, enabling a state to take measures prohibiting the import or export of nuclear, chemical and biological weapons and relevant material from which they are derived.[124] However, given (a) that a number of countries have adopted national export regulatory mechanisms to determine which dual-use items they can import and export[125] and (b) the ambiguity in scope of the untested security exception: challenges to the legality of national export measures may be made within the framework of the WTO dispute settlement procedures.[126] It is within these parameters that the potential for a breach of the GATT and corresponding state resort to countermeasures must be considered. It is with this that we come to look at the nature of rules governing countermeasures in the WTO system.[127]

The Dispute Settlement Understanding does not directly refer to countermeasures, but rather permits states to suspend the application of concessions as a last resort under Articles 3.7 and 22, which in relevant parts state the following:

> **Article 3.7 DSU**
> The last resort which this Understanding provides to the Member invoking the dispute settlement procedures is the possibility of suspending the

124 Art. XXI GATT states, in part, 'Nothing in this Agreement shall be construed: (b) to prevent any contracting party from taking any action which it considers necessary for the protection of its essential security interests: (i) relating to fissionable materials or materials from which they are derived; (ii) relating to the traffic in arms, ammunitions and implements of war and to such traffic in other goods and materials as is carried on directly or indirectly for the purpose of supplying a military establishment; (iii) taken in time of war or other emergency in international relations; or . . .'.

125 Most notable is the Export Administration Act (1979) in the USA and the system developed known as the Enhanced Proliferation Control Initiative. For a discussion of such national measures and their breadth, see Joyner, *International Law and Proliferation of Weapons of Mass Destruction*, chap. 3; D. Joyner, 'The Enhanced Proliferation Control Initiative: National Security Necessity or Unconstitutionally Vague?', *Georgia Journal of International and Comparative Law*, 32 (2004), 107. For other jurisdictions, see Beck et al., *To Supply or to Deny*.

126 The potential for challenges to national measures (prior to the WTO DSU) is the infamous USA–Czechoslovakia Dispute of 1949, where the USA refused to export certain dual-use drills to Czechoslovakia – an action challenged by the latter as inconsistent under the GATT rules. There was no resulting case. For more, see Joyner, *International Law and Proliferation of Weapons of Mass Destruction*, pp. 132–136.

127 See, generally, J. Pauwelyn, 'Enforcement and Countermeasures in the WTO. Rules are Rules: Towards a more Collective Approach', *American Journal of International Law*, 94 (2000), 335; L. Boisson de Chazournes, *Les contre-mesures dans les relations internationales économiques* (Paris: Pedone, 1992).

application of concessions or other obligations under the covered agreements on a discriminatory basis vis-à-vis the other Member, subject to authorization by the DSB of such measures.

Articles. 22.1–2 DSU

1. Compensation and the suspension of concessions or other obligations are temporary measures available in the event that the recommendations and rulings are not implemented within a reasonable period of time. However, neither compensation nor the suspension of concessions or other obligations is preferred to full implementation of a recommendation to bring a measure into conformity with the covered agreements. Compensation is voluntary and, if granted, shall be consistent with the covered agreements.
2. If the Member concerned fails to bring the measure found to be inconsistent with a covered agreement into compliance therewith or otherwise comply with the recommendations and rulings within the reasonable period of time determined pursuant to paragraph 3 of Article 21, such Member shall, if so requested, and no later than the expiry of the reasonable period of time, enter into negotiations with any party having invoked the dispute settlement procedures, with a view to developing mutually acceptable compensation. If no satisfactory compensation has been agreed within 20 days after the date of expiry of the reasonable period of time, any party having invoked the dispute settlement procedures may request authorization from the DSB to suspend the application to the Member concerned of concessions or other obligations under the covered agreements.

Owing to the presence of these provisions, as well as the exclusive dispute settlement clause contained in Article 23 of the DSU,[128] the ILC has taken the approach that the WTO regime is an express derogation from, and excludes, the general international law of countermeasures.[129] Others have argued that there is no such exclusion or derogation and Article 23 cannot be read to prohibit recourse to additional remedies under general international law.[130] Indeed, it would be pertinent to point out that it is hard to decipher whether Article 22 DSU should be considered as *lex specialis* on

[128] Art. 23 DSU states, in relevant parts, 'When Members seek the redress of a violation ... they shall have recourse to, and abide by, the rules and procedures of this Understanding.'

[129] See Crawford, *ILC Commentaries*, pp. 290–291 and nn. 813–814.

[130] For this position, see M. Garcia-Rubio, *Unilateral Measures as a Means of Enforcement of WTO recommendations and Decisions* (The Hague: Academy of International Law, 2001); P. Mavroidis, 'Remedies in the WTO Legal System: Between a Rock and a Hard Place', *European Journal of International Law*, 11 (2000), 763; Simma and Pulkowski, 'Self-Contained Regimes', 520.

rules governing reparations or countermeasures: given that both are aimed at ensuring compliance and cessation of the breach, this latter rationale cannot be used to support a determination on where the *lex specialis* attaches in terms of the rules on state responsibility.[131] Yet, even if one was to join the dominant position that the WTO system comprises a strong *lex specialis* on the law countermeasures, several issues remain to be resolved.

First, it may be reasoned that 'WTO members [are not permitted] from unilaterally resolving their disputes *in respect of WTO rights and obligations*'.[132] While it is clear that state A's WTO rights may be suspended as a countermeasure under Article 22 DSU, in response to a breach of WTO obligations, can they also be suspended for a breach of obligations contained in other treaties? Furthermore, even if state A breached WTO obligations, does not the *US-Section 301* panel decision leave open the question of whether a state B can take the countermeasure of suspending non-WTO obligations (e.g., obligations contained in other treaties between the parties)? Second, it is relatively clear from Articles 3.7 and 22 DSU that countermeasures are only permitted (a) when a recommendation by the DSB has been made and (b) upon implementation, in the case of non-compliance, and after certain procedural steps, when the countermeasure has been authorized by the DSB. These are procedural prerequisites that derogate definitively from the general international law of countermeasures, constituting condition precedents for non-proliferation law in the context of the WTO regime. Yet, this potentially lengthy process does not speak to the need for urgent countermeasures (as will be likely in the case of a severe WMD threat) – as one sees in Article 52(2) ILC Articles (section IV. ii. c, below). Third, given both the ambiguities concerning dual-use technologies and defining the application of the security exception, the likelihood is that one may be faced with a non-violation complaint (i.e., where there has been no actual violation but the benefits under the GATT have been impaired or nullified)[133] rather than a violation complaint, which if upheld and not rectified will definitively enable a resort to countermeasures. The problem is that in order to be defined as a countermeasure, a measure must be taken in response to a previous breach of an international

131 See, Simma and Pulkowski, 'Self-Contained Regimes', 521; J. Pauwelyn, *Conflict of Norms in Public International Law: How WTO Law Relates to other Rules of International Law* (Cambridge University Press, 2003), p. 230.

132 Panel Report, *United States – Sections 301–10 of the Trade Act of 1974*, 22 December 1999, WT/DS152/R, para. 7.46.

133 Pursuant to XXIII(b) of the GATT.

obligation. However, a non-violation complaint, if upheld, does not in fact establish a breach of any international obligation – even under the ad hoc system of the GATT (even if it does eventually provide standing to suspend concessions). Therefore, while non-violation complaints require the showing of harm,[134] this cannot be equated with a breach. Accordingly, it is dubious to classify any authorized suspension of obligations in response to an unremedied non-violation impairment as a countermeasure. Despite the rarity of non-violation complaints,[135] it is apparent their likelihood of arising in a non-proliferation context renders this a valid theoretical concern for the purposes of the present chapter. Fourth, despite the imposition of strict procedural conditions on the taking of countermeasures, the WTO regime sustains a close relationship with general international law on the substantive conditions that must be met to ensure the legality of any measures.[136] Indeed, this dependence is a necessity in some 'hard cases' in which the agreements are silent.[137]

Given the above analysis, it should be uncontroversial to state that Articles I, XX and XXI(b) of the GATT constitute rules which can govern exports and imports of WMDs as well as fall under the umbrella of non-proliferation law; and Articles 3.7, 22 and 23 of the DSU constitute *strong lex specialis* rules on countermeasures, both introducing strong procedural requirements on invoking states. It may also be stated that the scope of the WTO regime on countermeasures is not as well defined, nor as particularly strong a case for a self-contained regime, as first thought. The relationship between WTO provisions and a state's right to non-perform other treaty obligations is of central importance for future analysis. For the purposes of the present chapter it suffices to note that in the WTO certain rules constitute special rules on countermeasures in the area of non-proliferation law.[138]

[134] See Art. 26.1(b) DSU.

[135] GATT panels have found non-violations through nullification and impairment in only four out of fourteen instances in which they have been argued. They are an 'exceptional remedy'. See Panel Report, *Japan – Measures Affecting Consumer Photographic Film and Paper, Complaint by the United States*, WT/DS44/R, para. 10.402.

[136] See the truly thorough work of F. Perez-Aznar, 'Countermeasures in the WTO Dispute Settlement System: An Analysis of their Characteristics and Procedure in the Light of General International Law', thesis, Graduate Institute of International Studies, Geneva, 2005 (on file with author).

[137] See, generally, L. Bartels, 'Applicable Law in the WTO Dispute Settlement Proceedings', *Journal of World Trade*, 35 (2001), 513.

[138] This of course does not automatically translate to saying that non-proliferation law is a special regime in the context of the law of countermeasures – due to the clarifications identified in section IV.ii, below and as obviously applicable to the analysis on WTO law.

The UN Security Council Resolution 1929 (2010) and countermeasures In contrast to the WTO regime, where explicit provisions governing countermeasures were examined, the present subsection will look at how, despite the absence of any rules explicitly governing countermeasures, the UN Security Council has *implicitly and effectively eroded* available measures through the taking of coercive disarmament steps.[139] While such coercive steps have largely been targeted at specific countries (most notably North Korea and Iran, of late), they *effectively removed* valid countermeasures from the array of rights that a maligned state may otherwise use. Furthermore, some measures in their effect not only prevent available countermeasures from being used between states but also by states towards international organizations.

Bowett eloquently outlined the problematic in relation to the UN Security Council and the taking of countermeasures:

> *For, in principle, the Security Council could either authorize countermeasures or prohibit counter-measures.* In either case the question will arise whether such a decision by the Council will be regarded as conclusive of the legality, or illegality, of the measures taken. There is an apparent illogicality in making the right of a state to take countermeasures subject to carefully formulated conditions, but leaving the Security Council free to authorize institutionalized counter-measures, subject to no conditions. It is this illogicality which has seemingly worried the Special Rapporteur.[140]

This section will contend that the Council has implicitly and effectively restricted the right of Iran to resort to specific countermeasures. It does not argue the case for Iranian countermeasures, nor does it posit that Iran has invoked the right to countermeasures in a specific case. It does argue that Iran has the ability to justify specific actions by countermeasures, and that these have been curtailed by positions taken by the Security Council and the IAEA. This section will further show that Council action in the field of non-proliferation law has *effectively*, if not explicitly, removed the right to resort to such countermeasures that may entail the non-performance of specific provisions of certain

[139] See, generally, on the expansive nature of the UN Security Council's expansive legislative agenda in regards to non-proliferation law, J. Fry, 'Dionysian Disarmament: Security Council WMD Coercive Disarmament Measures and their Legal Implications', *Michigan Journal of International Law*, 29 (2008), 198; D. Joyner, 'The Security Council as a Legal Hegemon', *Georgetown Journal of International Law*, 43 (2012).

[140] D. Bowett, 'The Impact of Security Council Decision on Dispute Settlement Procedures', *European Journal of International Law*, 5 (1994), 89 (emphasis added).

non-proliferation treaties. The latter has been achieved by the Council adding another layer of obligations which are identical to those contained in non-proliferation treaties, except their source is not said treaties, but rather Chapter VII UNSC resolutions. Each will be considered in turn.

In UN Security Council Resolution 1929 (2010), the following two seemingly innocuous provisions were included:

> [In tenth preambular paragraph]
>
> *Noting* with concern that Iran has taken issue with the IAEA's right to verify design information which had been provided by Iran pursuant to the modified Code 3.1, and *emphasizing* that in accordance with Article 39 of Iran's Safeguard's Agreement Code 3.1 cannot be modified nor suspended unilaterally and that the IAEA's right to verify design information provided to it is a continuing right . . .
>
> [In operative paragraph]
>
> 5. *Decides* that Iran shall without delay comply fully and without qualification with its IAEA Safeguards Agreement, including through the application of modified Code 3.1 of the Subsidiary Arrangement to its Safeguards Agreement, *calls upon* Iran to act strictly in accordance with the provisions of the Additional Protocol to its IAEA Safeguards Agreement that it signed on 18 December 2003, *calls upon* Iran to ratify promptly the Additional Protocol, and *reaffirms* that, in accordance with Articles 24 and 39 of Iran's Safeguards Agreement, Iran's Safeguards Agreement and its Subsidiary Arrangement, including modified Code 3.1, cannot be amended or changed unilaterally by Iran, and *notes* that there is no mechanism in the Agreement for the suspension of any of the provisions in the Subsidiary Arrangement;[141]

At first blush, the cited parts of Resolution 1929 seem far more relevant from a treaty law perspective[142] rather than that of the law of countermeasures. Even though the Council's approach to treaty obligations is of considerable importance to how states may approach the question of countermeasures, there are two fundamental problems with the Council's approach in Resolution 1929.

First and foremost, the Council takes a rather inconsistent position on whether Iran may suspend performance of any provisions of its Subsidiary Arrangements, as part of its Safeguards Agreement. While

[141] UN Security Council Resolution 1929 (2010), 9 June 2010, UN Doc. S/RES/1929 (2010).

[142] See M. Wood, 'The Law of Treaties and the UN Security Council: Some Reflections', in E. Cannizzaro (ed.), *The Law of Treaties Beyond the Vienna Convention* (Oxford University Press, 2011), 244.

the cited preambular paragraph states that Code 3.1 of the Arrangement *cannot be* modified or *suspended unilaterally* owing to Article 39 of Iran's Safeguard Agreement, operative paragraph 5 merely notes that there is no mechanism for suspension of Agreement or Arrangement provisions contained in the former. Yet, paragraph 5 also relies on Article 39 of the Agreement (alongside Article 24) to argue that neither the Agreement nor the Arrangement can be amended or changed unilaterally. The inconsistencies are troubling.

(a) Between two different but apparently declarative statements of the law, or an interpretation thereof, the Council has changed its position regarding Iran's ability to suspend the provisions of its Arrangement: from outright prohibition, in its tenth preambular paragraph, towards a note that there are no mechanisms for suspension contained in the Agreement, in operative paragraph 5. This dilution can be partially explained by the following point.

(b) The Council used the same provision of the Safeguards Agreement, Article 39, first to argue that both unilateral suspension *and* modification of the Arrangement's provisions is prohibited (in preambular paragraph) and then to argue that Article 39 only prohibits unilateral modification or amendment: suddenly no mention was made of Iran's ability to suspend the application of certain Arrangement provisions. The Council's clear retraction of its position on Iran's ability to suspend its obligations is perhaps misguidedly well informed – given the content of Article 39 (the provision apparently supporting the prohibition on suspension): it only relates to extensions or changes to the Subsidiary Arrangement through mutual agreement between Iran and the IAEA.[143] It does not, in any way, shape or form, consider the ability of either party to suspend its obligations. The Council's tenth preambular paragraph, that suggested as much, imports the same irregular and, quite frankly, incorrect reasoning put forward by the IAEA in March 2009: reasoning that assumes that one can conflate the competence to amend a treaty with the competence to suspend performance of its

[143] Iran's Safeguard Agreement. Art. 39 states, in part, '*The Subsidiary Arrangements may be extended or changed by agreement between the Government of Iran and the Agency without amendment of this Agreement*' (emphasis added). Equally, Art. 24, cited in para. 5 of the Resolution 1929, is entitled 'Amendment of Agreement' and concerns only amendments of the Agreement.

provisions.[144] Not only is this plainly wrong if one were to interpret[145] the Iran Safeguards Agreement and the Subsidiary Arrangement, but it is also severely misguided as a matter of the international law of treaties.[146] The treaty provisions address amendment and modification; they cannot be extended to reach a statement of law governing the suspension of specific provisions – a matter that cannot be conflated with the suspension of the treaty.

The inconsistencies highlighted in (a) and (b) leave Iran's ability to suspend parts of its Safeguards Agreement and Subsidiary Arrangement in a precarious position. While the tenth preambular paragraph is not binding and the innocuous statement concerning suspension in operative paragraph 5 is not decisive,[147] certainly the former may be used to bolster a position that the IAEA is clearly sticking by (namely prohibiting a unilateral Iranian modification or suspension of the Agreement and Arrangement). This is clearly a dangerous proposition: for it not only removes the Iranian right to suspend its performance of certain provisions in the name of countermeasures[148] but goes so

[144] See Statement by the Legal Adviser, Meeting of the Board of Governors, March 2009, paras. 1–2 of Analysis: 'The implementation of the provisions of Subsidiary Arrangements can only be *amended or suspended* with the agreement of both parties to them ... The provisions *cannot be amended or suspended unilaterally* by the state. Thus Iran's failure to provide design information in accordance with the modified Code 3.1 as agreed to by Iran in 2003 is inconsistent with Iran's obligations under the Subsidiary Arrangements to its Safeguards Agreement' (emphasis added). Also cited in Joyner, 'The Security Council as a Legal Hegemon', 13.

[145] Wood, 'The Law of Treaties and the UN Security Council', 248 offers an interpretation.

[146] The Vienna Convention on the Law of Treaties treats amendment or modification of treaties differently from suspension. The VCLT has two entirely different parts for each (Parts IV and V, respectively). Indeed, we are not concerned with this differentiation, since the Resolution is not concerned with suspension of the treaty but rather suspension of its provisions (or performance thereof).

[147] The Council does not go so far as to preclude recourse to suspension measures contained in general public international law, only noting that no such measures exist in the Safeguards Agreement.

[148] An important distinction should be made between suspension of a treaty and suspension of the performance of a provision. The Council and the IAEA refer to the suspension of a treaty (the Safeguards Agreement and the Subsidiary Arrangement) and of the provisions contained therein. See also, Crawford, Third Report, paras. 324–325 (looking on the distinction and link between suspension of a treaty and countermeasures). On the topic of whether the Subsidiary Arrangement may be qualified as a treaty, see D. Joyner, 'The Qom Enrichment Facility: Was Iran Legally Bound to Disclose?', *Jurist Legal News and Research* (2010), available at http://jurist.law.pitt.edu/forumy/2010/03/qom-enrichment-facility-was-iran.php (accessed 2 April 2012) (arguing that the Arrangement is not a treaty).

far as to create a general position applicable to all states parties – a position which has not otherwise been contested by other IAEA states parties. Without seeking fully to argue the particulars of the Iranian case, this sort of measure may have a particular relevance given Iran's treatment by the IAEA – especially following its referral to the UN Security Council on 4 February 2006. The arguable case is that such a referral was not in compliance with the IAEA's own statute,[149] and inconsistent with previous IAEA practice in cases of clear non-compliance.[150] Should it be possible to construct an arguable case for a breach by the IAEA, then Iranian recourse to a suspension of its performance of the rights and obligations owed to the IAEA would constitute an operational right to take recourse to countermeasures. The Council's actions clearly proceed effectively to limit such recourse to a potential Iranian countermeasure. Despite this profound effect, it is too early to state that the Council has laid down a clear, coherent and applicable rule on the matter. What is has done is to go some way to support an incorrect position on the law – taken by the IAEA.

Second, and far more simply, it is contended that Security Council action in the area of non-proliferation law has removed any *effective ability* of states to resort to countermeasures in the face of unjust treatment. This has been achieved by the Council incorporating, as binding on member states, obligations identical to those contained in major non-proliferation treaties. This has the effect of making these same obligations being owed to different international legal actors.

[149] The argument to make in this regard is that in accordance with Art. XII(7)(c) IAEA Statute the referral to the UN Security Council is only permitted upon a determination of non-compliance. Such a determination by the Board of Governors has to be made on the basis of an inspector's report demonstrating said non-compliance. Not only was there no dispositive proof that there had actually been non-compliance by Iran but the Board of Governors' determination of non-compliance was made without any corroborating report by inspectors. For a description of the situation and conflicting legal approaches, see Joyner, *International Law and Proliferation of Weapons of Mass Destruction*, pp. 50–54; Calamita, 'Sanctions, Countermeasures, and the Iranian Nuclear Issue', pp. 1400–1402; Fry, 'Dionysian Disarmament', pp. 271–272; Joyner, 'Security Council', 11–13.

[150] Notable contrary examples of IAEA practice of non-referral (calling for constructive action, rather than mere reporting) to the Council despite non-compliance are: Japan and the unresolved issue of missing 200 kg of plutonium from the 1980s and South Korea's secret processing of plutonium and uranium enrichment. See, for a description of each, T. Ogilvie-White, 'International Responses to Iranian Nuclear Defiance: The Non-Aligned Movement and the Issue of Non-Compliance', *European Journal of International Law*, 18 (2007), 463–464 nn. 25 and 26.

Consequently, even if Iran felt aggrieved and took suitable countermeasures against the IAEA due to a previous breach, this would not preclude it from being in breach of the same obligations as owed to the UN Security Council. A clear example is demonstrable by operative paragraph 5 of UNSC Resolution 1929 (2010), where it '*calls upon* Iran to act strictly in *accordance with the provisions* of the Additional Protocol to the IAEA Safeguards Agreement that it signed on 18 December 2003'. The Council bound Iran by the provisions of the Additional Protocol by virtue of this resolution, and its wording. It did not make it party to the treaty, nor did it presume that Iran was at any point previously bound by the Additional Protocol by virtue of treaty law.[151] Therefore, any countermeasure that may be taken by Iran against the IAEA would absolve it of international responsibility against the Agency, but it would simultaneously be in breach of its obligations to the Security Council – where its wrongful acts would not be precluded. This phenomenon of creating identical but differently sourced obligations is also prevalent among a number of other non-proliferation Council resolutions.[152]

The preceding analysis has revealed that there are no direct rules on countermeasures in Security Council resolutions in the area of non-proliferation law. However, it should also be observed that UNSC Resolution 1929 (2010) may be read to have explicitly rejected the right of Iran to undertake a specific countermeasure. A more reasonable interpretation is that the resolution does not do this, but does lend support to the IAEA's legal position which explicitly rejects Iran's right to take recourse to the specific countermeasure of suspending the performance certain procedural treaty provisions. It is therefore problematic to state that Security Council action has given rise to special rules on countermeasures. Yet, its limiting effects on maligned states to resort to this general international law right cannot be doubted – even if it only forces them to make a tough political choice on which rights to obey and which not.

This concludes the analysis of relevant rules affecting *when* there is a right to resort to countermeasures. Different considerations have

[151] For an identical reading, see Wood, 'The Law of Treaties and the UN Security Council', 249.

[152] For a systemic and detailed review of each major resolution that not only echoed provisions of treaty law but imposed new obligations on certain states, see Fry, 'Dionysian Disarmament' (looking at UNSC Res. 487 (1981) (Israel–Iraq); Res. 582 (1986), 598 (1987), 612 (1988) and 620 (1988) (Iraq); Res. 687 (1991) (Iraq); Res. 1172 (1998) (India–Pakistan); Res. 1695 (2006), 1718 (2006) (North Korea); Res. 1696 (2006), 1737 (2006) (Iran); and Res. 1540 (2004)).

emerged from different categories of non-proliferation rules. These categories have ranged from mild specialness to strong forms of *lex specialis*, yet it is impossible to state the existence of categorical special rules across non-proliferation law. What has emerged is a modest conclusion that non-proliferation law's relationship with the *right to resort* to countermeasures under general international law is highly dependent on the specific treaty regime. Some treaties are silent on the role of countermeasures, but contain extensive mechanisms to determine a breach and compliance therewith. Others contain specific rules, which only govern a narrow type of countermeasures, while others still contain strong, settled, but not fully determinate rules concerning non-proliferation law. The question now becomes not whether there is a right to resort to countermeasures under general international law, or under special rules, or even when this right is triggered, but *what countermeasures may be taken* – given the above rules.

ii. What *countermeasures are permissible in non-proliferation law?*

Having previously addressed the questions of *who* may take countermeasures and also partially *when* they may be taken, this subsection will complete the analysis of the latter and also identify *what* countermeasures can be taken. This enquiry has two aspects: one that centres on revisiting the nature of the obligations contained across different parts of non-proliferation law,[153] and a second examining the role of urgent countermeasures and their relationship with certain non-proliferation provisions that lay down procedural prerequisites for the taking of countermeasures. Each aspect contains entirely different issues, with different conceptual foundations. Section III concluded that a small minority of substantive non-proliferation obligations could be considered as interdependent, under a law of state responsibility approach. A breach of these obligations enables a decentralized response, allowing all states parties to the obligation in question to take countermeasures. However, section III also concluded that not all substantive non-proliferation obligations, nor procedural ones, could be considered as interdependent (see, generally, section III. iii). Such an analysis was premised on the majority of non-proliferation treaties that contain *collective*

[153] Note that section III, above explicitly examined only the nature of obligations in identifiable non-proliferation *treaties*. Section IV has highlighted a number of non-proliferation obligations that may not be entirely collective in nature.

obligations.[154] Section IV. i should have clarified that some non-proliferation obligations are conceivably *bilateral.* Examples highlighted include those owed by Iran, and other states parties, to the IAEA;[155] those owed by specific states to the UN Security Council; and those owed as between each state party to each other bilaterally under the WTO.[156] The question of whether an obligation is *bilateral* or *collective* in nature is a prerequisite to determining both who may take countermeasures and whether such countermeasures are permissible.[157] Bar the cited examples, the vast majority of non-proliferation obligations are collective. The consequences of this will be examined in subsections (a) and (b), below, both of which relate to potential limitations on what type of countermeasures may be taken.

a. The apparent preclusion of reciprocal countermeasures for collective non-proliferation obligations

There is an important consequence in finding that the majority of non-proliferation obligations are collective: a state party taking countermeasures in response to a breach of collective obligations is *almost precluded* from taking reciprocal countermeasures comprising non-performance of a similar or the same collective obligations contained in the same multilateral treaty.[158] The caveat of *almost precluded* is important to

[154] Crawford defined these as those that 'are expressed (or necessarily implied) to relate to matters of the common interest of the parties'. Crawford, Third Report, para. 92.

[155] It is uncontroversial to state that IAEA Safeguard Obligations are bilateral insofar as they are contained in a bilateral Safeguards Agreement and Additional Protocol. These bilateral obligations may, however, become collective through the presence of extraneous treaty provisions. A clear example is the NPT framework. While under Art. III(1) NPT it is arguable that bilateral IAEA–state safeguard obligations may be collectivized, this is only so where the important caveat that such obligations are 'for the exclusive purpose of verification of the fulfillment of its obligations assumed under this Treaty with a view to preventing diversion of nuclear energy from peaceful uses to nuclear weapons'. It should be clear that, in theory, not all IAEA–state obligations might be collectivized – but only insofar as they meet the Art. III(1) caveat. Indeed, IAEA obligations contained in the IAEA Statute are not collectivized, but merely bilateral.

[156] On the bilateral nature of WTO obligations and provisions, see Pauwelyn, 'The Typology of Multilateral Treaty Obligations'.

[157] There is a valid argument to be made that certain other obligations are bilateral, such as those contained in Art. VI NPT, where they are owed between two specific groups of states. Roscini also alleges the bilateral character of certain NFZ treaty obligations. Cf. M. Roscini, 'Something Old, Something New: The 2006 Semipalatinsk Treaty on a Nuclear Weapon-Free Zone in Central Asia', *Chinese Journal of International Law*, 7 (2008), 593 n. 88.

[158] This is a slightly looser definition of 'reciprocal countermeasures' than that provided by Riphagen and Crawford. See, Crawford, Third Report, paras. 327–329 and n. 65. See also Crawford, *ILC Commentaries*, p. 282.

note. By way of example, should state A breach any provisions contained in the CWC, and should it be presumed that state B has standing to take countermeasures, then state B is still *technically capable as a matter of law* to take measures of non-performance of collective obligations contained in the CWC *against* state A. The law of state responsibility shall preclude the wrongfulness of state B's actions inasmuch as it may incur responsibility in regards to state A. However, given that the measure involves non-performance of a collective obligation, it shall not preclude state A's wrongfulness for its breach of obligation, which it incurs vis-à-vis all other states parties C to Z of the NPT.

The understanding that state B is *technically capable as a matter of law* to take countermeasures in this scenario *against* state A, but may retain responsibility for its actions as regards third states, arises out of a degree of legal ambiguity.[159] The inherent problem of taking countermeasures as regards collective obligations is that they *do not* per se *preclude* the taking of reciprocal countermeasures but they require the invoking state to make an *acute political decision*[160] between enforcing its right and incurring responsibility to third states. The problem is far more paradoxical for interdependent obligations, a subset of collective obligations, inasmuch that while breach of these obligations enables a decentralized response through third-party countermeasures, an invoking third state is clearly 'restricted' in its right to take recourse to reciprocal countermeasures.[161] The normative desirability to sustain treaty regimes based

[159] Art. 49(1) of the ILC Articles states that state B 'may *only* take countermeasures against a State which is responsible for an internationally wrongful act'. Therefore, state B may only take the countermeasure against state A, but this does not preclude that such a countermeasure may affect the rights of third states. The ILC Commentary takes the position that 'Countermeasures may not be *directed against* States other than the responsible State. In a situation where a third State is owed an international obligation by the State taking countermeasures and that obligation is breach by the countermeasure, the wrongfulness of measure is not precluded as against the third State. In that sense the effect of countermeasures in precluding wrongfulness is relative. It concerns the legal relations between the injured State and the responsible State.' Cf. Crawford, *ILC Commentaries*, p. 285.

[160] While clearly invoking a right is always a political decision, the nature of the political decision in the described instance is particularly acute. See, generally, H. Lauterpacht, *The Function of Law in the International Community* (Oxford University Press, 1933).

[161] The relationship between reciprocal countermeasures and interdependent obligations has long been a source of issue in the law of state responsibility. See, generally, for a discussion, J. Crawford and S. Olleson, 'The Exception of Non-Performance: Links between the Law of Treaties and the Law of State Responsibility', *Australian Year Book of International Law*, 21 (2001), 7. Furthermore, interdependent obligations cannot be

on collective (and, more specifically, interdependent) obligations has led commentators to reject the right to states to undertake reciprocal countermeasures *ab initio*.[162] However, this should not be mistaken as the current state of law. The only viable and technical limitation on the resort to reciprocal countermeasures for collective obligations is *political*.[163]

b. Self-existent obligations as limitations on the object of countermeasures in non-proliferation law

In contrast, an absolute limitation on the taking of any type of countermeasure emerges from the existence of certain self-existent non-proliferation obligations. Where the general international law of countermeasures may be considered applicable, as is the case for most non-proliferation treaties (see, section IV.i.a), it is clear that countermeasures could not in any event relate to several fundamental substantive obligations by virtue of Article 50(1) of the ILC Articles. These exceptions cannot be contested from a general international law standpoint, nor, in some cases, from a *lex specialis* perspective. An example of the latter concerns countermeasures not infringing on the obligations not to threaten to use or to use force – these have been codified in specific non-proliferation treaties.[164]

The central point of contestation is determining which obligations fall into the category of being so fundamental that they may not be considered subject to countermeasures. Some commentators have suggested that *all* self-existent obligations cannot be subject to countermeasures.[165] The case has therefore been put forward from exempting environmental obligations, non-fundamental human rights obligations, among others, from the object of countermeasures.[166] This approach has some appeal from a principled approach to self-existent obligations, and would bear

considered as necessarily 'intransgressible', effecting their automatic preclusion from the object of countermeasures. Cf. Crawford, *ILC Commentaries*, p. 291.

162 Dekker, *The Law of Arms Control*, 351. See also Hammarskjöld, UN Doc. S/3596, paras. 17–19, as cited in Crawford and Olleson, 'The Exception of Non-Performance', 21.

163 The political element is sharpened when one considers that if a state A breaches an interdependent obligation not only may all states parties take countermeasures but they may suspend performance of the treaty under Art. 60(2)(c) VCLT.

164 e.g., Art. 11 African NFZT (prohibition on armed attacks); Art. 1, Protocol 2, South Pacific NFZT (prohibition on threatening to use, or using, nuclear weapons); Arts. 3(1) and (2), Southeast Asia NFZT (prohibition to test, use or station nuclear weapons).

165 See, e.g., Pauwelyn, 'The Typology of Multilateral Treaty Obligations', 924.

166 See, generally, for environmental obligations, U. Beyerlin, 'State Community Interests and Institution-Building in International Environmental Law', *Heidelberg Journal of*

relevance for a number of non-proliferation treaties that contain environmental obligations.[167] Indeed, the prevalence of anti-dumping provisions in non-proliferation treaties may justify a fifth category of obligation to be added to the non-exhaustive list drawn up in section III. ii. a, above. Yet, however much a principled approach may require a broader understanding of self-existent obligations to be adopted,[168] the problem that occurs is that the ILC did not decide to base its Article 50(1) analysis on the notion of self-existent obligations. In this respect, the following analysis differs significantly from that of interdependent obligations and Article 42(b)(ii), above. The ILC's starting point for determining exceptions to obligations the object of countermeasures was in fact first peremptory norms and then those which emerged by *lex specialis*. It was only later in the ILC debates that fundamental substantive obligations were listed, and these were limited due to certain expressions of will by states.[169] However, in drawing up these substantive obligations, their self-existent character was not a functionally determinative criterion in the ILC's work.[170] To the extent that there may have been any reference, the ILC Commentary talked of 'intransgressible' obligations within the meaning referred to in the *Legality of the Threat or Use of Nuclear Weapons* advisory opinion – but this reference is far from clear. Indeed, it is arguable that attributes the court gave to 'intransgressible' obligations are far narrower and more demanding than the attributes that Fitzmaurice gave to self-existent or absolute obligations.

One may therefore be sympathetic to a persuasive principled argument that examines the core tenets of self-existent obligations (as the present author is – to a degree), in which case environmental obligations contained in non-proliferation treaties are precluded from being the object of countermeasures. Such an approach becomes more appealing if one accepts that the ILC's determination is not dispositive of the matter, and, even if it did not base its approach on the self-existent

International Law, 56 (1996), 605–611; Pauwelyn, 'The Typology of Multilateral Treaty Obligations', 924.

167 e.g., obligations prohibiting the dumping of radioactive waste: Art. 7(a)–(b) African NFZT; Art. 3(2) Treaty on a Nuclear-Weapon-Free Zone in Central Asia; Art. 7(1) South Pacific NFZT; Art. 3(3) Southeast Asia NFZT. See also Roscini, 'Something Old, Something New', 612.

168 See Tams, *Enforcing Obligations*, pp. 57–58 for an excellent example of how this may be done.

169 Crawford, *ILC Commentaries*, p. 51.

170 A point overlooked by the analysis of Pauwelyn, 'The Typology of Multilateral Treaty Obligations', 922–924.

nature of obligations, it should have done. However, even if this was accepted, it cannot also be accepted that all environmental obligations are of a standard-setting character, and certainly the approach to environmental obligations in certain NFZTs seems to support such an assertion. The point of contestation is therefore murky and requires more in-depth analysis than can be provided here. Suffice to say that the above analysis reveals that there are equally valid arguments for precluding countermeasures in regards to environmental obligations contained in non-proliferation treaties as there are for permitting them.

c. The potential expansion of the general law of countermeasures: urgent countermeasures in non-proliferation law

Having examined two possible sources of limitation on what countermeasures may be taken, this next point of analysis will examine what type of countermeasures may extraordinarily be permitted, given the content of the non-proliferation rules identified in section IV. i. That section examined different non-proliferation rules which may constrain, modify or exclude countermeasures under general international law. However, owing to the character of these rules there is a need to examine a specific type of countermeasure that may retain significant relevance for non-proliferation law: urgent countermeasures.

The examination of institutional treaty mechanisms, certain specific treaty specific countermeasure rules and those arising under the WTO and the UN Security Council, revealed the potential for specific treaty regimes laying down extensive *procedural prerequisites* before resort to countermeasures under the treaty or under general international law may be permitted. Although the present author contends that institutional treaty mechanisms and their accompanying rules do not establish procedural prerequisites as regards the determination of a breach and subsequent treatment of the breach, certain authors hold a different position (see, section IV. i. a, above). In some cases, the argument for the existence of procedural prerequisites is relatively strong – as in the case for the WTO, or for countermeasures of general interest under the CTBT and CWC (where a treaty body recommendation is first required) (see, section IV. i. b–c, above).

A central tension emerges from the above conclusion and the following central propositions on the law of countermeasures: (a) urgent countermeasures are not distinguishable from 'normal' countermeasures under international law;[171] (b) countermeasures must be regarded as equivalent to interim measures of protection;[172] and (c) facile recourse to countermeasures must be tempered by certain procedural requirements.[173] The tension manifests itself as follows: if some non-proliferation rules do lay down onerous procedural prerequisites, and are therefore not limited as under Article 51(1) ILC Articles, nor expeditious, then how can states take recourse to countermeasures as an effective interim measure. The need for urgent countermeasures under general international law permits a state to set aside the obligation to offer to negotiate (Article 52(2)), but if non-proliferation law lays down – as it does in some cases – more onerous procedural prerequisites, then what mechanism is there to set these aside in the name of urgency? The problem is that there is no clear way to manage this issue.

The nature of non-proliferation law also lends itself to countermeasures that must, in some cases, be taken in a time-sensitive manner (e.g., to prevent an international actor from obtaining WMD material etc.). The central problem is not merely the existence of procedural prerequisites, but that they are clearly not expeditious enough to do justice to such a scenario and there is no available rule in international law to set them aside where they apply. The Article 52(2) rule setting aside the obligation to offer to negotiate in cases of urgent countermeasures, while applicable to general international law, does not allow one to set aside treaty-specific procedural prerequisites. Accordingly, in the view of the present author, there are two ways to reconcile these issues. First, undertake a watered-down reading of the procedural requirements contained in non-proliferation treaties: in reaching the determination that apparent procedural prerequisites in non-proliferation treaties containing extensive institutional treaty mechanisms were not binding requirements, the present author has done precisely this. However, this approach is a little more difficult for those rules contained in Article XII(3) CWW, Article V(3) CTBT and the WTO. In such cases, the possibility for a watered-down reading is negligible. Rather, one must

[171] See J. Crawford, Fourth Report on State Responsibility, 2 April 2011, UN Doc. A/CN.4/517, para. 69; Crawford, *ILC Commentaries*, p. 53; J. Crawford, 'Counter-measures as Interim Measures', *European Journal of International Law*, 5 (1994), 65; but see limited incorporation of concept in Art. 52(2) ILC Articles on State Responsibility.

[172] Crawford, 'Counter-measures as Interim Measures', 68 (identified as his sixth principle); Arts. 49(3), 52(3) and 53 ILC Articles on State Responsibility (recognizing the temporary and reversible nature of countermeasures).

[173] Art. 52(1)(a)–(b) ILC Articles on State Responsibility.

resort to the second approach of reconciliation. Second, should the procedural prerequisites of such treaties be unable to function in an *expeditious* manner,[174] and therefore the way they should, then one must consider this a *procedural failure* by the treaty regime,[175] triggering a fallback onto the general rules of international law governing countermeasures.

Frankly, neither the first nor the second is satisfactory as normative readings of doctrine, but what must emerge from this legal analysis is a way to reconcile the need for urgent countermeasures in non-proliferation law with the apparent obstacles in specific treaty regimes to meet such a need. The present author advocates for a degree of liberalism in the reading of that which determines under what conditions urgent countermeasures are permissible.

iii. Conclusion

The present chapter has attempted to introduce a comprehensive approach to examining countermeasures in non-proliferation law. It has also done so with a view to examining the existence of special rules on three central questions: *who* may take countermeasures, *when* may such countermeasures be taken and *what* countermeasures are permissible. It was hoped that from an examination of these three areas, and the rules contained therein, a thesis on whether non-proliferation law was a special regime might emerge. It is regrettable to say that one has not. What has emerged is the identification of certain special characteristics in specific areas and a few, highly specific, rules which perhaps mark a special approach to countermeasures. However, these findings cannot be extrapolated to reach a more general conclusion on non-proliferation law being a special regime.

The central findings of this chapter have been (1) that non-proliferation treaties, in general, contain certain substantive obligations that may be qualified as interdependent. However, the majority of provisions (procedural, substantive positive peaceful and some substantial) cannot be so qualified, thus disabling a decentralized approach to

[174] This expeditious requirement was identified by Crawford, 'Counter-measures as Interim Measures', 68: 'Thus the purpose of the counter-measures should be regarded as met if (a) the *expeditious* procedure for determining the legality of the conduct in question is triggered' (emphasis added).

[175] The concept of a procedural failure by a regime was considered by the ILC in its ILC Report on Fragmentation, paras. 188–189.

countermeasures for the majority of provisions upon breach. (2) non-proliferation treaties and other treaties (e.g., WTO) contain provisions which curtail, modify or exclude the general international law of countermeasures to extremely varying degrees. These rules are of a varying degree of specialness at a general norm level, and in some cases highly case-specific (e.g., the UN Security Council, IAEA and Iran). The central point to note is that despite the presence of extensive treaty-specific institutions, the general law of countermeasures governs in most cases. (3) That given the *largely* collective nature of non-proliferation obligations, and the considerable presence of interdependent obligations, reciprocal countermeasures are in some cases *effectively precluded*, while environmental obligations could also be excluded from the object of countermeasures in non-proliferation law. Finally, it was found that urgent countermeasures should fall within the legal regime of non-proliferation law, but whether and how the law permits this is ambiguous.

It appears that in the context of non-proliferation law, the law of countermeasures has been of little use in elucidating a general thesis on whether the former is a special regime. This is quite an unremarkable result indicative only of the unnecessary hype that one finds in the rhetoric of fragmentation discourse. Nevertheless, it is hoped that this chapter will have contributed to clarifying the problematic underpinnings of certain state responsibility issues and identifying the applicable laws concerning countermeasures and non-proliferation law – and how one might approach them with a degree of legal pragmatism.

8

State responsibility consequences of termination of or withdrawal from non-proliferation treaties

DIETER FLECK

I. Introduction

In non-proliferation law the obligations of states are not confined to the accountability for breaches[1] and the examination of circumstances precluding the wrongfulness of certain action.[2] The potentially harmful effects of weapons of mass destruction and the prevailing lack of effective measures relating to complete nuclear disarmament make it imperative to consider further legal consequences. There is emerging consensus that state responsibility in this realm, as with respect to the protection of the environment, must go beyond the avoidance of wrongful acts. Even if the notion of an international liability for injurious consequences of acts not prohibited by international law has not yet entered into codified treaties, it may be accepted today that there is a general legal obligation for states to avoid transboundary harm in their activities,[3] whereas precise conditions and limitations of such obligation are still to be specified. The problem under discussion here may be compared with the situation of signatories of an international treaty as long as they have not signed it,[4] yet it is more difficult to solve in the absence of agreed standards on

[1] See Chapter 6, in this book, Matthew Happold, 'The "injured state" in the case of breach of a non-proliferation treaty and the legal consequences of such a breach'.

[2] See Chapter 7, in this book, Sahib Singh, 'Non-proliferation law and countermeasures'.

[3] See M. Koskenniemi, 'Doctrines of State Responsibility', in J. Crawford, A. Pellet and S. Olleson (eds.), *The Law of International Responsibility* (Oxford University Press, 2010), chap. 5, esp. p. 50; A. Boyle, 'Liability for Injurious Consequences of Acts Not Prohibited by International Law', *ibid.*, chap. 10.

[4] See M. Asada, 'CTBT: Legal Questions Arising from its Non-entry into Force', *Journal of Conflict and Security Law*, 7(1) (2002), 85–122.

positive law such as those provided with Article 18 of the Vienna Convention on the Law of Treaties (VCLT).

The present chapter will discuss legal consequences for withdrawal from non-proliferation treaties, including suspension and termination. The essential question outlined in the Introduction of this book – whether there are any specific rules in non-proliferation law which differ from the general rules of public international law or the rules of other special regimes, and if so, whether these peculiarities would justify the conclusion that non-proliferation law is a special regime – will be discussed with respect to treaty withdrawal and an answer will be sought in three steps of different size. First, I will briefly consider general conditions for withdrawal under the law of treaties (section II. i) and examine substantial and procedural limitations that have been introduced so far in non-proliferation law (section II. ii), topics that are discussed in greater depth in Chapter 5, above.[5] I will then try to identify existing gaps in treaty law as far as legal consequences of withdrawal from non-proliferation obligations are concerned (section III. i) and undertake an assessment of specific law and policy aspects of withdrawal from non-proliferation commitments (section III. ii). As the third step, relevant questions of dispute settlement will be explored (section IV). Finally, some conclusions may be drawn (section V).

II. *Lex lata* consequences of withdrawal

States which have committed themselves to non-proliferation of specifically destructive weapons should not be presumed as being free to withdraw from this commitment at will without certain consequences. But relevant tasks are complex and difficult to discern. This is particularly true for legal obligations in this field. The problems involved here go beyond the issue of reparation in the strict sense, as this would require a wrongful act, while withdrawal from a treaty is not necessarily wrongful. Yet the withdrawal may have harmful results regardless of whether these are caused by prohibited action or not. When a state withdraws from a non-proliferation obligation in violation of a treaty, material compensation will hardly be the issue, and other forms of reparation (restitution and satisfaction) are to be examined as part of a wider responsibility for the maintenance of peace and security. In the event

[5] See Chapter 5, in this book, Daniel H. Joyner and Marco Roscini, 'Withdrawal from non-proliferation treaties'.

of lawful withdrawal from a treaty obligation it is even more difficult to identify positive obligations. Such obligations may exist, however, even beyond the avoidance of wrongful acts.

i. General conditions for withdrawal

A termination of or withdrawal from a treaty obligation cannot *per se* be considered as a wrongful act, as it is generally accepted, although with certain limitations, under the conditions set out in the Vienna Convention on the Law of Treaties (VCLT). As this Convention entered into force only on 27 January 1980, has no retroactive effect, and formal participation by states is still limited, it does not directly apply to most of the existing non-proliferation obligations. Its provisions may, nevertheless, be considered as a codification of existing customary international law, to the extent that both *opinio iuris* and former or subsequent state practice would support this evaluation. Under Article 42(2) VCLT any termination of, or denunciation or withdrawal from, a treaty, or its suspension, may take place only as a result of the application of the provisions of that treaty or of the VCLT. Articles 54–59 VCLT provide that termination of or withdrawal from a treaty must take place in conformity with the provisions of the treaty or at any time by consent of the parties. Any denunciation or withdrawal must either be foreseen in the treaty, or it must be established that the parties intended to admit this possibility, or it must be implied by the nature of the treaty.

Unilateral withdrawal or suspension may be declared in the event of material breaches (Article 60 VCLT), irrespective of whether this possibility was expressly foreseen or at least implied when the treaty was concluded. Even when unilateral withdrawal was not explicitly provided for in the treaty text, a party may invoke the impossibility of performing a treaty as a ground for terminating or withdrawing from it (Article 61 VCLT), or it may base its withdrawal on a fundamental change of circumstances (*rebus sic stantibus*) that was not foreseen by the parties before, *if* '(a) the existence of those circumstances constituted an essential basis of the consent of the parties to be bound by the treaty; and (b) the effect of the change is radically to transform the extent of obligations still to be performed under the treaty' (Article 62 VCLT).

Hence the *pacta sunt servanda* principle does not generally exclude unilateral withdrawal from a treaty, even if the treaty was concluded with indefinite or unlimited duration. There may, however, be limitations deriving from contrary behaviour of a party (Article 45 VCLT). It may be noted in this context that the International Law Commission is considering a loss of a right of withdrawal even under wartime conditions if the party has expressly agreed on or 'acquiesced in the continued operation' of a treaty.[6]

ii. Substantial and procedural limitations

It is in this context that substantial limitations and procedural regulations of the right to withdraw from non-proliferation treaties needs to be revisited in the light of both specific national interests which have led to their conclusion and subsequent circumstances which may have substantially changed for one or more parties. The 1963 Partial Test-Ban Treaty (PTBT), the 1968 Treaty on the Non-Proliferation of Nuclear Weapons (Nuclear Non-Proliferation Treaty – NPT), the 1996 Comprehensive Nuclear-Test-Ban Treaty (CTBT) and likewise the conventions on nuclear-weapon-free zones have limited withdrawal to extraordinary events that have jeopardized the supreme interests of a party. Relevant treaties since 1968 require a withdrawing party to notify such events three months in advance, yet they do not give any other party a right to grant or deny approval of such notification.[7] The decision on withdrawal thus remains a result of auto-interpretation by the withdrawing party[8] tempered by the criterion of good faith.[9] The inclusion of the Security Council as a required recipient of advance notification was meant to provide a 'suitable forum for meeting security

[6] See ILC Draft Articles on Effects of Armed Conflicts on Treaties, http://untreaty.un.org/ilc/texts/instruments/english/commentaries/1_10_2011.pdf, draft Article 12: 'Loss of the right to terminate or withdraw from a treaty or to suspend its operation. A State may no longer terminate or withdraw from a treaty or suspend its operation as a consequence of an armed conflict if, after becoming aware of the facts: (a) it shall have expressly agreed that the treaty remains in force or continues in operation; or (b) it must by reason of its conduct be considered as having acquiesced in the continued operation of the treaty or in its maintenance in force.'

[7] J. Goldblat, 'Should the Right to Withdraw from the NPT Be Withdrawn?', research paper commissioned by the International Commission on Nuclear Non-proliferation and Disarmament (January 2009). Available at www.google.co.uk/url?sa=t&rct=j&q=&esrc=s&source=web&cd=1&ved=0CCcQFjAA&url=http%3A%2F%2Ficnnd.org%2FDocuments%2FGoldblat_Withdrawal_from_NPT.doc&ei=ZZ95T767KoHH0QWd5um1DQ&usg=AFQjCNFM7wcWnOf9JuZYW2X9lIJ494Xndw&sig2=hP8ZYxGs_BPk92ZDEz3SEw.

[8] N. Ronzitti, 'Problems of Arms Control Treaty Interpretation', in *The International Law of Arms Control and Disarmament*, Proceedings of the Symposium, Geneva, 28 February–2 March 1991 (Geneva: United Nations, 1991), 120.

[9] C. A. Cohn, 'Interpreting the Withdrawal Clause in Arms Control Treaties', *Michigan Journal of International Law*, 10 (1989), 849–871; E. Schwelb, 'The Nuclear-Test-Ban Treaty and International Law', *American Journal of International Law*, 58 (1964), 662–663.

preoccupations of the withdrawing Party',[10] and to allow for necessary action by the Council including delay or prevention of withdrawal.[11]

Similar withdrawal clauses (yet without reference to the Security Council as a required recipient) were introduced in bilateral treaties between the two military superpowers. Examples are the 1972 Anti-Ballistic Missile (ABM) Treaty, from which the USA declared its withdrawal on 13 December 2001, contending that several states and non-state entities had acquired, or were seeking to acquire, weapons of mass destruction, and that this posed a threat to US security. This was the first time that an arms control agreement was unilaterally denounced and – as the Treaty had been concluded bilaterally and its extension to the USSR successor states Belarus, Kazakhstan and Ukraine had not yet been ratified by the USA – US withdrawal resulted automatically in its termination, effective on 13 June 2002. In response, Russia had declined to ratify START II and notified on 14 June 2002 that it no longer considered itself bound by its terms.

The 1974 Threshold Test-Ban Treaty (TTBT), the 1976 Peaceful Nuclear Explosions Treaty (PNET), and again the New START signed in 2010 carry identical withdrawal clauses. In the last case, the possibility of withdrawal was mitigated by its limited duration.[12] In addition, further specifications on withdrawal were declared during parliamentary debates on ratification.[13]

[10] M. Shaker, *The Nuclear Non-proliferation Treaty: Origin and Implementation, 1959–1979* (New York: Oceana, 1980), p. 896.

[11] G. Bunn and J. Rhinelander, 'The Right to Withdraw from the NPT: Article X is Not Unconditional', *Disarmament Diplomacy*, 79 (April/May 2005).

[12] Art. XIV (2) of the New Start Treaty: 'This Treaty shall remain in force for 10 years unless it is superseded earlier by a subsequent agreement on the reduction and limitation of strategic offensive arms. If either Party raises the issue of extension of this Treaty, the Parties shall jointly consider the matter. If the Parties decide to extend this Treaty, it will be extended for a period of no more than five years unless it is superseded earlier by a subsequent agreement on the reduction and limitation of strategic offensive arms.'

[13] On 25 January 2011, the Russian State Duma adopted the draft law on the New START treaty ratification with two formal statements, one addressed to the Russian President ('As the US has withdrawn from the Soviet–US Treaty on the limitation of anti-ballistic missile systems, special significance has to be attached to maintaining missile defense systems and all their components at a designated level of preparedness for improvement in case of a military threat against Russia'), the other to the international community ('The State Duma considers the deployment of the US non-strategic nuclear weapons outside the US unjustified and not complying with today's Euro-Atlantic relations'). The US ratification text specifies that the correlation between strategic offensive weapons and missile defence addressed in the preamble 'does not impose a legal obligation on the

The 1972 Biological Weapons Convention (BWC), the 1990 Treaty on Conventional Armed Forces in Europe (CFE), the 1992 Open Skies Treaty and the 1993 Chemical Weapons Convention (CWC) expressly stipulated an unlimited duration without, however, denying parties a right to withdraw in extraordinary circumstances.[14]

On 10 January 2003, North Korea announced the reactivation of its withdrawal from the NPT which had been declared on 12 March 1993, but suspended on 11 June 1993, one day before effectuation. While initially different ways of interpreting the 2003 announcement had been open for discussion,[15] North Korea publicly declared on 10 February 2005 that it possessed nuclear weapons. The Security Council, unable to act in this situation, has left the matter to be dealt with through the six-party talks by North Korea, South Korea, Japan, China, Russia and the USA. It took until 2006 for the Council to request North Korea to retract its announcement of withdrawal, a reaction similar to that of 1993,[16] yet reinforced with the additional request to abandon all nuclear weapons and existing nuclear programmes in a complete, verifiable and irreversible manner.[17] Again, in 2010, the NPT Review Conference urged North Korea 'to return, at an early date, to the Treaty'.[18]

North Korea's withdrawal from the NPT raised a number of questions regarding not only whether this withdrawal was valid, but also what

parties', with the effect that the USA cannot be constrained in its missile defence activities. The Russian document asserts otherwise. Russian Foreign Minister Sergei Lavrov, referring in that context to the withdrawal clause in the event of an emergency, stated: 'We are convinced that the implementation of the full-scale global missile defense by the US will be precisely such an emergency.' See http://gsn.nti.org/gsn/nw_20110201_4215.php. The New START treaty entered into force on 5 February 2011.

[14] The CFE Treaty was adapted in 2002 to replace existing troop ceilings that were still arranged on a bloc-to-bloc (NATO versus Warsaw Pact) basis with a system of national and territorial ceilings and also to provide for more inspections and new mechanisms designed to reinforce states parties' ability to grant or withhold consent for the stationing of foreign forces on their territory. Owing to its dissatisfaction with the ratification process, especially over Western insistence on withdrawal of its troops from Moldova and Georgia, Russia suspended the original treaty and its amendments on 14 July 2007, effective 150 days later. See W. Zellner, 'Can This Treaty Be Saved? Breaking the Stalemate on Conventional Forces in Europe', *Arms Control Today*, 39(7) (September 2009).

[15] International Law Association, 71st Conference (Berlin 2004), 'Final Report of the Committee on Arms Control and Disarmament Law' (London: International Law Association, 2004), 493.

[16] SC Res 825 (1993), paras. 1–5.

[17] SC Res 1718 (2006), paras. 3 and 6. This request was again repeated in SC Res 1874 (2009), paras. 5, 6 and 8.

[18] 2010 Review Conference of the Parties to the Treaty on the Non-Proliferation of Nuclear Weapons, Final Document, NPT/CONF.2010/50 (vol. 1) (final para.).

consequences particular to a non-proliferation treaty regime may accompany withdrawal from the treaty. Relevant treaties are silent as to specific consequences in a case of withdrawal. It is also difficult to argue that there is a general legal obligation for parties to cooperate in good faith to find a solution in such an extraordinary situation. What appears to be good policy for states to meet existing challenges does not necessarily amount to a legal obligation. This may best be explained by a side glance to Article 41 of the Articles on Responsibility of States for Internationally Wrongful Acts,[19] which calls for an obligation 'to cooperate, to bring to an end through lawful means any serious breach' by a state of 'an obligation arising under a peremptory norm of general international law'. As explained in the Commentary,[20] it 'may be open to question whether general international law at present prescribes a positive duty of cooperation', yet Article 41(1) 'seeks to strengthen existing mechanisms' to this end. The Commentary confirms that states are under a 'positive duty under these Articles' to take a 'joint and coordinated effort' to bring to an end such breaches 'whether or not they are individually affected', even if the provision 'does not prescribe in detail what form this cooperation should take' and 'what measures' should be taken. Hence, Article 41 imposes certain duties of states in respect of cooperation in response to serious breaches of peremptory norms, and under Articles 42–48 any state, not only an injured state, is entitled to invoke the responsibility of another state. Measures to be taken under these Articles, beyond non-recognition of breaches, and non-assistance to perpetrators, which already reflect general international law,[21] should be further discussed in the light of the drafting history[22] and current challenges in post-conflict situations.[23] The lawfulness of measures, as called for by Article 41, must be a matter of careful assessment in which sovereignty

[19] UNGA Res. A/RES/56/83 (28 January 2002).

[20] J. Crawford, *The International Law Commission's Articles on State Responsibility: Introduction, Text and Commentaries* (Cambridge University Press, 2002), Commentary (paras. 2 and 3) to Art. 41.

[21] ICJ, *Legal Consequences for States of the Continued Presence of South Africa in Namibia (South West Africa) notwithstanding Security Council Resolution 276 (1970)*, Advisory Opinion, ICJ Reports 1971 16, 54, para. 118; 56, para. 126; *Legal Consequences of the Construction of a Wall in the Occupied Palestinian Territory*, Advisory Opinion, ICJ Reports 2004 136, 199–200, paras. 155–159.

[22] N. H. B. Jørgensen, 'The Obligation of Cooperation', in Crawford, Pellet and Olleson, *The Law of International Responsibility*, pp. 695–701.

[23] See, e.g., A. Cassese, '*Ex iniuria ius oritur*: Are We Moving Towards International Legitimation of Forcible Humanitarian Countermeasures in the World Community?', *European Journal of International Law*, 10 (1999), 23–30.

and responsibility are to be understood as mutually enforcing principles. One practical aspect will be the involvement of international organizations and in particular the Security Council.

While this is the imperfect legal situation in the case of serious breaches of peremptory norms of international law, many more uncertainties arise in the event of lawful withdrawal from treaty obligations. Do existing general principles suffice to delineate the behaviour of states in extraordinary circumstances? What limits are to be drawn from existing norms of international law? Is it correct to assume that legal constraints can only be found in new treaty law?[24] The 'obligations owed to the international community as a whole'[25] are, indeed, less than specified and sometimes even less than certain.

III. Legal and policy considerations strengthening non-proliferation

The absence of positive legal regulation of important consequences that unilateral withdrawals from non-proliferation treaties might entail raises the classical question of whether this may be considered as a 'gap' in international law, and how such a gap can be closed by means of legal interpretation.

i. Existing gaps in treaty law

Classical, as the discussion of legal gaps certainly is, any possible outcome will nevertheless be philosophically vague and subject to policy solutions rather than legal decision-making. Hans Kelsen has denied the possibility of any behaviour which is not the object of a legal norm. This is why, instead of 'gaps', he used to speak of 'negative legal regulation',[26] a term which would accept the non-existence of legal obligation in the given case. Sir Hersch Lauterpacht, acknowledging the possibility of gaps in the law, has denied that such gaps could necessitate *non liquet*,[27]

[24] See Goldblat, 'Should the Right to Withdraw from the NPT Be Withdrawn?'.

[25] 'Fragmentation of International Law: Difficulties Arising from the Diversification and Expansion of International Law', Report of the Study Group of the International Law Commission, A/CN.4/L.682 (13 April 2006), para. 492, published in *Report of the International Law Commission, 2006*, vol. 2, part II.

[26] H. Kelsen, *General Theory of Norms* (Oxford: Clarendon Press, 1991), pp. 131–132.

[27] H. Lauterpacht, 'International Law – The General Part', in E. Lauterpacht (ed.), *International Law: Being the Collected Papers of Hersch Lauterpacht*, vol. 1

whereas Julius Stone has argued that 'it should be left open to a tribunal, in the absence of contrary request by both parties, to decide that the authoritative legal materials and other resources available for judgment do not in the particular case enable it to make a binding judgment'.[28] Would then 'any absence of a legal prohibition ... constitute the presence of a legal permission'?[29] Judge Bruno Simma, in his declaration on the recent *Kosovo* Advisory Opinion, convincingly warned against a quick affirmative answer which would in his opinion reflect 'an old, tired view of international law ... famously expressed in the *Lotus* Judgment' that 'equate[s] the absence of a prohibition with the existence of a permissive rule'; the Court 'could also have considered the possibility that international law can be neutral or deliberately silent on the international lawfulness of certain acts'.[30] An excellent scholarly assessment of this discussion,[31] based on recent literature[32] and the ICJ Advisory Opinions on *Nuclear Weapons*[33] and *Kosovo*,[34] emphasizes that it is necessary 'to give a point of reference against which to measure the absence' of a certain rule,[35] rather than mixing that reference point with morals, political ideology or personal views on what the law should be in place of what the law is. The convincing conclusion is that '[g]aps *in law* are impossible; gaps *of prescription in behaviour* are common',[36] and hence it may be acknowledged that 'gaps are factors of uncertainty in

(Cambridge University Press, 1970), p. 94. See also H. Lauterpacht, 'Some Observations on the Prohibition of "Non Liquet" and the Completeness of the Law', in *Symbolae Verzijl: Présentées au Professeur J. H. W. Verzijl à l'occasion de son LXXXième anniversaire* (The Hague: Martinus Nijhoff, 1958), pp. 196–221.

[28] J. Stone, '*Non Liquet* and the Function of Law in the International Community', *British Yearbook of International Law, 1959* (1960), p. 160. See also J. Stone, *Legal Controls of International Conflict: A Treatise on the Dynamics of Disputes- and War-Law* (London: Stevens, 1954), pp. 152–164.

[29] Stone, '*Non Liquet* and the Function of Law in the International Community', p. 136.

[30] ICJ, *Accordance with International Law of the Unilateral Declaration of Independence in Respect of Kosovo*, Advisory Opinion of 22 July 2010, Declaration Simma, paras. 2 and 3, www.icj-cij.org/docket/files/141/15993.pdf?PHPSESSID=49855af6032557ef4a018dc9f9d3209d.

[31] J. Kammerhofer, 'Gaps, the Nuclear Weapons Advisory Opinion and the Structure of International Legal Argument Between Theory and Practice', *British Yearbook of International Law*, 80 (2009), pp. 333–360.

[32] See, e.g., U. Fastenrath, *Lücken im Völkerrecht: zu Rechtscharakter, Quellen, Systemzusammenhang, Methodenlehre und Funktionen des Völkerrechts* (Berlin: Duncker & Humblot, 1991).

[33] ICJ, *Legality of the Threat or Use of Nuclear Weapons*, Advisory Opinion of 8 July 1996, ICJ Reports 1996, 226.

[34] See n. 30, above. [35] Kammerhofer, 'Gaps', 354. [36] *Ibid.* 359.

international law', an uncertainty that is 'always a pragmatic factor of the interaction of real human beings with the ideal idea that is norms'.[37]

In international humanitarian law, the famous Martens Clause, named after the Russian delegate to The Hague Peace Conferences in 1899 and 1907, Fyodor F. Martens, provides a classic tool for closing gaps of prescription in behaviour. It provides that in cases not covered by international agreements, civilians and combatants remain under the protection and authority of the principles of international law derived from established custom, the principles of humanity and the dictates of public conscience.[38] This clause *first* offers a point of reference – 'the principles of humanity' and the 'dictates of public conscience' – against which the absence of a certain rule of international humanitarian law is to be measured. *Second*, it puts these two parameters on the same footing as state practice as historical sources of customary principles of international law, thus loosening, in the specific area of international humanitarian law, the requirements prescribed for state practice, while at the same time elevating *opinio iuris ac necessitatis* to a rank higher than normally admitted in international law,[39] even if it may be recognized that in developing this clause Fyodor Martens did by no means envisage such wide-reaching effect himself while he intentionally 'used loose language for the purpose ... of solving a diplomatic problem'.[40] Martens himself never referred to that clause in his many publications. This, however, did not exclude that the Martens Clause was given general importance in the development of international humanitarian law, and was reaffirmed in the 1977 Additional Protocols to the Geneva Conventions,[41] again confirmed in subsequent conventions,[42] and invoked by the ICJ in its *Nuclear Weapons* Advisory Opinion as 'an effective means of addressing the rapid evolution of military technology'.[43] Judge Mohamed Shahabuddeen in his Dissenting Opinion went further, describing the Martens Clause as a self-sufficient and conclusive authority 'to govern military conduct in cases in which no relevant rule

[37] *Ibid.* 360. [38] See Preamble, para. 8, of the 1907 Hague Convention (IV).

[39] Cf. A. Cassese, *International Law*, 2nd edn (Oxford University Press, 2005), p. 161; A. Cassese, 'The Martens Clause: Half a Loaf or Simply Pie in the Sky?', *European Journal of International Law*, 11 (2000), 193–202.

[40] Cassesse, 'The Martens Clause', 202.

[41] Art. 1(2) Additional Protocol I; Preamble, para. 4, of Additional Protocol II.

[42] See e.g., Preamble, para. 5 of the 1980 Inhumane Weapons Convention; Preamble, para. 8 of the 1997 Landmines Convention; Preamble, para. 11 of the 2008 Convention on Cluster Munitions.

[43] ICJ, *Legality of the Threat or Use of Nuclear Weapons*, para. 78.

was provided by conventional law' and even suggesting that the Clause operates to impose a prohibition of the use of nuclear weapons in any circumstances.[44] This position was generally shared by Judge Christopher Gregory Weeramantry, who stipulated that 'the applicability of those principles to the specific case of nuclear weapons cannot reasonably be in doubt'.[45]

While the Martens Clause is certainly of great importance for international humanitarian law, it does not have direct application on non-proliferation law, the latter being strictly treaty-oriented, based on reciprocity, continued cooperation and strict regulation of procedures for confidence-building – criteria not applicable in international humanitarian law.[46] Hence, there is no equivalent clause in arms control agreements that might be used for closing gaps of prescription in behaviour. In matters affecting the peace and security of mankind, any solution will be fully subject to an objective evaluation in the given case and will depend on cooperation between sovereign states and not without United Nations organs' participation, backed by the international community. While there are general principles of international security stemming from the danger of weapon of mass destruction (WMD) proliferation, any legal obligation is to be based on positive commitment and unequivocal rules.

Activities *de lege ferenda* have given support to the principle that the freedom of states to carry on or permit activities in their territory or otherwise under their jurisdiction or control is not unlimited. Based on proposals made by the International Law Commission, the General Assembly had commended articles on the prevention of transboundary harm from hazardous activities[47] to the attention of governments and invited them to submit comments on any future action in respect of these articles. Their provisions are designed to apply to activities not prohibited by international law which involve a risk of causing significant transboundary harm through their physical consequences. They require states to take all appropriate measures to prevent significant transboundary harm or at any event to minimize the risk thereof. States concerned will cooperate in good faith and, as necessary, seek the assistance of

[44] *Ibid.*, Dissenting Opinion Shahabuddeen, Part III.

[45] *Ibid.*, Dissenting Opinion Weeramantry, Part III, sections 4–5.

[46] See D. Fleck (ed.), *The Handbook of International Humanitarian Law*, 2nd edn (Oxford University Press, 2008), sections 1219, 1404.

[47] A/RES/62/68 (28 January 2008).

competent international organizations. Any authorization of relevant activities will, in particular, be based on an assessment of the possible transboundary harm caused by that activity, including any environmental impact assessment. Also, procedures for peaceful settlement of disputes are provided. Two years before, principles on allocation of loss[48] in such cases had likewise been commended as authoritative guidance for all states' conduct with a view to ensure prompt and adequate compensation for victims of transboundary damage, to take adequate response measures, provide for international and domestic remedies, and create specific international regimes as necessary. Specific non-proliferation aspects of the proposed articles and principles have not been discussed so far, but it would be logical to treat dangers incurred by WMD proliferation as being even more relevant to peaceful cooperation than a severe environmental impact of economic enterprise. As only nine states had submitted written comments,[49] the General Assembly invited further comments and recommendations on whether a convention based on the articles should be elaborated. It also asked for information on any practice in the application of the articles and principles and requested the Secretary-General to submit a compilation of decisions of international courts, tribunals and other bodies referring to the articles and principles. The General Assembly will take the matter up again at its 68th Session.[50] It remains to be seen whether states will be willing explicitly to extend their liability on a no-fault basis.

ii. Specific aspects of withdrawal from non-proliferation commitments

Any withdrawal from non-proliferation commitments raises questions as to its consequences for WMD proliferation and international peace and security. It is the threat of clandestine armament and its possible effects on WMD terrorism[51] that do require reconsideration of existing rules and the development of new forms of legal response. National security of states still adhering to the NPT as non-nuclear-weapon states may be jeopardized by the withdrawal of another state party. At the same

[48] A/RES/61/36 (18 December 2006).

[49] Report of the Secretary-General on the prevention of transboundary harm from hazardous activities and allocation of loss in the case of such harm, A/65/184 (29 July 2010) and Add. 1 (2 September 2010).

[50] See Report of the Sixth Committee, A/65/469 (11 November 2010).

[51] N. Ronzitti (ed.), *Coordinating Global and Regional Efforts to Combat WMD Terrorism* (Rome: Istituto Affari Internazionali, 2009).

time, any such withdrawal may cause them additional burden for implementation of the treaty. It appears necessary to balance out these negative effects in joint efforts together with the withdrawing party which should be held responsible to cooperate for this purpose.

1. The obligation to participate in the maintenance of peace and security It may be generally accepted that even for a state withdrawing from a non-proliferation treaty a specific obligation to participate in the maintenance of peace and security will prevail. It is this obligation that requires a continuing dialogue between affected states (possible countermeasures notwithstanding). To ensure peace and security all states are not only obliged to refrain from the threat or use of force (Article 2 para. 4 UN Charter) but also to take positive action for the settlement of any disputes (Article 2 para. 3 UN Charter). That obligation is pivotal, but it is an obligation of conduct, not an obligation requiring the achievement of a specific result.[52] This obligation requires the parties to settle both procedural aspects and the actual substance of their conflict. They must respond to proposals made and develop proposals as necessary for the solution of all pertinent issues.

To perform this task, parties are not left alone. They may submit their dispute individually or jointly to one of the United Nations' organs: the Secretary-General,[53] the General Assembly, the Security Council[54] or the ICJ. Article X(1) NPT explicitly provides that notice of withdrawal shall be given to the Security Council in addition to all parties to the treaty. Similar obligations are included in most nuclear-weapon-free-zone treaties, the BWC, the CWC and the CTBT. Even during early phases of decision-making prior to withdrawal from a non-proliferation treaty, Security Council involvement may have preventive effects and will assist in achieving sustainable solutions. Yet in the few events under discussion here, United Nations' activities remained rudimentary and no consistent state practice has evolved so far. It was only after certain reluctance in the

[52] C. Tomuschat, in Bruno Simma, Daniel-Erasmus Khan, Georg Nolte et al. (eds.), *The Charter of the United Nations: A Commentary*, 2nd edn (Oxford University Press, 2002), Art. 2 (3), MN 15.

[53] See S. Chesterman (ed.), *Secretary or General? The UN Secretary-General in World Politics* (Cambridge University Press, 2007).

[54] See V. Lowe, A. Roberts, J. Welsh, and D. Zaum (eds.), *The United Nations Security Council and War: The Evolution of Thought and Practice since 1945* (Oxford University Press, 2008).

case of North Korea[55] that the Security Council has now committed itself to address without delay any state's notice of withdrawal from the NPT,[56] and it remains open to test whether and how such commitments will materialize in future.

While the Security Council enjoys considerable discretion as to the determinations to be made and action to be taken,[57] it is fully in accordance with Charter principles that the Council should play an active role in this regard, carefully evaluating the reasons notified, considering all security interests involved, and operating in an objective and comprehensive manner. This requires active cooperation by states. A state withdrawing from a non-proliferation treaty must explain the extraordinary situation that has jeopardized its supreme interests. Its readiness to comply with this obligation is an important element on which the Council's recommendations or decisions under Article 39 of the UN Charter are to be based. While it may be open for discussion whether the international legal system should set effective limits upon the authority of the Security Council with a view to protect states from subjugation by a 'legal hegemon unbound by law',[58] the question is here whether the notifying state in accomplishing its obligations for peaceful settlement under Article 2(3) of the UN Charter must respond to any request by the Council, cooperate in positive solutions, and consider even a return to the treaty to achieve peaceful settlement of the dispute. Such openness for dialogue in situations of tension is a prerequisite for cooperation under the Charter system. This is all the more relevant in non-proliferation issues.

Where the Security Council remains inactive, meditation may still be sought by the Secretary-General, or the matter may be taken up by the General Assembly which could provide political guidance under Chapter IV of the Charter or request the ICJ to give an advisory opinion.

Specific aspects are to be considered under the terms and requirements of non-proliferation law. A state which is considered by the IAEA to be in possible 'non-compliance' with the terms of its safeguards agreement with the Agency is under a positive obligation to prove its compliance with the non-proliferation provisions of the NPT and to provide for remedies in the event of failure. This entails a special burden of proof for member states which may be different from general rules of

[55] See nn. 16–17, above and accompanying text. [56] SC Res 1887 (2009), para. 17.

[57] J. A. Frowein and N. Krisch, in Simma, *The Charter of the United Nations*, Art. 39, MN 4.

[58] D. H. Joyner, 'How Can International Law Protect States from the UN Security Council? Nuclear Non-proliferation and the UN Security Council in a Multipolar World', in M. Happold (ed.), *International Law in a Multipolar World* (New York: Routledge, 2011), p. 59.

court procedures but fully in consistence with state responsibility for the maintenance of international peace and security.

2. Prevailing responsibility for violations committed prior to withdrawal In its recent resolution on the issue, the Security Council also affirmed that a state remains responsible under international law for any violations of the NPT committed prior to its withdrawal.[59] That position is fully in accordance with Article 79(1b) VCLT. It was likewise expressed by many states during the last NPT Review Conference and included in the Final Document.[60] While at first sight this appears uncontroversial, there may be more specific questions about what sort of liability would remain for the withdrawing state. Withdrawal from a treaty obligation will normally end such obligation from the effective date of withdrawal, unless the obligation explicitly applies beyond that date, yet it does not cure any violations in retrospect. The withdrawing state rather remains responsible for any consequences of these former violations. It is bound to continue cooperation with the IAEA to reach a satisfying solution.

3. Continuing implications for safeguards In this context the question whether there are continuing implications of NPT withdrawal for existing safeguards deserves special attention. The basic document on which comprehensive IAEA safeguards agreements are modelled requires them to provide that they remain in force as long as the state is party to the NPT.[61] While this will exclude a simple perpetuation of obligations so agreed, the necessary amount of cooperation with the IAEA must be ensured, most importantly to secure compliance with safeguards obligations while these are still in force.[62] A viable solution might be to return to pre-NPT safeguards which were suspended after the conclusion of INFCIRC/153 safeguards agreements.[63]

[59] See n. 56, at para. 17.

[60] 2010 Review Conference of the Parties to the Treaty on the Non-Proliferation of Nuclear Weapons, Final Document, NPT/CONF.2010/50 (vol. 1), paras. 118–119.

[61] IAEA, *The Structure and Content of Agreements between the Agency and States Required in Connection with the Treaty on the Non-Proliferation of Nuclear Weapons* (INFCIRC/153, June 1972), para. 26.

[62] A. F. Perez, 'Survival of Rights under The Nuclear Non-Proliferation Treaty: Withdrawal and the Continuing Right of International Atomic Energy Agency Safeguards', *Virginia Journal of International Law*, 34 (Summer 1994), 828.

[63] IAEA, *The Agency's Safeguards System* (1965, as provisionally extended in 1966 and 1968) (INFCIRC/66).

There may be continuing obligations under existing bilateral agreements, depending on their terms.[64] This is the case for regional safeguards systems established under nuclear-weapon-free-zone treaties or the Euratom Treaty.[65] But in other cases IAEA safeguards would cease to apply in the withdrawing state. Possible terms and conditions for safeguards obligations of former parties to non-proliferation treaties should be explored further.

A different conclusion might be drawn for nuclear material and equipment a withdrawing state had received under certain conditions, e.g., that they will be used only for peaceful purposes. It may be difficult to define such conditions and secure compliance. A mere expectation on the part of the supplier or the exporting state[66] would hardly suffice. In any event this interpretation would not solve the problem of proliferation of know-how; neither could it work for indigenously produced material. Hence, clear safeguards that would endure in any case of withdrawal from the NPT should be established by agreement. Where such agreements are missing, cooperative solutions and/or Security Council recommendations or decisions under Chapter VII must be sought and implemented.

4. Dismantling or return of nuclear material and equipment A further issue which should be discussed in its political context is whether a withdrawing state may be required to dismantle or return nuclear material and equipment received by virtue of its membership in the treaty.

This subject was mentioned by states in NPT Review Conferences and Preparatory Committee Meetings, yet it has received little discussion by international legal scholars. Dismantling or return of material or compensation requires cooperation of the withdrawing state and would have to be materialized jointly with the IAEA. This again would require conclusion of an agreement. The Security Council has encouraged states to require as a condition of nuclear exports that the recipient state agree that, in the event that it should terminate, withdraw from, or be found by the IAEA Board of Governors to be in non-compliance with its IAEA safeguards agreement, the supplier state would have a right to require the return of nuclear material and equipment provided prior to such termination,

[64] J. Carlson, 'Withdrawal from the NPT: Consequences for IAEA Safeguards', research paper commissioned by the International Commission on Nuclear Non-proliferation and Disarmament (5 June 2009), available at http://icnnd.org/Documents/Carlson_NPT_Withdrawal.pdf.

[65] *Ibid.* 5. [66] As suggested by J. Carlson, *ibid.* 4

non-compliance or withdrawal, as well as any special nuclear material produced through the use of such material or equipment.[67] The last NPT Review Conference referred to that possibility, adding also dismantling clauses in this context,[68] but lacking consensus on the issue it refrained from making relevant recommendations for follow-on action.

A supplier state could, indeed, even be considered to be under an obligation to request dismantling or return of relevant material in the event of the recipient state's withdrawal from the NPT. Such request, stemming from general non-proliferation obligations as from the recent recommendation made by the Security Council, would require its inclusion in relevant agreements which will be more successful prior to delivery of supplies than in retrospect. Supplier states might also consider for such case to arrange for compensation for any technological and other assistance provided.

Considering the scarcity of relevant state practice, further efforts will be necessary to develop positive incentives to ensure non-proliferation of weapons of mass destruction and provide for continued compliance control activities.

IV. Relevant dispute settlement obligations

It may be still correct to conclude that in arms control law there is not so much a lack of verification machinery and national technical means as a lack of effective dispute settlement procedures.[69] While this may be regarded as a paradox situation – given the historical development of modern arms control law which had started with the almost forgotten 1899 Hague Convention for the Pacific Settlement of International Disputes and its reaffirmation in 1907 – certain legal achievements on the development of dispute settlement procedures and their practical usage should not be denied altogether.

As defined by the Permanent Court of International Justice, a dispute is 'a disagreement on a point of law or fact, a conflict of legal views or interests'.[70] While both types of conflict can happen in non-proliferation law, opposing legal views or interests may be particularly relevant here. Pacific settlement of non-proliferation disputes may be sought by

[67] SC Res. 1887 (2009), para. 18. [68] See n. 60, above at para. 121.

[69] Ronzitti, 'Problems of Arms Control Treaty Interpretation', 125.

[70] PCIJ, *Mavrommatis Palestine Concessions Case* (*Greece* v. *UK*) (Jurisdiction), Judgment of 30 August 1924, *PCIJ Reports*, Series A No. 2, 11–12.

diplomatic and judicial means, and as the latter are often not available owing to the lack of jurisdiction or its limitation to legal rights and obligations rather than a balancing of interests,[71] the former will prevail in most cases. The legal framework under Chapter VI of the UN Charter is fully applicable for a pacific settlement of arms control disputes, and while the establishment by the Security Council of a 'system for the regulation of armaments' (Article 26) is to be missed, many multilateral and bilateral treaties on arms control are available, and some of them provide and institutionalize dispute settlement procedures. Even if such procedures have not played a major role so far, they could offer positive incentives to ensure compliance with arms control obligations.[72] Traditional dispute settlement may be seen as being only of supplementary value here in comparison with more specialized mechanisms of compliance control,[73] but in contentious cases of withdrawal these mechanisms are often no longer available and a need for general dispute settlement cannot be denied.

The rather congruent dispute settlement clauses used in the CWC[74] and the CTBT[75] provide for a wide range of activities, including recourse to appropriate organs of the relevant convention and, by mutual consent, referral to the ICJ in conformity with Article 36(1) of the ICJ Statute. Provisions on the peaceful settlement of disputes are also included in treaties on nuclear-weapon-free zones.[76] No such clause is to be found in the NPT. But states and international organizations are not precluded from using such forms of dispute settlement even if no explicit provision was made for this purpose in the particular instrument.

[71] See ICJ, *South West Africa Cases* (Preliminary Objections), Judgment of 21 December 1962, ICJ Reports 1962 328: 'It is not sufficient for one party to a contentious case to assert that a dispute exists with the other party. A mere assertion is not sufficient to prove the existence of a dispute any more than a mere denial of the existence of the dispute proves its non-existence. Nor is it adequate to show that the interests of the two parties to such a case are in conflict. It must be shown that the claim of one party is positively opposed by the other.'

[72] See G. Cottereau, 'A Comparative View of Arms Control Disputes', in J. Dahlitz (ed.), *Avoidance and Settlement of Arms Control Disputes: Arms Control and Disarmament Law* (Geneva: United Nations, 1994), vol. 2, pp. 103–121.

[73] T. Marauhn, 'Dispute Resolution, Compliance Control and Enforcement of International Arms Control Law', in G. Ulfstein, T. Marauhn and A. Zimmermann (eds.), *Making Treaties Work: Human Rights, Environment and Arms Control* (Cambridge University Press, 2007), p. 272.

[74] Art. XIV CWC. [75] Art. VI CTBT.

[76] See Art. 25 Tlatelolco Treaty; Art. 21 Bangkok Treaty; Annex 4, Rarotonda Treaty; Annex IV, Pelindaba Treaty; Art. 11 Semipalatinsk Treaty.

While it would be unrealistic to expect any kind of obligatory dispute settlement procedures to be accepted and used in non-proliferation law, states may still be considered responsible to choose appropriate means of mediation when one party announces its withdrawal, or has effectively withdrawn, from a treaty. In this context rules of a *jus cogens* character, obligations *erga omnes*, and the maintenance of international peace and security in conformity with the UN Charter have to be considered.

V. Conclusions

This discussion shows that consequences of withdrawal from a non-proliferation treaty are regulated by relevant rules of international law deriving from the UN Charter, general obligations under the law of treaties and specific provisions of the treaty from which withdrawal is to be declared. All parties to a non-proliferation treaty are bound to observe their obligations stemming from the contents and purpose of the relevant commitment and ensure full respect for applicable rules even in the event of withdrawal from the treaty.

While more specific obligations will apply during the timeframe in which advance notice of withdrawal is to be given, enduring consequences will remain even after the effectuation of withdrawal and irrespective of whether explicit arrangements have been made for its implementation. These obligations are derived from the obligation to participate in the maintenance of peace and security, to cooperate in good faith in accordance with the principles and provisions of the Charter and to settle international disputes in such a manner that international peace and security, and justice, are not endangered. In particular there is an obligation for all members of the United Nations to remain open for dialogue in situations of tension and to avoid international relations becoming a hostage of any threat of or use of weapons of mass destruction. The withdrawing state remains under a positive obligation to participate in such activities. Even after withdrawal it continues to bear responsibility for any violations committed prior to withdrawal and continuing implications for safeguards must be observed. Under particular circumstances nuclear material and equipment must be returned to the providing state. Where it was found by the IAEA that a withdrawing state may be in non-compliance with an existing safeguards agreement, that state remains under an obligation to prove compliance or provide for remedies in the event of failure. Furthermore, there is a special responsibility for member states and competent organs of the United

Nations fully to respect relevant principles and rules and to support activities of pacific settlement of disputes.

The rules on withdrawal from non-proliferation treaties which have been described above largely derive from general Charter principles on the maintenance of peace and security, principles which are of a general nature and do not only apply to non-proliferation of weapons of mass destruction. Hence it is not the origin and nature of the rules that are special, but their consequences in the particular context. It must also be considered that further activities are necessary to meet the challenges of withdrawal from non-proliferation obligations, in particular to ensure perpetuation of safeguards on nuclear material and missile technology existing at the time of withdrawal, and to provide for dismantling or return of nuclear material and equipment in the event of termination of, or withdrawal from, treaty obligations. Particular activities are necessary with regard to those states that have developed nuclear weapons capacity, but remained or became non-parties to the NPT.[77] It is in this context and with this understanding that the rules on withdrawal from non-proliferation treaties are special rules of international law and thus tend to support the existence of a special regime in this area of law.

Whether this would justify the conclusion that non-proliferation law in its entirety is a special 'regime' or 'system' must be left open for discussion. It may be questioned whether the relevant rules are comprehensive enough to form or be part of 'a system'. To answer this question convincingly all rules identified in this book are to be compared and a comprehensive assessment must be undertaken whether and to what extent they differ from the general rules of public international law or the rules of (other) special regimes.

Irrespective of whether a special regime of non-proliferation law already exists or might emerge, it should be accepted that non-proliferation of weapons of mass destruction is too important to be left in its present status of imperfect legal regulation.

[77] See T. Lorenz and J. Kidd, 'Israel and Multilateral Nuclear Approaches in the Middle East', *Arms Control Today* (October 2010); B. Chellaney, 'Let Facts Speak for Themselves: India–IAEA Safeguards Agreement Fact Sheet'. http://chellaney.spaces.live.com/Blog/cns!4913C7C8A2EA4A30!641.entry; The Nuclear Threat Initiative (NTI), 'Pakistan Profile'. www.nti.org/country-profiles/pakistan/.

Conclusions

DANIEL H. JOYNER AND MARCO ROSCINI

The present book is fundamentally a study of the impact of primary rules (in particular, those on weapon of mass destruction (WMD) non-proliferation) on secondary rules, including those on the law of treaties and the law of state responsibility. The main purpose is to establish whether there are specific secondary rules, as well as underlying interstitial principles, present in WMD non-proliferation law that depart from or conflict with general rules of international law, or with specific rules and interstitial principles present in other special regimes. To the extent that such specialized rules have been found to exist in non-proliferation law, the question of whether these specialized rules can be considered as evidence lending support to the conclusion that WMD non-proliferation law is a special regime explainable by fragmentation theory has been considered by the contributors in the discrete subject assigned to each of them.

We have defined a 'special regime' as a system of interrelated primary and secondary norms addressing a certain problem, where the primary rules are supplemented by secondary rules specific to the regime in question. A 'special regime' exists whenever there is a pattern of similar clauses in treaties in a discrete area, without those clauses having necessarily to be present in all treaties in that area.[1] 'Special' does not necessarily entail uniqueness but implies a diversity from, and also a common systemic nature with, the general rules.

As several contributors have noted, and as we stated in the Introduction to this volume, fragmentation occurs not only within general international

[1] See Chapter 2, in this book, Andrew Michie, 'Provisional application of non-proliferation treaties', p. 81. The need for an 'attractor', that is, 'a set or point towards which a dynamical system evolves over time', is also highlighted by Fitzmaurice and Merkouris. Without such attractor or point of convergence, 'one cannot talk of a "special regime" but rather of *ad hoc* and relatively unconnected, both causally and systemically, solutions to a particular problem'. See Chapter 1, in this book, Malgosia Fitzmaurice and Panos Merkouris, 'Amendment and modification of non-proliferation treaties', p. 18.

law but also within special regimes. Indeed, even some non-proliferation treaties, which tend to be highly subject-homogenous, contain particular provisions that could potentially be classified as international environmental law, international trade law or international humanitarian law provisions. This is why the expression 'non-proliferation law' has to be used with caution, and why we have tried to do so. The risk, of course, is that qualifying a certain treaty as belonging to trade law or human rights law or environmental law or non-proliferation law can result in an unwarranted 'pigeonholing' of the treaty based on a 'wholly arbitrary choice between what interests are relevant and what are not'.[2] This fact generally argues that the analysis of specialness in special regime theory should primarily be conducted treaty by treaty and provision by provision in order to identify patterns. As Pauwelyn notes, '[a] conflict is rarely one between treaties or sub-systems of international law *in their entirety*, where one treaty or sub-system *in its entirety* needs to give way to another treaty or sub-system.'[3]

However, while each of the authors has proceeded accordingly and has looked to the provisions of discrete treaties within their topic of secondary rules to find specialness in the first instance, they have also considered whether there are patterns of specialness among non-proliferation treaties within their topic of secondary rule analysis. Such patterns of specialness, that is, multiple examples of the same or similar type of secondary rule specialness within non-proliferation treaties, can, we think, constitute evidence of specialness in secondary rules that transcends the individual treaties considered in the first instance, and constitute facts that have explanatory power about non-proliferation law more broadly.

As we argued in the Introduction, non-proliferation law is an issue area of international law that, in terms of its unique interstitial principles, exclusively subject-committed legal sources, and its complexity and epistemic capture by a discrete community of technical, policy and legal experts, both inside and outside of government, arguably make it a more

[2] 'Fragmentation of International Law: Difficulties Arising from the Diversification and Expansion of International Law', Report of the Study Group of the International Law Commission, A/CN.4/L.682, 13 April 2006, 18.

[3] J. Pauwelyn, *Conflict of Norms in Public International Law: How WTO Law Relates to other Rules of International Law* (Cambridge University Press, 2003), p. 10. Lindroos also notes that '[a]n abstract determination of an entire area of law as being more specific towards another area of law is not, in effect, realistic.' A. Lindroos, 'Addressing Norm Conflicts in a Fragmented Legal System: The Doctrine of *Lex Specialis*', *Nordic Journal of International Law*, 74 (2005), 44.

defensible subject for the identification of patterns and standard clauses and for the possible characterization as a special regime in at least certain aspects than would be possible with regard to other substantive areas of international law. We maintain that position, and think that where patterns of secondary rule specialness can be found in non-proliferation treaties, these patterns of specialness can be taken as at least probative evidence that there is specialness both at the particular treaty level as well as at the regime level on the subject of that secondary rule.

Let us proceed now, then, to a review and summary of the various chapter authors' inquiries into particular secondary rules. While in all cases noting the predominance of rules in non-proliferation law sources that are in harmony with general rules of international law, approximately half of the contributors to this book have identified in WMD non-proliferation treaties patterns of special secondary rules and legal practice that appear to lend support to the idea of non-proliferation law as a special regime pursuant to fragmentation theory, from at least those perspectives.

With regard to the law of treaties, Malgosia Fitzmaurice and Panos Merkouris identify a number of special amendment provisions deviating from the general rules contained in the Vienna Convention on the Law of Treaties (VCLT). This is, in particular, the case with the PTBT (Article II), the CWC (Article XV), the CTBT (Article VII) and the Pelindaba Treaty establishing the African nuclear-weapon-free zone (Article 19). In each of these provisions, all treaty parties may be bound by a post-ratification amendment approved by a majority of the treaty parties, in disharmony with Article 40(4) VCLT.[4] With regard to the CWC and the CTBT in particular, a bifurcated amendment procedure is provided where the 'tacit acceptance procedure' applies to amendments to technical and administrative treaty provisions. The reason for these special rules is the need to facilitate regularized updating of the initial text in the light of ongoing technological developments.

[4] Another element of specialness is the presence of amendment procedures for certain bilateral non-proliferation treaties such as the START, PNE, INF, ABM Treaties, while the VCLT only refers to amendments to multilateral treaties, as in bilateral agreements amendment/modification imply re-negotiation and subsequent new agreement (Fitzmaurice and Merkouris, Chapter 1, above, pp. 32–34). The main purposes of inserting procedures for the amendment of bilateral non-proliferation treaties are to leave the provisions not affected by the amendment out of the negotiating process and to be a safeguard against the possible dissolution of one of the contracting states.

The question, however, as in all of the discrete topics of treaty law and state responsibility law examined by the contributors to this volume, is whether the presence of secondary rules deviating from general international law or from the law of other special regimes in certain non-proliferation treaties is widespread and systematic enough to argue for the existence of a pattern of special rules, sufficient to constitute evidence supporting a conclusion that non-proliferation law is a special regime with regard to that particular secondary rule. In the case of amendment provisions, for example, other non-proliferation treaties follow the unanimity and majority rules of the VCLT and are in complete harmony with these general rules. If the answer is negative, the conclusion would be that non-proliferation law is not a special regime from this perspective, even though certain non-proliferation treaties can be considered special subsystems. In the context of treaty amendment rules, Fitzmaurice and Merkouris conclude that, notwithstanding their identification of a number of special amendment rules in certain non-proliferation treaties, there does not appear to exist in the rules and legal practice related to amendment of non-proliferation treaties a sufficient degree of coherence and systematicity as to constitute evidence of a special regime on this secondary rule.

On the other hand, Andrew Michie argues that with regard to secondary rules on provisional application of treaties there is a sufficiently well-established pattern of specialized law and legal practice in non-proliferation treaties to constitute evidence of a special regime. This pattern can be divided into three subcategories: bilateral non-proliferation treaties such as the STARTs, with limited provisional application provisions in deviation from Article 25 VCLT; global non-proliferation conventions such as the CWC and the CTBT, characterized by provisional application provided under a separate agreement establishing a preparatory commission; and subsidiary non-proliferation agreements such as the Plutonium Management and Disposition Agreement and its Protocols, where provisional application is provided consistently with Article 25 VCLT. Of all these provisions, perhaps the most special is the provisional application mechanism in the now terminated START I, which diverged from Article 25(2) VCLT in that the parties had the right to terminate the provisional application of the Protocol on the Joint Compliance and Inspection Commission, the Protocol on Telemetric Information, and the Memorandum of Understanding, without necessarily having to drop out of the treaty altogether. Notwithstanding superficial differences, Michie argues that the three typologies mentioned above are united by several common normative features: preparatory function, confidence building character, contractual nature of the treaty obligations, limited number of clauses provisionally applied which do not include the core non-proliferation obligations, and the ancillary role played by secondary provisional application rules in the process by which primary non-proliferation norms become customary international law.

In his chapter on interpretation of treaties, by contrast, Nigel White finds that there is no significant evidence of specialness in secondary rules of interpretation, either contained in or consistently applied to non-proliferation treaties. He argues that the general VCLT rules on treaty interpretation are sufficiently flexible so as to be in harmony with interpretive rules and practices related to non-proliferation treaties, so that there is no disharmony between the general rules of international law and the rules of non-proliferation law on this issue. He also finds no significant specialness in non-proliferation law rules on interpretation differing from rules of interpretation relating to other substantive areas of international law.

In their chapter on the violation of non-proliferation treaties and related verification treaties, Eric Myjer and Jonathan Herbach note that the breach of obligations contained in non-proliferation treaties can raise particular problems because of the dual-use nature of many of the materials regulated by such treaties. The evidence of breach may be particularly controversial and difficult to detect due to this fact. They note that, in order to address this difficulty, a number of non-proliferation treaties include within their terms either the creation of a specialized internal monitoring and verification mechanism, as in the case of the CWC/OPCW, or, as in the context of the NPT/IAEA, an obligation to conclude and maintain a separate special monitoring and verification treaty with an outside organization. These special mechanisms for determining and addressing treaty breach are sufficiently systemically present in non-proliferation treaties so as to comprise a set of specialized secondary rules and legal processes evidencing the special regime character of non-proliferation law with regard to secondary rules on treaty breach.

Daniel Joyner and Marco Roscini similarly find, in their chapter on treaty withdrawal, that non-proliferation law and related special regimes, particularly including United Nations law, contain a consistent and systemic set of special rules on this topic. In this area, a sustained pattern is clearly evident, with the 'extraordinary events' clause, modelled on Article IV of the 1963 Partial Test-Ban Treaty, included in virtually all non-proliferation treaties. Joyner and Roscini find that the 'extraordinary events' clause relaxes the general grounds to terminate a treaty, in particular the *rebus sic stantibus* and the *inadimplenti non est adimplendum* clauses. This is certainly not inconsistent with Article 54 VCLT, which allows the parties to a treaty to withdraw from it in accordance with the provisions of the treaty itself. What makes the 'extraordinary events' clause special is rather its uniqueness, that is, the fact that it is significantly different from (and broader than) withdrawal provisions in any other substantive area of international law.

As far as the law of state responsibility is concerned, Matthew Happold finds in his chapter on the legal consequences of treaty breach that non-proliferation treaties do not contain a significant number of special provisions on the consequences of breaches and the right to invoke such consequences. Happold argues that, although the general rules contained in the ILC Articles on the Responsibility of States for Internationally Wrongful Acts are flexible enough to suit the peculiarities of non-proliferation agreements, they however have little practical relevance in this area. Indeed, he argues that non-proliferation law is more focused on the prevention of the breaches and compliance monitoring than on dispute resolution and reparation. Non-proliferation law is thus characterized by the presence of progressively more institutionalized compliance control procedures, but this is not peculiar to non-proliferation treaties.

Dieter Fleck has, however, identified systemic and consistent special rules in non-proliferation treaties with regard to the consequences of treaty withdrawal: specifically, rules requiring cooperation with verification bodies to address consequences of breach occurring prior to withdrawal, rules ensuring perpetuation of safeguards on nuclear material and missile technology existing at the time of withdrawal, and rules providing for dismantling or return of nuclear material and equipment in the event of withdrawal.

In his chapter on countermeasures, Sahib Singh observes in relation to standing to take countermeasures, that non-proliferation law is special inasmuch as it is susceptible to allowing all states party to a non-proliferation treaty to undertake countermeasures for most, but not all, mainstay obligations. In relation to when countermeasures can be taken, Singh observes that while the general law of countermeasures prevails in most cases, non-proliferation treaties do contain provisions which curtail, modify or exclude the general international law of countermeasures to varying degrees. He notes that these rules are of a varying degree of specialness at a general norm level, and in some cases highly case-specific (e.g., the UN Security Council, IAEA and Iran). However, notwithstanding these discrete instances of special rules in non-proliferation treaties, Singh finds that a determination of sufficiently systemic specialness in non-proliferation treaties on this aspect of law cannot be made.

In light of the above, it can be concluded at least that non-proliferation law is a special regime with regard to secondary rules relating to the provisional application of treaties, mechanisms for determining and addressing treaty breach, withdrawal from treaties, and state responsibility consequences flowing from treaty withdrawal.

We therefore believe that this evidence can be taken to support the conclusion that non-proliferation law is a regime of international law characterized by a significant degree of specialness, explainable by fragmentation theory, and creating the legal conflict effects predicted by fragmentation theory. Andrew Michie in his chapter herein goes even further to argue that 'on what has been called the "sliding scale of specialness", non-proliferation practice may well be the strongest and most special in all of international law'.[5] While this is an assessment that we cannot verify through the evidence produced in this volume, it is our opinion that on the sliding scale of specialness non-proliferation law does appear to fall somewhere quite far along the spectrum toward specialness. We think that this special character of patterns of secondary rules in non-proliferation law is primarily due to the presence of specific interstitial norms underpinning this issue area of law.[6] Several interrelated interstitial norms in the area of non-proliferation law have been identified by the contributors to this volume: the significant impact that the conclusion of non-proliferation treaties and their violation have on national security, the very close relationship between WMD non-proliferation and the maintenance of international peace and security, the environment of dynamic political, security and technological change, the high level of technical elaboration involved, the need for confidence building. These extra-legal principles are all expression of what Michie effectively calls the 'cautious world of non-proliferation'.[7]

[5] See Michie, Chapter 2, above, p. 85.

[6] V. Lowe, 'The Politics of Law-Making: Are the Method and Character of Norm Creation Changing?', in M. Byers (ed.), *The Role of Law in International Politics* (Oxford University Press, 2000), p. 216.

[7] Michie, Chapter 2, above, p. 65.

This technically, politically and legally complex and dynamic issue area has also become 'captured' in terms of knowledge and influence by a discrete specialist community of experts. We believe that this is another cause of the high degree of specialization in secondary rules observed in non-proliferation law.

So what do our conclusions tell us about fragmentation theory, special regime theory and non-proliferation law? So much of fragmentation and special regimes literature is conducted on the macro theoretical level and makes predictions about what that theory means in practice. What we first hoped to accomplish with this volume was to look at a specific, concrete, substantive area of international law of interest to us, and to see if special regime and fragmentation theory could help us understand how this substantive area of law has been constructed, and how it interacts with both the general rules of international law, as well as with other substantive areas of international law.

We believe we have shown that fragmentation and special regime theory does have explanatory power when applied to non-proliferation law and that this will aid in understanding non-proliferation treaties, and will become a useful analytical tool for non-proliferation law specialists to employ in future work.

Second, at the same time we hoped that conducting a concrete case study of special regime and fragmentation theory in this thorough, systematic way, and in a real and complex area of law in which we have qualitative expertise, would in a reflective sense itself contribute to understanding of special regime and fragmentation theory.

We believe we have made such a contribution in the comprehensive design of this study, in the application of special regime theory both to specific treaties as well as to a normative regime, in considering the criteria for establishing specialness at both of these levels, and in clarifying the role of interstitial principles in underlying and shaping the contours of special rules.

INDEX